Praise for *The Family* by

"David Laskin's *The Family* is a vivid, utter[...]
forces that have shaped modern history. We[...]
ism, fascism, mass migration, assimilation, and the like—only from a distance, as vast, impersonal abstractions. But in Laskin's magnificent book we see them in the intimate details of actual lives, deftly followed through a tangle of triumph, accommodation, and often unbearable suffering. An extraordinary achievement." —Stephen Greenblatt, *New York Times* bestselling author of *The Swerve: How the World Became Modern*

"As rich and poignant as any novel, only all true and impeccably researched. David Laskin tells the moving and tragic story of three distinct filaments of his ancestral family—and in the process brilliantly captures the dynamism, industry, and sorrow of the Jewish experience in modern history, from the family's roots in a shtetl in Eastern Europe, to Israel, Manhattan, and the darkest reaches of the Holocaust." —Erik Larson, *New York Times* bestselling author of *In the Garden of Beasts*

"A true triumph of historical storytelling . . . David Laskin is a magical searcher into the past. . . . His generations of Cohens could be your Johansens, Smiths, Lopezes, Schmidts, O'Houlihans, even my Scottish peasant forebears. . . . *The Family* will touch you, heart and soul." —Ivan Doig, National Book Award finalist for *This House of Sky*

"I read *The Family* without stopping, except sometimes to weep (and occasionally to chuckle). Through the stories of members of David Laskin's large, dispersing family, history sharpens into individual lives and deaths and losses and becomes personal and vivid and tragic." —Edith Pearlman, National Book Critics Circle Award winner and National Book Award finalist for *Binocular Vision*

"I was utterly entranced by David Laskin's *The Family*. Tracing three strands of his fascinating ancestry, Laskin takes us on an epic journey deep into the heart and soul of the twentieth century. The story is haunting, heartfelt, and deeply moving. And in the end—as Laskin eloquently points out in a beautiful, almost mystical, epilogue—his telling of it weaves another bright silver thread into the fabric that binds all of us together." —Daniel James Brown, *New York Times* bestselling author of *The Boys in the Boat*

"'Fate and chance and character make and break every generation,' David Laskin tells us in this personal, highly moving history of his family. At once heartbreaking and gloriously triumphant, it's finally a story of love. Yes, a big unyielding, often rollicking and humorous history of one generation's prevailing love for the next. A wonderful achievement."
—Philip Schultz, Pulitzer Prize–winning author of *Failure*

"David Laskin's *The Family* is an elegantly evocative meditation on the Jewish diaspora of the twentieth century. Deeply emotional at times, *The Family* is both harrowing and uplifting. Highly recommended!"
—Douglas Brinkley, author of *Cronkite*

"What a story! Scholars and scribes, Zionists and revolutionaries, Holocaust martyrs and the inventors of the Maidenform bra all march through these pages. *The Family* is the twentieth-century history of the Jews writ small."
—Jonathan D. Sarna, Joseph H. and Belle R. Braun Professor of American Jewish History at Brandeis University

"A banquet of Jewish history, as lived by one exceptional American family, across four generations and on three continents, the worst things endured and the best things relished."   —Edward Ball, author of *Slaves in the Family*

"An ambitious, experimental look at exodus, acclimatization, and culture with a cast as diverse as any family photo album . . . Were this fiction, it would read much like the novels of Leon Uris and other spinners of historical sagas."
—*Kirkus Reviews*

"[A] window into the enormity of the events that is comprehensible but also fundamentally humane. . . . *The Family* contains multitudes—the fabric of a dark and bloody century most of all."   —James McAuley, *The Daily Beast*

"*The Family* belongs on the shelf next to Daniel Mendelsohn's *The Lost* as a response to Saul Bellow's lament that American Jews 'should have reckoned more fully, more deeply, with' the Shoah."   —*The Oregonian* (Portland)

"[David Laskin] urges us to see the workings of history not merely as a list of dates, places and events, great men and great ideas, but as a tapestry whose threads include the lives of flesh-and-blood human beings. . . . [He is] a storyteller who has given his own family chronicle all of the depth and detail of a great novel while, at the same time, honoring the truth of their lives."   —*Jewish Journal*

PENGUIN BOOKS

THE FAMILY

David Laskin is the bestselling author of *The Children's Blizzard*, which won the Washington State Book Award and Midwest Booksellers' Choice Award for nonfiction, and *The Long Way Home: An American Journey from Ellis Island to the Great War*, which also won the Washington State Book Award. Laskin writes for *The New York Times* and *The Washington Post*. He and his wife, the parents of three grown daughters, live in Seattle.

THE
FAMILY

—

A JOURNEY INTO
THE HEART OF
THE TWENTIETH CENTURY

—

DAVID
LASKIN

PENGUIN BOOKS

PENGUIN BOOKS
Published by the Penguin Group
Penguin Group (USA) LLC
375 Hudson Street
New York, New York 10014

USA | Canada | UK | Ireland | Australia | New Zealand | India | South Africa | China
penguin.com
A Penguin Random House Company

First published in the United States of America by Viking Penguin,
a member of Penguin Group (USA) LLC, 2013
Published in Penguin Books 2014

Copyright © 2013 by David Laskin
Penguin supports copyright. Copyright fuels creativity, encourages diverse voices, pro-
motes free speech, and creates a vibrant culture. Thank you for buying an authorized edition of this book and for complying with copyright laws by not reproducing, scanning, or
distributing any part of it in any form without permission. You are supporting writers and
allowing Penguin to continue to publish books for every reader.

Photograph credits
    Insert page 2 (top): © World Monuments Fund
    15 (bottom): United States Holocaust Memorial Museum, courtesy of Esther Ancoli-
Barbasch. The views or opinions expressed in this book and the context in which the image
is used do not necessarily reflect the views or policy of, nor imply approval or endorsement
by, the United States Holocaust Memorial Museum.
    16 (bottom): Maidenform Collection, Archives Center, National Museum of American
History, Smithsonian Institution
    All other photographs courtesy of the author and his family

THE LIBRARY OF CONGRESS HAS CATALOGED THE HARDCOVER EDITION AS FOLLOWS:
Laskin, David.
The family : three journeys into the heart of the twentieth century / David Laskin.
pages cm
Includes bibliographical references and index.
ISBN 978-0-670-02547-3 (hc.)
ISBN 978-0-14-312589-1 (pbk.)
1. Kaganovich family. 2. Jews—Belarus—Biography. 3. Laskin, David, 1953– 4. Jews,
Belarusian—United States—Biography. 5. Jews, Belarusian—Palestine—Biography.
6. Valozhyn (Belarus)—Biography. I. Title.
DS135.B383A155 2013
929.20973—dc23   2013017047

Printed in the United States of America
10 9 8 7 6 5 4 3 2

Set in Minion Pro with Brandon Grotesque
Designed by Daniel Lagin
Maps by Virginia Norey

To my cousin Benny Kahanovitz,
who saved the letters and shared the history

לבן דודי בני כהנוביץ

שהציל את המכתבים וחלק את ההיסטוריה

גלמי ראו עיניך ואל ספרך כלם יכתבו ימים יצרו ולא אחד בהם

Your eyes saw my unformed body;
all the days ordained for me were written in your book
before one of them came to be. (New International Version)

Thine eyes did see mine unformed substance,
And in Thy book they were all written—
Even the days that were fashioned,
When as yet there was none of them. (Jewish Publication Society)

—PSALM 139.16

CONTENTS

FAMILY TREE OF
SHIMON DOV HAKOHEN
AND BEYLE SHAPIRO

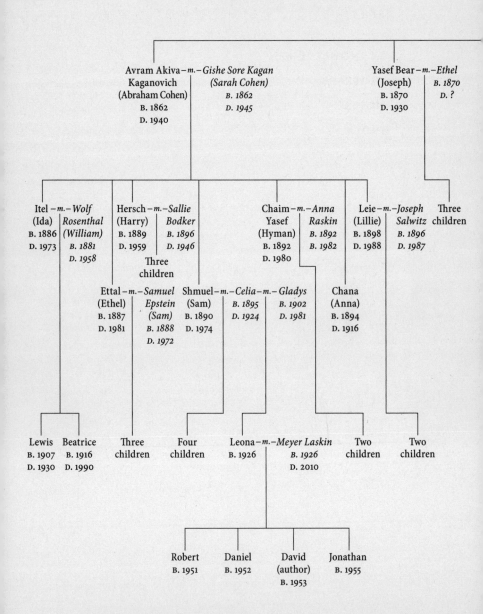

Avram Akiva – *m.* – *Gishe Sore Kagan*
Kaganovich   *(Sarah Cohen)*
(Abraham Cohen)   *B. 1862*
B. 1862   *D. 1945*
D. 1940

Yasef Bear – *m.* – *Ethel*
(Joseph)   *B. 1870*
B. 1870   *D. ?*
D. 1930

Itel – *m.* – *Wolf*
(Ida)   *Rosenthal*
B. 1886 *(William)*
D. 1973 *B. 1881*
         D. 1958

Hersch – *m.* – *Sallie*
(Harry)   *Bodker*
B. 1889   *B. 1896*
D. 1959   *D. 1946*
         Three
        children

Chaim – *m.* – *Anna*
Yasef   *Raskin*
(Hyman)   *B. 1892*
B. 1892   *B. 1982*
D. 1980

Leie – *m.* – *Joseph*   Three
(Lillie)   *Salwitz* children
B. 1898   *B. 1896*
D. 1988   *D. 1987*

Ettal – *m.* – *Samuel*
(Ethel)   *Epstein*
B. 1887   *(Sam)*
D. 1981   *B. 1888*
             D. 1972

Shmuel – *m.* – *Celia* – *m.* – *Gladys*
(Sam)   *B. 1895*   *B. 1902*
B. 1890   *D. 1924*   *D. 1981*
D. 1974

Chana
(Anna)
B. 1894
D. 1916

Lewis   Beatrice
B. 1907   B. 1916
D. 1930   D. 1990

Three
children

Four
children

Leona – *m.* – *Meyer Laskin*
B. 1926   *B. 1926*
              D. 2010

Two
children

Two
children

Robert   Daniel   David   Jonathan
B. 1951   B. 1952   (author)   B. 1955
                          B. 1953

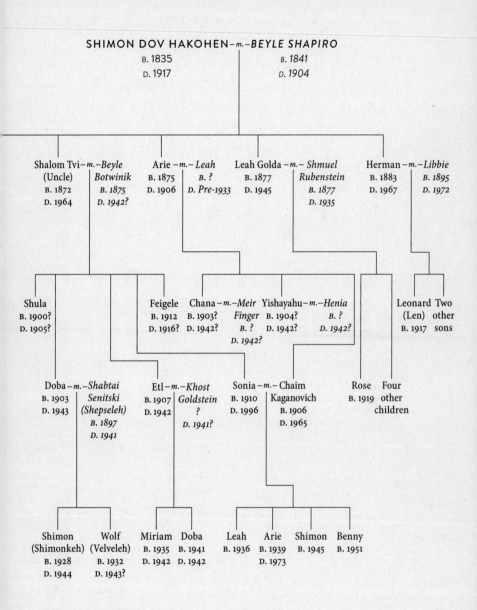

SHIMON DOV HAKOHEN – m. – *BEYLE SHAPIRO*
B. 1835   B. *1841*
D. 1917   D. *1904*

Shalom Tvi – m. – *Beyle*   Arie – m. – *Leah*   Leah Golda – m. – *Shmuel*   Herman – m. – *Libbie*
(Uncle)   *Botwinik*   B. 1875   B. *?*   B. 1877   *Rubenstein*   B. 1883   B. *1895*
B. 1872   B. *1875*   D. 1906   D. *Pre-1933*   D. 1945   B. *1877*   D. 1967   D. *1972*
D. 1964   D. *1942?*   D. *1935*

Shula   Feigele   Chana – m. – *Meir*   Yishayahu – m. – *Henia*   Leonard   Two
B. 1900?   B. 1912   B. *1903?*   *Finger*   B. 1904?   B. *?*   (Len)   other
D. 1905?   D. 1916?   D. *1942?*   B. *?*   D. 1942?   D. *1942?*   B. 1917   sons
               D. *1942?*

Doba – m. – *Shabtai*   Etl – m. – *Khost*   Sonia – m. – Chaim   Rose   Four
B. 1903   *Senitski*   B. 1907   *Goldstein*   B. 1910   Kaganovich   B. 1919   other
D. 1943   *(Shepseleh)*   D. 1942   *?*   D. 1996   B. 1906   children
      B. *1897*   D. *1941?*   D. 1965
      D. *1941*

Shimon   Wolf   Miriam   Doba   Leah   Arie   Shimon   Benny
(Shimonkeh)   (Velveleh)   B. 1935   B. 1941   B. 1936   B. 1939   B. 1945   B. 1951
B. 1928   B. 1932   D. 1942   D. 1942   D. 1973
D. 1944   D. 1943?

INTRODUCTION

I t all started, like so many family stories, with a plausible fiction—honest mistake, faulty memory, bit of embroidered imagination that got repeated so many times it became family truth. My mother told me that her cousin Barbara told her that Barbara's parents had always insisted Stalin's notorious henchman Lazar Kaganovich was a relative of ours. "Iron Lazar," one of the prime culprits in the "famine genocide" that killed millions in Ukraine in 1932 and 1933, does indeed share my mother's family name—Kaganovich or Kahanovitz ("son of Kagan") in Russian, HaKohen ("the priest") in Hebrew, Cohen in English—and there is some family resemblance in the old photos. He was born in 1893, the same decade as my grandfather Sam and his brothers, one of whom distinctly remembered that even as a little boy Lazar was mean and nasty—a mass murderer in the making. Here was the clincher. If Lazar Kaganovich was my grandfather's cousin, that meant he was also cousin to my grandfather's sister Itel, known to the world as Ida Rosenthal, the founder of the Maidenform Bra Company. What a story! While one cousin was raking in millions selling bras and girdles the other was engineering the famine that killed as many as 7.5 million people in Ukraine. The Entrepreneur and the Madman. From Madison Avenue to the Kremlin. Uplift and Oppression. *I dreamed I was in the Politburo in my Maidenform bra. . . .*

Too bad it isn't true. At least the part about Lazar. When I pressed my mother for more details—exactly *how* were we related to this monster? where does he fit on the family tree? who's in touch with his descendants?—she drew a blank and suggested I e-mail our cousin Shimon Kahanovitz in Israel. Shimon has an interest in family history, my mother said, and he'll know, if anyone does. I wrote Shimon a breathless message outlining my exciting new idea, and asked what he knew about our kinship to "the Wolf of the Kremlin." Shimon's response was brief and definitive: "Many years ago I asked my mother Sonia about him. She told me that Lazar Kaganovich is not part of the family."

End of story. Or rather, end of one story, beginning of another.

Shimon's phrase "not part of the family" got me wondering. Who exactly was part of this family of Cohens and Kaganoviches and where were we all? I knew about the relatives in Israel—I'd met Shimon and one of his nieces many years earlier—but I had no idea how or why or when they had ended up in the Middle East while the rest of us went to the States. Back in the 1960s and 1970s, my mother's parents, Sam and Gladys Cohen, used to visit Israel for a month or two every year. They sent us Jaffa oranges; I wrote them aerogrammes on thin blue sheets that a fold and a lick magically transformed into thin blue envelopes. When they got back home, they always had a lot to say about Uncle—whose uncle or why he lacked a first name I never knew and never thought to ask. That was more than forty years ago; I was a teenager, barely interested in my American relatives let alone distant kin in Israel. "Uncle," the oranges, and the aerogrammes lodged in my mind. Everything else washed over me and kept on going.

But now that I had opened a line to Shimon, I was curious—more than curious, "beguiled," as Alice Munro described herself when she began "rifling around in the past" in search of her own family's story for her autobiographical collection *The View from Castle Rock*. I began peppering Shimon with e-mails, and bit by bit the story emerged. Shimon explained that the reason I have relatives in Israel is that his parents, Chaim and Sonia, both of whom were first cousins of my grandfather, made aliyah (literally "ascent") to Palestine in 1924 and 1932, respectively. Chaim and Sonia could have gone to New York like my grandfather Sam and his sister, Itel, and their siblings and parents, gotten hired by Maidenform or the wholesale business (flatware and small appliances) that Sam and his two brothers ran, pulled down a tidy salary, and moved to the suburbs. But instead they chose the Holy Land. They were young, wildly idealistic Zionist pioneers—*halutzim* is the Hebrew word—bent on reclaiming the Land through "the conquest of labor." In the 1920s, Chaim and his comrades tried to farm a parched rocky slope in the mountains above the Sea of Galilee and later helped found a cooperative agricultural village north of Tel Aviv. Sonia ran the family farm, raised four children, set a sumptuous table any Jewish mother would be proud of. Together they suffered malaria, poverty, an unforgiving climate, the hostility of Arab neighbors, and decades of relentless toil—and they survived to witness the violent birth of a new nation. In photos Shimon sent me, the young Chaim and Sonia look as tan, gorgeous, and happy as movie stars.

So no, Stalin's willing executioner does not hang on our family tree. Instead, through Sonia and Chaim, we have a stake in the story of Israel.

But there's more. The mysterious Uncle turned out to be Sonia's father, Shalom Tvi Kaganovich. He was, by all accounts, a loving, sweet-tempered man who, together with his pious wife, Beyle—my grandfather's aunt—ran a mildly prosperous leather shop and factory in a small village near Minsk. When Sonia went to Palestine in 1932, Shalom Tvi and Beyle remained behind with their two other daughters, sons-in-law, and grandchildren. The parents and sisters worried constantly that Sonia would be lonely or hungry or hot or poor or forced to eat nonkosher food or taken advantage of by randy *halutzim*. The terrible irony, of course, is that nine years later, all of them were imprisoned by the Nazis—all except Shalom Tvi, who by chance had come to visit the family in New York, in July 1939, two months before the Second World War began, and thus escaped the catastrophe.

As a child writing aerogrammes to my grandparents in Israel, I knew about the Holocaust, but somehow it never occurred to me that the Holocaust had anything to do with my family. I dimly recall hearing that Uncle's family was "trapped" in Europe after he had come to the United States in 1939. Yet I never asked what happened to them, never wondered about why they had stayed and suffered while the others emigrated and prospered. Though they were my grandfather's aunt and first cousins, I never heard him mention any of their names. Two clicks on a Web site conjured their photos onto my computer screen—these relatives I never knew I had. Why was the name of the wicked Lazar Kaganovich batted around at family gatherings but never a mention of Doba, Etl, Shabtai, Khost? I took it for granted, as I studied the photos, that I would never learn anything more about them. What they experienced under the Nazis, I assumed, had been erased. I was wrong on all counts. Two years of research and travel to our towns and cities in Belarus and Lithuania have yielded staggering discoveries.

I thought I knew about the Holocaust—or Shoah ("catastrophe") as it is called in Hebrew—but my knowledge was made of clichés and blind horror. I thought I knew about my family but I discovered that I knew almost nothing. My grandparents and great-grandparents came to America to escape the ethnic and religious hatred that had poisoned Jewish life in Eastern Europe for centuries—and I had always assumed they succeeded. They did well in America; we, their descendants, are still enjoying the fruits of their hard work and imagination. We are living the lives they wanted for us. But despite their best efforts, they could not keep us from the nightmare of history. The three branches of my mother's family endured and enacted the great Jewish upheavals of the twentieth century—mass immigration to the United States, the founding of Israel, and the Shoah. My grandfather and his first cousins fought in two world wars, ran two successful businesses, copied Torah scrolls, planted citrus groves in Palestine, lived in a mansion by the sea on Long Island, and watched tanks draped in swastikas grind through the boulevards of Vilna. One family—three fates. The story had been hiding in plain sight all my life. It took a shattered myth and a sifting of the remnant shards to make me see it.

I am a product of the baby boom. I grew up in a plush leafy suburb of New York City with other privileged kids from Eastern European Jewish backgrounds. Madison Street on the Lower East Side, where my grandfather lived in a cold-water tenement flat with his parents, two brothers, three sisters, and a boarder, is less than twenty miles as the crow flies from my parents' house in Great Neck—but there may as well have been an ocean between them. Though I knew my grandparents were immigrants, I had no idea where precisely they had come from (Russia? Poland?) or why they had left—and I never thought to ask. I knew I was Jewish because they were Jewish, but what did being Jewish mean for a child born on Long Island in 1953? At the reform synagogue my parents made me attend, I hated the repetitive prayers, the rabbi's faux-folksy tales about Minsk and Pinsk, the defensive pride, and the self-congratulating liberalism. I quit when I was sixteen. By then I had found my true spiritual home in literature, and Judaism seemed like an archaic, artificial barrier between me and the great world of fiction, poetry, drama, epic I longed to inhabit. The older I got, the more I thought of myself as different from my family, especially the Cohen side. I had no head for business; my Judaism had dwindled down to culture, cuisine, and Bible stories; I forgot the Hebrew that had been drummed into me. I belonged to Greenwich Village, London, Paris, Rome, maybe James Joyce's Dublin—certainly not to Jerusalem, Vilna, Minsk. As for my immigrant relatives, they struck me as a bunch of stout people with accents who got together at holidays to eat too much and talk too loudly. Itel, of course, was rich and famous after the Dream Campaign made Maidenform a marketing icon, but she was remote, chilly, imperious, more like a boss than an aunt (oddly, though all of her siblings adopted their Americanized names, she was always Itel in the family, even if they called her Ida in her *Time* and *Fortune* profiles). My grandparents loved us, plied us with delicious heavy food, tolerated the Sephardic pronunciation of Hebrew prayers we had learned at the reform synagogue (they adhered to the Ashkenazic pronunciation—"Shabbas" not "Shabbat"). They spoke to us rarely and reluctantly of the "Old Country." My family, I assumed, was about business, not history. History belonged to pioneers in their prairie schooners, young soldiers mown down at Gettysburg, west African slaves chained in the holds of wooden ships, sons and daughters of the American Revolution. Not to us.

Now I see how wrong I was. History made and broke my family in the twentieth century. My grandparents and their cousins were born into a world of tradition and religion that had lasted for centuries and died in the course of four years. In America, my grandparents, great-aunts, and -uncles were part of a huge influx of immigrants—some 23 million between 1880 and the 1920s—that transformed the culture, economy, accent, complexion, and politics of the nation. Sonia and Chaim's struggle to make a new

life in Palestine was as heroic—and tragic in its consequences—as the settling of the American prairie. Sonia's father, Shalom Tvi—the "Uncle" in
my grandparents' stories—in his own modest way stood at the crossroads
not only of the family but of the Jewish twentieth century. He left Europe
on the brink of the abyss, watched helplessly from America as war swallowed his family, frantically awaited word or sign or scrap of news. As a
child growing up, I heard about the oranges Uncle sent from the orchard,
the modern appliances he brought with him from New York to his daughter's farmhouse at Kfar Vitkin, the palms that grew by the beach on the
Mediterranean where he loved to swim. No one told me that during the
six and a half years he lived in the same house with my mother and her
parents, Uncle went out of his mind with anxiety over the fate of his wife,
two daughters, two sons-in-law, and four grandchildren in Europe. Were
he alive today to read these words, Shalom Tvi would shake his head in
humility and deny it, but in his life, his loss, his wanderings, he connected
the three branches of the family and bound them together, emotionally and
morally. Though they lived on three continents, they were a real family
joined by love, need, guilt, worry, religion, culture, cooking, sense of humor,
and outlook on life—in short, by Jewishness.

I don't know why my grandparents and parents never spoke to me
about the Shoah. But I know they were not alone. Saul Bellow mused eloquently on this question in a letter he wrote to Cynthia Ozick in 1987: "We
(I speak of Jews now and not merely of writers) should have reckoned more
fully, more deeply with it. Nobody in America seriously took this on and
only a few Jews elsewhere (like Primo Levi) were able to comprehend it
all. . . . Growing slowly aware of this unspeakable evasion I didn't even
know how to begin to admit it into my inner life. Not a particle of this can
be denied."

I am not proposing to take on this "unspeakable evasion" but rather to
give light, life, words to one facet of it—my family's facet. The stories I never
heard occurred at the same time and to the same family (the same generation of cousins) as the founding of Israel and the businesses booming in
New York. The three stories—the three branches of the family—belong
together. They twine into one inextricable strand. This story, then, is not

about the branches in isolation but about the tree. That tree has stood many thousands of years—and, God willing, will stand many thousands more.

My grandfather, great-grandfather, great-great-grandfather, and great-great-great-grandfather were Torah scribes—and for all I know the tradition goes back to the days before the Diaspora. The texts I compose and redact are not sacred, but I am a kind of scribe as well. I count myself proudly among the people of the book. I commit to paper the stories of those who came before me. What we have done, what we have lost, what remains, what we can pass on—this is the scope of my work. The family work, as I now understand.

Though I have ceased to attend synagogue and don't claim my ancestors' knowledge or share their faith, I have come to love and revere the Judaism that sustained my family through the generations. The more I learn about them, the more amazed I am by the breadth and originality of their lives. Their daring, their drive, their inventiveness and ambition and confidence and secret melancholy strike me now like something out of Dos Passos or Isaac Bashevis Singer. They were giants; wittingly or not, they enacted epics. They gave me so much, these fierce, passionate immigrants—my life, my freedom and privileges, my education, my identity, my country. The least I can do is give their stories back to them.

CHAPTER ONE

VOLOZHIN

He sat at the Torah and at God's service in holiness and purity, wielding the scribe's pen and fashioning crowns for his Creator.

—S. Y. AGNON, "THE TALE OF THE SCRIBE" (1919)

Shimon Dov HaKohen was one of God's secretaries, a scribe who laid down the law stroke by black stroke on the scraped, sanded hides of animals. The son of a scribe, the father and grandfather of scribes, Shimon Dov was a member of the Jewish priestly caste that traces its ancestry (through the male line) back to Moses' brother Aaron, the first high priest of the Israelites. The biblical Ezra also stood in this line—"Ezra the priest, the scribe of the Law of the God of heaven." Ezra HaKohen, HaSofer—Ezra the priest, the scribe—was therefore Shimon Dov's spiritual father and very possibly his blood ancestor as well, since science and scripture eerily concur that the Kohain DNA has remained intact all the way back to Aaron. It sounds as fantastic as a letterless shepherd discovering the Dead Sea Scrolls in a desert cave while the ash and radiation of the Second World War still circled the globe, but there is an unbroken strand of genes and tradition that connects Aaron, shoulder to shoulder with Moses, asking Pharaoh to "let my people go," to Ezra weeping and tearing his garments before the fallen Jews of Jerusalem to gentle-eyed, white-bearded Shimon Dov inking his parchment by the window of a small wooden house in a market town at the fringe of the Russian Empire.

Shimon Dov, for all his august lineage, was a humble, ordinary man—learned, devout, meticulous, good to his diminutive wife, openhanded with their six children, slow to kindle with either anger or joy. But when he sat down at his table in the town of Volozhin, closed his eyes to pray for perfection, and took up his quill pen, Shimon Dov glowed with God's radiance. His forked beard was so long that it brushed the soft surface of the parchment when he bent his head to write. Ever at hand were a turkey quill and a pot of special ink, always black. And a book, The Book, open to the page where he had left off. "All day he sat in his house communing with his soul in solitude, completely within the frame of the Torah," novelist S. Y. Agnon wrote of a scribe at work. "He sat secluded and isolated and no one was with him except His Name, may He be blessed. . . . From morning to evening the quill wrote on the parchment and beautiful black letters glistened and alighted on the parchment as birds upon the snow on the Sabbath when the Song of Moses is read." "You must never, ever touch anything," Shimon Dov's children and grandchildren whispered to one another as quill scratched parchment and the beautiful sacred Hebrew calligraphy spread across the scroll from right to left in dense, orderly lines. Precisely 304,805 letters composed the 79,847 Hebrew words of the Torah, the first five books of the Jewish scriptures, and Shimon Dov knew every stroke as intimately as a tailor knows his thread or a soldier his gun. Not a thunderer before kings, not a prophet raging against the sins of his people, not a seer or a tzaddik ("righteous one") singled out for a sacred mission or possessed of a shape-shifting staff—but a member all the same of an honored literate family that kept alive the book that had kept alive the Jews for more than three thousand years. When Shimon Dov died in 1917, his son Shalom Tvi instructed the mason to carve these Hebrew words onto his gravestone: "Son of Chaim, scribe of the Holy Book, he followed his father's way, he was strong in Torah, he will rest with the hands of the Kohanim." Hands are also carved on the patriarch's gravestone—hands of the priest, HaKohen, raised and spread in blessing; hands of the scribe, HaSofer, curled in painstaking toil. How many times had Shimon Dov risen in shul to recite the *birchat kohanim*, the priestly blessing that none but a Kohen can perform? *May the Lord bless you and keep you; may the Lord make His face to shine upon you, and be gracious to you. May the Lord lift up His countenance upon you, and give you peace.*

A crane or a crow flying from the Baltic to the Black Sea in the spring of 1875, the year Shimon Dov's oldest son, Avram Akiva, turned thirteen and thus by Jewish law became a man, would have looked down on a vast expanse of rolling green—pale green fields, darker green woods—stretching nearly a thousand miles along the western fringe of the Russian Empire. This was the Pale of Settlement where the tsars had decreed that their Jews must live. The occasional city—Warsaw, Lodz, Vilna, Minsk, Kiev, Odessa—blotted earth and sky with its spires and smokestacks and hives of roofs, and then the planted and forested countryside took over again. Every few miles the verdant patchwork bunched into the gray-brown corduroy of village, town, or shtetl—little town—and then relaxed into green again. Abel, Eiragola, Chelm, Slutsk, Zaskovichi, Kielce, Žeimiai, Karczew, Okup, Nowogródek, Piaseczno, Stargard, Biala, Rakov, Tuchin, Eishyshok—each shtetl name had its own peculiar linguistic knot tied by the language or dialect of the region, but the places themselves were remarkably similar.

A main street, usually named for the city it led to, entered from the fields at one end of town and disappeared into them at the other; a few blocks of wooden houses set in small garden patches fanned out around the main street, the houses of Jews and the houses of gentiles barely distinguishable but usually in separate enclaves. The center of town was left blank to make suitable space for an onion-domed Russian Orthodox church or a towered and spired Catholic church or sometimes both. The church plaza formed an obvious marketplace, and around its periphery stood the stalls and shops of the shtetl's merchants, most of them Jews. There was also a place for Jews to worship and study, but this was usually tucked down a side street, discreetly out of sight of the loftier churches and built not of brick or stone or plaster but of rough plain wooden boards and beams. The synagogue was unadorned inside too but for a bit of fine carving on the ark and the exquisite embroidery and metalwork that encased and crowned the ark's hidden contents, the one gem that every devout Jew held more

THE NORTHERN PALE OF SETTLEMENT, CIRCA 1900

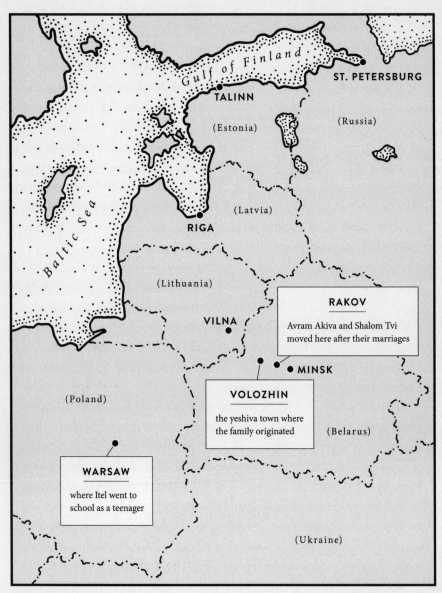

RAKOV

Avram Akiva and Shalom Tvi moved here after their marriages

VOLOZHIN

the yeshiva town where the family originated

WARSAW

where Itel went to school as a teenager

In 1900, the family lived in two neighboring towns–Volozhin and Rakov–in the Russian Pale of Settlement. (Current borders are indicated with — · — · — · —; names of current nations are in parentheses.)

precious than life itself—the scroll of the Torah—to which Shimon Dov or one of his fellow scribes had devoted years of their lives to hand lettering.

The family of eight lived in Volozhin, a town about midway between Vilna and Minsk of some five thousand inhabitants (half of them Jewish). Volozhin had one unique glory that made it stand out from all other shtetlach. In 1803, a yeshiva had been started here, and for the better part of a century this school flourished as the most renowned and revered institute of Talmudic study in Eastern Europe, and thus the world. Shimon Dov had no wealth to speak of; his house was low and flammable, his family large, his income small, his prospects dim. But to live beside the Volozhin yeshiva during its golden age was a priceless blessing. Shimon Dov grew up hearing stories of how this kingdom of wisdom had come to be established in Volozhin, and he passed the stories on to his children. The tale always began in 1726 when a six-year-old boy named Elijah ben Solomon Zalman stood before the Jewish elders in the Great Synagogue of Vilna, the Pale's preeminent city of piety and culture, to discourse on a passage of scripture. No one could believe that so young a child could be so learned, but by the age of ten Elijah, soon to be known simply as the Gaon—the "genius"—of Vilna, had outstripped any teacher in the depth and breadth of his mastery of the Talmud. Like many of God's chosen, the Vilna Gaon was difficult. As a young man, he lived a life of ascetic focus bordering on madness. To stretch his time for study, he limited himself to two hours of sleep per day; he kept the windows of his chilly house shuttered against the distractions of the world and immersed his feet in cold water to maintain mental acuity. But in the course of his seventy-seven years, this brilliant, eccentric, irascible scholar reinvented and reinvigorated Torah study. Eschewing the dialectical hairsplitting of the so-called *pilpul* (pepper) method, the Vilna Gaon brought clarity, straight thinking, and direct engagement with the biblical text to the pursuit of Jewish knowledge. He also waged holy war against the noisy, joyous, populist style of Jewish worship known as Hasidism, which was spreading wildly through the Pale in his day.

According to family lore, Shimon Dov's father, Chaim, founded the Volozhin yeshiva as a bastion of scholarship in the Gaon's anti-Hasid campaign—but family lore is wrong. Shimon Dov was born in 1835: there is no way his father could have been old enough to start a yeshiva in 1803 and still have been in shape to sire a son thirty-two years later. The yeshiva's founder was indeed named Chaim—not Chaim HaKohen but Chaim ben Yitzhak, known as Chaim the Volozhiner. This Chaim was the prize student and disciple of the Vilna Gaon, and he made the school the prime exemplar of his master's pedagogy and discipline. In time, the Volozhin yeshiva became the pattern and inspiration for yeshivot all over Lithuania, the Pale, and eventually the New World and the Holy Land as well. "Whoever wanted to learn Torah traveled to Volozhin," became a byword of the day. "It was the Torah center of the great Russian Jewry," wrote a honey-tongued Yiddish historian, "a holy place for searching souls, a mighty workshop of spiritual richness. Thousands found protection in her shelter, drank from her sources, absorbed her spirit, and became intoxicated by her aroma. Jewish lads, talented and strong willed, scraped their feet walking from remote places to bask in the light of her Torah, to breathe her scholarly atmosphere, to catch at the wings of the Divine Presence." The Hebrew poet Hayyim Bialik, who studied at the Volozhin yeshiva in the 1880s, said it was the place where "the soul of the people was forged."

Shimon Dov had breathed this intoxicating atmosphere in his youth, and someday, God willing, his firstborn, Avram Akiva, would breathe it too. But first the boy must complete his apprenticeship. Already, at thirteen, Avram Akiva had proved himself an able and ready assistant. Already he was serious, determined, assured beyond his years, maybe a bit of a know-it-all. Other bar mitzvah boys trembled when the Torah was unrolled before them for the first time. What if they accidentally poked a hole in the parchment with the pointer? What if their nose dripped and smudged the text? Avram Akiva had no such fears. He knew that the sacred scroll was strong enough to endure his clumsiness and congestion, because he had spent his childhood absorbing the occult art and science of fabricating it. When his father needed ink, Avram Akiva went to the forests surrounding Volozhin to gather gallnuts—the hard, gnarled, tannin-rich balls that gall wasps create when they implant their larvae in oak trees. The boy plucked the gallnuts off the trees, and at home he boiled them in reeking pots on his mother's stove and then mixed their essence with gum arabic, copper sulfate, and soot to make the velvety pitch-black indelible ink with which his father wrote the words of God. The preparation of the writing surfaces also fell to the apprentice—the smoothing on his father's worktable of the pliant rectangles of parchment, the backs of which he coated with powdery plaster. With a rose thorn affixed to a stick, Avram Akiva incised the parallel lines that would guide his father's hand when the scribe took up the quill and, impregnating its tip with gallnut ink, summoned forth the diamonds, crowns, daggers, and petals of the Hebrew alphabet.

At fifteen or sixteen, his apprenticeship over, Avram Akiva duly enrolled in the yeshiva. He took his place on a bench in the dimly lit hall and gave himself over to the exacting regimen of prayer and study, study and prayer, days and nights of argument, analysis, explanation, insight, refinement, all to wring out a few more precious drops of the dew of Talmudic enlightenment. A couple of hours of sleep in a narrow bed shared with a brother or a boarder, meals wolfed down without ceremony or savor, and then back to the yeshiva to continue his studies—that was the life the scribe's teenage son embraced with all his soul and all his might. Avram Akiva was lucky, for he was at the yeshiva in the latter half of the 1870s, during the directorship of Rabbi Naftali Zvi Yehudah Berlin, known as the Netziv, a brilliant dynamic scholar who ran the school for more than four decades and brought it to its peak. Under the Netziv, the student body, which had been around fifty when the school was founded, grew to as many as four hundred *bochurim* (yeshiva boys) from all over Europe and even Britain and America. The Netziv enforced the yeshiva's policy that prayer and study must go on round-the-clock, twenty-four hours a day, seven days a week, 365 days a year. This wasn't just scholarly zeal. The Netziv was convinced that if the light of Torah study ever went out, even for a second, then the primordial void would rise up once more and swallow the universe. And so with back bent, eyes bagged, brow furrowed, his days as pinched and monotonous as a monk's, Avram Akiva kept the world spinning on its axis.

The youth sat with the sages at the table of Torah—but when his studies were over, Avram Akiva returned home to follow his father in the craft of the scribe. In the hierarchy of Volozhin, scribe was a decided step down from rabbi or Talmudic scholar. Ancient and honored though his profession was, the scribe *copied* books, he did not compose or interpret them.

The scribe's work straddled the worlds of labor and learning, craft and spirit. On the one hand, Shimon Dov and his son worked with their hands, like bakers or clock makers, not solely with their minds, like the scholars at the yeshiva—and in this pious community, the life of the mind, the mind bent on Torah, was all that counted. Everything else was deemed more or less a waste of time. On the other hand, what Shimon Dov's hands produced was the very staff of Jewish life, far more sustaining than bread, more precise and beautiful than any clock. Without the work of the scribe, the Torah would have vanished in a generation like thousands of other scrolls from antiquity; and without the Torah, Jews would have vanished, dissolved like salt into the common sea. In the Diaspora, Torah was the Jewish homeland and the scribe was the archivist of his people, the custodian of sacred memory, the linguistic historian.

The scribe and his son kept their people alive while the Netziv and his students at the yeshiva kept the universe from slipping into the abyss. Avram Akiva sat at his father's worktable and began assisting in writing the tiny scrolls that the faithful hung as mezuzot upon the doorposts of their houses and bound each morning upon their arms and foreheads in the leather boxes of the tefillin. The boy soon came to know the texts by heart. He mastered the technique of correcting errors by scraping the mistaken letters or blots off the parchment with shards of glass. He learned to repair damaged faded scrolls, to sew the old parchment pieces back together and reattach them to the wooden rollers called the trees of life—*atzei hayim*. To him fell the infinitely fussy task of unrolling the teffilin scrolls and inspecting them for dirt and decay. Patience became second nature. With every pen stroke, he had to wait for the thick glossy ink to set and adhere to the parchment, for gallnut ink is not absorbed but bonds to the surface of the animal skin as it dries. Reverence and ritual portioned out his days. Avram Akiva listened as his father murmured aloud or even chanted every letter of every word he wrote, never relying solely on memory, since each quill stroke was blessed. The son knew instinctively when his father had come to one of the Names of God, for the scribe would pause to collect himself and take a deep breath before inking the Name, which once written cannot be erased. One day, when he was old enough and skilled enough, Avram Akiva would write the Names in a Torah scroll on his own.

In the course of a year, Shimon Dov might complete a single Torah—assuming he had a commission for a Torah that year. The real bread and butter of the business were mezuzot and tefillin, which were always in demand. Still, it wasn't much of a business—though business was obviously not the point. Fortunately, Shimon Dov had a wife who earned enough from her small grocery to keep their growing family clothed and fed (it was the same for Hayyim the Volozhiner, who, after founding the yeshiva, had run it on the income from his wife's textile mill). Six children the couple produced over a span of twenty-three years—five sons and a daughter raised on the proceeds of sacred texts and staple foods.

The scribe and his family were among the pillars of their community, but never the central pillar. They knew this and it rankled them. They were short, these Volozhin Kohanim, but they stood tall in their own estimation. At once earthy and self-important, egotistical and insecure, recalcitrant and easily cowed, ambitious and anxious, they hummed with contradictions. They did God's work but their women fed them. They sought the blessing of sages but gazed jealously at their richer, more learned, more accomplished neighbors. They bore a great name but no great deeds were attached to it. Ezra and before him Aaron were their progenitors, but 150 generations of hunch-shouldered exiles stood between them. The scribe kept the Book alive, but it was the Book of a people without a home, without rights, without enforceable laws, without means, without respect, and seemingly, in the Russian Pale of Settlement in the late 1870s, without hope of gaining any of these.

Things happened in Volozhin but nothing seemed to change. The yeshiva burned down one hot summer day, and a new yeshiva was built—as austere and resplendent as a Greek temple with pure white walls, unadorned pilasters, high windows, a peaked red roof. Students kept flocking here from all over Eastern Europe. Prosperous fathers still tried to snag prize Volozhin scholars as husbands for their pampered daughters. Imperial authorities swept into town, inspected the yeshiva, interrogated the rabbis, ordered that secular subjects and Russian language be taught—and the rabbis once again found ways to circumvent or accommodate government control while ensuring the uninterrupted flow of Torah study. The wheat harvest failed. Prices rose. Rubles changed hands from peasant to shopkeeper, merchant to banker, banker to prince. But in Volozhin none of it raised more than a ripple. An epoch was grinding to its close, but behind the walls of the yeshiva, study and prayer went on as always night and day. Shimon Dov bent over his parchment with his pious sons beside him.

In the pure white temple of knowledge, the *bochurim* prayed through the minutes and hours and weeks and months of the Jewish year. They believed that their devotion sustained the world that Hashem had summoned out of darkness and given to the sons of Adam. "Hashem, His will, and His word are all one and the same," declared the founder. The *bochurim* devoted their lives to fathoming His word: His will was beyond them.

CHAPTER TWO

THE MOVE TO RAKOV

I t was a time when angels glimmered before the righteous in the watches of the night. The Gaon of Vilna was studying on one such night when an angel appeared and offered to reveal the secrets of Torah without struggle—a flash in the mind and he would know all. Sleepless and fierce as ever, the Gaon sent the angel back to heaven. "I have no desire for any understanding of Hashem's Torah that comes through any intermediary," he declared. "My eyes are lifted only to Hashem, that He reveal my portion in His Torah, according to my own lifelong efforts."

Lifelong effort powered the Gaon, but to truly worship Hashem, joy was also required. In Volozhin, every Shabbat and every holiday, the sound of voices singing and chanting in unison pulsed through the walls of the yeshiva and out into the streets and courtyards beyond. When the last echoes died, the *bochurim* began to dance. They whirled into the square outside the yeshiva and in a triumphant line crossed the marketplace, marched to the house of the Netziv, called him forth to join them, and danced him back to the yeshiva to resume their studies. Dance, song, blessing, celebration—all joy always led back to study.

On cold winter nights, the children of Shimon Dov could see the light of hundreds of candles falling onto the snow from the high windows of the yeshiva. Volozhin may have been poor and shabby, but the candlelight burned gold on the white courtyard and flashed jewels from the surface of the drifts. The scribe's children felt as if they lived in an enchanted holy realm, a true "Jewish kingdom of strength and purity."

One night when he was six years old, Shalom Tvi, the third son, was walking home from his cheder—Jewish elementary school—when he came upon a stooped old man staggering along with a cane. The high holidays had passed; autumn was well advanced; the streets were dark and wet and covered with fallen leaves. Young as he was, Shalom Tvi could see that the man was lost. "Grandpa, give me your hand," the boy said kindly, "and I'll take you home." Shalom Tvi took the man's cold dry palm in one hand and with the other he held his lantern high. Only when they reached his house did the old man let go; then he turned to the boy and said slowly in Yiddish, "Thank you very much. I am going to give you a blessing. May you have light your entire life, light throughout your journey." Shalom Tvi never forgot. And indeed the blessing was received on high. From that time forward the boy had his own angel watching over him.

The children of the scribe needed all the heavenly help they could get. Money came seldom to God's secretary; trouble overtook them despite their righteous deeds. When Shalom Tvi was nine and Avram Akiva nineteen, the Russian tsar was assassinated and rioters fell on the Jews. Alexander II had freed the serfs and abolished the twenty-five-year mandatory military service for Jewish boys—but radicals hated him and, after many attempts on his life, finally cut him down with a bomb in St. Petersburg in March of 1881. Jews were blamed (two Jewish women were involved in the plot) and in the ensuing months vicious pogroms flared throughout the Pale. The next year the new tsar, Alexander III, enacted the so-called May laws, forbidding Jews to live, or own land, in agricultural villages. Uprooted rural Jews poured into the already overcrowded shtetlach and city slums. One of the tsar's advisers stepped forward with a bold new solution to the empire's "Jewish problem": one third will die, one third will emigrate, one third "will be completely dissolved into the surrounding population." There were some 5 million Jews living in the Pale at that time: the tsar's councilor was dreaming of ethnic cleansing on an unprecedented scale.

But life went on. The year the May laws were enacted, Avram Akiva wed at the age of twenty and left Volozhin to settle in the nearby shtetl of

Rakov, the home of his new wife, Gishe Sore. The newlyweds shared the names of the first Jewish couple—Abraham and Sarah (Sore is the Yiddish form of the Hebrew name Sarah). Like her husband, Gishe Sore had been born to the priestly caste—the family went by the name Kagan and they had roots in Rakov going back at least to the eighteenth century. Gishe Sore, the oldest of three children, was born in 1862, the same year as her future husband; she was small, sharp, competent, and pious—in short, an excellent wife for the learned son of the Volozhin scribe. Avram Akiva found his wife's shtetl a step down from the yeshiva town where he had grown up, but in time he came to appreciate its advantages. With three thousand residents (two thirds of them Jews), Rakov was small and sleepy, but proximity to the regional center of Minsk made it more convenient and more prosperous than Volozhin. There was plenty of work for the young scribe, and when it came time to pray, he had his choice of four synagogues, all clustered together in a compound near the market. Rakov's market square boasted seventy shops, most of them owned by Jews. Avram Akiva soon became accustomed to the racket and dust of the twice-weekly markets, Monday and Friday, when peasants converged on the town to buy, sell, and drink. At the Friday market, as the sun neared the western horizon, a man came striding through the square shouting, "It's Shabbat!" and all the Jewish shopkeepers closed up and went home. At one end of town, a dreamy lake reflected the twin brick towers of the Catholic church; at the other end, an ancient Jewish cemetery dozed in a grove of twisted pines. Even the humbler families had big gardens bursting with cucumbers, carrots, potatoes, and sorrel, and a clump of fragrant peonies to brighten the spring. Rakov's soil was sandier than Volozhin's and the countryside around it was flatter—fields of grain and dense green woods rolled out to the horizon in every direction. On summer Shabbat afternoons, after shul, Avram Akiva and Gishe Sore strolled out of town on Granary Lane past apple and pear orchards and into the dappled forest where children gathered mushrooms under the firs and poplars. The land belonged to gentiles, but a Jew could own the sky and the intoxicating smells that rose from the earth.

The young couple took a house by the lake and settled in for a long marriage. Theirs was a good match. Avram Akiva, though poor, was respected for his knowledge of Torah, for his name, his trade, and his standing as the firstborn son of a Kohain. Fierce and unyielding on the Word of God, he was mild in everything else—a tolerant, generous man, content with little, comfortable in his skin, wise beyond his years. Gishe Sore was expected to serve as his intermediary with the world and she stepped up briskly to the task. While Avram Akiva devoted himself to Torah, she ran the household and earned the money. She milked the cow each morning; every spring she planted a large vegetable garden around the house and tended it through the warm months. And like her mother-in-law, she went into business, running a general store that catered to the neighborhood families and the peasants who flocked to Rakov on market days. A barrel of herring and a barrel of kerosene held pride of place in the center of Gishe Sore's shop; cupboards, drawers, and shelves were crammed with flax oil, tobacco of various grades, matches, clay pipes, needles, thread, buttons, kerosene lamps, and sharp little knives cased in red pouches. If your boot soles flapped, you paid for a dab of the tar she kept ready in a pitcher for quick repairs. Like all Jewish shopkeepers, Gishe Sore extended credit— sooner or later, everyone paid, and if they didn't she could chalk it up as a mitzvah. Her store was not in the central marketplace but near the lake that the family lived on—a picturesque spot on sunny days with views of the Catholic church rising from the green glassy water. A small river with the marvelous name Svishloshz drained the lake. In the winter blocks of ice were cut from the river, and every spring Jews came here to dip out the clearest, cleanest water to use in making their Passover matzo. Idlers fished from the bridge and in the summer children swam naked in the shallows. Since it was miles to the nearest train station at Olechnowicze, everything and everyone arrived or departed by foot or cart. The newspaper from Minsk that Gishe Sore subscribed to—she was the only woman on her street to take a daily—carried stale news, but it was better than no news.

In any case, the news that mattered most concerned the family. In the middle of March 1883, word came that Avram Akiva's forty-two-year-old mother had given birth to a healthy baby boy. On the first day of spring, Avram Akiva and Gishe Sore went to Volozhin to attend the bris of his new brother, Herman. When the mohel had done his work and the baby was soothed and tucked into his cradle, the family sat long over cake and schnapps. There was much talk that day about the strange doings at the yeshiva. The current crop of *bochurim* seemed to be fired up with new passions, grievances, and laments. The students had organized a boycott of the town butchers and bakers, who they claimed were depriving them of the proceeds from a tax on yeast; things had grown so heated that a few irate butchers had threatened the students with cleavers. But there was more. All of a sudden, the yeshiva was mad for Palestine. This was not the first upwelling in Volozhin of fervor for the Land. Chaim the Volozhiner and the Vilna Gaon had been early supporters of what came to be known as Zionism, breaking ranks with traditionalists who argued that the return must wait until *after* the Messiah had come. At Chaim's urging, Jews from Volozhin and the surroundings raised money to support a colony of the pious in the holy city of Tzvat (Safed) in the Galilee. But the young hotheads of 1883 were rallying around something entirely different: return not for the sake of prayer but to build a self-sustaining Jewish homeland. A year earlier a group named Hovevei Zion—Lovers of Zion—had dispatched a tiny band of idealists to plant the first Jewish agricultural colony near Jaffa. Rishon LeZion—First to Zion—was now barely clinging to life, but that only goaded the zeal of the Volozhin students. Even the Netziv, though he officially banned Zionist organizations on the grounds that "one does not suspend Torah study for the sake of a mitzvah that can be done by others," privately sympathized with the cause. The patriarch kept his views to himself, but his older sons were clearly intrigued by these rumblings of Jewish life beyond the Pale.

God blessed Gishe Sore with a child on July 20, 1884, but Itka, as they named the daughter, did not survive infancy. Many years later, Gishe Sore confided to one of her daughters-in-law that she had accidentally smothered a baby to death when she rolled over in her sleep—and this may have been how Itka died.

A year and a half later, on January 9, 1886, Gishe Sore bore Avram Akiva another daughter. This one they named Itel. Itka and Itel are apparently variants of the Hebrew name Esther, so Itel was likely chosen to remind her parents of the daughter they had lost. The new baby was healthy and robust in every way except size. Even in a family so chronically compact, Itel was tiny—maybe four feet eleven at her zenith—with a mass of unruly dark hair, deep-set eyes, and a rounded solidity that would always tend toward stoutness. But in character Itel more than made up for her stature.

Avram Akiva and Gishe Sore were faithful servants of the Lord. They eschewed the so-called Jewish Enlightenment—Haskalah—that had spread to the Pale from Germany. Not for them the heretical fads—folkism, socialism, Yiddishism, assimilationism—that godless youths shouted about in the cities. The scribe and his wife preferred it quiet. What their fathers and mothers had done before them, they did now. What God demanded, they gave. So why did Hashem in his infinite wisdom decree that the first surviving fruit of their marriage should be a revolutionary?

Practically from birth, Itel defied all expectations of what a Jewish child, and especially a Jewish daughter, should be in the waning years of the nineteenth century. If the parents were hoping for sweet, pious, yielding, and obedient, they were sorely disappointed. Seven more children followed in rapid succession (another daughter, three sons, two more daughters, and a baby who died in infancy), though none ever challenged Itel's will, daring, and absolute authority. Itel knew that she was right about everything that mattered, and she laid down the law in the two children's bedrooms. In time, not even the parents stood up to her. "Don't manage me," Itel once told a friend. "My parents couldn't do it and neither can you."

Gishe Sore was a famously bad cook. Her matzo balls were like glue, her chickens raw. When she baked, the children left the center of the bread untouched because it had the consistency of wet paper. The mother wheedled; the children defied her. Such a scandal—a Jewish child wasting food. So Itel took charge. On her mother's behalf, she commanded that every crumb must be consumed, and the younger ones cleaned their plates. When she caught her mother watering the cow's milk to make it go further, Itel made her stop. Milk, after all, was one of the few palatable things that came out of Gishe Sore's kitchen.

Only Avram Akiva was untouchable. Itel did not always follow her father's dictates, but she knew better than to challenge him to his face. Apparently, Avram Akiva did not challenge her too much either. By force of character, Itel got a pass, even from a very early age. It didn't matter that she was tiny and clearly not destined to be a beauty. It didn't matter that the family was large and their means small. It didn't matter that she was born into a world where Jews had few rights and Jewish women fewer still. Itel, without asking permission, gave herself rights. She assumed the privilege of speaking her mind, making her own rules, acting on her own beliefs. And her parents wisely—or helplessly—did not stand in her way.

Childhood was brief in those days, pleasures scanty. In the summer Itel and her sisters swam naked in the lake (well screened from the prying eyes of boys). She carried water from the lake to the house in a pair of buckets yoked across her shoulders and milked the cow in the shed out back. When her three brothers were old enough they went to cheder, but Itel and the sisters stayed home. No matter how bright or curious, girls were not admitted to cheder—and certainly not to yeshiva. What early education Itel got, she picked up from her mother, and she learned about life in the streets and shops and fields of Rakov. Especially the shops.

In 1898, when Itel was twelve, the family's business interests in Rakov doubled. That March, Avram Akiva's younger brother Shalom Tvi married a young Rakov woman named Beyle Botwinik, who had inherited a thriving company that manufactured and wholesaled animal hides. Shalom Tvi, twenty-six at the time of his marriage, moved to Rakov and joined his wife in running the leather business. At a stroke, the affable, dimpled, good-looking third brother became the wealthiest member of the HaKohen family. Avram Akiva, though a decade older, was delighted to have his brother in town, and the two grew close during these years. In time, some of their children grew close as well.

Shalom Tvi was a lucky man, for his bride was pious and rich and she connected him with a Rakov family of substance, imagination, enterprise, and many members. Beyle herself was one of fourteen children, and among her relations there were scholars and Zionists, revolutionaries and philanthropists, even one young man who fought beside Trotsky during the Russian Revolution. Four years younger than her husband, Beyle at twenty-two already had the calm demeanor and steadiness of a mature woman. Her features were fine, her figure tidy, her eyes alight with a sterling character. "My mother was a *tzadeke*—a very charitable God-fearing woman," one of her daughters said years later. "She would bake *challot* on Fridays which she would distribute to all of the poor. There were very poor people in Rakov, and I would go and give them out. Each person would bless me."

So Shalom Tvi had done well for himself. The dimples just discernible beneath his neatly trimmed beard were much in evidence in those days. Beyle's parents and uncle lived in a compound of houses on a large oblong piece of property on Kashalna Street—the lane that ran between the marketplace and the Catholic church—and they gave the newlyweds a corner of their lot to build on. The young couple put up a nice new house with two bedrooms, a living room and dining room, and even a water barrel in the kitchen that Shalom Tvi, always clever with gadgets, equipped with a faucet. Their children would remember the house and garden, even the outhouse that their father built, as bathed in golden light. A gentile maid came in to clean, fetch water in pails from the communal well, and do the laundry. In her ample fenced yard Beyle grew fruit and vegetables—and what the family didn't eat fresh she pickled and stored in the cellar. In the hall outside the kitchen stood a tall cabinet stocked with glass jars of preserves, and at the top of the house they had a *boidem* (storage attic) with racks and hooks for hanging laundry. Every morning Beyle walked through her garden and opened the gate to the courtyard that she shared with her parents and her uncle and aunt. Every night the gate was shut, the porch was swept, and the couple had their gleaming house to themselves. Many years later, when a rare sweet evening breeze blew over the desert of Palestine where she lived, their daughter Sonia would breathe deeply and murmur, "It smells like Rakov."

Beyle and Shalom ran their business with the traditional division of labor: Beyle looked after the shop in the Rakov market and schmoozed customers, Shalom Tvi traveled the countryside buying hides and tinkered with the machines in the small factory. Though the business was hers originally, Beyle let her husband have top billing in the company name— Kaganovich and Rubilnik Leather Goods (Kaganovich is the Russian form of the name HaKohen). But she remained as active as ever, even after she had children. Like her sister-in-law Gishe Sore, like wives of scholars and scribes and teachers and small businessmen and peddlers all over the Pale,

Beyle was a member of the sisterhood of the working Jewish mother. Gishe Sore was a terrible cook, because between the grocery store, the garden, the cow, the laundry, the seven children, and the duties to her husband the scribe, who had time to stand around a sizzling pan? Beyle's children later complained that her letters were never more than three lines, but where would she find the time to write more? Itel grew up watching women spend the day on their feet in perpetual motion while men sat, nodded their heads, and moved only their fingers, their eyes, and sometimes their lips. No wonder the women's section of the shul resounded with laughter and chatter every Shabbat: it was the one time in the week when they could sit and relax. Women had no urge to argue with angels in the middle of the night—they were grateful if they could grab five hours' sleep. Jewish mothers in the Pale were efficient managers, brilliant improvisers, shrewd negotiators, practiced schmoozers, nimble stretchers of every kopek. They juggled multiple tasks. They toted columns of figures in their heads. They rolled with market conditions beyond their control. They learned from past mistakes and planned for an uncertain future. In short, they were ideal models for how to succeed in business, and their lessons were not lost on bright girls like Itel.

In the Russian annals of the family, the wives are all but silent. They worked, they sacrificed, they looked after their families, they faded into their husbands' shadows. Between them Gishe Sore and Beyle bore at least nine daughters, starting with Itel. It was the lot of these daughters to emerge from the shadows, break the silence, leave a mark on the world that everyone recognized as theirs. Gishe Sore and Beyle were not timid, but they were obedient and they did what was expected of them. Their daughters were different. They did what no one expected. Starting with Itel.

CHAPTER THREE

THE MAKING OF A REVOLUTIONARY

tel took it for granted that she would work for a living like her mother and grandmother before her—but not in a grocery store. Forever fussing with jars and sacks and barrels, dickering with peasants, bartering foul-smelling kerosene for eggs and vegetables, keeping the books, sweeping the floor—it would kill her to be chained to the daily round of small-town retail. So what was left? The daughter of a scribe did not work in a factory. Itel was not cut out to be a lady's maid, cook, or governess. So she learned to sew. Before her thirteenth birthday, she was apprenticed to a Rakov dressmaker to be instructed in the arts of measuring, cutting, basting, fitting, embroidering, lining, pleating, and hemming; and soon her shy younger sister Ettel joined her. The girls proved to be wizard seamstresses, quick, nimble, astonishingly intuitive in translating fabric into fashion, and when their apprenticeship was done, Gishe Sore bought them a sewing machine of their own and set them up in a corner of the house. The Kaganovich sisters: quality clothes at affordable prices. Rakov did not generate enough orders to keep them occupied, and so in the slack periods Itel traveled to nearby Minsk and not so nearby Warsaw to drum up business—daring behavior for a teenage Jewish girl back then. Volume duly increased—word spread that these diminutive sisters had something special—but the uptick in business was nothing compared with the upheaval in Itel's consciousness. Rakov at the turn of the last century was sunk in deep, seemingly unshakable sleep. But Warsaw—for a girl with Itel's temperament, Warsaw was pure intoxication. Itel became drunk on life's possibilities. "She was never really a seamstress," a relative said, "she was always an entrepreneur." *Always* is stretching it a bit. The entrepreneurial spirit awoke when Itel first went to Warsaw.

In 1901, the year Itel turned fifteen, her uncle Yasef Bear emigrated to America—the first of Shimon Dov's family to depart from the Pale. It was the tremor of a seismic shift that no one recognized at the time. An opportunity arose, a path was chosen for reasons long forgotten, one door shut and another opened. No landmark, monument, or even a scrap of paper commemorates this private earthquake. But a large family lives and prospers today as a consequence.

Yasef Bear, Shimon Dov's second son, was thirty years old, married, and the father of three young children when he left Volozhin by himself and sailed to New York. He passed through Ellis Island and made his way to Hoboken, New Jersey, where he eventually found work as a teacher in a Hebrew school. Joseph Cohn, as he called himself in America, established the beachhead in the New World—and other family members followed quickly. Herman, the youngest, was nineteen when he joined his brother, in 1902; the next year Joseph sent for his wife, Ethel, their son, and two daughters. When none of them was attacked by Indians, lost in the wilderness, or converted to Christianity, Avram Akiva and Gishe Sore decided it was safe to send an emissary from their own family. Ettel, the second daughter, had come down with typhoid and the parents thought a change of climate would do her good. So in July 1904, the seventeen-year-old girl boarded a ship in Hamburg and made her way to Ellis Island. She moved into Uncle Joseph's house in Hoboken, shared a room with her cousins Sarah and Rachel, and went to work in a dress factory.

All over the Pale, the shtetlach were emptying. Those left behind felt small and abandoned. With the departure of Joseph and Herman, only two of the scribe's six children—the fourth son, Arie, and the daughter, Leah Golda—remained in Volozhin to comfort the aging parents. Even the famous yeshiva had closed—shut down by order of the tsar's government, in 1892, when the Netziv refused to include secular course offerings. "The third temple is destroyed," wailed Volozhin Jews as they stood by the locked doors and shuttered windows. Some swore they heard a soft sobbing sound coming from deep within. Though the yeshiva later reopened, the prestige and preeminence of Chaim the Volozhiner's original academy was gone forever. The old and the precious were vanishing before their eyes and nothing good arose in their place.

Itel reversed the customary sequence in the stages of growing up: first she went to Warsaw to look for work, then she stayed there to go to school. In the Russian Empire at the time, Jews were admitted into public schools on a quota system based on population, with the number of Jewish students capped between 3 and 10 percent depending on the region. Warsaw, because of its size, had a fairly generous allotment of places for Jewish students, and somehow Itel, despite the fact that she had received no formal education, managed to snag a spot in a gymnasium (a school that roughly straddles American high school and the first years of college). She studied math and Russian, initiating a lifelong passion for Russian literature and a proficiency with numbers that would come in handy in the years ahead.

Itel was seventeen years old and a student at the Warsaw gymnasium when anti-Jewish riots broke out in Kishinev on April 6, Easter Sunday, 1903. The accounts published in underground Jewish newspapers electrified her—electrified every Jew in the Pale of Settlement. There had, of course, been pogroms before in the cities where Jews and gentiles lived together in desperate poverty—but this was *her* pogrom, the one that seared the consciousness of *her* generation. The young had assumed the twentieth century would be different—modern times, a new age. Trams ran up and down the stately boulevards of Warsaw; electric lights blazed in shopwindows; women smoked openly in public; young Jewish girls left their families and struck out on their own. Yet in the provincial capital of Kishinev people still believed in the ancient blood libel—the hideous lie that Jews required gentile blood for their religious rituals. A child had been found dead in a village; an anti-Semitic writer claimed that local Jews had slain the child to use the blood to make Passover matzo. Word spread in the usual way and the fabrication took on a life of its own. Starting on Easter Sunday, the holiday that traditionally triggered pogroms, the city of 125,000 people erupted in three days of uncontrolled violence. Nails were driven into the heads of Jewish men and the eyes of Jewish women; Jewish women were raped, their breasts hacked off, their stomachs torn open; Jewish babies were tossed out of windows with their tongues cut out of their mouths. Itel read the eyewitness accounts and burned:

> *The riot was now at its height. Windows had gone, the frames were following, the stoves had been smashed and the furniture and crockery broken up. Pages of scripture and of the sacred books lay scattered on the ground. Piles of feathers were to be seen in the courtyard and all around the house. Feathers and down flew about in the air and covered the trees like hoar-frost. In the midst of this mad inferno, in the din of destruction and wild laughter and savage roars and cries of terror, the thirst for blood awoke. The rioters at this point ceased to be men. Their first rush was for the shed; they found there but one man, the glazier Grienschpoun. A neighbor . . . was the first to stab the glazier in the neck. The unhappy man rushed out, but they seized him and dragged him on to the roof of the outhouse, where they finished him off with sticks and cudgels. . . .*

Civil authorities stood by while the citizens of Kishinev killed forty-nine Jews, wounded some five hundred, ransacked and looted over a thousand Jewish residences and businesses, and left two thousand Jewish families homeless.

It was "the last pogrom of the Middle Ages and the first atrocity of the twentieth century." A few weeks later, when the blood was dry but before it had been scraped off the walls and paving stones, a young Russian Jewish poet named Chaim Bialik (a former Volozhin yeshiva student) traveled to Kishinev at the behest of the Jewish Historical Commission of Odessa to interview survivors and report on what he heard. Bialik's response was an epic poem, a prolonged howl of agony and shame that he titled "In the City of Slaughter."

Descend then, to the cellars of the town,
There where the virginal daughters of thy folk were fouled,
Where seven heathen flung a woman down,
The daughter in the presence of her mother,
The mother in the presence of her daughter,
Before slaughter, during slaughter, and after slaughter! . . .
In that dark corner, and behind that cask
Crouched husbands, bridegrooms, brothers, peering from the cracks,
Watching the sacred bodies struggling underneath
The bestial breath,
Stifled in filth, and swallowing their blood! . . .

Crushed in their shame, they saw it all;
They did not stir nor move;
They did not pluck their eyes out; they beat not their brains against
    the wall! . . .

They died like dogs, and they were dead!
And on the next morn, after the terrible night
The son who was not murdered found the spurned cadaver of his father
    on the ground.
Now wherefore dost though weep, O son of man?

Bialik's indictment of Jewish passivity, Jewish terror, Jewish helpless-
ness in the face of gentile violence galvanized a generation. It certainly
galvanized Itel. Everywhere she went young Jews were in an uproar. Slender bespectacled students announced that they were quitting school and
moving to Palestine to work in the vineyards. Sons and daughters of shopkeepers gathered in the corners of coffeehouses to whisper about the weapons they needed for underground cells. Emigration to America spiked,
doubling in the year after Kishinev. A new wave of Zionist fervor—the
ecstatically idealistic Second Aliyah—began to build. The word suddenly
on everyone's lips was *self-defense*. Never again would they stand by
while their women were raped and their children hacked with axes. Never
again would they be cornered in attics, chased into cellars, stabbed in

the neck by laughing neighbors. No city would ever again be a city of slaughter.

In the welter of post-Kishinev Warsaw, Itel was exposed to every shade in the radical spectrum. Each faction assured her that if she signed on with them, a new revolutionary day would dawn—while the other factions were certain to plunge the world into immediate and irredeemable doom. She chose to join the Bund.

Itel had known of the Bund—the socialist Jewish labor organization that held sway in the Pale in the late nineteenth and early twentieth centuries—before she went to Warsaw. She was twelve years old when the organization emerged in 1897. But she was old enough to thrill to the story of how the first Bundist agitator infiltrated Rakov.

One Friday evening in winter, when the pious were ushering in the Sabbath bride as usual with song and prayer, a handsome young man with a disturbing little mole on his nose appeared at the door of the prayer house used by the shtetl's young breakaway congregation. The youth was tall, his smile was broad and pleasant, his greeting of "Sholem Aleichem" set everyone at ease—and so when he politely implored the congregants to take one of his pamphlets home and read it ("but please not in the presence of your parents"), they all readily complied. They assumed this young fellow was a new-hatched *magid*—an itinerant preacher—come to spread God's love. "Until late in the night, each of us was immersed in this thin pamphlet," one of the congregants wrote later, "and something new, strange, and not understood came to us from its pages. It seemed to be written in Yiddish; yet it was not the familiar language or the familiar words. What words! Beyond understanding! Words like 'conspiracy,' 'expropriation,' 'confidence,' and many more which we had never heard." The next morning, they gathered again for Sabbath prayer and conferred. *Did you read? I did read. And what do you think? I did not understand.* Happily, the charming young pamphleteer with the mole was on hand to explain. Smiling the same irresistible smile as the day before, the stranger removed his overcoat and revealed his *rubaska*—the traditional long Russian shirt that flows from shoulders to calves—colored a bright red and cinched by a bright red band around his waist. The innocent young Jews of Rakov were so dazzled by the smile, the red shirt, the mysterious pamphlet, the confiding manner that no one had the nerve to tell the man to cover his head in the presence of God. He begged permission to talk, and soon it became clear that this was no *magid* and his enchanting words had nothing to do with God. The young man was in fact a representative of the newly established revolutionary socialist workers' party—the Bund—and he had come to Rakov from Minsk as part of a concerted program of agitation and recruitment. Rakov's breakaway congregation was won over to a person. "All of us, as one, signed up for membership then and there. And thus, instead of a rabbi to teach us the lessons of 'Ein Ya'akov,' that young man was teaching us, every evening, the lessons of the Bund and of the revolution."

The story of the handsome stranger with the mole and the pamphlet and the red shirt made a deep impression on the young Itel. Five years later, a seventeen-year-old student and a garment worker roiled by the Kishinev atrocities, she was ready to don the red shirt herself. She attended secret meetings in shuttered back rooms (secret because the Bund was illegal), she read pamphlets by the score, she listened to shining-faced comrades sing the Bund hymn:

We swear our stalwart hate persists
Of those who rob and kill the poor:
The Tsar, the Masters, Capitalists.
Our vengeance will be swift and sure.

Earth with its heaven hears.
Witness: the bright stars,
And our oath of blood and tears.
We swear. We swear.

Itel swore too. She had always been headstrong, outspoken, impatient, entitled. She had always lashed out against injustice. Now, the Bund gave her a way to channel her energy and ego into something larger than defying her parents and lording it over her brothers and sisters. With the Bund she had an ideology and a platform for organized resistance. She was a party member. She was a comrade. She was a fighter in the revolution. By a strange twist, history gave Itel, the born revolutionary, a revolution to join just as she crossed the threshold into maturity. Not merely talk of a revolution—but an inchoate mass struggle that was escalating, coalescing, and spreading through the Russian Empire. The Bund, from its founding in Vilna in 1897, had pledged to overthrow "those who rob and kill the poor." Now, in the aftermath of Kishinev, the Bund leadership passed a resolution calling for members to "organize armed resistance." Itel swore the oath of blood and bullets. When she left Warsaw to return to Rakov, she was a committed Bundist prepared to take up arms against the tsar and his reactionary henchmen.

The return home cannot have been easy. Avram Akiva and Gishe Sore wanted only security and piety for their children—the boys should be scholars and scribes; the girls should be plump happy wives. And now they were harboring a bomb thrower under their roof. How could the scribe of God have sired a daughter who never set foot in shul except to attend a Bund meeting? The parents were not blind. No Hebrew prayer was ever on the child's lips; no sign of respect ever dimmed her wicked eyes. She smoked cigarettes—a daughter of a Kohain, smoking in public. And soon there was talk of a young man, an admirer, a revolutionary no less, who followed her to meetings and hung on her every word. Where would it end?

It was true. Itel was in love. Wolf Rosenthal was five years older, strapping (at least compared with her), dark-haired, clean-featured, not quite handsome but certainly striking, with the intense black burning eyes of a fanatic or madman. The piercing gaze and gruff barking voice were deceptive: though he looked like a Jewish Rasputin, Wolf had a kind heart, a healthy young man's appetites, and the undying fidelity of a born husband. Wolf gazed adoringly as Itel, all four feet eleven inches of her, stood up at Bund meetings and thundered to the rafters about the overthrow of the tsar, the rights of all working people, the bourgeois self-delusions of Zionism (the Jewish faction that the Bund opposed most fiercely in this period), the liberation of women from the shackles of tradition. He was smitten. She was smitten. The revolution had come. Desire, like the will of the people, was irresistible. What were they waiting for? It would have been a crime against nature not to act on their feelings—and a crime against freedom to hide or lie about their relationship. Their mothers could only pray that the neighbors didn't ask too many questions.

On Friday, February 12, 1904, Itel's grandmother, Beyle, died in Volozhin at the age of sixty-three. Beyle (she shared the name with her daughter-in-law, Shalom Tvi's wife) had been lovely in her youth, with pale sad eyes that sloped down at the corners, high cheekbones, and a full finely chiseled mouth—and as an older woman she carried herself with serenity and pious resignation. A good wife for Shimon Dov, a good mother to her sons and daughter, a member in good standing of the Volozhin synagogue. With Beyle's passing, the scribe had only a son and a daughter left in Volozhin— the rest of the family was either in Rakov or the United States.

The day after Beyle's death was the Shabbat of Mishpatim—the Sabbath of the laws—when the faithful gather to read the section of Exodus (chapters 21 to 24) devoted to Jewish law. *If a man come presumptuously upon his neighbor, to slay him with guile; thou shalt take him from Mine altar, that he may die. . . . I will send my terror before thee, and will discomfit the people to whom thou shalt come, and I will make all thine enemies turn their backs unto thee.*

At the appointed moment before the service ended, Shimon Dov stood and keened and recited the mourner's kaddish for his wife.

That same month Russia went to war with Japan and the world of bearded scribes and wooden synagogues was shoved another step closer to the brink. The Russo-Japanese war was a classic imperialist face-off—senseless, blundering, impelled not by opposing ideologies or ethnic rancor but by the naked greed of neighboring powers competing over resources. Russia provoked; Japan reacted; obstinacy on both sides prevailed; and a year and a half of bloodshed ensued. For Russia, it was a disaster, and the herald of worse disasters to come. The tsar, deluded by the vastness of his empire and the swagger of his army, promised his people a swift shining victory and instead handed them military disgrace, diplomatic embarrassment, economic slump, and political chaos. Japan astounded the world by taking out more than half the Russian naval fleet at the start of hostilities—and went on to inflict a series of military humiliations on land and sea. With the tsar's forces crumpling, popular opinion in Russia swung rapidly from patriotic fervor to disillusionment to revolutionary ferment. Workers grew restive as the military drained off manpower and deprived families of much-needed seasonal income. The assassination of the minister of internal affairs in July 1904 threw the government into turmoil. With every setback on the battlefield and policy zigzag at home, the autocracy appeared shakier.

All of this was pure oxygen for radicals. By the late summer of 1904, Russian cities and towns were astir with meetings, rallies, political banquets, and proclamations. Could the end of the empire be at hand at last? Bundists, socialists, Bolsheviks, Mensheviks prayed devoutly at their godless shrines and organized feverishly.

For Itel and Wolf, it was a moment when everything blissful seemed to converge—power, youth, love, sex, new knowledge, revolution. Cramped at home, Itel escaped to the Rosenthals' house where the atmosphere was freer and the views more liberal. The Rosenthals displayed a portrait of Moses Mendelssohn, leading light of the Haskalah, in their parlor, and beneath the philosopher's humane, clean-shaven gaze, Itel and Wolf endlessly discussed and argued, plotted and exulted. Wolf's father was a great Talmudic scholar, a teacher, and a *maskil* (a proponent of the Haskalah) who read widely in both Hebrew and secular literature, collected books on a range of subjects, professed liberal political views, and, to the disgust of his Bundist offspring, embraced Zionism. With the Rosenthal library at her disposal, Itel embarked on an ambitious course of study—not in the Talmud but in the works of the towering figures of world literature: Tolstoy, Turgenev, and Dostoyevsky in Russian; I. L. Peretz, Sholem Aleichem, and Mendele Mocher Sforim in Yiddish; and foreign authors like Jules Verne, Zola, and James Fenimore Cooper in Yiddish translation. (Years later Wolf's youngest brother, Moe, then living in America, was amazed to find *Twenty Thousand Leagues Under the Sea* in an English "translation": he had read the book in his father's library and assumed it was a Yiddish classic.) Chaim Yasef, Itel's younger brother, though only eleven years old, got wind of the riches of the Rosenthals' library and began tagging along to borrow books and eavesdrop.

As the war with Japan dragged on and the revolutionary fervor mounted, Itel and Wolf and their fellow Bundists began stockpiling weapons in preparation for the uprising they knew was imminent. Caches of knives, clubs, and guns were hidden away under beds and at the back of closets. Trips were made to Minsk to proselytize Jewish workers. Wolf's oldest brother and the brother's fiancée lived in Minsk and kept a printing press on which they ran off revolutionary pamphlets and broadsides. The young people were playing a dangerous game and they knew it. Police spies were everywhere, and Bundists were being arrested in droves—4,467 of them rounded up and imprisoned between June 1903 and July 1904. Wolf's brother and his fiancée were arrested when their landlord falsely told the police that they were using the press to print counterfeit bills. Sentenced to three years in Siberia, the couple married hastily in prison so they could remain together.

Danger "only raised the level of enthusiasm," Wolf recalled half a century later. Being "persecuted, suppressed, and hunted down by the authorities" gave the endeavor "the halo of heroism." Besides, the political crisis was coming to a head. All over Russia, revolutionaries, Jewish and gentile alike, but overwhelmingly gentile, were on the move. Intellectuals and workers were banding together in unions. Students took to the streets in Moscow, Kharkov, Odessa, Kiev, and St. Petersburg to call for an end to the war and to demand free elections open to all. In the capital, a shadowy charismatic priest named Father Gapon was gathering support from oppressed factory workers, common laborers, and rootless peasants. Father Gapon was something of an enigma. Some whispered that he was in the pay of the tsar's secret police. Others dismissed him as a charlatan. But his heroic stature among the disaffected masses grew steadily. That summer and autumn, the Rakov Bundists held secret meetings in houses at the edge of town and in the surrounding woods where they could talk without being overheard and practice firing their weapons without accidentally killing someone. "A forest of pine trees, green and fragrant, a clear brook, the chirping of the birds on the treetops—here was the cradle of the Bund in Rakov," one comrade recollected. "Here we held our meetings, and here the young men of Rakov first heard about the revolution and about socialism. Here, also, were our first loves." Itel learned how to shoot a gun. Wolf's oldest sister did too. Even if revolution never came, the knowledge of weapons would be useful in the event of a pogrom.

This was something unheard of in the Russian Pale. Not since classical antiquity had Jews taken up arms to combat oppression and change the world they had been born into.

Then disaster struck: Wolf was drafted. Having suffered defeat after defeat during 1904, the Russian army was hungry for manpower, and young Jewish men, though unworthy of every other civil right, were deemed good enough to swell the ranks of the doomed defenders of Port Arthur in Manchuria. Wolf knew what happened to Jews in the tsar's army. Like every Jewish child in Russia, he had grown up hearing stories of the "military martyrdom" inflicted on his kind: boys as young as twelve called up for terms that stretched to twenty-five years (since then reduced), brutalization at the hands of gentile recruits and sadistic Russian officers, censorship and confiscation of letters from home, religious observance and identity beaten out of them, promotion into the officer corps strictly barred. Bund leaders, fearful that Jews would be accused of treason if they resisted or deserted en masse, called on its members to report for duty when they were drafted and then to agitate from within the ranks. But Wolf had other ideas.

Wolf duly reported to training camp, bringing with him a trunk and a few spare rubles. When the time was right, he distributed the rubles where they would be most useful, grabbed his trunk, and quietly strolled through the camp gates. At the first opportunity, he stripped off the soldier's tunic and trousers, unpacked the civilian clothes that he and Itel had carefully folded into the trunk, made the change, and continued on his way—his brief stint in the tsar's army over. Wolf had arranged for a final rendezvous with Itel—hastily and in secret. After promising his undying love and extracting her promise of the same, he slipped across the border and made his way west to Rotterdam. Young Jewish draftees were doing the same all over the empire. A few coins in the right hands, a word whispered by a comrade in a border town, and many a deserting Jewish soldier was tucked into a load of hay or bundled on the back of a peasant's cart. By the start of the new year, 1905, Wolf, along with 2,350 other passengers, was on board the *Rotterdam* bound for New York.

But by then, the situation in Russia had changed dramatically. At the end of December, a massive strike at a St. Petersburg munitions plant had triggered a chain reaction of sympathy strikes and by the first week of January the capital was without electricity or newspapers. Father Gapon chose this moment to stage a mass demonstration. On the morning of January 9, 1905, which happened to be Itel's nineteenth birthday, Father Gapon led a march of the oppressed through the streets of the capital. The plan was for six columns of protesters—striking factory workers and their families, students, peasants—to converge on the vast cobbled square before the Winter Palace, where the priest hoped to present a petition to the tsar. The demonstrators began assembling in the city outskirts around dawn. Checkpoints were set up to screen for weapons, and the presence of women and children carrying icons and chanting the mournful hymns of the Orthodox church added a calming note. To the poor of Russia, at least the non-Jews, the tsar was still a revered figure—more father than king—and they had turned out on this winter Sunday to beg for his mercy in the presence of God. When Father Gapon and his column reached the Narva Arch—a Roman-style monument that commemorates Alexander I's victory over Napoléon with an arch straddling a major arterial south of the Winter Palace—they paused. Facing them were ranks of soldiers, mounted and on foot, with rifles loaded and cocked. The officer in charge gave the order and a bugle was sounded—the command to open fire—but none of the protesters heard it over the singing and chanting and shuffling of feet. In any case, the shots rang out before the crowd could possibly have dispersed. Thirty fell dead in the first volley, including members of Gapon's guard, though the priest himself escaped unharmed. The slaughter continued all afternoon as marchers en route to the Winter Palace were stomped, shot, and bayoneted by the tsar's army, then trampled by their fleeing comrades.

By conservative estimates, some 1,000 people were killed or wounded on Bloody Sunday (the official government count was 130 dead and some 300 wounded, but journalists put the number of casualties at 4,600). The bullets, hooves, and blades of the tsar's protectors had also killed his people's faith. Their father had betrayed them. Their petition was unread; their demands were ignored; their grievances dismissed. Russia's Jews had never had any illusions about the benevolence of their ruler, but the empire's vast gentile population had always held the tsar blameless for their suffering. No longer. From the blood of Bloody Sunday rose the Revolution of 1905—and from 1905 came the Revolution of 1917. The fate of an empire was sealed in an afternoon.

The fact that Bloody Sunday fell on Itel's nineteenth birthday was a coincidence. Who could blame her, though, if she took it as a sign? All over Russia, young revolutionaries were on fire at the news. Bloody Sunday was the moment they had been waiting for. In the immediate aftermath, strikes broke out—some four hundred thousand workers in the major cities walked off their jobs in protest within hours of the slaughter. The numbers were most impressive and solidarity most intense in the Bund strongholds of the northern and western sections of the Pale. Warsaw, Vilna, Lodz, cities with large well-organized Bundist operations, were all but shut down. Bund organizers moved swiftly to capitalize on the popular outrage. "Comrades! We have flooded the earth of Russia with our blood, and now freedom is blooming from this earth," one Bund leader exhorted the ranks of the new "soldiers of the revolution." "Attack the stores where arms are sold! Everyone get a gun, a revolver, a sword, an ax, a knife! Arm yourselves! . . . Let us give up the blood of our hearts and receive the rights of human beings!" It was the zenith of the Bund's power and influence and glamour.

In Rakov, the local Bund came out of hiding and organized strikes at some of the larger factories; Rakov workers declared their solidarity with revolutionaries in the bloodstained streets of the capital. Thanks to the Bund, Rakov's Jews had weapons; thanks to the uprising, they had political will and momentum. Now what they needed was a leader. With Wolf in America—he had arrived at Ellis Island on January 26 with $1.50 to his name and the address of an uncle in Manhattan in his pocket—Itel stepped up to the task. Every Monday and Friday—Rakov's market days—Itel stood in the market square to rail against the injustice of the autocracy. Commanding beyond her years and height, she was a fiery orator and a born leader. And her moment—the moment of all Russia's downtrodden workers—was at hand.

The strikes continued into February and March. The peasants joined the uprising. There were rumblings of mutiny in the army. Riga, Warsaw, Lodz saw bloody street battles. Students shut down the universities; doctors and lawyers and journalists voiced their support for the workers. Pogroms, always the shadow of upheaval in Russia, erupted in the Pale—though in many places armed Bundists were able to counter the violence. In fact, the Bund seemed to be unstoppable in those first magnificent months of 1905. "It could achieve everything, reach everyone," one Bundist declared with fierce, hopeful pride. "The word of the Bund was law; its stamp worked like hypnosis. . . . It was legendary."

Sadly, the legend was no match for the flypaper of custom and the noose of authority. In the way of small towns, Rakov's police chief was a customer at Gishe Sore's shop, and he strolled in one day to give her a bit of friendly advice. Either her rabble-rouser of a daughter stop making speeches in the marketplace or he would personally have the brat arrested, spanked, and thrown in jail.

Itel had no intention of rotting in Siberia like Wolf's brother and sister-in-law. And anyway, her heart was in New York.

In April of 1905, as the last patches of snow retreated to the depths of the pine woods, Itel left Russia and its revolution in the care of her fellow Bundists. She packed up what she could call her own, tucked away a slip of paper with the address of her uncle Joseph in Hoboken, and bid farewell to her mother, father, three younger brothers, and two small sisters. A horse-drawn wagon brought her to the nearby town of Olechnowicze and there she boarded a train that took her, after many changes and border crossings, to Rotterdam, the same port Wolf had embarked from three months earlier. "I couldn't live without him," Itel confessed later. It was like something out of a novel: they were each other's first love and only love. They would never be apart again.

Together, Itel and Wolf would bring revolution to America—though it proved to be a very different kind of revolution than the one they had fled.

The year of revolution was a year of tragedy for the family of Shalom Tvi. Worldly and easygoing, Shalom Tvi had settled comfortably into his new life in Rakov. His wife's family was rich, the leather business brought in a tidy income, there was enough work to keep him busy but not so much that he couldn't enjoy life. And enjoying life was important to Shalom Tvi. Not a scholar like his brother Avram Akiva, not a revolutionary like his niece, not a restless seeker after fortune like the relatives in America, Shalom Tvi was a charming, faithful, self-possessed man, and he and Beyle should have reaped the blessings of a large, loving family.

It was not to be. In the first years of their marriage, Beyle bore her husband two daughters—Shula, named for Beyle's mother, in 1900; and Doba, round and adorable, three years later. But in the year of revolution, Shula died. No record survives of what disease or accident carried off the firstborn child or the exact date of her passing. More than a century later she is still faintly, sadly, remembered.

CHAPTER FOUR

THE BOYS

The 1905 revolution went on without Itel and Wolf. All spring and summer, demonstrations, mutiny, and assassinations were rampant in Russia. Since the uprising had blown the lid off government censorship, newspapers were free to report on the protesters' demands and the growing solidarity between workers and intellectuals. Every day, there was a fresh account of a policeman or government official gunned down or ripped to pieces by a bomb. The countryside was literally on fire as peasants torched the manor houses of the great landowners and divided the estates. As the year went on, spontaneous local flare-ups spread and merged until they took on the character of a true national revolution. The climax came in October, when a general strike spread from Moscow and St. Petersburg to the far reaches of the empire, shutting down the railroads and crippling the economy. Cornered and desperate, the tsar issued a series of concessions known as the October Manifesto granting his subjects limited democratic representation along with an array of civil liberties, including freedom of religion. Bundists hailed the "Days of Freedom," but the violence continued unchecked.

Then the violence metastasized. A group calling itself the Black Hundreds—a proto-fascist confederation of die-hard tsarists, Russian Orthodox zealots, arch-nationalists, ethnic purists, urban workers, displaced peasants, and drunken thugs—took to the streets in counterrevolution. Once more, Jews were targeted. "The root of all evil, the root of all our misfortunes is the Jews," proclaimed one of the insidious leaflets that circulated through Russia's cities. "Soon, soon a new time will come, friends, when there will be no Jews." In October and November of 1905, the Black Hundreds instigated the deadliest pogroms in Russian history. Over one thousand Jews were slain in some six hundred communities, primarily in Ukraine. For three days the anti-Semitic violence raged in Odessa. Scores died in Kiev, Zhitomir, Ekaterinoslav. Kishinev exploded again. Isaac Babel, who lived through the Odessa pogrom as a boy of eleven, described the ecstatic release of anti-Semitic rage in his sketch "The Story of My Dovecote":

> A young muzhik [Russian peasant] was smashing a window frame in the house of Khariton Efrussi [a wealthy Jewish wheat merchant]. He was smashing it with a wooden hammer, his whole body steeped in the movement. He breathed in deeply, smiled in all directions the gentle smile of drunkenness, of sweat and hearty strength. The whole street was filled with the crackling, crashing song of shattering wood. . . . Old men with painted beards were carrying the portrait of a neatly combed Tsar, banners with sepulchral saints fluttered above the religious procession, inflamed old women were running in front of it. When the muzhik in the vest saw the procession, he pressed the hammer to his chest and went running after the banners. . . .

Though Bundists fought back, they were no match for the Russian mob. The revolution had become "drenched in a torrent of Jewish blood," one Bundist wrote in despair.

Fearing that violence would spread to their own shtetl, Rakov Bundists dispatched a delegation to Minsk to purchase more weapons—two Finnish knives and seventy rubber clubs—but Itel's brothers stayed out of it. One revolutionary was enough for the family. The three sons of Avram Akiva—Hersch now seventeen, Shmuel sixteen, and Chaim Yasef thirteen—were not inclined to make speeches in the marketplace or fire guns in the forest.

The boys were becoming men in a world that was splitting beneath their feet, but they were still Kohanim, descendants of Aaron, the sons and grandsons and great-grandsons of priests and scribes. A daughter might play at insurrection; it was a son's duty to protect his father's name and the family reputation. But what future could they expect in a country where a thousand Jews were slaughtered in the street while their king tutted about the "brazen, insolent way" of the victims? The boys looked around at the shul, the market, the fields, and the woods and saw no future for themselves. To work as a butcher, carpenter, tailor, shoemaker was out of the question for the sons of the scribe. But they were too restless and ambitious to settle down to a life of Torah. "It would please the parents," Chaim Yasef wrote, "but the sons were not agreeable." And so, between tradition and revolution, they chose a middle course. They learned to fix watches.

Hersch was apprenticed to a watchmaker in the nearby town of Smargon, and in 1906 his younger brother Chaim Yasef joined him. The brothers rented a room in the house of a local freight carrier ("the conveyance was his own back") and on every morning but the Sabbath they went off together to Mr. Rudnick's little shop, in the center of town, to master the craft of repairing clocks and watches. Hersch, with a bit of experience under his belt, was paid two rubles a week; Chaim Yasef a quarter of that. The boys worked hard, dined on crumbs, and lived like monks—but during the year they spent together in Smargon they forged a bond that endured all their lives. The apprenticeship was like boot camp, and the brothers emerged from it comrades—though they never ceased to be rivals.

Avram Akiva and Gishe Sore's seven surviving children were arrayed symmetrically by gender—two girls, then three boys, then two more girls. Having three sons one after another in the space of four years is a sure formula for internecine warfare, and the Kaganovich boys were no exception. Whenever they were together under one roof, the atmosphere turned stormy. Hersch, the first son, was a born diplomat—funny, calm, soft-spoken, nice-looking—but where Hersch put out fires, Chaim Yasef, the domineering youngest son, started them. Where Hersch negotiated, Chaim Yasef provoked. Once he truly became a man, Chaim Yasef had a rough barking voice, which he used, mercilessly, on those he considered his inferiors. If you quailed, Chaim Yasef barked more; if you barked back, he backed off. The person Chaim Yasef barked at the most was Shmuel, the middle brother. He was born to be insulted. Thin-skinned and bighearted, Shmuel was tense, stocky, loyal, and volatile. Shmuel grew up to be the most pious of Avram Akiva's children—he was the only one of the sons who learned the art of the scribe from his father—but being close to God did not make him serene or confident. Little things set him off, especially things done by his brothers, and then you never heard the end of it. Later in life, Shmuel became intensely jealous, even a touch paranoid, about the bond between his brothers. That jealousy first became acute during the year when Hersch and Chaim Yasef lived together in Smargon. For whatever reasons, the family decided that Shmuel, instead of apprenticing with the other boys, should follow his older sisters to America. And so, in 1906, Shmuel sailed for New York and missed out on the ticktock boot camp. He never really broke into the rough easy camaraderie that Hersch and Chaim Yasef developed in Smargon. He was a good Jew, a hard worker, and an upright man. But he was not the favorite son or the favorite brother, and he knew it.

Premature death touched the family again in the year the boys left Rakov for apprenticeship and America. Avram Akiva's brother Arie died in Volozhin at the age of thirty-one. The only one of Shimon Dov's five sons who had chosen to remain in Volozhin, Arie was married and the father of two small children—a daughter, Chana, and a son, Yishayahu (the Hebrew form of the name Isaiah). But in 1906, with his wife Leah nine months pregnant with their third child, something happened—whether disease or accident has been erased by time. When the baby was born, they named him Chaim—*life*—after Shimon Dov's father. But Arie died before his new son was a week old. Chaim's bris took place during his father's shiva—an inauspicious way for a Jewish son to come into the world.

"Repairing watches or clocks is fascinating and interesting, to those who love the work," Chaim Yasef wrote of his apprenticeship in Smargon. "You get to revive a dead watch or clock by adjusting and replacing worn or broken parts (which part you had to make yourself). There was no such thing in those days or in that town as replacements parts, so when you finished your work and brought the watch back to normal, useful life, you got a great feeling of professional pride." However gratifying, dead clocks were not enough to keep Chaim Yasef's brother Hersch in Smargon very long. In June 1907, the oldest Kaganovich son put apprenticeship behind him and made his way to Antwerp, where he boarded the Red Star Line's *Samland* and set sail for New York. His older sister Itel, now Mrs. Ida Rosenthal, paid the fare, and she and Wolf, now William, were on hand to meet Hersch when he arrived at Ellis Island on June 28. Harry Cohen, as Hersch Kaganovich promptly restyled himself, was eighteen years old and five feet three inches tall, with dark hair and brown eyes. Bent on becoming an American as quickly as he could, he moved in with his relatives and went to work.

That left fourteen-year-old Chaim Yasef alone in Smargon, the last of Avram Akiva and Gishe Sore's sons in the Russian Pale. To save money, Chaim Yasef gave up the room in the freight carrier's house and set up a folding cot in the watch repair shop. "I became my own chambermaid. As companions I had the repaired clocks that struck the hour and half hour and the repaired alarm clocks that would go off at all hours of the night. The shop was located in the building where the owner lived so I was given the privilege of heating water on his stove to make breakfast usually consisting of a roll and tea."

Chaim Yasef was a proud, lonely, brooding teenager in Smargon. He took umbrage at the snobbish aunt who offered to pay him to stay away lest her pampered children be contaminated by a poor watchmaker's apprentice who slept in the shop. He dreamed of landing a job at a fancy clock shop in Moscow or Petersburg. Preoccupied with his own sensitive feelings and glittering prospects, the boy failed to notice that all thinking people in the Pale were plunged in blank despair that year. By 1907 it was apparent that the revolution had failed utterly: after the Days of Freedom came the Years of Reaction, when hope of reform was crushed, pogroms raged, the Bund withered, and the net of surveillance tightened. Though the tsar had agreed in 1906 to an elected assembly—the Duma—it was dissolved after a few months of mostly ineffective debate and toothless investigation of official corruption. Freedom withdrawn is worse than no freedom at all. Now, in the aftermath of revolt, a drizzle of ash settled over the land. Hooligans of the Black Hundreds prowled city streets like wolves. The economy stagnated. Those who suffered and those responsible for the suffering blamed the Jews for everything—the incitement to revolution, its failure, the sour revulsion that followed. Infected by the general virus, Rakov sweated, shivered, and cracked its aching joints. "The economic situation in our town is bad," wrote one of the Botwiniks. "Poverty is on the increase, and emigration is getting stronger from day to day." New Catholic churches were built in the neighboring villages—seemingly a matter of indifference to Jews, but in fact it hit the Kaganovich family hard. As Polish and Belarusian peasants flocked to churches closer to their farms, attendance at Rakov's church fell off—with the result that there was less traffic at Gishe Sore's general store. A Catholic merchant opened up a competing store in town—and priests urged their parishioners to boycott Jewish shops and buy only from their fellow Catholics. Business declined further.

Avram Akiva and Gishe Sore agonized about joining the exodus to America. Itel, Ettel, Hersch, and Shmuel—now calling themselves Ida, Ethel, Harry, and Sam—were already in New Jersey and urging them to sell out, pack up, and get out of Russia. The American children did the math— they had become very skilled with numbers: if the parents sold out in Rakov, if the sisters and brothers pooled their earnings, if the younger ones got jobs, if they all worked hard, if God smiled on them and gave them health, then they could live comfortably in America. They could live free— and they could live together.

Concern for their next-to-youngest daughter also factored in. Chana had developed an alarming cough—possibly a reaction to the damp atmosphere near the lake. The Rakov doctor thought a change of climate would do her good, and maybe there were better doctors in the New World.

The parents turned to Chaim Yasef, the oldest child still at home, for advice. "I see no future here," the boy intoned with the wisdom of his seventeen years. "If I stay, it will not be in this town. One thing Rakov does not need is another watchmaker."

By the spring of 1909, they had made up their minds. Gishe Sore and Avram Akiva found a buyer for the house by the lake, the cow, the calf, the garden. Rubles changed hands and the store that had fed the family for so many years passed to another shopkeeper. Avram Akiva assembled all the bits of parchment he had on hand—tiny scrolls for the mezuzot, pages for the Passover Haggadoth and Purim megillahs, beautifully lettered prayers—and sold them to pious friends. The family went to Volozhin to say farewell to Shimon Dov. They found the patriarch hale but wizened and more alone than ever after Arie's death. Avram Akiva asked for and received his father's blessing. The men prayed together for the souls of the dead and the health of the living. Father and son must have known that they would never see each other again.

Before their departure, Rakov's mayor, who lived on the same street, made a state visit to wish them Godspeed and to announce solemnly that he had never seen a more upstanding shopkeeper or finer homemaker than Gishe Sore (he had clearly never tasted her cooking). Most painful was the parting with Shalom Tvi. The brothers had become inseparable during their decade together in Rakov, and despite their differences, they were alike in the ways that mattered. Once Avram Akiva and his family left, Shalom Tvi, Beyle, and their two daughters (Doba was six and the baby, Etl, was two) would have to keep the Kaganovich name alive in Rakov on their own. Shalom Tvi promised to visit one day. Avram Akiva promised him a clean bed and a place to say his prayers in New York.

The end was a rapid blur. The last walk to synagogue. The last reading from the Torah. The last tears shed at the graves of the two babies Gishe Sore had lost and buried in the Rakov cemetery. The last meal in the creaking wooden house by the lake. The last breath of the blue and white lilacs that bloomed in profusion all over town. Finally the day of departure was upon them. A horse and wagon dragged them through green meadows and dark pine woods to the rail station at Olechnowicze. A train took them northwest toward the coast. There was a fifteen-minute stop at the Smargon station, and the uncle (but not the aunt) came to the platform to bid them farewell and praise young Chaim Yasef for his hard work and ambition. Like everyone, the uncle said he hoped to visit them one day. In America.

The train rattled through Vilna with its many magnificent synagogues and narrow streets teeming with Jewish workers, teachers, beggars, and revolutionaries. Through Kaunas crouched behind its immense brick fortresses. Through the grain fields that in a decade would cease to be Russia. As the land flattened and the trees grew stubbier, they could sense the pull of the sea. And then, all at once, through the train windows, there it was—the Baltic—430 miles across from Stockholm to Petersburg, tinged with gray even at the balmy cusp of summer, as if winter were curled beneath its surface.

No time to marvel at the miracle of horizonless water or explore the beckoning chaos of the dockside streets of Libau. The Russian-American Line's *Russia*—a sleek black barracuda of a ship—was waiting to carry them to New York.

It was the season of lingering twilight and the heavy perfume of fruit trees. But no flower's scent could penetrate the acrid smoke rising from the *Russia*'s funnels or the reek of oil, wet cloth, rancid food, and vomit that permeated its steerage. Europe faded to a brown smudge. The continent had been the family's home for a thousand years—probably more. None of them ever again set foot on Russian soil.

CHAPTER FIVE

LOWER EAST SIDE

Gishe Sore thought she knew about America from her children's letters, from the bits and pieces that appeared in the Yiddish and Russian newspapers, from the gossip she picked up in the store and the rumors that spread from neighbor to neighbor. But now she saw that she hadn't understood the first thing. Who knew that New York was islands—one tiny island for the colossal statue, another for the immigrants, a long narrow blade of an island for the millions of people who had come before her and the new ones pouring in beside her from every corner of the world?

The crossing in the *Russia's* third-class compartment had made them all sick. The ship stank; the food was worse than anything she cooked. But now that they had trudged up and down the endless stairs in the palace of the immigrants, had their eyes and hair examined, sworn they were neither bigamists nor anarchists, received the coveted stamp on their papers, found their luggage, piled through the door marked "Push to New York," and fallen into the arms of their American children, Gishe Sore's insides had settled at last. Now, on the morning of June 1, 1909, with her shoes touching American soil for the first time, she was terrified.

Her American children—not children anymore but glossy adults in expensive clothes—took charge of everything. Gishe Sore let herself be guided to the dock at the edge of Ellis Island, where a ferry was waiting to take them across the harbor to Manhattan. She looked where the American children pointed. She listened to them explain: that was New York City—Manhattan—their new home. She stared at the treeless forest rising from the point of land surrounded by slopping brown water. To her it didn't look like a place where people lived, but she submitted. What choice did she have? One hour in America and already everything was topsy-turvy: the children led, the parents shuffled along behind.

The ferry docked at the Battery and all the new immigrants spilled out with their luggage, their baskets, their screaming children, their heavy reeking foreign clothes. Gishe Sore waited and sweated while the American children found a taxicab. It took an eternity to cover the couple of miles from Ellis Island to their flat. She gazed through the cab window at the shadowed canyons where dark-suited people milled on every corner and rushed along the margins of every street and disappeared into or emerged from gaping holes in the pavement. The canyon walls shrank block by block as they inched their way across the tip of Manhattan—but as the buildings became humbler, the life on the streets grew denser. They passed beneath the ramps leading up to the Brooklyn Bridge and crossed into the Lower East Side. East Broadway, Catherine Street, Allen Street, Henry, Madison—*their street.* Instead of houses set in fenced gardens, there were just buildings, ugly brown and gray and black buildings, all more or less the same height, all perforated by dirty opaque rectangular windows, all pushed together with no air or light between them. Every street, every housefront, every roof, every corner was perfectly, drably geometrical—not a curve or curl to soften the right angles—but the effect was shoddy, haphazard, sprawling, and dirty beyond belief. Hebrew letters painted on awnings and stenciled on shopwindows brought no comfort—the signs were too pressing, the messages too clamorous. Outside the storefronts more stuff for sale spilled out onto the streets—food, clothing, household items, cast-off junk heaped on pushcarts and rickety tables or hauled around by plodding blinkered horses. The ugly buildings were defaced by ugly grillwork—fire escapes strewn with laundry, children, boxes, crates, stray bundles, broken furniture, more junk. Not a green leaf or patch of brown earth anywhere; not a wisp of shade in the profligate light of June, not a path to walk down or a bench to sit on and chat with the neighbors. And such neighbors—in such numbers. Gishe Sore would be lost forever the first time she ventured out alone. She would be robbed, cheated, pushed into an alley, or tripped down cellar stairs. She would die and no one would ever find her.

They pulled up to 195 Madison Street—a tall narrow six-story redbrick and limestone-trimmed tenement house indistinguishable from all the tenement houses on all the other streets of tenements. The bars and ladders of a fire escape ran up the left side of the building; sooty stone scrolls, shields, and flowers framed the second- and third-story windows. *This was the place where they had to live?* Two blocks from the commercial madness of East Broadway; two blocks from the filthy snout of the East River, smelling of fish, ships, and garbage; three blocks from the brain-rattling racket of the elevated train; three blocks from the playground of the Henry Street Settlement; practically in the shadow of the construction site of the twin-towered Manhattan Bridge. Every three blocks they passed more people than the entire population of Rakov. Half a million Jews packed the one and a half square miles of the Lower East Side in 1909: 702 people per acre in the densest acres. It was one of the most crowded places on earth, and all of them seemed to be swarming outdoors on the June afternoon that Gishe Sore and her family arrived. Aside from the crisscross steel girders of the Manhattan Bridge at the end of the street, it was all tenement houses as far as she could see. Tenements and bodies. In every room of every building, bodies fought for a ray of light and a sip of air. Bodies slept four to a bed and on two chairs pushed together; bodies sat hunched over sewing machines in parlors and sunless back bedrooms and at kitchen tables heaped with cloth and thread; bodies ate, slept, woke, and cleared out for the next shift of bodies to cycle through. Toilets in the hall or in courtyard outhouses; windows opening, if they opened at all, onto fetid air shafts; no privacy; no escape from the racket and smell of neighbors; no relief from summer heat or blasting winter furnaces. *This was the place her American children had brought them to live?*

They climbed, the seven of them clattering up through the stink of chicken fat, fried onions, boiled cabbage, and overflowing toilets. The stairs were dark and battered. They stopped on the third floor, and one of the

American children opened one of the doors. Their flat was at the rear, facing north into the rear windows of another tenement building across a tiny garbage-strewn courtyard. Four dark tiny rooms with 350 square feet between them ran one after another to the building's back wall; only the room at the end of the chain had windows that admitted any light. There was a sink in the kitchen but no hot water. They shut the door but they couldn't shut out the smell or the noise. Gishe Sore, stony-faced, tried not to cry. "For mother, it was shocking," one of the children recalled. "She was used to a large house with plenty of ground, and here were four tiny rooms for eight persons." Eight persons because even though Ethel, Sam, and Harry had been on their own in America for some years now, they were expected to move in with their parents. The three boys, though no longer boys—Harry was now twenty; Sam nineteen; Hyman (as Chaim Yasef would call himself) seventeen—slept in one room; the three girls (Ethel and her little sisters, Chana, now Anna, and Leie, now Lillie) in another—just like in Rakov. "At least the whole family is together again," Gishe Sore kept repeating to console herself. As if eight were not enough, to eke out a few extra pennies they soon took in a boarder, nineteen-year-old Isidore Gordon, who bunked in with the brothers. The family was crowded—but everyone was crowded at 195 Madison Street. The tenement's sixteen apartments housed 115 people—all of them Russian Jews or the children of Russian Jews. Sam and Chana Chadman, upstairs, had eight kids; the Fibes, who lived under the roof, had five kids and three boarders; the Shulbergs had seven in their flat; Abe and Goldie Greenberg had eight. The same thing next door at 197 Madison Street, the same across the street, the same on Henry Street to the north and Jefferson Street to the east. "If a dog came around he'd have to prove he was Jewish before they let him in," one immigrant said of his neighborhood, "that's how Jewish it was." That was the Lower East Side in 1909. All twelve tribes of Israel, plus of course the Kohanim, lived between Delancey and Allen.

Some immigrants forever grieve for their "real" homes, the predawn smell of baking bread, the glaze of rain on cobblestone, the echo of bells in the alley. Others step off the boat, fill their lungs with the raw unfamiliar air, and get to work. They never look back because they never have a moment to spare or an urge to regret. Itel was one of these. When she fled the tsar's police and arrived in Hoboken on April 25, 1905, she had twelve dollars and the address of her father's brother Joseph in her pocket—406 Newark Street, Hoboken—but what she carried in her head proved to be far more useful than anything in her luggage. Uncle Joseph, a Hebrew schoolteacher, had been charged by Avram Akiva with looking after his daughter, housing and feeding her, and keeping her safe and proper (i.e., not too flagrant about the romance with William). But Itel (she never surrendered her original Yiddish name with family and intimate friends) had other ideas. She had not escaped the tsar's police only to be policed by a pious uncle. Within weeks of her arrival, she quarreled with her aunt and decided to strike out on her own. Enlisting Ethel as a roommate, she found a two-room cold-water basement apartment, also in Hoboken, for ten dollars a month. William, then working as an unpaid apprentice garment worker on the Lower East Side, could come and go freely. Itel had everything arranged to her liking except a job. Ethel was employed in a Jersey City dress factory—but there was no way in hell that Itel was going to chain herself to a factory sewing machine six days a week while some cigar-chomping foreman barked at her. So she resuscitated the old Kaganovich sisters dressmaking partnership from Rakov. She and Ethel bought a Singer machine for $11.98 (on installments) and began making dresses in their basement flat. Uncle Joseph steered the mothers and sisters of his students their way—and word spread through Jewish Hoboken that the Cohen sisters would whip you up a lovely stylish dress to order for seventy-five cents. Soon they were charging three dollars a dress and working from morning until dark. "We did not have a life of glory," Ethel commented drily years later. But they made a living.

Itel and William were married on June 10, 1906, in an Orthodox Jewish ceremony arranged and paid for by William's uncle Max (one of the prosperous Botwinik family that Shalom Tvi's wife, Beyle, belonged to). A traditional Jewish ceremony to please the family; a gorgeous white wedding dress of French wool with a straight skirt that fell just shy of the ankle to please the bride (who designed and sewed it, naturally); and a traditional American honeymoon to Niagara Falls to please the newlyweds. They took a week off from work and then set up housekeeping in a Hoboken railroad flat. William tried to make a go of a candy store, Itel went back to making dresses, Ethel, complaining of the damp, left Hoboken for a dressmaking job in Manhattan. A year into the marriage, William was diagnosed with tuberculosis. Convinced that cleaner, drier air was essential for his health, the couple relocated to a small resort town in the Catskill Mountains north of the city. It was a crippling move financially since Itel's work dried up and their income dwindled to next to nothing. But William soon recovered (the diagnosis proved to be wrong) and within the year they were back in Hoboken. They found a first-floor flat in a tidy low-rise building at 212 Willow Street on a block of brownstones and four- and five-story apartment houses near the Hudson River. It was a blue-collar neighborhood of German, Irish, and Italian bartenders and chauffeurs, porters and butchers, dockworkers and mill hands—not a single Jew among them aside from the Rosenthals. Lewis, their first child, was born on August 10, 1907, and a Polish maid named Stosia Radzekowki—a gentile—was hired to look after the baby. Even after the rest of the family arrived in 1909, Itel and William stayed put in Hoboken. They wanted no part of the Lower East Side: no Jewish neighbors; no Jewish help; no tenement house; no haggling on Hester Street; no sweatshop. And no Jewish religion for them or their children. In a break with tradition that mortified Avram Akiva and Gishe Sore, Lewis, the first grandson, had not been circumcised. Itel and William refused the rite that had been inflicted on Jewish male infants for thousands of years. The coming generation, the American generation, would grow up with rituals and beliefs that had been chosen, not mindlessly inherited from their forebears.

At forty-seven, Avram Akiva looked like a biblical prophet. His graying beard flowed over his chest; his eyes were dark and piercing; his shoulders were square, his posture upright, his expression stern and melancholy. But the appearance was deceiving. Under the beard lurked a wise, gentle soul. The scribe was not one to cast out a daughter for breaking God's covenant or to love a grandson less for the sins of his parents. Though thirty years earlier Avram Akiva had studied beside the finest Jewish scholars in the world at the Volozhin yeshiva, at heart he was not a zealot but an obliging, practical man, willing to bend when necessary, careful to fight only the battles that counted. So he kept his thoughts to himself about his first grandson's failure to be circumcised. And when the American children told him he had to change his name, he shrugged and went along. Avram Akiva Kaganovich did not sound American, they said; no one but a Jew would be able to pronounce it. From now on, in New York, he was Abraham Cohen and Gishe Sore was Sarah. Anyway, what did a name matter? Call him what they wanted, he would always be a stranger and a sojourner in this new land, like the first Abraham in Hebron. If it made them happy that he should sign his name Abraham Cohen, he'd sign. God knew who he was.

Mild and tolerant Abraham Cohen might be, but he was not blind. In New York, the American children told him, a man had to have a paying job, so he got himself set up in a small concession selling religious books, tefillin, and mezuzot in a Rivington Street synagogue. Every morning he walked to work up Essex Street, across East Broadway, Hester, Broome, Delancey; every evening he walked back to the cold-water flat on Madison. Every walk through the cauldron of commerce seared his senses anew. He couldn't take three steps without being jostled, shouted at, solicited, implored to buy. Boys who should have been in cheder hawked the *Jewish Daily Forward* on street corners. Grown men, idling in candy shops, blew smoke from cigars and sucked egg creams from straws. Peddlers cried "I cash clothes!" over and over in a kind of dirge as they hauled their carts through the streets. Women openly peddled their bodies to passing men. On his first Shabbat in New York, Abraham was stunned to see men and women, Jews all of them, bartering and selling, buying and eating, passing money from hand to hand. *Handling currency on the Sabbath*—unheard of in Rakov. Even on Kol Nidre night, the eve of Yom Kippur, the holiest day of the Jewish year, the shops were open, the streets were full, Jews went on wheeling and dealing and shouting and swearing as on any other night. It was like spitting in God's face. Synagogues were everywhere—depending on whom you asked, the Lower East Side had 500, 800, 1,000 shuls in those days, more than Minsk, more than Vilna—but all those houses of prayer and study did not make New York a holy city. Abraham saw soon enough that these so-called shuls were not true synagogues but small provisional tabernacles set up in dance halls or shop fronts by *landslayt*—people from the same village or region back in Russia. Every shtetl with a sizable presence in New York had its own *landsmanshaft*—a benevolent association that provided insurance, sick benefits, and burial plots for *landslayt*—and many *landsmanshaftn* also formed congregations. Forty or fifty former neighbors from the Pale would gather on Shabbat in an upstairs tenement room or vacant store or even a converted church fitted with an ark and some benches. On a special occasion, like a bar mitzvah, there might be a bottle of whiskey and an extra dollar for the rabbi. Rakov's exiles prayed at Beth David Anshei Rakov, at 225 Clinton Street; and the Volozhin community davened at 209 Madison Street, just a few doors down from the family's tenement, in a pretty little mission church that had been made over into the Etz Chaim Anshei Volozhin. Rivington Street alone had eighteen *landsmanshaft* shuls jostling with its beer joints, butcher shops, bakeries, and soda fountains. Thirty more on Columbia Street, thirty-eight on Henry Street, more than a dozen on Orchard Street. So there were plenty of places to pray, but to Abraham, these makeshift sanctuaries of brick and cork and soot and smudged gray windows lacked the savor of grace. In Rakov, generations of Jews had darkened the wooden beams of the old synagogue with the exhalations of their souls—but in New York even prayers were muttered in haste between one deal and the next. The Lower East Side was the capital of Jewish America, but barely 12 percent of Jews attended synagogue. Sam went to shul with his father on Saturday, said his morning prayers, showed respect—but the other two sons quit going through the motions the minute the old man wasn't looking.

Abraham spent his days selling prayer books to a few old gents on Rivington Street and regretting that he no longer worked as a scribe, but his children had no time for piety. Every morning they rushed out to work—every evening they rushed off to English classes, Yiddish variety shows, meetings, God knows what. Everyone was doing the same. Racing against the American clock. Looking for a gap in the fence they could slip through. No one set foot on Madison Street who didn't have to be there—no one left unless he got lucky, figured out an angle, found a way to elbow through the crowd. Prayer fell on deaf ears here. Only money charmed open the door. "Success, American style . . . was all very simple," wrote immigrant poet

Harry Roskolenko. "Don't work for others. Work for yourself. Don't be a wage slave."

Success, American style, meant nothing to Abraham. What little money he earned he saved. He kept his own counsel, walked uprightly, salvaged what he could of the old ways. Abraham never really learned English, but he understood more than anyone realized.

Letters from Rakov were eagerly anticipated, passed from hand to hand, pored over and sighed over and quoted from until the paper grew limp and tattered. The letter from Shalom Tvi that arrived on Madison Street early in April 1910 brought one special bit of news: Beyle had given birth to yet another daughter—her fourth, counting the baby who had died during the 1905 revolution. So seven-year-old Doba and three-year-old Etl now had a new little sister named Sonia—a black-haired beauty with a healthy set of lungs. Everyone marveled that God should give Shalom Tvi only girls while the rest of the siblings had at least one boy each. Without a son, who would say the kaddish for Shalom Tvi when he died? If this kept up, there would be no more Kohanim in Rakov.

Aside from the birth of Sonia, there was the usual recitation of town gossip, business setbacks, and hand-wringing over the state of the Jewish community. Zionism remained strong among Rakov's youth and many were learning Hebrew, but emigration to Palestine had slackened off because of the unstable political situation in the Land. The shtetl had raised seventy-three rubles for the Jewish National Fund to buy up arable plots from Arabs. The police were cracking down on Jewish shopkeepers under a new law that forbade stores to open on Sundays and Christian holidays. The fate of Rakov's Jewish library was uncertain—it had closed shortly after the family left for America, then reopened, now who knows. Jewish firefighters had been forbidden to carry their own flag in the anniversary celebration, even though most of the Rakov fire brigade were Jews. And so on. Abraham and Sarah read Shalom Tvi's letter over and over. They thought about the lake, the old wooden shul, the vegetable garden behind the house, the trees that would soon be blooming in the orchards. If they regretted anything, they kept it to themselves. They had left the land of the pogrom and come to the land of opportunity. Things were bound to improve.

In their first spring in the New World, the 1910 census was taken, and the family duly added eight new names to the national roll. Sarah was at home on Monday, April 25, when census enumerator Harry Barewitz came calling. Where else would she be? The others had jobs or school to attend, but Sarah, who in Rakov had stocked the shelves and kept the books, now stayed at home and burned the cooking. Her sons and daughters told her that there was no need to run a shop anymore. In America, the children worked—the mothers kept house. So it was Sarah who opened the door to Mr. Barewitz the census enumerator and answered the questions he was required to ask. The family name was now Cohen. Nine people lived in the flat including the teenage boarder. She and Abraham were both forty-seven; Ethel (the former Ettel) was twenty-two; Harry (Hersch) was twenty; Shmuel (nineteen) had become Solomon (Mr. Barewitz made a mistake—it should have been Samuel); Chaim Yasef (seventeen) was now Hyman; Chana (fifteen) was Annie (another error—the family always called her Anna); Leie (twelve) was Lillie. The two younger daughters attended public school, but everyone else had a good-paying job. Ethel was a dressmaker in a dress shop; Harry was a salesman for a jewelry store; Sam operated a machine in a leather factory; Hyman was a watchmaker in a jewelry shop; Abraham was a "merchant in a bookstore working on his own account." The only one without a "trade or profession" was Sarah. She told Mr. Barewitz to write "none" beside her name.

Sarah had lived at 195 Madison Street for almost a year when the census enumerator showed up that Monday in April—but the rawness and strangeness still had not worn off. No garden, no cow, no neighbors she knew to gossip with, no work, no sky she could see, not even a glimpse of the sidewalk from the grimy rear-facing windows. Sarah had been right to tremble when the family first threaded these streets. Hester Street would never replace the Rakov market. The faces on the sidewalks would never look familiar. She would never grow accustomed to the noise and crowds. She would never again feel that the place she lived was scaled to her comprehension. Even the language foamed at her ears without penetrating her brain. Hyman, enrolled in English classes at the Educational Alliance, already sounded like he had lived in America all his life. Sam owned a cheap set of the complete plays of Shakespeare—in English—and boasted that he had read every one of them. *Hath not a Jew eyes? Hath not a Jew hands, organs, dimensions, senses, affections, passions?* But Sarah would have no part of this brave New World. They talked about how large and grand and rich America was, but when she looked out the window, all she saw was the rear wall of the tenement across the courtyard with another frightened Jewish lady staring back at her.

CHAPTER SIX

THE BIRTH OF A BUSINESS

S am was the shortest of the three brothers and even when he was nineteen it was clear he was going to be the stoutest. Not proud, not stuck on himself, not bent on taking charge, Sam was approachable, tractable, eager to please, someone you could confide in, kvetch to, commiserate with. His forehead was high and smooth, his hair thin and brown and wavy, eyes small, dark, and deep set. When he wore his gold wire-framed glasses he looked like a Russian poet. But Sam was no poet. Sam was a born salesman who at the age of nineteen had gotten himself yoked to a machine in a leather factory. In later years, Sam never said a word to his kids or grandkids about this chapter of his life—where he worked, what kind of machine he operated, whether the factory made belts or shoes or coverings for furniture. He was not especially handy nor was he patient. He was intolerant of both stress and monotony, so whatever he did for twelve or fourteen hours a day in whatever dusty loft or converted stable or unventilated back room must have been soul-destroying. There was certainly noise that never stopped and lubricated steel parts that never quit moving. "Machines, needles, thread, pressing cloths, oil, sponges—and the all-embracing smells of bodies, steam, and anger," wrote one Lower East Side immigrant of the cloak-making factory where his father toiled. "These were the ever-present elements of the garment industry, but there was no oil to soothe away the anger." The windows were sealed shut even in the summer heat. The fan, if there was a fan at all, blew only in the office where the boss worked. No radio. No bathroom break. Twenty minutes, maybe half an hour for lunch. Eight crummy dollars in your pocket after a six-day week. Leather is heavy, smelly when it's being processed, hard to cut or stitch, suffocating to spread and move around in close airless spaces. Sam and leather cannot have been a good match. His uncle Shalom Tvi and aunt Beyle ran a leather business back in Rakov, and maybe Sam had helped them out in the factory now and then. But it was one thing to work for your father's good-natured brother and another to have some ruthless foreman breathing down your neck. Sam was educated, a son of the scribe, born to the priestly caste—whatever shame or rage he felt at working for strangers on the hides of cows he never spoke of it. He never spoke of wolfing down a few bites of lunch with the other sullen, sweaty workers. He never spoke of the lousy wages, endless days, aching muscles, head-splitting racket. He never spoke of strikes—and those were banner years for protracted, ferocious strikes among Lower East Side garment workers. He never spoke of any of it, but the facts and circumstances speak for themselves. Sam was a born salesman. He had a salesman's voice—as warm and enveloping as chicken soup and so richly guttural that even his English sounded like transliterated Yiddish. He loved being out on the street, wheeling and wheedling. He loved to schmooze, to kibitz, to hear the talk of the trade. But necessity trumped love in those years. The family could not live without the eight dollars a week that Sam added to the twelve that Harry made and the ten that Abraham and Hyman each pulled in. So Sam, who had missed out on the apprenticeship in Smargon that boosted Harry and Hyman into the watchmaking business, gritted his teeth, pushed his spectacles up his low-bridged nose, and worked a machine in a leather factory.

Sooner or later everyone got a break—sooner if they kept their eyes open and their head down. Sam's break came in the shape of a clock. Actually, it was Harry, the smooth, smart oldest son, who came up with the idea that made it happen. Harry figured that with so many shop fronts vying for attention on the Lower East Side, the way to stand out was to put a clock in the window. A nice big display clock would make people check the time—time is money, they were always saying—and once they stop they'll want to take a look at what's for sale, maybe step inside and spend a little money.

A clock is like free advertising, Harry told the brothers. And we'll be the ones to sell them. Or rather Sam will. Sam who could sell a cross to the Pope, water to a drowning man, a razor to a rabbi. Sam will peddle display clocks to all the shops on Hester, East Broadway, Ludlow, Essex. No cash down—payable on the installment plan—twenty-five cents a week. Who's gonna say no?

So Sam started out to sell. One morning he turned up on East Broadway with a bulging sack swinging from his hand. Eyeglasses gleaming, shoulders squared for battle, he pushed open the door of a candy shop and strode to the counter. The sack was opened and a big electric clock was extracted and set down on the counter.

A lot of guys tossed him out, but that never stopped Sam. Nothing stopped Sam so long as you didn't insult him, laugh at him, or call him a greenhorn. The word *no* was not in his vocabulary. Throw him out the door and he'd climb in the window. Bar the window and he'd come around the back.

Sam was good. But the business model was crappy. The average sale was ten dollars—which at a quarter a week meant forty weekly trips to collect. Forty trudges up East Broadway or dodging the pushcarts on Hester Street's Pig Market. It was a punishing routine and the cash barely trickled in. No way to make a living. So the brothers put their heads together again and came up with a better idea. Kienzle Clock Company, the German-based manufacturer where Hyman worked, was starting a new line of quality alarm and musical clocks. Hyman could buy the clocks in bulk from Kienzle at the wholesale price and Sam could sell—*for cash*—to select outlets and peddlers.

So Sam set out with a sack of chirping clocks, and at the end of the day he returned home with an empty sack and ten dollars of profit in his pocket. The same thing the next day, and the next. Sam quit peddling the display clocks altogether. The brothers had something better.

They called a family meeting. The Cohens were a distinguished family, bearer of an ancient name—and now for the first time in hundreds of years they had an opportunity within reach that matched their ability and ambition. It was time to stop working for others. It was time to make a success of themselves, American style. Harry knew jewelry. Hyman knew timepieces. Sam knew how to sell. Abraham knew how to command respect. Why not pool their resources in a family firm? What the sons proposed to their father was to take the chirping alarm clock idea and expand it into a full-fledged wholesale operation specializing in silverware, clocks, and cut glass.

The father stroked his beard. The boys held their breath. The wife and daughters sat with their hands in their laps. If Abraham said no, the idea would die on the spot.

Finally, the father broke the silence. *I have over a thousand dollars in savings*, he told his sons. *What I have I'll combine with what you have.* How on earth had Abraham accumulated that much money? And to give it all to them, just like that, to start a business?

One of them—nobody remembers who but it was probably Harry— proposed a name: A. Cohen & Sons.

Abraham Cohen had never been a wage slave. With a business in the family, his sons and grandsons would never have to be wage slaves either. The father gave his blessing and A. Cohen & Sons was born.

By November 1911, they had found an empty storefront to rent at 126 East Broadway—a redbrick five-story tenement building with ground-floor retail space. Two big cast-iron-framed windows on the street, a tall black door, a storage cellar. They signed a year's lease at fifty dollars a month. It was a prime location on the Lower East Side's main commercial artery— East Broadway, "the sentimental heart and the battling mind of our ghetto," was lined with coffeehouses, newspaper offices, schools for rabbis, Zionist organizations, and the headquarters of Jewish charities. Their shop front stood a block from the newly opened Garden Cafeteria, where Yiddish journalists, writers, intellectuals, and union organizers gathered to schmooze and drink tea; a block and a half from the Educational Alliance, where every self-improving immigrant took night classes; another half block from the headquarters of the *Jewish Daily Forward* going up at 175 East Broadway—at ten stories, the tallest and finest building in the neighborhood, complete with marble columns and carved busts of Marx and Engels.

They hired a painter to dab the company name on one of the windows in gold letters etched in black—A. Cohen & Sons, Importers & Jobbers—and in January 1912, the company opened for business. Abraham was president. Harry and Sam were co-proprietors. Hyman, at eighteen, was too young to be listed as a legal owner, but the three brothers were equal partners from the start and they would always draw equal salaries. Once there was enough profit to draw a salary.

In the first months they ran the business in their spare time. Sam kept peddling, Hyman held on to his position with Kienzle, Abraham retained the concession at the Rivington Street shul. Harry worked the neighborhood taking orders during the day, and Hyman came in at night and all day Sunday to package up what Harry had sold. The Cohen brothers were middlemen, buying from manufacturers and selling to retailers, though many of their retailers were in fact pawnbrokers or custom peddlers who hawked merchandise door-to-door and street to street. They were always squeezed for cash, always scrambling to eke out a few more days and a few extra dollars of credit. A year after they opened for business the company's net worth was $3,091.79—$91.79 more than the initial investment.

The Cohen brothers were not pioneers or visionaries; they had not hit on some essential new product or revolutionary process; they were not going to corner the market, make headlines, or have their names emblazoned on college libraries or hospital wings. But they were eager and determined and they kept an eye cocked for the angle or niche. Hyman figured out a way to make inroads into the silverware market by selling direct to the proprietors of Catskills boardinghouses and vacation farms that catered to urban Jews. If the guests kept kosher, the landlady needed twice as much flatware—one set for meat, another for dairy. They set their sights on the Lower East Side's huge Italian population, second only to the Jews. The neighborhood's Italian groceries, in addition to purveying salami, olive oil, canned tomatoes, and parmesan cheese, also carried cheap housewares—vases, candlesticks, clocks, and bowls—that were exchanged for coupons collected by loyal customers. Some wholesaler had to supply these housewares—why shouldn't it be A. Cohen & Sons? It was pure Lower East Side: Jewish boys wholesaling the tchotchkes that Neapolitan shopkeepers used to entice Sicilian housewives to part with their money. Sam was soon doing so well on the salami circuit that he quit peddling alarm clocks. The end of an era for him—and the start of a new one for the company.

Inevitably, they brought their familiar roles and rivalries into the business and then back home to the flat on Madison Street. Harry, though diplomatic, had a fuse. Sam's skin was the thinnest. Hyman liked to claim credit for whatever succeeded and assign blame for what failed. It was an explosive mix. The boys had always bickered, but once they were in business together their fights became epic and operatic. Soon their father's primary job was to keep his sons from one another's throats. Abraham was not a tyrant, a bully, a ranter, or a table banger—he didn't need to be. In the family, his word was law; and in the family company, his word brought the sons to order and guaranteed that business was conducted honestly, equitably, and humanely.

But how the hell did they figure out how to run a business in the first place, these jumpy young men and their otherworldly father? The Cohens had left a small faded market town at the margin of Europe for "the capital of capitalism, the capital of the twentieth century, and the capital of the world." What made them swim to the surface so fast? Commerce seethed in every crevice of the Lower East Side, but most of it was two-penny trading, a peddler's sack, a candy shop, a sewing machine whirring by a tenement window. What gave the Cohen boys the chutzpah to start a wholesale business and the shrewdness to succeed? Money might, on the face of it, seem to be the obvious motive, but judging from the choices they made later on when they all had some dollars in their pockets, money was not central. The brothers liked to be comfortable and openhanded, but none of them was hounded by the plutocrat's craving for bottomless coffers. They didn't care all that much about power either, at least outside the confines of the family. They wanted to win, but not crush the competition. They didn't live large, run after women, hobnob with famous people or politicians. Nor did they work to please God. God was their father's concern. The sons started a business because in America *they could*. In Russia, a Jew had no choice. Except for the most exalted or brilliant, there was no possibility of owning land, joining a profession, securing a place in government or academics. But in America, by law, a Jew was the equal of anyone (even if the law was often subverted or skirted by family wealth, social connections, schools, clubs, churches, and codes). In America, as long as your skin was white, industry and energy were rewarded no matter what your last name was, and imagination could make you a fortune. The American playing field was far from level, but at least Jews were allowed on it. Which may explain why some Jews, the Cohen family among them, were determined to play like gentlemen. Nothing pleased Hyman more than to hear a gentile corporate executive praise him for his "attitude." Meaning, he did not act like a grasping, uncouth immigrant jobber. Hyman made it a matter of pride that he would be *more* upstanding, *more* rigorous, *more* square and scrupulous and clean-cut and aboveboard than the next fellow. Never let it be said that the Cohen brothers were cheap chiselers.

The boys, in short, made a mad rush to Americanize. All of them became naturalized as U.S. citizens. They did their best to lose their accents; they shaved every morning and wore sober three-piece suits with starched collars that covered their necks. Sam even sported a top hat. Never let it be said that the Cohen brothers were greenhorns. They knew which avenue to open a business on, where to bank, how to avoid getting cheated, how to order a good meal in a fine restaurant, and so what if it wasn't strictly kosher. Lots of other Jews their age were joining Zionist youth groups, sing-ing Hebrew songs, going off to training camps to learn how to be farmers in Palestine. That was not their dream. A different ideal motivated the Cohen brothers—an ideal compounded of self-interest, tribal and family loyalty, ambition, business savvy, and a burning desire to fit in with the American mainstream that was surging up the avenues of New York in a mighty torrent. Maybe in their heart of hearts they felt they were better than the rest, a cut above, Kohanim who could raise their hands in priestly blessing. It was not a family renowned for modesty. But they scaled their dreams to reality. They didn't want to conquer America—they simply wanted their American slice. So they pooled their resources, threw in their lot together, and, to the sound of shouting voices and slammed doors, made common cause. They would never cease to be Jews, but from the moment they set foot on Ellis Island they had ceased to be *Russian* Jews. From now on they were Americans, and as Americans they would rise or fall.

CHAPTER SEVEN

SOCIALIST IN A BLACK SATIN DRESS

tel heard all about the business that her brothers and father were trying to make a go of on the Lower East Side, but she really couldn't summon much interest in A. Cohen & Sons. By 1912, Itel and William had a burgeoning business of their own to run. Without advertising, without even hanging a sign in her window, Itel at the age of twenty-six had become Hoboken's premier dressmaker. Well-to-do matrons from Jersey City and even Manhattan trekked to the shop on the ground floor of the Rosenthals' house on Washington Street to commission gowns and frocks from the seamstress with the *goldene hent*—golden hands—though "seamstress" did not begin to cover Itel's job description. In the course of seven years, the penniless Bundist revolutionary had realized the ur-American dream: she had become a successful small business owner. Itel and William had always shared quarters with their sewing machines, but at last they had an entire house to themselves, on the more prosperous stretch of Hoboken's main commercial artery, with enough room to live and work on separate floors—downstairs for the business, upstairs for the family (Lewis, their son, was five years old). Six girls worked in shifts at the three Singer treadle sewing machines in the workroom. There was even a reception room at the front of the house where ladies could relax and flip through fashion magazines while waiting their turn. Itel had always been formidable: now she had the means to make a formidable impression. When a fashionable new client arrived in a chauffeur-driven car, Itel was on hand to greet her, usher her into the reception room, and ply her with charm. Charm was Itel's stock in trade. The ladies loved Itel's dresses, but also they loved Itel. She made them feel special. It was Itel who helped the new client decide on which pattern suited her best and Itel who took the woman's measurements—bust, waist, hips, thighs, shoulder, back, neck—while chatting away amiably in her throaty Yiddish accent. From the back of the shop, unseen but unceasing, came the noise of sewing machines, and, over the mechanical chatter, William's deep bass voice booming out commands, comments, reprimands, praise. Initially, William had come on board to lend a hand with stitching and ironing, but with the volume of business they were handling now, he had become more of a floor manager, keeping the machines in working order, directing the flow of production, checking the workmanship of every sleeve and collar. "The Jewish needle made America the best-dressed nation in the world," Jacob Riis wrote; he might have been talking about the Rosenthals of Hoboken.

One girl to one dress, with two days to get the job done—that was the method that Itel and William decided worked best in their shop. It wasn't exactly the assembly line at Ford, but it kept production ticking along smartly. When a new order came in, Itel selected one of the girls and walked her through the infinite fussy design and fabrication details, and the girl took over from there. After the seamstress had roughed out the pattern, cut the cloth, and basted together the garment sufficiently so that it could be tried on, the client returned for the first fitting. Itel helped the woman into the dress and then the golden hands went to work tugging, gathering, tucking, pinning, pinching, scrawling marks with tailor's chalk. The woman was assured that she would love it and she believed it implicitly— Itel's assurance was a force of nature.

All of the seamstresses knew that Itel and William would never let a dress go out the door unless every stitch was perfect, uniform, and invisible. If there was the smallest flaw, it was ripped and repaired.

The girls worked hard—six days a week from eight in the morning to six at night for a dollar a day, an hour for lunch, and the month of August off—but Itel and William worked harder. Itel did evening fittings for women who were occupied during the day; she and William were in the shop most Sundays to catch up on paperwork and tie up the thousand loose ends of running a small business. William, more of a Jewish mother than his wife, took enough time off from work to make sure that Lewis was clean, healthy, well fed, well loved, and put to bed every night with a story and a kiss. He even learned to cook on the maid's day off. Itel got the glory, and naturally she and William got the lion's share of the money—but the seamstresses knew they were comparatively well paid and well treated. Itel could be cold and calculating but she was also charismatic: she deployed what one relative called her "flamboyant charm" to maximum advantage with both customers and employees. She didn't just want to be the most successful dressmaker in Hoboken—she wanted to be the best. She expected nothing short of perfection and she got it.

Success spurred Itel to reinvent herself—at least outwardly. She would never be a beauty—she was too short, too stocky, too penetrating and quizzical in her expression—but she learned to make the most of what she had. She started taming her frizzy dark hair into smooth waves that framed her round fleshy face and she took to wearing stylish black satin dresses. She and William had always been readers, and now they added the works of Mark Twain, Jack London, and Shakespeare to their shelves of Yiddish and Russian classics. When they could tear themselves away from the shop, they crossed the river to attend Yiddish plays and variety shows on the Lower East Side and the occasional performance at the old Metropolitan Opera house on Thirty-ninth and Broadway.

The two of them were naturalized in 1912 and that November William cast his first vote in a presidential election, for the perennial Socialist Party candidate Eugene Debs (women in New Jersey were not granted the vote in presidential elections until 1920). It was a proud moment when William, along with more than 900,000 other socialists (nearly 6 percent of the total vote), marked his ballot for Debs in the historic four-way contest that swept Democrat Woodrow Wilson into office over Republican incumbent William Howard Taft and Bull Moose Party candidate Teddy Roosevelt. The Rosenthals may have become small business owners with money in the bank and workers on the payroll, but they hadn't abandoned the political ideals for which they had been hounded out of Russia seven years earlier.

Itel was still a socialist—a socialist in a black satin dress. The *Forward* was their newspaper; immigrant lawyers/politicians Morris Hillquit and Meyer London were their heroes; left-wing political rallies and lectures their milieu. "I am a socialist because I cannot be anything else," proclaimed the brilliant, eloquent Hillquit, who took 21.23 percent of the vote in his 1908 run for Congress in New York's Ninth District. "I cannot accept the ugly world of capitalism, with its brutal struggles and needless suffering, its archaic and irrational economic structure. . . . If I were alone, all alone in the whole country and the whole world, I could not help opposing capitalism and pleading for a better and saner order, pleading for socialism." So pleaded firebrand seamstress Clara Lemlich when she led 20,000 fellow shirtwaist operators out on a general strike that shut down sweatshops and factories all over the city for weeks in the fall and winter of 1909. So pleaded union leader Rose Schneiderman at a memorial for the 146 workers, most of them Jewish and Italian immigrant girls in their teens and twenties, who burned or jumped to their deaths when the ten-story Triangle Waist Company building on Washington Place caught fire on March 25, 1911. So pleaded Itel and William and tens of thousands of like-minded Jewish immigrants on the Lower East Side, Brooklyn, the Bronx, Hoboken, and Jersey City. It was the heyday of Jewish socialism in America and every shade of revolutionary radicalism from anarchism to Socialist-Zionism flourished wherever Jews lived and worked. On May Day, tenement fire escapes blossomed with red flags; on March 28, union halls rang with the "Marseillaise" to commemorate the short-lived Paris commune of 1871; every election season the Jewish streets and auditoriums filled with foot-stomping fist-clenched rallies for socialist candidates.

The high-water mark came in the midterm elections of 1914. On the evening of November 3, a crowd of fifty thousand gathered in Seward Park across from the Forward Building to await the results of the battle for the Twelfth District congressional seat between Democratic incumbent Henry M. Goldfogle and Socialist Party challenger Meyer London. The crowd stood fast through the night as rumors swirled and special editions of the Yiddish newspapers posted conflicting results. Finally, around 2 A.M., the *Forward* issued an extra proclaiming that Meyer London, a poor Jew born in a Ukrainian shtetl, had become the first Socialist Party member to be elected to the United States Congress, and the crowd went wild. Ten thousand delirious socialists, singing and dancing to the strains of the "Marseillaise," stormed the Forward Building. Editor Abe Cahan, toiling through the night in the editorial office, was summoned to make a speech. Dawn had broken when a car bearing London inched its way through the tenement-lined streets. The crowd was so thick on East Broadway that the car had to stop before it reached the *Forward* headquarters; London climbed on the roof to deliver his acceptance speech. "Organize, friends. Carry on the great struggle for the liberation of the working class. Build strong unions. Join the Socialist Party and carry on the fight for freedom till the final victory." The crowd celebrated until 8 A.M. Then they slowly dispersed to put in another day in the sweatshops, factories, storefronts, and pushcarts.

This was the political climate that Itel and William lived in and breathed. Though the Bund had outposts in America, they preferred the Workmen's Circle—the *Arbeter Ring* in Yiddish—a Jewish fraternal order that fostered socialist ideology, Jewish values, education for needy children, and affordable health insurance for working people. Itel and William signed on with the Workmen's Circle Rakov chapter, attended lectures, supported strikes and unions, and more or less practiced what they preached in their dress shop. They didn't turn the business into a collective, but they did pay the seamstresses a fair wage and treated them humanely. Itel cut a striking figure at raucous, sweaty union hall rallies—but in those days Jewish socialists came from all walks of life, every rung on the social ladder, and every shade of religious belief or disbelief. Socialism was the norm in enlightened Jewish America in the decade before the Great War. It was what bright kids, striving workers, and cultured, self-made immigrants subscribed to. It gave Itel and William a touch of ramparts glamour, and it connected them to the world outside Hoboken—indeed, to the world outside of the United States, since socialism was always aimed at "workers of the world." William's ties with former Bundist comrades would draw him back to Rakov for a final visit in the 1930s.

"A man either had God or socialism or he was in business," one Lower East Side immigrant wrote, "but then, with some intellectual and psychological variants, he could be involved in all three and not feel contradictory." Itel and William were involved in two of the three without feeling contradictory. Itel's brothers across the river pretty much limited themselves to business. Socialism was not for them and God was their father's affair, but if Itel wanted to wave the red flag, who were they to judge? In America, success spoke louder than politics and faith—and Itel and William were by any measure successful, certainly more successful than Harry, Sam, and Hyman. Itel was hobnobbing with upper-crust ladies, or at least taking their measurements and money, while the boys squeezed nickels out of pawnbrokers and peddlers on Hester Street. By Jewish custom and tradition, the sons were supposed to be the heavenly bodies around which the mother and daughters orbited, but that's not how it was in the Cohen family. Itel, the socialist capitalist, was the star, and the rest of them trailed along behind her. She wouldn't have had it any other way.

CHAPTER EIGHT

FIRST WORLD WAR

Shimon Dov expected the world to end in a burst of divine radiance. There would be a knock on his door and he would open to utter clarity, absolute knowledge, perfect peace, and overwhelming joy: the Messiah had come at last! The scribe and his offspring in Volozhin and Rakov and New York and New Jersey, and all the Jews in Russia and Europe, in Vilna and Warsaw, Berlin and Moscow, London and Rome and Vienna, even the Jews in China and Africa and Australia and South America would rush to their synagogues to praise God and then stream as one people, one redeemed body, back to Jerusalem, where the Temple would stand again in all its holiness and might.

Shimon Dov did not expect his world to end with a bullet fired from an assassin's rifle into the proud pampered body of the heir to the Austro-Hungarian throne. For Shimon Dov, for Europe's Jews, the assassination of the archduke Franz Ferdinand, on June 28, 1914, ushered in the age of the anti-Messiah. It took three decades to complete the mission—and when it was done, the earth, at least one smoldering chunk of it, was emptied of justice, joy, clarity, light, and love. Shimon Dov at the age of seventy-nine saw it begin. He was blessed that he did not live to see it end.

When the news reached Volozhin that Germany, on August 1, had declared war on Russia, three old friends—Fayve the tailor, Oyzer the postman, Naftoli the bookbinder—were gathered as usual in the Klayzl synagogue on Vilna Street. The talk, of course, turned to the future. Their country was now at war with the most powerful, most modern, most heavily armed nation in Europe. What would happen to them, to their families, to their beloved shtetl? *Nothing to worry about*, Oyzer the postman told his friends resolutely. Russia was not only immense but immensely strong. So strong that she could choose to fight where she wanted. Siberia, the Caucasus, the fertile plains of Ukraine, the deserts of Manchuria: the tsar controlled all of this territory and he would fight where his commanders advised him to fight. Volozhin was safe—they could all relax. With a huge empire under his belt why would the emperor pick their little town for a battlefield?

While Oyzer held forth, Nahumke, a graduate of the yeshiva, was sitting nearby, ostensibly immersed in a book. But the yeshiva man looked up when there was a pause and launched into a story—a *true story* he insisted: There once was a poor Jew in Volozhin with six ugly daughters, one nastier than the next, all of them impossible to marry off. One day the *shadken*—the matchmaker—appeared at the house of the poor Jewish father to announce that he had found a most impressive match: the only son and heir of Count Tyshkevitch, the nobleman who owned forty thousand acres of estates and forests surrounding Volozhin. There was just one problem: the prospective groom was a goy. The poor Jew was outraged, but his wife was intrigued—and so, after much soul-searching and beard-tugging, he summoned the *shadken* back and gave his consent. "Wonderful," replied the *shadken*. "Now we have to go see if the count and his son are agreeable."

"The moral of the story," Nahumke told his friends, "is that even though Russia may claim she will fight where she chooses to fight, first she needs to get the consent of Germany and Austria. Are you sure that they would agree to do battle in those precise places and not here in Volozhin?"

Nahumke was prophetic. A little more than a year later, the German army was virtually on their doorstep.

———

Shimon Dov was convinced they had been spared. When Russia mobilized, half a million Jews were called up to fight in the tsar's army, but his sons and grandsons were not among them. Avram Akiva and his three boys were safe in America. The same with Yasef Bear, Leah Golda (who had emigrated with her family in 1911), Herman, and all of their sons. Arie was dead, and Arie's two sons, Yishayahu and Chaim, were too young to be drafted. The only ones left within range of the imperial recruiting officers were Shalom Tvi and his family in Rakov. But, praise God, Shalom Tvi had only daughters—four of them once Feigele, the youngest, was born in 1912, two years after Sonia. Shalom Tvi himself was forty-two the summer war was declared—too old for the army. The news was dire—immense battles were being fought in the Pale, shtetlach were on fire, Jews were being evacuated, robbed, killed, denounced as traitors—but at least the family was safe.

Shimon Dov clung to this belief for as long as he could before the reality of the Great War closed in. In the initial chaotic months, the opposing armies had made a series of rapid advances and retreats in the borderlands of Eastern Europe, "swaying back and forth in Poland and in Galicia," as one Yiddish daily reported, and fighting "every inch of ground in Jewish towns and villages." But in the spring of 1915, the swaying stopped and the movement turned decisively in one direction: east. The Germans mounted a push into Russian territory and the tsar's army was powerless to halt it. The heavily fortified Lithuanian city of Kaunas fell in the middle of August; Smargon, where Harry and Hyman had done their apprenticeship, was overrun at the start of September; and Vilna, the regional capital, with its large cultured Jewish population, was in German hands by the middle of September. At the end of September the Eastern Front congealed along a line that sliced south through the Pale from the Baltic to the Red Sea.

The line fell so close to Volozhin that on maps the name was bisected. The yeshiva town was now a besieged outpost on the Eastern Front—still inside Russia but close enough to the line of battle that Shimon Dov was within range of artillery and in earshot of machine-gun fire. At night the eighty-year-old patriarch awoke to the repeating earthquake of exploding shells. Week after week, he watched two endless currents flow in opposite directions along the town's main street: Russian soldiers and Cossacks

THE EASTERN FRONT IN
THE GREAT WAR, CIRCA 1916

Gulf of Finland

PETROGRAD
(ST. PETERSBURG)

TALINN

(Estonia)

(Russia)

Baltic Sea

(Latvia)

RIGA

(Lithuania)

VILNA

taken by the German
army in September 1915

RAKOV

where Shalom Tvi
and his family lived

MINSK

(Poland)

VOLOZHIN

Shimon Dov was trapped
here after the war broke out

(Belarus)

WARSAW

**GERMAN-HELD
TERRITORY**

**RUSSIAN
TERRITORY**

(Ukraine)

In 1916, the front line that separated Russian and German forces in the Great War fell just a few miles west of where the family was living. (Current borders are indicated with — · — · — · — ; names of current nations are in parentheses.)

moving west with their supply wagons and unwieldy artillery pieces mounted on limbers, while refugees from evacuated towns and villages streamed east. The Volozhin marketplace filled with the homeless, the wretched, the hungry and dispossessed. Yeshiva boys were routinely dragged from the school by Russian military police, marched off in shackles to Minsk, and thrown into the Russian army—or prison. The tsar's government, deeming all Jews potential traitors, ordered mass deportations from shtetlach at the front. Some 600,000 Jews were sent packing into the Russian interior, and as many as 200,000 Jewish civilians were killed behind the Russian line. Peasants from the surrounding farm villages were also being evacuated en masse. With winter looming, those remaining in Volozhin wondered where they were going to get food.

The neighbors warned Shimon Dov that it was now a capital offense to speak Yiddish in public. The Russians had noticed that Germans could understand Yiddish—which is essentially a German dialect—and they accused Jews at the front of passing secrets to the enemy. Yiddish speakers were suspected of spying, and spies were shot on sight.

Behind their hands, the neighbors whispered that the shtetlach that had fallen to the Germans were the lucky ones. Russian soldiers raped, plundered, and torched Jewish homes, just as they always had. Cossacks were desecrating synagogues, smashing headstones, digging up Jewish graves because they believed that Jews buried their dead with their money. But the Germans were different. German soldiers were civilized, law-abiding. When they wanted something, they paid for it. Or so they thought in Volozhin.

Rakov, twenty-five miles east of Volozhin, was a day's march from the front—far enough that Shalom Tvi did not have to worry about forced evacuation, but close enough to absorb the shock waves. It turned out that Shalom Tvi was wrong when he assumed he was too old to be drafted. After the losses of 1915, the desperately depleted Russian army was pressing every able-bodied man under fifty into service. Rakov was picked clean, but somehow Shalom Tvi escaped. Maybe his leather business was considered critical to the war effort (saddles, straps, coats, gloves); maybe he secured an exemption because he had four small children to feed; maybe his angel interceded on his behalf. Whatever the reason, Shalom Tvi managed to remain at home during the war to look after his family and their business.

Rakov families that could afford it sent their wives and daughters to Minsk "lest they fall prey, Heaven forbid, to the lust of the soldiers and Cossacks," as one resident wrote. Shalom Tvi and Beyle had no relatives in Minsk and lacked the means to pay for lodging, so it's likely that the mother and daughters stayed put. Day by day, they watched the town swell with refugees. "Old and young, men and women, were carried by the huge wave, heading to the interior of Russia. And they all passed through Rakov," wrote one of their neighbors. "They would congregate in the market square, blocking the roads with their wagons, boxes, sacks, furniture, and bundles. Bundles upon bundles, of all kinds, holding the poverty which was somehow saved from the jaws of destruction. Sighing and choked weeping filled the air. They would sit, like mourners, on the ground, hungry and thirsty." Shalom Tvi listened in horror as the refugees told how Jews in the opposing armies were forced to fight against their fellow Jews—brother against brother. Again and again, a story was repeated of a Jewish soldier who was about to make the fatal plunge with his bayonet when he heard the enemy cry out in Hebrew, "Shema Yisrael!"—"Hear O Israel"—the first words of the most essential Jewish prayer. Had Shalom Tvi been drafted, this might have been his fate.

No record has come down of how Shalom Tvi and Beyle survived the first years of war. That the business suffered is certain. "The World War brought complete ruin and destruction to the industry of Rakov," wrote a shtetl historian. "Because of the economic difficulties and the drafting of the farm workers, the farmers and estate owners stopped buying the agricultural machinery which was produced in Rakov. Many of the factory owners (or as they were called: 'Mechanikers') were drafted into the army; others left Rakov and were spread all over the globe. As a result, factories were shut down, and the end came to the industry of which Rakov was famous for generations." By January 1916, with the front line more or less fixed, the flow of refugees ceased and Rakov surrendered to its winter torpor. Occasionally a convoy of ambulances careered through town bearing wounded or frostbitten soldiers; then the frozen silence closed in again.

Word came that Volozhin, which had been sealed off by the Russian army due to its proximity to the front, was on the verge of starvation. The yeshiva was emptying as *bochurim* were drafted or imprisoned. Those who remained struggled to keep the light of Torah shining, but they were slowly dying of hunger because the townspeople had no food to spare. In a neighboring shtetl, Cossacks lounging in the synagogue ripped up the Torah scroll and used pages of the Talmud to roll cigarettes: Volozhin's holy books would be next. A letter appealing for emergency aid was smuggled out of the yeshiva and delivered to Rakov's community leaders. After much soul-searching, Rakov residents finally decided to hold back a portion of the food they had been distributing to refugees and send it to the Volozhin yeshiva instead. A sleigh was loaded and Rabbi Kalmanovitch set out. The *bochurim* received him like Bar Kochba, and the women of Volozhin got busy making bread and noodle kugel. And so the revered yeshiva, having risen from the ashes of nineteenth-century fires and the enforced closure by Russian authorities, survived for another season.

Two years into the war, Shalom Tvi and Beyle's youngest daughter, Feigele, fell ill with scarlet fever. It tore the parents' hearts to see their four-year-old so weak and undernourished, but how could they feed the child properly with soldiers and stragglers plundering the garden, and with milk, eggs, and meat so hard to come by? Everyone suffered in the towns near the front, but the young and old suffered most. The doctor was summoned and medicine was prescribed—no one remembers what it was, though it must have been very strong. Feigele was put to bed in a room by herself so as not to infect her sisters. Miserable and frightened, the child drifted in and out of burning sleep. Her mother had told her that the medicine would make her better—so why not take more and get better faster? The medicine was on the table beside the bed. When no one was looking, Feigele opened the bottle and drank it all down at once. Her parents found the empty bottle and the tiny cold corpse. "It's impossible to describe my mother's feeling," Sonia, six years old at the time, told her own children many decades later. In the family photos taken after Feigele's death, Beyle looks stricken. She never stopped blaming herself. She never recovered. Next to the 600,000 refugees, the millions who had already died of bullets and shells, and the millions more who would die in the battles and influenza epidemic to come, a tragedy in a darkened bedroom is a speck of dust. But for the parents who lost their daughter, this is the history that matters.

Shalom Tvi and Beyle were both devout, strict in their observance of the commandants. But they wondered how God could let them go about their lives—unwitting, heedless—while their beloved child poisoned herself to death.

In March of 1916, the Russians tried to punch their way back toward Vilna with a massive offensive—more than 350,000 men, 282 big guns, a huge stockpile of artillery shells and poison gas, cavalry, infantry, machine guns, bayonets—the combined arsenals of traditional and modern industrial warfare. All to little or no avail. "Epic confusion" snarled the Russian push. In the end, the Germans held on to Vilna; the Russian army suffered losses of 100,000 men, and 12,000 more succumbed to frostbite. The Eastern Front remained where it had been.

The winter of 1916–1917 was a bitter one. The cold and snow were so intense that roads and rail lines became impassable and food deliveries were disrupted to Russian cities; what food got through was fantastically expensive due to rampant inflation. In Rakov, there were so few vigorous men left that the Russian authorities began pressing the elderly into forced labor. "They were put to work digging trenches, cutting down trees, and other forms of hard labor, in exchange for dry bread and water," recorded one resident. "One cannot describe the great suffering of the town people during that period." In Volozhin, still on the front line, all trade had come to a halt; a stamped permit was required to enter or leave.

Shalom Tvi managed to secure a permit for his father. A congenital worrier, Shalom Tvi had been going out of his mind at the idea that his eighty-one-year-old father was living all by himself in a starving town at the front. He greased a palm, got the necessary papers stamped, and brought Shimon Dov to live with him and his family in Rakov. The scribe had precious few possessions. He took up hardly any room in his son's house. Pious, charitable Beyle did everything she could to make her father-in-law comfortable.

The long years of war had eroded the patriarch's will to continue. Who would want to live in a world where Cossacks shredded the sacred Torah and rolled tobacco in the pages of the Talmud? On February 4, 1917 (12 Sh'vat, 5677), with temperatures plunging across Russia and food shortages worsening, Shimon Dov HaKohen died. His body was laid to rest in the Rakov Jewish cemetery, the cemetery of exile. The deceased grandchildren—Shalom Tvi's daughters Shula and Feigele and the two babies lost to Avram Akiva and Gishe Sore—may have been buried nearby, but the stones of the children have disappeared and only Shimon Dov's headstone remains at the back of the cemetery near the fence. "He was strong in Torah, he will rest with the hands of the Kohanim," reads the Hebrew inspiration—and a pair of hands, the thumbs almost touching, the fingers spread in priestly blessing, hovers over the text. It was a comfort to Shalom Tvi that his father's grave was at the cemetery's far edge. Descendants of Aaron are forbidden to enter a cemetery—but Shalom Tvi could walk to the side and gaze through the railing at the patriarch's grave while he recited the mourner's kaddish. As long as Shalom Tvi remained in Rakov, his father's soul would be attended to.

Abraham and Sarah were already in mourning when word reached Abraham that his father had died in Rakov. A few months earlier, their daughter Anna, a delicate black-haired girl of twenty-two, had been diagnosed with tuberculosis. On the advice of a doctor, Anna was packed off to a sanatorium in New York's Catskill Mountains, but it was too late to do her any good. Anna died on November 1, 1916, and Harry was dispatched to bring the body home. Sarah had now lost three of her nine children—two buried back in Rakov, and now Anna, dying alone in a sanatorium at an age when most young women were just starting their lives.

With the death of Shimon Dov, the mantle of the patriarch passed to Abraham, the firstborn son. And finally Abraham was in a situation worthy of a patriarch. After eight years in America, the golden door had creaked open for him a bit. The business was now bringing in enough money that the family was able to leave the Madison Street tenement and move into a clean modern apartment building in the Brooklyn neighborhood of Williamsburg, a short stroll from the East River. No more cold-water flat on the dingy courtyard. The Roebling Street apartment had steam heat and unlimited hot water.

The war in Europe was bringing prosperity to neutral America, and the Cohens and their business rose with the tide. Now when Abraham wrote to his brother in Rakov, he sent a little money along. And judging by Shalom Tvi's letters, the family in Rakov was going to need all the help they could get. Russia was once again in turmoil, and who knew where it would lead or when it would end.

On March 8, 1917, a month after the death of Shimon Dov, Petrograd, as Russia's capital was now called, erupted in protest. It was International Women's Day, and thousands of disgruntled women—textile workers, students, peasants, even a scattering of society ladies—marched in the street to decry the lack of bread. Police and Cossacks were called in, but they were powerless to suppress or disperse the crowd. For some reason, no one had thought to issue whips to the Cossacks that day—an oversight with serious consequences. The uprising was reminiscent of 1905—with this signal difference: after three years of war and a winter of food and fuel shortages and unbearable breadlines, not only the people of Russia but also the army had reached the breaking point. The strike of March 8 (February 23 in the old-style Julian calendar that was still in use in Russia) turned out to be the gust that brought down an empire: it was the start of the Russian Revolution. The following day the strike doubled in size, and two days after that, soldiers called in to quell the uprising turned on their officers in open mutiny. The Petrograd chief of police, rounding on the protesters with a bullwhip, was surrounded, forced from his horse, disarmed, beaten with a piece of wood, and then shot through the heart with his own revolver. One week after the women of Petrograd took to the streets shouting "Bread!" the tsar was persuaded to abdicate. On March 21, the imperial family was placed under arrest.

Romanov rule was over. Yet it was far from clear what would take its place. In the power vacuum that followed the autocracy's collapse, an unwieldy power-sharing arrangement emerged in which a provisional government, representing the elites (progressive politicians, liberal landowners, bourgeois professionals and intellectuals), ruled side by side with the Petrograd Soviet, a grassroots council of workers, soldiers, and radical politicians that was modeled on the soviets (councils) that had sprung up during the 1905 revolution. The assumption, or hope, was that the dual power arrangement would in time evolve into a single democratically elected government, but that was not what happened. As of March 15, 1917, Russia had no head of state—but it was still committed to fighting a devastating war. Had the world been at peace, revolution might have ushered in a stable, possibly democratic future. But revolution in the midst of world war proved to be catastrophic.

The Jews of Rakov and Volozhin and a hundred other shtetlach at the front erupted in wild euphoria at the news that the tsar had fallen. But joy, as always in Russia, was tempered by anxiety. Revolution had exploded and fizzled before; upheaval yielded freedom first, then repression and pogroms. Meanwhile, the war continued, practically at their doorstep. Though more and more soldiers were melting away and returning to their villages, though the officer corps was in shambles, though radicalized workers and soldiers were demanding with rising stridency that Russia pull out, still the fighting on the Eastern Front went on with no end in sight. Rakov and Volozhin Jews were giddy with their new rights, but their sons, those sons who remained after two and a half years of slaughter, were still being marched off to fight and die.

Of the three Cohen brothers, Hyman was the most taken with Germany. He loved the precision of German workmanship on clocks and watches, and his first job in New York, before A. Cohen & Sons got started, had been for the German-based Kienzle Clock Company. When Kienzle's president came over to inspect the New York operation, he was so impressed with Hyman that he offered to bring him back to Germany and train him in the manufacture of clocks. Hyman would have jumped at the offer had his mother not refused to let him go.

When Europe went to war in the summer of 1914, Hyman was naturally sympathetic to the German side. He was not alone. Even if they didn't share Hyman's love for German craftsmanship, the majority of American Jews supported Germany because it was fighting against Russia, the land of the pogrom. Russia's enemy was their friend—it was as simple as that. The pro-German stance was reinforced by stories and letters that came from the Pale attesting to how much better Jews fared in territory conquered by

Germany. Under the Germans, there was no rape, no plunder, no desecration of synagogues. German officers billeted in Jewish homes were considerate, even kind. Germans laid down the law, but it was the same law for Jews and gentiles. So even though England and France were more appealing politically and socially than the Central Powers (Germany, Austria, and the Ottoman Empire), Jewish America had very little appetite for the Allied cause. Jewish socialists abhorred the war as a capitalist plot to distract workers from their legitimate struggle. Jewish moderates worried about the consequences of an Allied victory for their relatives still in Russia. Apolitical Jews shrugged their shoulders and thanked God that they had gotten out. But the consensus was that a Jew would have to be crazy to fight on the same side as the tsar.

Everything changed when revolution broke out in Petrograd. With the tsar gone, with Russian Jews granted full civil rights, suddenly the world was a different place—not only on Nevsky Prospect but on East Broadway. Even William and Itel's beloved *Forward* abandoned its socialist-pacifist stance to declare, "There is nothing more to discuss. Feelings dictate, reason dictates, that a victory for present-day Germany would be a threat to the Russian Revolution and dangerous for democracy in Europe." The revolution for which Itel and William had been chased out of Russia twelve years earlier had resurged and triumphed at last. At a stroke, American Jewry renounced Germany and realigned itself with the Allies. On March 20, five days after the tsar abdicated, twenty thousand American Jews packed New York's Madison Square Garden, shouting and dancing in the aisles to celebrate the revolution.

They were dancing on an earthquake. That same day, President Woodrow Wilson assembled his cabinet secretaries in Washington, DC, and sought their advice on the situation with Germany. Wilson had been reelected the previous November on the promise to keep America out of the war, but in the late winter of 1917 that promise seemed doomed to be broken. On February 1, the Germans announced their intention to resume unrestricted submarine attacks on Atlantic commercial shipping, and several American vessels were sunk by German torpedoes in the following weeks. In March, as revolution swept Petrograd, the American press intercepted and published the so-called Zimmermann telegram, in which

Germany's foreign secretary, Arthur Zimmermann, was instructed to secretly enlist Mexico as Germany's partner in a war against the United States. Zimmermann was told to dangle the promise to "re-conquer the lost territory in Texas, New Mexico, and Arizona" as an incentive for Mexico to join with Germany. Public pressure on the Wilson administration to deal with German aggression had been mounting all winter, and the Zimmermann telegram was, in the minds of many, the tipping point. Wilson felt he no longer had any choice. He presented the options to his cabinet, and on March 20 they voted unanimously to go to war. Two weeks later, Wilson made his case before Congress. "The world must be made safe for democracy," the president exhorted America's lawmakers—and the lawmakers agreed. The Senate reached its decision on the night of April 4—82 voted for war, 6 against. In the predawn hours of April 6, the House vote was tallied: 373 members of Congress in favor, 50 opposed.

Had the family stayed in Rakov, Abraham's three sons would have been drafted into the Russian army and sent to the front. But now, just when revolution had freed Russia's Jews, the war had crossed the ocean and crashed into their home in Brooklyn. None of the boys was safe from conscription after all.

June 5, 1917—National Draft Registration Day—dawned fair and mild over New York City with a soft breeze out of the south. The temperature had approached eighty the previous day—and what green there was in the city looked bright and fresh and miraculously clean. Nowhere more miraculous than in the tiny garden of the narrow three-story Williamsburg row house at 73 South Tenth Street, where the Cohen family had just moved from Roebling Street. At last, Abraham and Sarah had a home of their own—not a couple of rooms off a shared hallway but a whole house rising out of God's earth with a bit of grass in front and a small bed in back where Sarah could grow a few flowers and vegetables and remember her garden in Rakov. Harry and Hyman were careful when they left the house that morning not to crush a single precious leaf or blade underfoot. Freshly shaved, neatly dressed, and nervous as hell, the brothers walked together to the local polling place to register for the draft. Every male between the ages of twenty-one and thirty-one was doing the exact same thing—not only in

New York City but from coast to coast all over the country. Citizen, immigrant, naturalized, disabled, disaffected—it made no difference: all had to register for the draft that Congress had been forced to reinstate in order to bulk up America's paltry army of 210,000 men (seventeenth in the world). Harry was twenty-eight, Hyman was twenty-four—right in the bull's eye of Uncle Sam's ten-year draft target—and so, they went off to do their civic duty along with 10 million other American males.

Sam, who was twenty-seven, wasn't with them because Sam was now a married man with a place of his own. Four years earlier, he had married a girl named Celia Zimmerman, a fellow Russian Jew, and the couple was now keeping house on John Street—not in Williamsburg, like the rest of the family, but in Brooklyn's Vinegar Hill neighborhood near the Manhattan Bridge. The two houses, though just a couple of miles apart, were in different precincts, so Sam had to go off by himself to register that morning. But before he could get out the door, Sam had to deal with his wife. Celia was flighty and high-strung and two months pregnant, and this war was making her frantic. *What if they took him? What if he never came back? What if he came back with his legs blown off?* In truth Sam was worrying himself.

It was the cusp of summer, but in Brooklyn and Manhattan it felt like the Fourth of July. At the stroke of seven when the registration stations opened, the whole city filled with the joyous noise of church bells tolling, horns blasting in the harbor, factory whistles shrilling. The avenues were bedecked with flags and bunting, and in the parks, bands and choruses belted out patriotic songs and marches. You couldn't walk ten blocks without hearing the National Anthem. Eight hundred interpreters stood by to assist foreign-born registrants at the 2,123 stations that had been set up not only at polling places but also in storefronts, schools, barbershops, even funeral parlors. "I do not anticipate any trouble," said Mayor John Purroy Mitchel (the so-called Boy Mayor of New York, who would die the following year at the age of thirty-eight while training with the fledgling air force). "But if there is any trouble, the police will be ready." Indeed, in Williamsburg, the city had deployed one hundred extra policemen to break up protests threatened by socialists; a machine-gun squad, thirty-five motorcycle police, and two hundred cops armed with rifles were on hand—just in case.

The city was "prepared for anything short of invasion" reported the *New York World*—but the registration of some 610,000 New Yorkers unfolded peacefully. There was certainly no trouble from the Cohen brothers. Harry and Hyman filled out their cards under the watchful eye of registrar Edward P. Kearney, while Sam submitted his card to one D. H. Leary at Precinct 152. Though all three were citizens now, none of them showed much appetite to serve in the armed forces of their adoptive country. On line 12 of the registration card, in the space beside the question "Do you claim exemption from draft (specify grounds)?" Harry wrote "Yes break up the business and support of father and mother." Sam wrote "Weak lungs." And Hyman wrote "Yes. Support of mother."

Six weeks later, there was a lottery drawing in Washington, DC, to determine the order in which registrants would be called up, and as luck would have it, all three of the brothers received very low numbers. Hyman, convinced that his civilian days were numbered, managed to get himself invited to the Catskills summer resort where his sweetheart, Anna Raskin, was vacationing with her family. Might as well make time while there was still a chance. Hyman could be gruff and scrappy, but he pitched as much sweet woo to lovely Anna as the senior Raskins would tolerate. By the time he returned to Brooklyn late in the summer, the couple had evidently reached an agreement. Sam and Harry, meanwhile, toiled away at A. Cohen & Sons and anxiously checked their mail.

The U.S. War Department intended to have 687,000 new recruits in uniform by autumn, and the first round of call-up notices went out at the end of August. Sam was one of the lucky recipients—but the army didn't want him. At his physical, the examiners concluded he was too nearsighted to pick off German soldiers. In any case, he was short and stout and married and claimed to have weak lungs, so all in all not very promising soldier material. Harry was also refused. So that left Hyman. He got the call a few weeks after returning from what he called his "long date" in the Catskills. The War Department ordered him to report to his Brooklyn draft board for processing and warned that he was now "in the military service of the United States and subject to military law. Willful failure to present yourself at the precise hour specified constitutes desertion and is a capital offense in time of war." Hyman showed up at the appointed hour and got in line for his physical with hundreds of other tense young Brooklynites. Medium in height and build, good-looking in a kind of hooded way though none too muscular after years shuffling papers and schlepping flatware samples, Hyman was a perfectly adequate specimen of Jewish American manhood. Neither flat-footed, alcoholic, myopic, or sexually degenerate, Hyman passed his physical with flying colors. The examiners told him to get dressed, go back to work, and await the next communiqué from Uncle Sam. It wouldn't be long.

All that summer and autumn, as the United States shambled into war, violence and uncertainty convulsed Russia. The Germans had facilitated Vladimir Lenin's return to Petrograd, in April, on the assumption that the Bolshevik leader would further destabilize Russia, and they were right. Fierce, grim, and disciplined, Lenin pushed for the extreme solution. He demanded that the bourgeois provisional government be overthrown at once and replaced by a government of those at the bottom of Russian society—urban workers, disaffected soldiers, and the disenfranchised rural poor. Russia must withdraw immediately from the world war; rural estates must be broken up and redistributed; food must be made affordable for the starving masses. Large angry crowds took Lenin's call for "all power to the Soviets" to the streets. The message hit a nerve—even Lenin was surprised by how rapidly the ranks of his supporters swelled that summer. In June, Alexander Kerensky, a moderate socialist who was then minister of war and would shortly take over as head of the provisional government, launched a disastrous military offensive that only played into the Bolsheviks' hands. Morale collapsed in the army; desertions increased exponentially. In the first week of July, the streets of the capital filled with half a million armed deserters and militant, radicalized workers. In September, the Moscow Soviet went over to the Bolsheviks, and on October 23, the Bolshevik Central Committee called for the armed overthrow of Kerensky's provisional government.

The triumph of the so-called October Revolution was swift and all but bloodless, at least in the capital. Led by Trotsky, the Bolsheviks stormed the

Winter Palace on the night of November 8 and took control of the government. "We shall now proceed to construct the socialist order!" Lenin proclaimed in his harsh monotone to a rapturous crowd.

In Rakov, hundreds of jubilant young Jews marched to the marketplace to the strains of the "Marseillaise" blared out by the band of the revolutionary Russian army. "How bestirred were our hearts!" wrote a nephew of Sarah's named Zelig Kost, who was among the marchers. "The whole town rose with us, the marchers, like waves in a stormy sea. We had great hopes. We sang about a new emerging world, a superior world where the tortured Jewish people would find their rightful place. Ah! How quickly the illusion vanished."

A scant seven months had passed between Lenin's return and the raising of the red flag over the Winter Palace. A "decree on peace" was the new leader's first proposal to the Congress of Soviets. It was approved unanimously.

Peace was what the people most fervently hoped for. But as Zelig Kost and his young comrades in Rakov discovered, peace was the first illusion to vanish after the revolution.

Hyman turned twenty-five on November 5, a Monday, three days before the Bolsheviks seized the Winter Palace. A full day of work lay ahead of him at A. Cohen & Sons. Though Hyman and Harry were no longer roommates—Harry, at the age of twenty-eight, had finally left home and moved into a place of his own on West 150th Street in Manhattan—they were still brothers and partners, and they still spent every day but the Sabbath working together side by side. Nonetheless, Hyman felt compelled to sit down that morning and write Harry a long, emotional letter. His orders from the War Department were due to arrive any day, and the birthday letter had the urgent self-dramatization of a young man face-to-face with his own, possibly heroic, death.

"You know me to be a poor writer," Hyman began, but he needed to explain his "present feelings in my own poor way." He had recently heard at a lecture that "when a boy enters his twenty-fifth year he at the same time enters into manhood, and a man should therefore take inventory of himself, look over and examine carefully what he has done in the past, and make new plans for the future." And so:

> I have taken inventory of my self to-day and I can tell you that with the exception of a few minor things not even worth mentioning I was pleased with my past work and I started to make plans for the future, but I couldn't go very far, and didn't make many plans, as at the start of my planning I remembered my self that this birthday came in a month in which I may have to give up all my plans for a while, as our government will very soon start to do all the planning for me.

Hyman waxed nostalgic over the five and a half "very pleasant" years he and Harry had spent as business partners:

> We struggled together when everything about looked complete failure, and we were, and are, both sharing the honor now that we have brought for our business a little success and its good name in the "business world."
>
> I am approaching very rapidly the day when I'll have to stop for a while to take active interest in the business, and while I appreciate the hard work Sam has done for us, we know that he only can do hard inside work (labor) and he couldn't run the business even for a week. I therefore want you although you will have to work much harder, [to] do some of my work, follow my principals [sic], and also protect, and take care of my interest as well as of your own, during my stay in the "National Liberty Army."
>
> To Harry Cohen my friend I have this to say, we have been friends for a very long time, our friendship started in 1906 in the little city, or town of Smargon, Russia, when we worked to-gether in the little old Watchmaker's shop owned by Mr. Rudnick. You undoubtedly remember how you worked for 2.50 Rubbels [sic] a week, and with your small salary we lived to-gether in a little room 10 X 6. . . . When in 1909 I came to this country to-gether with our parents and our sister Lillie and our late sister Anna, our friendship was resumed, and in fact we were

*more united, and if on one or the most two occasions we had a misun-
derstanding it only kept up for a few hours, our friendship couldn't
stand much longer.*

Moved by his own eloquence, Hyman signed off emotionally:

> *We have seen brothers drifting apart from one another, but we have
> always stuck together, we were real brothers, and as my brother I don't
> ask any more but I demand of you in other words I draft you to take
> good care of our parents, protect them, support them, and keep up their
> spirits. . . . Take care of my interest, and when I'll return, and I hope in
> the very near future, we will start life again as the best Partners, Friends,
> and Brothers one for all, and all for one. Unity the key of success. Yours
> for an early and general world Peace your Partner your loving brother
> your Friend Hyman.*

Hyman's induction orders arrived in the mail two weeks later and he
reported as instructed to Camp Upton out in the scrub flats of central Long
Island. The 77th Division—the so-called Melting Pot or Times Square
Division, assembled from raw immigrant recruits from the ghettos of the
Lower East Side, Brooklyn, and the Bronx—was training at Camp Upton
when Hyman got there. The division's commanding officer despaired
when he learned that the men he was in charge of spoke forty-three
different languages—"the worst possible material from which to make
soldier-stuff."

Hyman soon found out that anti-Semitism was rampant in the army.
He wised up fast: if a guy called you a kike, there was no use whining to
your sergeant—you had to deal with it with your fists. Anyway, it wasn't
just Jews. Hunkies, Pollocks, Guineas, Chinks all got razzed, picked on,
shoved out of the chow line, denigrated as hyphenated Americans or not
American at all. While the Ivy League officers perused Madison Grant's
1916 best seller *The Passing of the Great Race*, which claimed that "the
wretched, submerged population of the Polish Ghettos" was polluting
the "splendid fighting and moral qualities" of America's old "Nordic" stock,
the draftees—20 percent of them foreign-born—traded ethnic insults and

occasionally came to blows. Hyman never breathed a word of it in his letters home. What would be the point?

"No one is allowed to leave the barracks," Hyman wrote home on December 10. "Whatever may turn up we are getting ready and are singing in the barrack our camp songs Pack up Your trouble in your old kit bag and smile smile smile and also Where do we go from here?" (The latter ends with the memorable refrain: "Where do we go from here, boys? Where do we go from here? Slip a pill to Kai-ser Bill and make him shed a tear, And when we see the en-e-my we'll shoot them in the rear, Oh, joy! Oh, boy! Where do we go from here?")

Around Christmas, Hyman returned home to Brooklyn on a three-day pass. He and Anna had one last date—dinner and a show in Manhattan. Back at Camp Upton a couple of weeks later, Hyman received word that Sam's wife, Celia, had safely delivered twins on January 9—Dorothy and Sidney, a girl and a boy, the first great-grandchildren of Shimon Dov. Three days later, Hyman's unit was finally issued their "complete field outfit"—rifle, bayonet, ammunition, mess kits, and metal water bottle. On January 17, they were ordered to assemble in the bitter cold at the rail platform for the train to Long Island City. Here they boarded ferries bound for a pier in New York harbor. Stowed like steerage passengers on the lower deck of a British troop ship—"We were just live freight," wrote Hyman—they set out across the Atlantic. The crossing proceeded without incident until the final day, when, eight hours shy of Liverpool, Hyman's ship collided with one of the freighters. Sirens wailed as passengers and crew were ordered to evacuate to lifeboats. "Here, I learned how men react in emergencies," said Hyman. "Strong men prove to be panicky and weak men become strong, some cry, some pray, some sing. I was among those who sang. Normally, I don't carry a tune." Upon inspection, the damaged ship was deemed seaworthy—and so the weak and the strong, the tuneful and the teary, reboarded and steamed on to Liverpool. After a few days regrouping in dank unheated wooden-floored tents at a camp near Winchester, they boarded ships at Southampton and crossed the channel.

"Arrived safely," Hyman cabled from LeHavre on the Normandy coast on February 3. "Feeling great love to all."

He spent his first two months of war marching, training, and feeling sorry for himself because not a single letter reached him from the States. All the replacement recruits from Camp Upton were in the same boat: because they were constantly on the move, shuffled from unit to unit, neither their mail nor their pay caught up with them. "We began to feel we were all among the forgotten men," Hyman lamented.

Finally, on March 10, 1918, his permanent assignment came through. The forgotten men were piled into dun-colored French rail cars—no American soldier failed to remark on the words "40 *hommes*, 8 *chevaux*" (40 men, 8 horses) prominently stenciled on the side—and transported to the city of Toul east of Paris. Hyman reported to Company K, 18th Infantry, First Division. The company's commanding officer, Captain Joseph Quesenberry, a boyish twenty-three-year-old honors graduate and former football player from the New Mexico College of Agriculture and Mechanic Arts in Las Cruces (now New Mexico State University), informed Hyman of the great honor that had befallen him: he had landed in the fabled Big Red One. The First Division prided itself on being first in every way: it was the oldest division in the U.S. Army, the first American division to arrive in France after the United States entered the war, the only American division to parade through the streets of Paris on July 4, 1917, the first to fire a shell at the German line, and the first to suffer casualties. When Hyman and the other replacement troops fell into line at Toul, Captain Quesenberry laid out their sacred mission: "The First Division has been in every war the country was in. It came out with honors every time. I expect to maintain the good name of the division in this present conflict, so we can wear the Red One [the divisional insignia] with pride." There was another First Division first that involved the captain personally—on March 15, he had participated in an attack in which the Americans took their first German prisoners of war. After bouncing around for five months, Hyman was at last in a permanent outfit with men who had "pride in their company, regiment, and division."

Above all, pride in their commanding officer. "He was a great officer, a soldiers' soldier," Hyman wrote of Quesenberry. "He was the idol of our outfit." The 250 men in Company K were ready to lay down their lives for their young captain. Hyman felt the same.

"There is no doubt that it will be a shameful peace," declared the newly empowered Lenin when faced with the dilemma of how to extract Russia from the war, "but if we embark on a war, our government will be swept away." The most the Bolsheviks could hope for was to minimize the shame. This they botched as well. Peace negotiations with the Germans opened in the city of Brest-Litovsk three days before Christmas of 1917 and culminated in a dramatic stalemate in the middle of February 1918. The Russian delegation under Trotsky announced that Russia was pulling out of the war but refused to commit to any kind of peace treaty. "Neither peace nor war" was Trotsky's sly position. The Germans' response was to mount a rapid push east into Russian territory. In five days, the German army advanced 150 miles, swallowing more Russian territory than in the previous three years. With Petrograd in imminent danger, the Bolsheviks moved the government to Moscow. On February 23, the Germans made one last ultimatum for a peace treaty, and Lenin conceded: "It is a question of signing the peace terms now or signing the death sentence of the Soviet Government three weeks later." The treaty of Brest-Litovsk was formalized on March 3 and it was indeed shameful. Russia lost not only all of its western territories—Poland, Finland, Estonia, Lithuania, Ukraine, most of Belarus—but a third of its population, a third of its arable farmland, more than half of its industry, and nearly 90 percent of its coal mines. The dismembered former empire would devote what remained of its resources to a protracted civil war.

Rakov and Volozhin were now under German control. After three years near the front line and six months of lawlessness following the Bolshevik revolution, Shalom Tvi and Beyle were subjects of the Ober Ost—the German name for the territory they had taken from the Russians during the war. The regime change came as a huge relief. The family had lost everything during the chaotic "neither peace nor war" weeks in February, when a gang of armed bandits and deserters took over Rakov and terrorized the townspeople. "For three days they rioted, looted, and plundered, with no one to stop them," one resident wrote. Sonia, now almost eight, and her two older sisters, Doba and Etl, were hidden away in a closet while the marauders went from house to house. Their mother crept into the garden at night to bury the family's money and silver. Then, a week into March, the Germans rolled in and the reign of terror came to an end. The girls emerged from hiding. Beyle went to the market to see if there was any food for sale. Shalom Tvi salvaged what he could of their shop and factory. The family, like all of Rakov's Jews, had high hopes from the Ober Ost. The provisional government had been powerless. The Bolsheviks had brought nothing but plunder and chaos. Maybe under the Germans life would return to normal.

And indeed for a while it did—or something that approached normal. German officers requisitioned rooms in the finer houses in town, but they treated the home owners, Jews and gentiles alike, with respect. Germans did not steal from Beyle's garden as the Russian soldiers had. Shops reopened in the market. The peasants once again trundled into town on Monday and Friday, bought and sold, got drunk, and staggered back to their villages. Relatives of Shalom Tvi in a nearby shtetl had a German officer billeted in their house, and the daughter reported that he was a perfect gentleman who did everything he could to keep the family safe and comfortable. When Passover came on March 28, the German authorities made sure that Rakov's Jews had kosher flour to bake matzo. Shalom Tvi was astonished when a couple of German Jewish soldiers showed up at shul for Shabbat services. Germany's Jews were far more assimilated than Russia's, and most of the German-Jewish soldiers who occupied the shtetlach were appalled by the poverty and backwardness of the *Ostjuden*—the Eastern Jews. But for a few, the life of the shtetl stirred some deep atavistic longing. "On the earth this is the last part of the Jewish people that has created and kept alive its own songs and dances, customs and myths, languages and forms of community, and at once preserved the old heritage with a vital validity," wrote one German Jew serving with the Ober Ost.

After nearly four years of war, Shalom Tvi and Beyle did not expect much from their new rulers. The Germans were better than chaos and banditry—but they were occupiers, not angels, and they could be just as ruthless as the Russians when they were crossed. There were stories of German soldiers jeering at the Jewish townswomen whom they had forced to scrub a market square on hands and knees; and Germans giving Jewish laborers soup crawling with worms. "Jews are living here in considerable numbers: a cancerous wound of this land," one German officer reported after taking charge of his district in the Ober Ost. Another officer declared that Jews were loathsome "because of the ineradicable filth which they spread about themselves." A good German was better than a Russian, Shalom Tvi concluded, but a bad German was worse than anything. The German high command had had almost four years to impose *Deutsche Arbeit*—German Work—on the Ober Ost; by the time they took Rakov, they had their Germanizing policies down to a science. They restored order, but they also took all the best food, grain, and livestock and sent it off to Germany. "We ate what the [German] soldiers threw away, including potato peels from the military kitchen," one boy wrote.

Shalom Tvi could not help noticing that Rakov's German occupiers were hungry and ragged too. These were not the grinning, singing, strapping youths who had marched off to war in the summer of 1914—but an exhausted army of the very old and very young. Shalom Tvi had seen four occupying forces come and go in quick succession in the year since his father's death. The Germans were tolerable as long as they lasted, but frankly, he was dubious that they would last long.

Shalom Tvi and Beyle's youngest daughter, Sonia, was eight years old when the Germans entered Rakov. She retained no memory of the foreign soldiers marching into town, the new flags and posters, the punctilious officers, her parents' cautious relief. What she did later remember from this time was being punished for setting foot in a church.

Sonia was a born adventurer, confident and curious; when her heart was set, she did what she wanted—even if it got her into trouble. One day late in the war, Sonia noticed crowds of people in their finest clothes converging on the Catholic church, just a stone's throw from their house. Sonia slipped out the gate and followed the people up the lane. When she reached the church, she saw there was a wedding. One of the teachers at the Polish Catholic seminary was marrying a seventeen-year-old girl from a wealthy gentile home, and the celebration was large, noisy, and colorful. As the guests in their finery climbed the steps and disappeared into the big double doors beneath the pointed brick arches, Sonia decided she had to follow them. It was beautiful inside the church—far more beautiful and mysterious than

Rakov's cozy wooden shul. The ceilings were so high she had to crane her neck to see to the top, and there were paintings framed in gold wherever she looked—paintings of beautiful women and a sad suffering man. "It was so quiet there," Sonia remembered, "with not even the sound of a fly buzzing around. The walls were covered with many different pictures of Jesus, the crucifixion, the resurrection, his mother Mary, and more. This was the first time I had ever entered a church." But not all the images were lovely. Sonia noticed a knot of guests gathered in the shadow at the back. She crept over to see what they were doing—no one paid any attention to her, she was so small and quiet. "I saw that they were all spitting onto a certain place, and when I looked closer I saw the figure of an old Jewish man with a big nose, dressed in a red cape, labeled 'The Traitor Judas Iscariot Who Betrayed Jesus.'"

Sonia fled from the church and ran home. She couldn't help blurting out what she had done and seen to her parents. Her father was furious. "He said that it was forbidden to Jews to set foot in a church. I had to swear a *neider* [vow] of 40 days of silence."

Forty days of silence—when the child felt like howling at the top of her lungs. But this was the vow that Jews in Europe had always imposed on one another: when you wanted to scream, keep your head down and your mouth shut; don't look; don't fight back; hide.

Sonia could not understand what she had done wrong. "It was simply that it was very interesting to me to see inside," she said. Wasn't it punishment enough to discover that in their church the Christian neighbors secretly spat upon the dirty Jew? She wondered if they spat on the gates of her own house while their backs were turned. She couldn't fathom this hidden hatred. It didn't seem right that their churches had domes and steeples and stained glass and pictures framed in gold while everything Jewish was so shabby and sad. Even the Christian cemetery was a gardenful of flowers, while the Jewish cemetery where her grandfather was buried struck Sonia as a place of "total destruction, poverty, and the feeling of exile—that's what I felt." Sonia was once walking through the Christian cemetery when her eyes fell on an inscription in Russian—*I'm already home, you'll come to visit soon.* She wondered what it could possibly mean. The Christians had a home right here on earth—why did they need another? In Rakov's

Jewish cemetery, the cemetery of exile, trees grew but not a single flower bloomed. When her father went there to pray for her grandfather's soul, he stood outside the rusted fence like a beggar. Why couldn't a Jew have sweetness and beauty too?

At the end of March 1918, around the same time that Rakov was absorbed into the Ober Ost, the Germans launched a massive push aimed at decisively ending the stalemate along the Western Front. The Americans had still barely gotten their noses bloodied in the war: now that the spring offensive had put the Germans within striking distance of Paris, the time was at hand for the Americans to show what they were worth. The First Division was chosen to mount the counterattack, and on April 6, 1918, Sonia's first cousin Hyman boarded one of the hated "40 *hommes*, 8 *chevaux*" train cars and headed up to the front line in Picardy. On the train ride across northern France, Hyman saw smooth round hills just greening up in the first flush of spring and blackened stumps of villages that had been shelled to oblivion. He saw women and children, sometimes waving, sometimes staring stonily; he saw men, but only old men or young ones who were bandaged or missing limbs. He saw church steeples and hedgerows and delicate jade green fronds that by summer would explode in drifts of red and pink poppies. He detrained in a sector that looked a lot like the countryside around Rakov, only hillier. He scrambled to find places to sleep. He listened to the rumors of imminent attacks. He pined for letters—"I have not heard a word from anyone since I left the States," he wrote his parents, "days have turned into weeks and weeks into months and even the months are turning and turning and still not a word from any one of you." He pined for Anna. He became a crack marksman with a Springfield bolt-action rifle.

On the night of April 24, Company K took up its position about a mile from the village of Cantigny. Hyman, scoping out the terrain, understood at a glance what they were up against: the Germans had chosen an elevated position on the top of a chalk rise that commanded the countryside to the west. When it came time to fight, Company K would be slogging uphill without any cover into the teeth of German machine guns.

But first they had to survive the ceaseless barrage of German artillery.

As soon as the regiment dug in near Cantigny, huge volumes of high explosive shells and canisters of poison gas rained down on them from some ninety German battery positions. German airplanes whined overhead, spitting down rounds of machine-gun fire. "The shelling did not come in bursts," wrote one soldier, "but was continuous and apparently was meant to break down the morale of the new occupants of the sector." Food carts were blown up or held back by the intense shelling, and the men counted themselves lucky to get one cold meal a day. For a week they lived on "a slice of meat, a spoonful of sour mashed potatoes, a canteen of water, a canteen cup of coffee, a half-loaf of bread, a beautiful country and sometimes a sunny sky."

On the evening of April 27, German shells started landing with such deadly accuracy that Captain Quesenberry decided to move his men to a safer position. It was either move or get blown up. Around eight o'clock that night, the men were engaged in digging a new trench in a less exposed position when the shell with the captain's name on it came in. Quesenberry had listened to a thousand shells whistle and detonate—but this one was different. The shriek was directly overhead; the flash was blinding; the concussive blow immediate, deafening, and suffocating. On contact, the high-explosive shell casing disintegrated into a thousand hot splinters of steel. Some of these splinters tore into Captain Quesenberry's arm and leg.

"We held our position," wrote Hyman, "but Captain Quesenberry, the idol of our outfit, was hit and severely wounded." A soldier with Company K who saw Captain Quesenberry fall testified that "he was taken away in an ambulance and I understand died on the way to the hospital, from loss of blood." But Hyman gave a different account:

> Four of us carried him into the church basement of the town, which was now a field hospital. We found many of our men lying there waiting for first aid and evacuation. The medics seeing the captain attempted to give him first aid. He refused treatment and ordered the medics, "don't touch me until all my men are treated."

The army's Graves Registration Service recorded that Captain Quesenberry died of shell wounds on April 28, the day after he was hit. The twenty-three-year-old captain was buried in the temporary American military cemetery at Bonvillers, though later, at the request of his father, his remains were disinterred and returned home to Las Cruces.

The men of Company K carried on without their beloved captain. For a month they endured ceaseless pounding outside of Cantigny. Then, on the morning of Tuesday, May 28, they were ordered to take the village. It was Hyman's first taste of combat. At the dot of 5:45 A.M., the combined French and American artillery opened up with everything they had and blasted away for an hour. When the guns fell silent, whistles shrilled up and down the line and the infantry moved out in waves toward the German stronghold. By 7:20 A.M., the Big Red One had taken Cantigny. The hard part would be fending off the inevitable German attempts to take it back.

Hyman's unit was supposed to form "working and carrying parties" to supply ammunition and water to the units at the front of the assault. Hyman remembered it like this: "Our company was ordered to get to the top of the hill and dig in. Make no advances. Just dig in and defend our position. Our company reached the assigned positions. We lost many of our buddies while digging under fire." These heavy casualties occurred during the ferocious counterattacks that German forces began mounting around 9 A.M.—seven counterattacks that went on for two days. Company K's carrying parties made easy targets as they tried to run supplies to the front; their losses mounted quickly.

"We were under continuous fire," wrote Hyman. "The German Army tried to retake the position, but our regiment held on. Cantigny was ours, and remained so."

Though it looked like an insignificant knob on the map of the Western Front, Cantigny was a jewel much prized by the German high command because it represented the westernmost point on their line—the deepest they had penetrated into French territory. Paris was a mere seventy miles away. A German victory there would not have significantly altered the course of the war, but it would have dealt a stinging blow to American morale. The First Division made sure that that did not happen. They paid a stiff price, but in the end, the Americans fought off the ferocious German counterattacks and prevailed. Captain Quesenberry was dead, many of his men were killed or wounded in the course of the battle, but Hyman and the boys who remained held their position—and the Big Red One held Cantigny.

When new recruits were rotated into Company K to fill the places of those who had fallen at Cantigny, Hyman had bragging rights. He had been there first. He had acquitted himself honorably in the first major American engagement of the war, and the first victory of the First Division. A decade earlier he had been tinkering with watches in the Russian Pale. Now he was a warrior.

Two months later, the 18th Infantry saw action again at Soissons. It was Hyman's last battle in the Great War.

Hyman had always admired square-jawed, starched-collar, old-line WASPs—and his new boss was a prime specimen of the type. Six feet tall, ramrod straight, broad chested, and steely eyed, Colonel Frank Parker, commander of the 18th Infantry, was a son of coastal South Carolina, a graduate of West Point, a gentleman and a scholar who spoke fluent French and taught young soldiers the art and science of modern war. He was also, apparently, one hell of an inspiring leader. Colonel Parker certainly inspired Hyman on the morning of July 17, when he stood in a clearing in the Compiègne Forest surrounded by his regiment—3,500 strong—and exhorted his men to fight and die:

> *Men, tomorrow we go over the top. Back home the war is a fight for the survival of Democracy. You just forget it. Tomorrow you and I fight for our own lives. Those of you who have no will or desire to live can start out by giving your life away. My advice is to go out and fight for your life and the lives of your buddies alongside of you. Starting tomorrow the whole world will be watching our activities. God be with you.*

Hyman had no idea on that July morning that he was about to be marched into the battle that turned the tide of the war. "You in America know more about the war in one day [from reading the newspapers] than we soldiers find out in a whole month," Hyman wrote the family back in Brooklyn. Men on the ground are seldom aware that they are making history, but history would be made in the wheat fields at Soissons in July 1918.

During their spring offensive, the Germans had punched a salient—a bulge—in the line between Soissons and Reims, from which they hoped to storm the Allies' ranks and march on Paris. At this weary stage in the conflict it was little more than a desperate gasp of hope and both sides knew it. But the Marne Salient had been stuck like a thorn in the Allies' side. The longer it remained, the more it goaded them. In July, the Allied command decided the moment had come to extract the thorn and start pushing the Germans back to their own borders. The First and Second American Divisions, along with the First Moroccan Division (which included the French Foreign Legion), were handpicked to do the job. Parker's 18th Infantry would spearhead the push. "No more glorious task could have been assigned to any troops," one of the regiment's officers declared.

Hyman set out for the front with a full pack at dusk on July 17. Within minutes it was pouring down rain. Men, horses, mules, and transport vehicles became snarled in an epic jam on the narrow muddy French roads:

Blinding flashes of lightning illuminated the countryside momentarily and gave the moving columns of men glimpses of a scene such as they would witness only once in a lifetime. Every road, every track and every field was filled either with trucks, wagons, artillery or moving columns of men. Here and there the French cavalry could be seen threading their way through the maze of tangled men, trucks and animals. . . . Clothing, packs and equipment of all kinds were soaked until they added many extra pounds for the men to carry. Strange oaths of the Orient mingled with those of Europe and America.

In one burst of lightning the serene neoclassical façade of the royal Château de Compiègne appeared at the end of a long straight line of trees and then vanished: a glimpse of heaven in the midst of hell. The sky cleared before dawn and by first light Hyman stood blinking and shivering in the crossroads village of Coeuvres—two intersecting streets packed almost wheel to wheel with rows of French artillery. There was to be no preliminary shelling. It was so quiet Hyman could hear birds heralding the dawn. At the dot of 4:35 a French artillery captain gave the signal to lay down the first salvo of the rolling barrage and two thousand big guns opened up simultaneously. The divisions to the south did the same thing at the same time. A thirty-mile wall of fire blazed, died, and blazed again.

Hyman understood that his time had come. Crouched like a boxer stepping into the ring, he gripped his Springfield rifle in both hands and moved out. About a thousand infantrymen fanned out in the first wave. Once Hyman cleared the scrubby woods around Coeuvres, he was in open wheat fields—fresh golden waist-high grain swaying in the morning sun for mile after mile on rising ground. A beautiful sight to behold if it weren't for the sudden flash of machine-gun fire and the black fountains of dirt that spouted where German shells detonated. Every now and then Hyman heard a cry and then a pockmark appeared in the wheat where one of the men fell and bled. By noon the wheat in every direction was speckled with dots of moving khaki and littered with pockmarks. Hyman kept moving ahead. The German fire was too intense to evacuate the wounded—as for the dead, they swelled and blackened in the summer sun until the battle was over and the chaplains and burial details could tend to them. Hyman didn't stop; he tried not to look at the wounded or hear their pleas for water. His orders were to go forward into the bullets and bombs. He fired his rifle when he had a target, ducked his head instinctively at every explosion, crawled on his stomach through the wheat when a burst of bullets came, and rose again to put one foot in front of the other. Even though every fiber of his being wanted to turn and run, he advanced. He had had no sleep and precious little food for thirty-six hours. Adrenalin kept hunger and the dull ache of sleeplessness at bay—adrenalin and fear. "No man is fearless in battle," wrote one of his comrades of that day, "but most well-trained soldiers hide their emotions." Hyman had lived through Cantigny. He hid his fear and pushed on.

July 18, the first day of the Battle of Soissons, was long and grueling. German resistance stiffened through the morning hours. Enemy machine guns spat at them from every rise and from behind every stone farm building. Casualties mounted. In their few months of combat, Americans had learned to hate German machine gunners. Word was that *Boche* officers ordered their machine gunners to chain themselves to their weapons and keep shooting until they were killed. They mowed down your buddies in perfect rows and then, when you were about to take them out, they jumped up with their hands in the air shouting "*Kamarad!*" Even though artillery killed more men in the Great War, machine guns aroused more fear and rage among the troops.

Through the endless hours of daylight, Hyman listened to the peculiar "zeep-zeep" of machine-gun bullets whizzing past him "like insects fleeing to the rear." That night, he bedded down in a shell crater for a few hours of sleep, and the next day he and the other guys who had made it through were up and at it again. Captain Robert S. Gill, who had replaced Joseph Quesenberry as commander of Company K, told his men they had advanced farther into hostile territory than any other unit in the sector. Now they had to do it all over. Their objective—the heights of Buzancy, south of Soissons—was still seven miles away.

The second day, July 19, went badly. Resistance was ferocious, forward motion painful. Those German machine gunners were living up to their reputation. Hyman and his comrades in Company K were now so far out ahead of the rest of the division that they were taking horrific flanking fire from the left. Cover was all but nonexistent in the wheat. By day's end, 60 percent of the regiment's officers were gone—dead, wounded, missing, captured—and nearly all the noncommissioned officers (the corporals and sergeants who were in charge of the individual platoons) had fallen. Even doughty Colonel Parker, shaken by the number of casualties, begged to be relieved. Another officer complained that his men were "so exhausted . . . that it was often necessary to take hold of them and shake them to get their attention." But First Division commander Major General Charles P. Summerall was implacable. The assault continued.

July 20, the third day, fell on the Sabbath. Hyman was still in the wheat. He was still being savaged by machine-gun and artillery fire. Sometime in the course of that bright hot summer day Hyman's luck ran out. He was gassed with mustard.

They called it mustard because it reeked of garlic and mustard, and they called it a gas, but in fact mustard gas is a thick oily amber-colored liquid like toxic molasses that volatilizes above freezing. Of the three types of poison gas introduced during the Great War, mustard was the most insidious, the most excruciating, and by far the most lethal. It was delivered in glass bottles packed inside artillery shells: when the bottle burst, the mustard escaped and transformed itself into a heavy vapor that crept along the ground and oozed into trenches and dugouts. By the time Hyman smelled the reek and got his gas mask on, it was too late. Mustard, as Hyman quickly discovered, did not have to be inhaled to inflict pain and injury and death: the gas ate at any piece of flesh it came in contact with, inside or outside his body. The vapor fixed itself to the sweat on Hyman's neck and raised excruciating blisters that swelled and broke and wept plasma for days and refused to heal. Had he not been wearing his mask, the mustard would have blinded him and flayed away his bronchial tubes. Men who inhaled it vomited and bled internally; they choked and gagged and gasped for breath. The pain was so intense that victims had to be strapped to their beds or they would tear at themselves or bash their head against the wall. The oily vapor saturated clothing and refused to dissipate, so doctors and nurses were gassed with mustard when they treated soldiers who had been gassed. Those who died suffered for a month or more before death released them.

Hyman never talked about the agony he suffered. "On the third day, we were attacked with mustard gas," he wrote later. "I became a casualty. Taken to the field hospital, put in an army ambulance to a railroad station; put in a hospital train and sent to a French hospital in the city of Angers, far from the front."

The Battle of Soissons raged on without him for one more day. At the end of Sunday, July 21, the fourth day of fighting, the American soldiers still in action accomplished their mission of cutting German supply routes at the neck of the salient and driving the Germans back to a line running south from Soissons; the German retreat from the salient would continue for another month. Soissons was chalked up as a success—but the price was ruinous. A thousand men in the regiment's Third Battalion had gone into battle alongside Hyman on the morning of July 18; only seventy-nine returned when the regiment was withdrawn on July 22. The First Division Infantry as a whole suffered casualty rates (dead, wounded, gassed, missing) of 50 percent, and 75 percent of the infantry's field officers were knocked out. "The flower of the American Army had been cut to ribbons," wrote one soldier in the regiment.

The generals, however, had cause to celebrate. For the first time since

September 1914, the German high command had ordered a general retreat. Appalling as the casualties were, Soissons proved to be the beginning of the end of the war.

For Hyman, the war was over. "It would be foolish for me to say that I am well for this letter is written in a Hospital," he wrote home on July 22. Two days later, he elaborated a bit—though he was clearly distraught and disoriented. "I am not well enough just now to go under the same strain that I was under recently while at the front. . . . I lived through days that a fellow does not have to make [illegible] to remember and if God will be as kind to me in future operations, as he has been in the last, then [these] days will always live in my memories." Whatever memories he carried, Hyman never again wrote or spoke of them. "What's done is done," he told the family.

The blisters raised by the mustard gas eventually closed and healed, though he would always have scars on the lower part of his chin and on his neck behind his left ear. Hyman remained in French military hospitals long enough to get thoroughly bored and restless. While nurses changed his dressings, he argued with the other wounded guys about which American state was the best ("I certainly have a heck of a time when I tell the Westerners and Southerners that New York is the only place"). In September he was well enough to go to Yom Kippur services. He boasted in a letter to his parents that "it is a known fact the First Division has done wonderful work." It shamed him that the division was still in combat while he convalesced behind the lines. Indeed Company K, its decimated ranks filled out with replacement soldiers, fought at Saint-Mihiel and the Argonne, the massive American engagement that brought the war to an end on November 11, 1918.

Hyman finally returned to the States in February 1919. He went back to work in the business, married Anna, fathered two children. But in ways that counted, ways he would never speak of, Hyman's life was not the same. He had been in war. He had seen men get torn apart by exploding shells and bleed to death in a wheat field; he had marched into machine-gun fire and shot his rifle at enemy soldiers; he had been burned and scarred by poison gas. Hyman had passed a test that every man wonders about. His uncles and cousins in Russia had endured occupation and revolution, but they had not been in the army; his brothers in America had spent the war building the business. Hyman alone had worn the uniform. It wasn't his choice to be a soldier. But he did his duty and was proud that he had. "What's done is done," Hyman said when his family asked about the war. But that wasn't the whole story. To soldiers like Hyman—Jews, immigrants, naturalized Americans—the war made a critical difference. They all knew the stereotypes—pants presser, watchmaker, pale-faced scholar, slacker, coward. They knew the skepticism of the likes of Captain Quesenberry and Colonel Parker and Major General Summerall. *Is it possible to make soldiers of these fellows?* Hyman had seen for himself the new respect in the eyes of his officers and comrades after he returned from battle. It was a point of honor that the percentage of Jews in the U.S. Army was higher than in the civilian population. Two thousand American Jews were killed in action in the Great War; Jewish American casualties topped ten thousand; 72 percent of Jews in uniform served in combat units. Sarah had been devastated when her son was drafted, but she wept tears of pride when he came home to Brooklyn safe and mostly sound. Hyman's service bound the entire Cohen family more closely to America. One of their own was a Doughboy. When the Purple Heart—the American military medal bestowed on those wounded or killed in action—was reinstituted in 1932, Hyman was awarded one retroactively. He wore it proudly all his life.

It was different for the children and grandchildren of Shimon Dov who remained in the Old Country. An armistice was declared, a treaty was signed, but in Rakov and Volozhin, revolution and civil war continued. Indeed, the treaties that formalized the cessation of hostilities in 1919 proved to be less the end of the Great War than the beginning of the next one.

CHAPTER NINE

PIONEERS

On November 2, 1917, British foreign secretary Arthur James Balfour wrote a letter to Walter Rothschild, Second Baron Rothschild, informing him with "much pleasure" that "His Majesty's Government view with favour the establishment in Palestine of a national home for the Jewish people." Balfour vowed that his government would "use their best endeavours to facilitate the achievement of this object, it being clearly understood that nothing shall be done which may prejudice the civil and religious rights of existing non-Jewish communities in Palestine, or the rights and political status enjoyed by Jews in any other country."

The Balfour Declaration, as Britain's new stance on the Middle East came to be known, transformed Zionism, at the stroke of a pen, from collective dream to political reality. World events hastened its realization. When the Ottoman Empire collapsed during the Great War, the British took control of a huge swath of the Middle East, including all of Palestine and Jordan. Under the terms of the British Mandate for Palestine, Britain became the de facto governor of the Holy Land, and the Balfour Declaration became state policy. Zionist claims and aspirations remained controversial, even in the Jewish community, but they would henceforth play a part in all negotiations over the future of the region.

The Balfour Declaration marked a turning point with immense consequences for the lives of millions of people, including two of Shimon Dov
HaKohen's grandchildren. Balfour's brusque, three-paragraph letter was
addressed to "Dear Lord Rothschild," but Shimon Dov's grandson Chaim
and granddaughter Sonia would count themselves among its recipients.

When the United States entered the Great War, the American army was
rudimentary, its arsenal skeletal. The War Department was so famished for
steel that its hungry eye fell on women's corsets. The hourglass figure then
in vogue called for constriction of the waist and elevation of the bosom,
and such feminine engineering required steel ribbing. Because bayonet
blades and shell casings required steel too, there wasn't enough for both
weapons and corsets. Bernard Baruch, the Jewish financier who managed
the nation's flow of military equipment and supplies through the War
Industries Board, issued a plea for American women to abandon their corsets. Some twenty-eight thousand tons of metal, enough to construct a
battleship, were thus diverted to the war effort.

Once fashionable women shed their ribs of steel, there was no going
back.

The corset ban altered not only the way women dressed but how they
walked and danced and worked and ultimately how they lived their lives.
From a tear in the fabric of history emerged new fashion, new economy,
new mores, new freedom, new lifestyle. And Itel, with her uncanny knack
for being ahead of the curve, in this case literally, was on hand to make the
most of it.

The Balfour Declaration and the passing of the corset, events connected only by time and war, would redraw the map of the world for a
generation of young Jewish cousins just coming into their own.

The Great War was still raging in Europe in the winter of 1918 when Itel
broke off diplomatic ties with the city of Hoboken. The breach was precipi-
tated by a blizzard—two feet of snow with waist-high drifts dumped on the
East Coast during a stretch of frigid weather. Snow is always inconvenient
for the small business owner—but this was worse than usual because William was stranded in Manhattan and Itel had to fend for herself. When a

Hoboken cop told her she had to promptly clear the considerable expanse of sidewalk that wrapped around her corner house/dress shop, Itel hit the roof. "I couldn't ask a maid to do it, she would have quit," she fumed. The cop refused to lend her a hand. So that left four-feet-eleven-inch Itel to battle the drifts by herself. "I was not built for snow shoveling," she noted drily. "I resolved right then that I wouldn't spend another winter in Hoboken." And she didn't.

Itel and William gathered Lewis, now eleven, their two-year-old daughter, Beatrice, and the child's nursemaid and crossed the river to Manhattan; sewing machines, dress forms, ironing boards, and bobbins followed behind in a horse-drawn wagon. They set up shop and housekeeping at 611 West 141st Street, between Broadway and Riverside Drive, nine blocks south of where Itel's brother Harry was living. Officially, the neighborhood was called Hamilton Heights after its most illustrious former resident, founding father Alexander Hamilton, who'd had a farm here at the turn of the nineteenth century, but people thought of it as Harlem. Not the elegant Harlem of Sugar Hill brownstones or the flashy louche Harlem of Lenox Avenue jazz clubs or the slum Harlem of tenements filling up with poor blacks from other parts of the city and the rural South: West 141st Street was immigrant Harlem, meat-and-potatoes Harlem, drab industrious Harlem of six-story brick apartment buildings and wide sidewalks shoveled by someone other than Itel. Itel and William turned the living and dining rooms of their ground-floor apartment into the dress shop, installed the children and maid in the back bedrooms, and got down to work. "Mrs. W. Rosenthal, Gowns," read her business card. They even had a telephone— Audubon 6917. Most of the Hoboken clients remained loyal, and new ones came knocking soon enough. Friends had been urging Itel for years to relocate to Manhattan. Now she realized they were right. Thirty-two years old, crackling with energy and itching with ambition, Itel was now a *New York* dressmaker. Her dresses, their skirts growing shorter by the month, were selling for as much as eighteen dollars each. The big pond suited her.

Itel's timing was impeccable. When the war ended and the 1920s began to roar, she was firmly ensconced in Manhattan with her platoon of seamstresses ready to make beautiful uncorseted New York women even more beautiful. One of those women was the director of the nursery school that Beatrice, called Bea, attended. This was clearly a nursery school director with taste and style and ready cash, for not only did she employ Itel to make her dresses but when she needed a hat she frequented Ferlé Heller's ultra chic millinery on West Fifty-seventh Street, just a few steps away from the posh precincts of Bergdorf's, Bendel's, and Jay Thorpe.

One day in 1921 the nursery director was browsing Ferlé Heller's latest confections when a small elegant woman with a musical English accent accosted her. *Where on earth had she picked up the divine dress she was wearing? Such craftsmanship, such detail and flair. Who was the dressmaker and how could she find her?* The bedazzled Englishwoman was Enid Bissett, the proprietress of a dress concession called Enid Frocks, which occupied a corner of Ferlé Heller's millinery. Mrs. Bissett's praise was not bestowed lightly, for she had seen plenty of lovely dresses in her day. In her youth, she had waltzed and shimmied her way across the vaudeville palaces of Europe as the female half of the Dancing Bissetts. When she crossed the Atlantic with her husband, Joe, she glided from show biz to couture, though she still had many useful connections in the theater. Refined and beguiling, Enid Bissett was one of those naturally stylish women whom people with more money and less taste like to have around. Though no longer in her first youth, she had the slender angular figure that looked wonderful in the sheath dresses just coming into fashion. Fifth Avenue socialites, Broadway starlets, society-page matrons, and flapper demimondaines who wanted to look like her flocked to Enid Frocks. Sophisticated ladies with money to spare paid Mrs. Bissett to make them look and feel beautiful.

Now, thanks to little Bea's nursery school principal, Mrs. Bissett had discovered Itel. A meeting was duly arranged and Mrs. Bissett made her way uptown to Hamilton Heights. She had a look around the dress shop, the whirring Singers, the girls bent over their works in progress. She liked what she saw, she liked Itel, she liked the intense quiet industry of the workshop. She decided to see how Itel did with some Vogue patterns for suits and dresses—essentially work on spec. Itel delivered, and Mrs. Bissett was more impressed than ever. "That little woman on 141st Street makes the others look like amateurs," Mrs. Bissett confided. Itel was pleased but not surprised. She had never had any doubts about her superiority.

Mrs. Bissett made a proposal: she would provide the designs and fabrics; Itel would transform them into flawless dresses. The tastemaker and the dressmaker were perfectly suited to be partners. Mrs. Bissett had the contacts, Itel had the drive. Mrs. Bissett knew how to make a splash, Itel knew how to make clothing—or rather, at this stage, how to get other skilled women to make clothing to her order. Neither of them was afraid to try something new, as long as impeccable standards were maintained. They were a winning duo and their moment was at hand. Every fashionable woman in New York, it seemed, wanted an Enid Frock executed in the workshop of the Jewish seamstress with the golden hands. As the orders rapidly piled up, Mrs. Bissett came back with another proposal: they would go into business together on the condition that Itel give up her own customers and devote her workshop entirely to Enid Frocks. To seal the deal, Itel would need to pay in a cash investment of four thousand dollars.

Four thousand dollars was just about all the money she and William had. Her brothers advised against it. Fashion was notoriously fickle. What if the fancy ladies moved on and Enid Frocks fell from favor? Itel was a seamstress—what did she know from business? Even Ferlé Heller thought it made no sense for Itel to stake so much of her money and security. "Enid can afford it," the milliner told her, "but you will sink whatever you have."

Itel had a powerful instinct for opportunity and to her this looked like opportunity supreme. It was her chance to leapfrog the jobbers, the schleppers, the sweaty crowded middle and go right to the glittering peak of money and glamour.

She weighed the risks, calculated the potential profit, and made her decision. In the summer of 1922, Itel and William Rosenthal and Enid Bissett became equal shareholders in a newly incorporated company called Enid Frocks, Inc.

Business was good from the start and it just kept getting better. Day in, day out, the shop door of the stone-clad, vaguely French Renaissance building at 36 West Fifty-seventh Street would swing open and another lovely customer—patroness, Mrs. Bissett liked to say—breezed in. Rich, of course, fashionable, bobbed, cloche-hatted, displaying the requisite inches of ankle and lower calf. The ideal Enid Frocks type. Alas, Itel knew at a glance that, when the dress was done, neither she nor the new patroness would be 100 percent happy. The problem was the patroness's bust. The problem, to be precise, was that she *had* a bust. Soft yet firm, full and swelling, round, smooth, perfectly symmetrical, the perfumed essence of American femininity made flesh—this lovely pair of breasts was doomed to be squashed into submission by the dictates of 1920s fashion. The flapper style du jour called for dresses to drop with barely a bulge or curve from neck to knee, and in order to achieve this sticklike silhouette a woman wore a flattener—"a towel with hooks in the back," as Itel described it. These hideous mammary mashers were marketed under the trade name Boyish Form, which pretty much said it all. Itel knew from sad experience that no Enid Frock ever looked right when worn over a Boyish Form bandeau. It was a crime and shame for a chic well-endowed lady to spend upward of three hundred dollars, a fortune in those days, for her Enid Frock and come away with a less-than-perfect fit because of the cursed flattener. "It was a very sad story," Itel sighed. "Our cheapest dress sold for a hundred and a quarter, and it just didn't fit right. Women were told to look like their brothers—that was just not possible. Nature made women with a bosom, so nature thought it was important. Why argue with nature?"

Mrs. Bissett had a brainstorm. She grabbed a Boyish Form bandeau, sliced it down the middle of the front with a pair of scissors, took the two edges and shirred each one to a small bridge of elastic so that they formed a pair of slightly bulging pockets. William was summoned to take a look. "If you want to wear something like that," he harrumphed, "at least let me make you a nice one." William was an artist, a *male* artist, and by the time he was done, it was very nice indeed. Satin shoulder straps were added; the pockets—the primordial cups—were fashioned of fine ivory-pink cotton net trimmed with silk rosebuds in pink and jade; the elastic center piece was shiny and striated; three tiny hooks were affixed to the back. Mrs. Bissett christened the garment Maiden Form to distinguish it from the hateful Boyish Form bandeau.

Itel saw at once that her frocks fit better with a Maiden Form brassiere sewn into the bust or worn separately underneath, but it took the partners a while to realize what a hot commodity they had on their hands. At first every woman who purchased an Enid Frock got a Maiden Form bra for free. When the ladies came back marveling at how good the bit of mesh and elastic made them look and feel, Itel offered to whip one up custom for twenty-five to fifty dollars a pop. She also kept a bowl of one-dollar ready-made bras on a table in the shop. The dress business kept booming— bras were just a sideline, a novelty item that the seamstresses ran off in their spare time. It was Broadway that made Maiden Form a star.

Mrs. Bissett may have moved uptown to cater to the carriage trade, but she and her husband, Joe, were still chummy with Broadway actors and actresses (especially the latter in Joe's case)—and Joe's female chums became the brassiere pioneers. Broadway had been lit up with energy and hot jazzy new music since the Great War ended, and it was ablaze the year the bra was born. Jerome Kern, Florenz Ziegfeld, Oscar Hammerstein II, and George and Ira Gershwin were cranking out one hit after another. Singing-dancing-shimmying starlets like Marilyn Miller, Billie Burke, Josephine Baker, and Adelaide Hall reigned as showbiz princesses (royalty without civil rights in the case of Baker and Hall, who were black). Chorus girls who strutted onstage half naked in George White's *Scandals* at the Globe Theater or *Ziegfeld Follies of 1922* at the New Amsterdam had no qualms about trying out a slinky new undergarment that made them look sexy, even if it broke with fashion. "The acting trade were the first customers because they were brave enough to uplift," Moses (Moe) Rosenthal, William's brother and later the company's general manager, said. Where brave busty showgirls led, ordinary busty women were sure to follow. Transgression was in the air in 1922. Women had won the right to vote two years earlier; they smoked in public and no one batted an eye (Itel herself put away four packs a day); they scandalized their mothers with their clothes, dances, drinks (illegal as of January 1919), and love affairs. F. Scott Fitzgerald's *The Beautiful and Damned* was a best seller that year, and he and Zelda were the toast of the town. Nowhere was the spirit of transgression headier and more pungent than on New York's Forty-second Street. What better locale to kick up a lingerie revolution? Joe Bissett hit every specialty shop between Forty-second and Fifty-ninth streets. He placed Maiden Form bras and racy little counter cards touting their virtues in the Astor Shop, in the Hotel Astor, and the Regina Shop, abutting the renowned Palace Theater vaudeville house. If a manager was reluctant to place an order, Joe got one of his chorine pals to sashay into the shop, demand a

Maiden Form, and storm out in disgust when told they didn't carry them. The next day a salesman came calling. "It was an extreme product but was accepted there [the theater district]," said one of the early salesmen.

Getting it accepted elsewhere required greater powers of persuasion. "I would take it out, and when I showed them this little bit of bra, all hell would break loose," recalled Jack Zizmor, who became a top salesman. "If it were the husband, he would call to his wife, 'Come over here and see what this crazy guy is trying to sell me!' They laughed and they ridiculed us, and said, 'This is a fly-by-night thing. It will die out next week, next month, next year.'" They didn't laugh for long. Within months the company was doing enough business that Itel and Mrs. Bissett had to take over the top two floors of the West Fifty-seventh Street building—the fifth floor for a workshop and the sixth-floor attic for processing and shipping orders. Ten employees were hired, most of them in sales. William, who had eleven siblings, put the arm on brothers and sisters. In 1923 the company had to relocate four times; that's how fast it was expanding. In 1924 they registered the name Maiden Form as their trademark.

The Maiden Form bra was the quintessence of the 1920s—fun, novel, vaguely risqué, easy to mass-produce, perfectly promotable, seemingly frivolous but in fact eminently practical and instantly indispensable. No one had heard of a brassiere in 1920. By 1924, all the fashionable women had to have one. The daughter and granddaughter of scribes had stumbled on one of the pure products of America.

Nineteen twenty-four, the year that cemented the cornerstone of Itel's fortune, was also the year that the first of Shimon Dov's grandchildren made aliyah—literally "ascent"—to the Holy Land. After two thousand years, a Kohen returned to the place where Jews had become Jews.

Itel was not the only revolutionary in the family. In Volozhin, her first cousin Chaim, the third child of Shimon Dov's son Arie, fomented revolution by deciding all by himself that the time had come to end the exile. Chaim would not spend his life poring over sacred texts or dripping gallnut ink onto parchment. He shunned laws decreed by strangers and customs enforced by a stateless people. America—increasingly difficult to enter after the tight new immigration quotas imposed that year—held no appeal either. Eighteen-year-old Chaim wanted revolution, but not in Russia. Zion alone consumed his young heart.

Though he was barely shaving, Chaim was ready to be a pioneer. He tossed out the *kippah* (skullcap) and the boxes and straps of the tefillin. He exchanged the somber garb of the ghetto for a farmer's rough open-necked shirt and a pair of sandals. He sang but he refused to pray. Prayer was for shtetl Jews. Love and contempt—pure, unmediated—propelled the boy out of exile and into the Holy Land. With him the line of the scribe blazed a third road.

Impulsiveness, stubbornness, and self-reliance came naturally to Chaim. He had taken his first breath in the shadow of tragedy, and turmoil was all he had known. Born in 1906, when Russia was still in the throes of the 1905 revolution, Chaim lost his thirty-one-year-old father, Arie, before he was a week old. Arie's widow, Leah, was left with three children—a daughter named Chana, a toddler son, Yishayahu, and the newborn, Chaim. Leah remarried and bore her second husband a son, Shlomo. So Chaim grew up a middle child in a broken and mended family, a stepson raised beside a full son. He was eight years old when the Great War began and Volozhin starved and trembled on the front line. The war ended the year he turned twelve. The year of his bar mitzvah, another war broke out: Soviet Russia and newly reunited Poland clashed over their boundary, and Volozhin promptly fell to the advancing Polish army—though later the Russians regained control only to lose it again. After living under five different governments in the first dozen years of his life, Chaim became a citizen of Poland under Chief of State Józef Piłsudski. Rakov was also on the Polish side of the border after the Polish-Soviet war, and Vilna was absorbed into Poland in 1922 after much wrangling with the newly formed nation of Lithuania. To Chaim and his family, Polish sovereignty made no difference. Polish, Russian, Bolshevik, capitalist—it was all the same. Chaim was a proud, lonely, defiant kid with a jut to his jaw and large liquid brown eyes peering out at a world not even sages could comprehend. Jews died and Jewish homes burned under Piłsudski just as they had under Lenin, Kerensky, Nicholas, and Alexander—"same old story," as Isaac Babel wrote: ". . . shrieks, whips cracking, shouts of 'dirty Yid.'"

In Volozhin, devout Jews cautiously reopened the yeshiva, which had been shuttered since 1915. But Chaim chose to study in Vilna at the Tarbut Gymnasium (Zionist high school), where instruction was in Hebrew and love of the Land wafted through the classrooms like the scent of Jaffa oranges. Devout old men muttered that it was a sin to speak the sacred tongue outside of shul, but Chaim didn't care. He never went to shul anyway. Yiddish was the language of oppression and fear. When he made his ascent to the Land, he would speak only Hebrew.

Chaim was aware that he couldn't simply pack up and leave the way his cousins had when they immigrated to America. To live in the Land, you had to train; you had to prepare; you had to be part of a group. By 1920, two generations of Zionist settlers had been trying to survive in Palestine. The first waves had come close to disaster because they knew nothing about farming, about finding work, about the climate, the food, the Arabs. They brought their dreams but they had no idea how harsh reality was. Chaim was determined not to make those mistakes. He didn't just declare himself a Zionist: he transformed himself into a pioneer. After the Great War, Zionism raged through Eastern Europe the way Hasidism had raged through the Pale at the end of the eighteenth century. Volozhin and Rakov and a thousand other shtetlach like them were full of headstrong boys and girls bent on returning to the Jewish homeland as farmers, swamp drainers, road builders. A score of Zionist organizations sprang up to absorb and channel all this ardor—youth groups; political parties; secular, religious, and quasi-military factions; bands of like-minded idealists who pledged to learn and practice and sing and dance together and one day to make aliyah together. Chaim chose to join HeHalutz. "The Pioneer" is the usual translation for HeHalutz, but in a Zionist context the word connotes something much more romantic—not just an agricultural settler but an ecstatic acolyte bent on mystical union with the Jewish soil through the sacrament of labor. Chaim and his pals started a HeHalutz chapter in Volozhin. They put out a newspaper called *Der Shtekel-Dreier* denouncing the degeneracy of life in exile and heralding the glorious national homeland that awaited them in Palestine. A photo of Zionist leader Theodore Herzl hung on Chaim's wall, but his true hero was Joseph Trumpeldor, the handsome, one-armed Russian army officer who had founded HeHalutz. "I am not a person," Trumpeldor declared after making aliyah in 1911. "I am the pure embodiment of service, prepared for everything. I have no ties. I know only one command: Build." Chaim's ardor grew all the fiercer after Trumpeldor was killed at the age of thirty-nine while fighting off Arabs in the Upper Galilee. In his dreams, Chaim would take the hero's place. He would plow and plant and make the desert bloom; if necessary he would water the crops with his blood. But first he must learn how to work. Not the degrading Diaspora work of keeping shop, peddling merchandise, brokering, smuggling. Chaim must master the noble labor of the *halutz*.

He and his group took up residence in the house of Bernshteyn the blacksmith. They hardened themselves by working at the Volozhin sawmill. They spoke and sang in Hebrew. They worked the soil, albeit Polish soil. Chaim was short and boxy but lean with broad shoulders, thick dark hair combed straight back from his forehead, and a stern, commanding demeanor. His olive skin would not burn under the fierce sun of Palestine; his stubbornness and passion would serve him well. Chaim toughened up like a soldier in boot camp. He was among the first of his comrades to win the certificate confirming his readiness to make aliyah. Now came the moment of truth. The *halutzim* believed that you could not be a Zionist in exile: the only true Zionists were Zionists in the Land, in Eretz Israel.

In the late autumn of 1924, at the glorious, precipitous age of eighteen, Chaim departed Poland for the Holy Land. He never set foot in Europe again.

The voyage began with horse and cart and song. Trailed by friends and families, Chaim and his fellow *halutzim* set out in a long convoy of wagons. The birch groves were yellowing, the pines black and dripping in the misty air. At the outskirts of town, a peasant stopped his work, stared at the procession, and shouted across the autumn stubble, "Damn Jews, to Palestine!" *They were going!* They were going as fast as they could and precisely so they would never hear such a shout again. To hell with ignorant peasants. To hell with churches full of pious supplicants spitting at pictures of the dirty Jew. To hell with snow and mud and jackboots kicking in the door. Chaim and his comrades raised their voices even louder to the strains of "Artza Alinu"—a Hebrew folk melody powered by a toe-tapping rhythm: *We ascended to the land, we've ploughed already and sown too, but we have not yet reaped.*

At the town of Horod'k they parted ways: the *halutzim* climbed aboard the train bound for Warsaw; the friends and family members stood on the platform and waved their handkerchiefs. Then in a cloud of smoke and soot, Chaim lurched into his future.

He had never been farther from home than Vilna. He had never seen the sea. He had never looked out at a horizon that wasn't low, green, smooth, settled. No matter. The images in the train window went by in a rattling indifferent blur. He felt not the slightest twinge of curiosity or nostalgia. It had required a terrific effort of will for Chaim to shake off the dust of exile. So many talked and dreamed and sighed but finally subsided back into the humid green. To *act*, to cut his ties with everything familiar and *go*, Chaim had to be as fanatical as Lenin. Eastern Europe passed before him like a rotten corpse. The scenery was so much pasteboard and tinsel. The other passengers, those not bound for the Land, were trivial, inane. Even the startling appearance of the sea was worthy of notice only because the same water laved the shores of the Land. For Chaim, for his fellow *halutzim*, Zion was the sole reality. Only the Land had meaning.

At the Romanian port of Constanta they boarded a ship and set sail southbound on waters that Roman galleys had plied two millennia earlier. Down the western edge of the Black Sea, through the straits of Bosphorus at Istanbul, across the Sea of Marmara, into the blue Aegean, around the storied islands of Turkey's western coast, and then, once they had cleared Rhodes, a straight shot southeast to the port of Haifa. Chaim's excitement became all but unbearable in the final hours at sea. For two thousand years his family had lived as strangers and sojourners. He had claimed for himself the honor of being the first to return.

Chaim stood on the ship's deck as Haifa Bay opened before him in an immense blue arc sweeping nine miles north to the ancient citadel of Acre. His first glimpse of the Holy Land was a crinkly brown smudge rising from the sea—the heights of Mount Carmel, freshly washed by the November rains. A Carmelite monastery crowned the summit; terraces of olive groves, vineyards, and carob trees ran along the flanks; palms etched their fronds against the sky. Beaches came into view as they neared the harbor. The water turned a deep royal blue. Red and white blocks of buildings—limestone walls, red-tiled roofs—rose in clusters near the shore and climbed to the base of the mountain. The ship dropped anchor and Chaim and the other passengers disembarked onto an open barge; they crossed the last stretch of water on a deck crammed with piles of cargo: until the British dredged the sandy harbor in 1933, this was the only way to get from ship to shore. Chaim finally allowed himself to exult in the warm air, the luminous sky, the smell of brine and spice and smoke, the utter unexpected strangeness pressing at every sense.

He stepped from the boat to a wharf backed by train tracks. Arabs sat on the ground next to blankets and rugs covered with produce—the Haifa vegetable market. If he wept or danced or fell to his knees and kissed the soil when he finally came ashore, he never mentioned it to his family. No Zionist arrived in Palestine with a still pulse or dry eye. Probably he danced. Chaim was always a great dancer. The joyous circle dances of the pioneers were his form of worship.

Chaim was lucky to have disembarked at Haifa. Most settlers in those days landed at the seedy old Arab port of Jaffa, sixty miles to the south. Situated on a long, low-lying stretch of sand (since swallowed up by Tel Aviv), Jaffa was the preferred port because of its proximity to Jerusalem, but it has always been awkward to approach by sea. The shallow harbor is so beset by rocks that passengers and their luggage had be off-loaded into tipsy dinghies and rowed to shore, and as soon as they landed they were swarmed by hawkers, beggars, street vendors, shills for every kind of shady business. "This was not my idea of the new life," future Prime Minister David Ben-Gurion recalled of his arrival at Jaffa early in the century. "It was worse than the Plonsk I had come from."

Disillusionment came, sooner or later, to everyone. No Zionist who stayed in Palestine escaped it. No matter how exalted the arrival, how hot the tears of joy or the gush of gratitude, the dust of disappointment eventually settled on all of them.

Sweating copiously in their European clothes, Chaim and his comrades made their way from the port to their guesthouse. Haifa called itself a city, but with a population of twenty-five thousand it was a small city with dramatic topography and a salubrious climate, peacefully shared by Jews and Arabs. Chaim saw his first camel and his first palm tree. He saw white-robed Arab traders gathered at the cactus hedges that grew outside the city gates. He saw the tidy little German colony of tile-roofed cottages and tree-lined streets that members of the Templer sect founded in the 1860s and still maintained as an incongruous little corner of Gemütlich-keit. He saw the deep velvety shadows that the white houses cast on the unpaved roads. He packed away his European clothes. There was rail ser-vice between Damascus and Saudi Arabia, with a stop at Haifa. Chaim and his comrades made their way to the train station, an elegant Renaissance toy of a building with a dainty clock tower and banks of high windows. The young men wanted to get to the Galilee as quickly as possible.

They discovered that "quickly" was not in the lexicon of Palestinian transport in 1924. In fact, the train they took was notorious even in Pales-tine for its agonizing pace—so slow, the old hands said, that you could walk faster. Chaim squinted through the dust-grimed window at the dust-grimed landscapes—the drab coastal plain, the black-soiled Jezreel Valley, the humped blue mountains that rumple this sleeve of a country from north to south. What he saw was not encouraging. The Jezreel was "still mostly stony desert, infested with malaria, typhus, and marauding Bedouin tribes-men," wrote Arthur Koestler, who made aliyah two years after Chaim. "The hills bordering the valley were dotted with Arab mud villages, dissolving by an act of natural mimicry in the violet haze of earth and rock. Down in the plain sprawled the first Jewish pioneer settlements, a conspicuous eye-sore with their white, cubic, concrete buildings." The earth "had not seen a plough for a millennium and a half." The air swarmed with mosquitoes, flies, and cockroaches. The rudimentary Jewish settlements—"dismal and slumlike oases in the wilderness, consisting of wooden huts, surrounded by dreary vegetable plots"—were even more depressing than the Arab mud villages. The pioneers lived in "ramshackle dwellings in which only the poorest in Europe would live, as an alternative to a discarded railway car-riage." *Aradi muat*—dead land—was what the Turkish rulers had called huge swaths of the country, and dead most of it remained in 1924. Wher-ever Chaim looked, he saw "but thorn and thistle, ruined cities, dens of wild animals, and death's shadow."

The sun had probably long since set by the time the train reached Smakh (today's Tsemach Junction) at the south end of the Sea of Galilee—Kinneret in Hebrew. But even in the dark, even in November, Chaim could sense something soft and seductive in the atmosphere here. He climbed down from the train and the warmth enveloped him like an embrace. Haifa was balmy compared with Poland, but the shore of the Sea of Galilee (not a sea at all despite its name, but a large freshwater lake) was warmer still because of its situation nearly seven hundred feet below sea level—the lowest body of freshwater in the world. Chaim ended his journey on foot, walking the mile or so from the train station across a bridge that spanned the Jordan River near the spot where Jesus was baptized, around the bottom of the lake, and finally to the walled compound of the Kinneret Colony, one of the early noncollective settlements. It was a walk to stir the soul. The bare mountains seemed to rise right from the surface of the water. The dense air held and heightened the perfumes of the earth. Land forms, stark and monumental, were barely nicked by rooftops and saplings. When the sun rose over the Golan Heights the next morning, a flood of light saturated every color. "The Kinneret was like a woman for my father," one of Chaim's sons said many years later. "He fell in love."

He was not alone. The Kinneret had an almost mystical allure for the early Jewish pioneers. An oven in the summer, isolated from the coastal settlements, hemmed in by mountains, vulnerable to Arab attacks, the region fostered the cocky independence at the heart of Zionism. Jews came here initially because the land was cheap and water plentiful; inspired by the beauty and the heat and the camaraderie, the young settlers invented new ways to live and work the land. The kibbutz, the moshav (cooperative agricultural village), the germ of a Jewish defense force, a training farm for women—all originated in the Kinneret.

Was it I who long ago
rose with dawn to fill the fields
by the sweat of my brow?

Was it I who bathed in the innocent blue
—under a peaceful sky—
Of my Galilee, my own Galilee?

NORTHERN PALESTINE UNDER
THE BRITISH MANDATE, CIRCA 1924

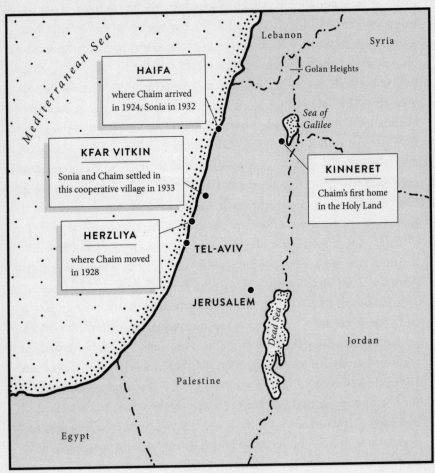

Palestine as Chaim and Sonia knew it in the 1920s and 1930s.

So wrote the Hebrew poet Ra'hel, who resided at Degania, the first kibbutz, in its early years and returned to the haunting landscape again and again in her verse. Ra'hel always spoke of her time in the Kinneret as the happiest in her life; when she died of tuberculosis at the age of forty-one, she was buried in the tiny cemetery beside the lake (the preferred resting place for Israel's early Labour Party elite).

By the time Chaim arrived, Jews had been farming by the lakeshore for a decade and a half—long enough to understand what they had let themselves in for, long enough to love the land regardless. Malaria was epidemic, the summers were long and torrid, the work never ending, the isolation deadening. But in the mythology of the *halutzim*, the Kinneret had something of the aura of the American West. Chaim, though he would suffer every hardship that the region could inflict, was smitten from the first— and for life.

Chaim was an extremist. Had he been milder, he would have been content to work at one of the Kinneret's well-tended lakeshore farms or join the kibbutzniks at Degania. But that was too tame for him. Instead, he ascended a thousand feet above the lake to the tiny, struggling settlement known as Kvutza Har (mount) Kinneret. A *kvutza* is a collective similar to a kibbutz, but smaller and modeled economically on the family—and the *kvutza* on the Kinneret mountainside where Chaim went in the autumn of 1924 was one of the smallest and most precarious. The original settlement, founded in 1920 by ninety *halutzim* from Russia, Ukraine, and Lithuania, had dwindled down to twenty members before disbanding, after three starving years, by order of the Jewish Agency (the organization that oversaw Zionist settlements). Now Chaim and a small group of young bachelors, two married couples, and one baby went back up the mountain to try again. Even in November, even in their shorts and sandals, they were perspiring heavily by the time they ascended through the rocks and brown grass and reached the "village"—really just three rough cabins, each measuring thirteen by twenty-six feet, with one kitchen between them, a storeroom, and a bakery. The piddling runoff from a spring, which turned out to be too saline to be potable, trickled through the rocks. On breaks in the slope the previous settlers had planted a rudimentary vineyard and orchard, straggling fields of wheat, barley and legumes, patches of tomatoes: all of it was suspended above the lake like a frayed hammock over the deck of a ship. Everything else was precipice. Gray scree slashed the slopes above, tufts of sunburned grass lapped at the edges of the farm fields, blue water beckoned at the bottom. In time there would be livestock—nine milk cows and their calves, a small flock of sheep, eight mules, one hundred chickens—but in those first days nothing broke the silence but the hiss of wind in the grass, the occasional spatter of autumn rain, the distant cry of a circling hawk, and the keening of jackals at night.

Fifteen years earlier, Chaim's cousins had gaped in dismay at the cramped shabby tenement flat on Madison Street that would be their first home in America. The arrival at Har Kinneret hit Chaim just as hard, though he was too proud to admit it. He slept on boards laid over empty gasoline cans in a room packed with snoring unwashed comrades; he choked down the salty water of the spring until his gut rebelled and his lips cracked and he was forced to haul up cans of sweet water from the lake; his hands split open and his back cramped from the toil of coaxing crops from such stony ground. But at least it was holy ground. At least, and at last, it was honest toil.

It rained. Since Chaim had arrived at the onset of winter, his first experience of the Middle East was not its fabled scorching sun but the intermittent winter torrents that found their way in through every crack of the cabins and cut gullies into the mountainside. The newcomers, however, did not have the luxury to wait for fair weather. They intended to grow all of their own food, so Chaim and the other settlers got to work building a chicken coop and cowshed for the animals and preparing the ground for spring sowing. Chaim dared not complain. A month ago, he had been in Volozhin scoffing at the degenerate life of the Diaspora—how could he disgrace himself now by whining about blisters, aching muscles, a stomach perpetually growling with hunger? He learned to pace himself, to share the workload, to tolerate and even enjoy a diet poor in meat and rich in olives, greens, and tomatoes (which Eastern Europeans considered inedible). Weak tea in a tin cup was his sole indulgence. "We dreaded comfort," said Ra'hel. "We yearned for sacrifice, for torture, for prisoner's bonds, with which to sanctify and exalt the Name of Homeland."

While he worked, he sang. When the work was done, he danced.

We are, we are, we are . . .
Pioneers, Pioneers
On burning fields
On barren fields of waste.
We cover the stony fields
With golden bloom.

He fell in love. Etl, one of two girls from Volozhin who had made aliyah with Chaim, was daring—no girl broke with her family and traveled to Palestine in 1924 unless she had guts and backbone—but she was delicate. Her hair fell in dark waves to her shoulders, her arms were elegantly rounded, her eyes dark and brimming. By day, Chaim and Etl worked side by side on the mountain, and at night they sang and danced. In the spring, when the rains stopped, they walked together at dawn through the spring grass and wildflowers. On the Sabbath they scrubbed the communal kitchen clean, ate pancakes and fish, and, dressed in their white Sabbath clothes, descended the mountain to visit other pioneers in the settlements beside the lake. When the heat arrived at the end of April, they swam. In summer, when the huts became unbearable, they slept under the stars.

They were just shy of twenty, the same age Itel had been when she ran away from Rakov to follow William to America. Their families were far away. Everything in this ancient land was new—everyone around them was young and promiscuous—nothing was forbidden. In the heat of the Kinneret, Chaim and Etl reinvented their lives from one day to the next. The world blazed with possibility.

But strength was essential to survive. "In those days we were a band of comrades," wrote one of the Kinneret pioneers, "and in our devotion to the country we said that anyone who left it was like a man running away in battle." Etl, Chaim's beloved, was one of those who ran away. Tens of thousands did the same. Conditions in Palestine were too harsh; they couldn't take the rigors of communal life; their bodies and spirits were shattered by the grind of daily agricultural labor. They pined for green pastures, forests full of streams and mushrooms, coffee, cobblestones. Even the most robust among them came down with malaria and could not regain their health. They returned to their shtetlach in Europe, they tried their luck in

America, they committed suicide in droves (depression and suicide were "rampant" in the early collectives). They had "dreamed of a life rich in heroic deeds and poetry," wrote one *halutzah* (female pioneer), "and lacked the imagination to find poetry in the task of sheep-tending among the barren hills, or heroism in the act of following the plow through the long, blazing Jordan Valley days." "Every single person who left the country left the mark of his failure on the workers who stayed," wrote one *halutz* who stayed.

Etl's mark of failure fell most painfully on Chaim. She left him behind in the beautiful inferno of the Kinneret, went back to Volozhin, married, bore three children—and twenty years later she and her family were killed by the Nazis. Chaim never forgot her.

Chaim and his comrades worked their hearts out at Har Kinneret, but the settlement was doomed. Because they were chronically strapped for cash and food, the most able-bodied among them went down to the lakeshore to hire out with road-paving crews. They all tried to get by on less; they pushed themselves to the limit of their endurance. But in the end, the location defeated them. The mountainside was too remote, resources too limited, arable land too scanty. Flies tortured them by day and mosquitoes at night; malaria was epidemic. Chaim remained at Har Kinneret for two years. Then he called it quits.

Itel summoned her brothers to a meeting. It was 1925 and business was booming. Not just the bra business, but the business of America. Automobiles, radios, bootleg liquor, ready-to-wear dresses, costume jewelry, kitchen appliances, stocks and bonds—all the accessories of consumer capitalism were taking off explosively. A. Cohen & Sons boomed along with the rest. Thirteen years old in 1925, the family business had been restructured from a partnership to a corporation, with Abraham as its first president, Harry as treasurer, Sam as vice president, and Hyman as secretary. That year they finally pulled out of the Lower East Side and moved their offices and showroom uptown to the relatively swank environs of 584–586 Broadway (between Houston and Prince)—thirty thousand square feet in a stately Italianate stone palace on Manhattan's prime commercial artery. It set them back eleven thousand dollars a year in rent, but the Cohens could afford it: they were now respectably on the map in every sense. The patriarch had put aside his religious book concession to devote himself to the company's silverware department. Over the years, Abraham's expertise in flatware patterns had become Talmudic: when the big manufacturers wanted to launch a new line, they solicited his opinion about its aesthetic appeal and sales potential.

All three brothers were married now with families of their own. Sam and Celia had four children—two more sons born after the twins. Celia was not handling it well. There were days Sam returned from work to find the children screaming and hungry, the baby's diaper unchanged. More worrisome, Celia became increasingly unstable under the strain of raising a large family. Her sudden death late in 1924, six months after the birth of her youngest son, Marvin, has never been explained. One story that circulated in the family was that she was so unhinged, or unhappy, that she went out undressed, possibly naked, on a frigid night and contracted a fatal infection. Left alone with four small children, Sam was desperate. What saved him was a match made within a year of Celia's death with a distant relative named Gisri Gelperin (Gladys, in America), a recent immigrant from a shtetl near Rakov. Quick, funny, vivacious, dynamic, as well as a fantastic cook and born manager, Gladys took over the household and made Sam a truly happy man for the first time in his life.

Married life was more stable for the other two brothers. Harry and his wife, Sallie, had a son, and soon a daughter and another son arrived. Hyman and Anna had lost their first baby—a stillbirth—but in 1925 Anna was pregnant again. The three brothers, all in their thirties now, were becoming men of substance, like their father. It was only natural that Itel should seek their advice on an important business matter.

Itel hated it when men, even her own brothers, towered over her. As soon as the boys showed up for the meeting, she told them to sit down and stay seated. That way they'd all be at the same level. She got right to it. Itel said she wanted their opinion—though in fact the only opinion she truly valued was Harry's. Here was the situation. At the age of thirty-nine, she had come to a crossroad. She and Enid Bissett had been in business together for three years selling quality dresses out of the Fifty-seventh Street shop and manufacturing bras for distribution at lingerie shops and counters all over the city. Dress orders were still brisk, but the bras were flying out the door. Their operators in Manhattan couldn't keep up with demand, so William had enlisted his sister Masha Hammer in Bayonne, New Jersey, to turn her kitchen into a mini workshop. Masha installed three sewing machines and brought in two girls to run them while she took the third herself. Within six months they had to move to a bigger house and set up more machines in the living and dining rooms. Uplift was all the rage, Itel told her brothers as the room filled with her cigarette smoke. The bra was a potential gold mine.

What did they think? Should she quit the dress business and put everything into the Maiden Form brassiere? "Everyone comes to a fork that will decide their life," Itel said. "If you're afraid to go, if you stand still or stand back, then nothing happens." This was her fork, her chance to make something happen.

So, nu? What would they do in her shoes?

Her brothers responded as Itel suspected they would. Dresses would be around forever, but the bra was a fad, a bubble. Sooner or later it would go bust—and then what? Itel should stick with what she knew. Run with the bra while it lasted, but keep the dress business to fall back on. Why sink an ongoing successful concern—and for what? For underwear? Itel might be older, but they had been in business a lot longer. They could tell her a thing or two about product lines, establishing trust, building credit, expanding into new markets. You didn't make money over the long haul by throwing out your bread and butter. Sure, those new Brazilian onyx ashtrays Hyman had insisted on buying were taking off—everybody smoked and drank these days and an ashtray balanced on the tail of a bronze dolphin made a swell gift. But did that mean they should drop the dresser sets of combs and brushes nestled in sateen-lined boxes, the alarm clocks, steak knives, waffle irons, and all the rest of the stuff they'd been wholesaling profitably for over a decade and gamble everything on ashtrays? It made no sense.

Voices got loud and heated. Tempers flared—tempers always flared when the boys had a meeting. Itel wrapped it up, thanked her brothers, and gave them that gracious smile they knew all too well. The smile that meant *I'm going to do exactly as I please.*

And so she did. Enid Manufacturing Company, as the business was now called, pulled the plug on dresses and put everything into bras. William, as chief designer, filed a series of patents for bras "adapted to support the bust in a natural position" without flattening and without coarse seams to irritate the tender tissue. They moved the sewing machines out of Masha's house and into a proper industrial facility on Eighteenth Street in Bayonne. Soon they had forty operators whirring away. Joe Bissett stepped up as sales manager. Reps fanned out across the country—George Horn handled Brooklyn, Harry Miller had Manhattan, Joe Feller took the Midwest, Al Siegel covered the East Coast, a guy named Plastrich got California. The reps found out fast that their boss was none too reliable. "Joe Bissett was, in my opinion, a hot and cold sales manager," salesman Jack Zizmor recalled of the early days. "If he liked an account, they could get anything. If he disliked an account, or if it were small, he didn't give them very much. You had the impression that he was a guy who knew all the answers, but who didn't. He was essentially a showman and a playboy. Many a day I would have to go to a hotel where I knew he was, find him, and tell him that he was needed back at the company. He seemed to be busy doing two jobs!" Itel knew about Joe's second "job" and she didn't like it. "Mrs. Rosenthal did not have a halo," said Zizmor. "She was a normal human being and there were plenty of times that she would get good and angry." A showdown with Joe was inevitable, though there was no question who would win. Itel was the boss and everyone knew it. William—"the most liberal, fairest minded man I have ever met in my life" in Zizmor's estimation— was the company's creative genius. But Itel held the reins of power. What Itel decided, William endorsed.

Years later, a callow young man, introduced to Itel for the first time, tried to break the ice with the glib opener, "I understand you're with Maidenform." "I *am* Maidenform," was her withering reply. So it was in the beginning and ever would be.

"Soon the accounts practically opened themselves," said the Brooklyn rep, George Horn. "The name was known. You were never turned down. You could always show your line, and the numbers showed themselves. No shop would ever open without Maiden Form."

Family lore has it that Itel, William, and Mrs. Bissett invented the bra, but lore is wrong. In fact, bras of various types had been around for half a century when Mrs. Bissett turned her shears on a Boyish Form bandeau. By 1925, as the breast began to rise again on fashionable torsos, plenty of other American companies were patenting, manufacturing, and selling brassieres in lingerie shops and department stores. But Maiden Form had the cachet, the mystique, the name. And, Itel made very sure, the quality. A bra requires the most precise design and fit of any garment. "Two stitches more or less at the top of a dart can make all the difference between comfort and discomfort," according to one top designer. Itel saw to it that Maiden Form bras were the best made, most comfortable, and best known on the market. The Bundist seamstress from Rakov turned out to be genius at branding. She had had no training in business; she was a short, stout, chain-smoking immigrant with an accent; temperamentally and culturally, she had more in common with Yiddish stage and screen star Molly Picon than with Henry Ford. Yet she would take her place beside Ford as a captain of industry. Only in America.

Chaim forsook the mountain aerie of Har Kinneret but he didn't go far. On his days off, he had gotten to know some of the settlers around the lakeshore, and one of the families at the Kinneret Colony, a walled settlement of eight farmhouses about half a mile up from the water, took him on as a hired hand. So Chaim's love affair with the Kinneret had a second chapter, softer and more idyllic than the first.

The Kinneret Colony (Moshava Kinneret in Hebrew), founded in 1908, was not a collective like Har Kinneret but a settlement of individual farmers: each family worked alone, bought and sold by themselves, and profited (or lost) on their own. In making the move, Chaim gained a private life, cash wages, more freedom to think for himself—but he lost his standing as an equal among comrades. Up on the mountain, every voice counted; decisions were made by committee; they all had their noses in one another's business and expected other noses in theirs. Now he had a boss who gave the orders, made the decisions, and controlled the finances. Luckily for Chaim, Yizhak Cohen was a good boss with a lovely generous wife and six beautiful boisterous sun-bronzed children (three girls and three boys, two of whom were twins). Chaim moved into the rickety shed beside the Cohens' cramped flat-roofed house and got to work. Yizhak and Leah had been in the colony for a decade now, and by the time they took on Chaim their farm was humming along nicely, with a dairy, vegetable garden, and sixty acres of cultivated fields, most of it planted with tomatoes and cucumbers. Leah was famous for her cheeses and sour cream. She baked bread in an oven in her yard and washed the children in an outdoor shower under a fig tree. Yizhak kept current with the latest agricultural practices and had family connections to the local flour mill. It was the custom at the Moshava Kinneret to treat hired help as part of the family, with a place at mealtimes—so Chaim became a kind of older brother to the Cohen kids. On hot breezy afternoons he took them sailing on the lake. On stifling nights he slept outside on the roof of the main house. His workdays began before dawn when he and the other farmers and hired hands left the compound through a gate in the security wall, climbed the flanks of the mountain with their tools, and tried to get as much done as possible before the valley became an oven. Chaim learned to keep one eye cocked for trouble. Most of the Arabs in the nearby villages left them alone, but there was the occasional raid or random theft—hence the wall around the compound. He became adept at loading a hay wagon just right—full to the point of overflowing but precisely balanced so that it wouldn't tip over when it hit a rut. On Shabbat, he cleaned himself in the outdoor shower, dressed in white, and gathered with the other young farmworkers. He didn't care how hot it was or how much his body ached—he would dance all night, gulp down a glass of tea, and go out once more to the burning fields. The girls noticed how muscular and handsome he was. He wore his dark hair long and oiled back. The Cohen children were not the only ones Chaim took sailing on the lake.

He hoped the dream would last forever. What ended it—and nearly killed him—was illness.

One morning Chaim woke up on fire with fever; a few hours later, the fire went out and ice gripped him. When he tried to stand, he collapsed. When he began to burn and sweat again, he saw visions and heard voices. Then the chills returned, setting his teeth to chattering and turning his tongue to flannel. Chaim had come down with malaria—epidemic in Palestine in those years, and especially acute in the Kinneret because of the torrid climate and the extensive swampland adjoining the lake. Chaim's bout began with a simple mosquito bite. Red itchy bumps tormented him for a while and then passed, or seemed to. But while he had been scratching, the parasites injected by the mosquito were silently coursing through his bloodstream, feasting on the hemoglobin in his red blood cells and leaching out toxins. By the time the fever was kindled, it was far too late for Chaim to slow the ravaging of his system. Some malaria victims die of their first bout within hours: the explosion of millions of red blood cells deprives the body of oxygen, starves the brain, and induces a fatal coma. Others, harboring the parasites in their livers for years, dwindle away into anemic ghosts of their former selves. That's what happened to Chaim. In time the cycle became as predictable and maddening as the tides: days of fever and chills, followed by a few fever-free days that roused the hope that the sickness had run its course, then another high tide of agony. "We used to work immediately before and after the attacks of fever," wrote one pioneer. "We worked and suffered. At ten o'clock the fever would increase suddenly; our limbs trembled, heads ached, and everything fell out of our hands. Twelve o'clock, and it is impossible to go on." But somehow they did go on.

Chaim was almost certainly infected numerous times—and even though his body developed some immunity, a new strain always emerged to fell him again.

The Kinneret was "the enchantress-bride, who led her bridegrooms to doom," as one early settler put it. "For a worker plagued by the vicious circle of disease there was no way out unless he chose to abandon the 'cruel enchantress' to recuperate in a healthier climate." After four enchanted years, Chaim was forced to make this choice. He had become a skilled, experienced farmer and a trusted comrade. He had filled out some, despite the malaria, and at twenty-two his face had lost its chiseled delicacy. He loved the Cohen family, he loved the lake and the bare corrugated mountains and the camaraderie of young idealists working together far from their homes. But he knew that it would kill him to stay in the Kinneret.

Chaim had heard about a new colony being organized in the coastal sand dunes north of Tel Aviv. Herzliya, named after the great Zionist founding father Theodore Herzl, had particular appeal for Chaim because it relied exclusively on Jewish labor, instead of hiring out menial jobs to Arab workers. Toward the end of 1928, he gathered his few possessions, bid farewell to Yizhak and Leah and their six children, and headed west across the narrow neck of Palestine to start over.

In Rakov, the year 1928 brought joy to the family of Shalom Tvi and Beyle: their first grandson was born on February 5. Doba, the plump, sweet, oldest daughter, had married the previous year and moved to Vilna with her husband, Shabtai Senitski. At twenty-five, Doba was old to be marrying—though Shabtai, the new husband, was over thirty, a string bean of a man with a high forehead, furrowed brow, and a beaky nose. Never mind the gawky appearance, Shabtai—everyone called him Shepsel or Shepseleh—was kind and intelligent, clean and well dressed, a good earner with a successful practice as an accountant. He came from a learned and cultured family, and he and Doba were able to afford a comfortable apartment across the street from the university's chemistry faculty and just up the hill from Vilna's Old City. It was an echt bourgeois neighborhood of stone-and-brick apartments and offices, built to endure. The carved lintels, tall lacquered portals, pilasters, and courtyards were quite a step up from what the Kaganovich sisters had grown up with in Rakov. Doba persuaded her husband to name the baby Shimon in honor of her grandfather. Shimon Senitski, though not a Kohain because the priestly status passed only from father to son, was nonetheless a healthy baby boy with fair hair and round wondering eyes, and his parents cherished and pampered him. Word of the new arrival spread from Vilna to Doba's first cousin Chaim in Palestine and to Itel, Harry, Sam, Hyman, and the many other cousins in the States. Another Shimon to carry the line of the scribe into the future.

Itel had more proximate reasons to rejoice that year: Sales of Maiden Form bras hit half a million. In fact, the bras were moving so briskly that the operators in the Bayonne factory were having a hard time keeping up with orders. Itel and William and William's sister Masha, drawing on their long experience with needle and thread, devised a streamlined new production process. Instead of having each operator sew a complete bra from start to finish, as Itel had done with her dresses, they broke the fabrication down into separate units and assigned each unit to an individual operator: one person handled only the binding, another did the joining, another worked on the shoulder straps, another affixed the labels, and so on. It was like the Model T assembly-line approach applied to lingerie. "We took a book out of the library on production efficiency," Masha recalled, "but I told them, 'Don't worry about it. I'm doing it efficiently without that book. I'm doing it better than the book.'" William hired his brother Moe to take charge of the factory. Moe turned out to be a crack general manager—tough, intimidating, eagle eyed. With Moe breathing down the operators' necks, the Bayonne plant became a quiet and extremely productive factory floor. "In those days, everybody had his head down," recalled Stella Kotowski, the assistant plant manager. "You didn't talk! You just did your work, very quietly. We were so close to the boss and he was always looking right at us! We came to work at eight in the morning to five in the afternoon, with an hour for lunch, and with no breaks." Moe was scary, but production spiked under his iron rule.

Enid Manufacturing (the company name did not become Maiden Form until 1930) relocated its headquarters to 245 Fifth Avenue, at Twenty-eighth Street, a few blocks from the site where the Empire State Building would soon rise as the world's tallest freestanding building. Itel was convinced that the only way to grow was to advertise, and she commissioned a fledgling ad campaign of black-and-white sketches (photography was way too risqué) of slinky women lounging around in their bras and slips. "Maiden Form Loveliness" read the copy line. "The new contour—siren rather than flapper— rounded yet slender." Clergymen chirped that it was indecent, but the company shrugged and kept moving forward. In 1928, the first Maiden Form ad appeared in *Harper's Bazaar*. They had scaled the heights of elegance.

Joe Bissett's days were numbered as sales manager. Mrs. Bissett, ailing, had pretty much withdrawn from daily operations and decisions. The company still bore her name, and she and Joe still held a one-third share, but in every other way the business belonged to Itel and William. Now that they could afford to splurge a little, the Rosenthals left Hamilton Heights for a stately brick apartment building right off Central Park West, at 18 West Seventieth Street. Lewis, now a graduate of Columbia College, was bound for Columbia Law School. Beatrice, thirteen, attended the Ethical Culture School, a few blocks from the apartment. They had a live-in Czech maid named Marie and a car (though it was usually in the shop because William, as one associate put it, "had more accidents than anybody ever had driving a car. Mrs. Rosenthal would take six aspirins before she got into the car with him"). Their neighbors were solid respectable lawyers, doctors, manufacturers, and stockbrokers—hardly an immigrant among them aside from the maids and baby nurses.

Itel had always separated herself from the rest of the family, both geographically and emotionally, and Abraham and Sarah knew it was pointless to try to reel her back in now. The parents had better luck keeping their other children in their orbit. Abraham and Sarah made the classic hopscotch of early twentieth-century Russian Jewish immigrants—from the Lower East Side to Brooklyn and, when finances permitted, from Brooklyn to the Bronx. In 1924, the family bought both units (up- and downstairs) of a duplex house at 1819 Andrews Avenue, a street of modest brick row houses in the University Heights neighborhood (named for New York University, which had its main campus in the Bronx from 1894 to the early 1970s). Abraham and Sarah lived upstairs with Ethel and her husband Sam Epstein and their three kids (Bernard, Inda, and David). Sam and Gladys and their five kids (the twins Dorothy and Sidney, Lester, Marvin, and Leona, Gladys's only child to survive infancy) lived in the downstairs unit. It was a schlep to the business on Lower Broadway, but the house suited Abraham and Sarah because it was in a nice predominantly Jewish neighborhood, it had a bit of a backyard where they could put up a sukkah during Sukkoth (Sarah had given up on vegetable gardening), and above all because it was a five-minute walk to the shul. Abraham was a founding member of the Hebrew Institute of University Heights—one of the great Orthodox synagogues of the Bronx, with more than 1,500 congregants in attendance during the high holidays. The patriarch might be president of a going wholesale concern in Manhattan, but he was a man of God before he was a businessman. Each day before work, he taught a Talmud class at the shul. On Saturday his discourses on the Mishna were packed. When the synagogue started a religious school, they named it Akiva Academy in his honor. Shimon Dov would have been proud.

Chaim moved from the Kinneret to Herzliya to regain health and strength, but his first impression of the place sent him reeling. An unpaved rutted track delivered him to a collection of huts and barracks set in a wasteland of sand. Instead of mountains ringing a gorgeous lake, dunes speckled with brown scrub rolled out in every direction. Goats from the nearby Arab village of Ijlil al-Qibliyya browsed the low hills. Spindly citrus orchards surrounded the identical rows of workers' houses (which had replaced the original tents), and two dozen acres of banana trees, planted the year before, flapped their tattered green banners in the sun.

Herzliya was founded in 1924 as a training center for *garinim*—Zionist youth preparing to relocate to collectives and cooperative farms—and a strong Labor Zionist ethic prevailed. Once he got over his shock, Chaim fit right in with the young, idealistic comrades.

Chaim had come to Herzliya to work, not to supplant Arab workers— but it happened nonetheless. Whatever land and livelihood Jewish workers gained, Arabs lost: the equation was fixed and inescapable. Herzliya was a small, tightly organized Jewish outpost—really a tiny Jewish world unto itself—and Chaim lived and worked there without a thought about who had owned and grazed this land before him. The first wave of Zionists had relied on Arab workers because they were cheap and skilled, and because Jews were considered too intransigent and expensive to make good farmworkers. But by the time Chaim made aliyah in 1924, things had changed. Now "Hebrew land, Hebrew language, Hebrew labor" was the rallying cry. It was a point of pride for Chaim and thousands like him to join colonies and collectives where everything, even the most menial tasks, *especially* the most menial tasks, was done exclusively by Jews. The intent was not to squeeze out the Arabs but rather to establish their own self-sufficient independent settlements, villages, regions, and, one day, God willing, nation. "Not to dominate—not to be dominated" was the formula David Ben-Gurion endorsed. Peaceful coexistence. Side by side but separate in this sliver of a land. Why not?

It was a beautiful dream, part and parcel of the wild blind idealism that the *halutzim* brought with them. But it was doomed from the start. "You want to found a state without bloodshed?" sociologist Ludwig Gumplowicz demanded of Theodore Herzl. "Where have you ever seen such a thing?"

Chaim had come to Palestine to work, not to fight. But fighting was inevitable given the ambitions of the Zionists and the deep roots of the

Arabs. All it took was an irritant—an economic downturn, a sudden spike in Jewish immigration, a squabble over holy places—to bring the latent violence to the surface. There were isolated incidents from the start of Jewish settlement—thefts, harassment, destruction of Jewish property, the occasional ambush or sniper attack—but more organized and widespread anti-Zionist rioting broke out in 1920. More Jews would have been hurt had the Zionists' rudimentary militia Haganah ("Defense" in Hebrew) not turned out to oppose the attacks. This was something else Jews had taken into their own hands in Palestine—Hebrew self-defense. Mobilized under the command of militant Zionist Ze'ev Jabotinsky, cofounder with Joseph Trumpeldor of the Jewish Legion during World War I, Haganah was still shadowy, decentralized, illegal, and amateurish. When even bloodier anti-Zionist rioting roiled the port city of Jaffa, in May 1921, and spread to the surrounding agricultural settlements, Haganah once again stood up to the attackers.

The *halutzim* had made aliyah to farm, not to fight. But if they had to fight in order to farm, they would. Only the next time they would be better prepared.

By the late 1920s, Haganah service had become all but mandatory for workers on the collective and cooperative farms. Chaim was ripe for recruitment. Soon after he settled in Herzliya, the local Haganah leadership approached him about enrolling in their commanders' course. The induction ceremony was like a sacred ritual. Chaim was ushered into a darkened room lit by a single candle. The door was locked. He sat at a table with a revolver and a Bible in front of him and, with the officers looking on in silence, recited the militia's oath: "I swear to be faithful all the days of my life to the Haganah organization, to its constitution, and to its duties as defined by the high command. I swear to dedicate all my powers and even to sacrifice my life to defense and to the war for my people and my homeland, for the freedom of Israel and for the redemption of Zion." The oath bound Chaim to strict secrecy. If he so much as betrayed the existence of the organization or revealed to an outsider the location of an arms cache (*slik* in Haganah slang), he would pay with his life.

Chaim trained for six months, from January to the start of July 1929. Five nights a week and Saturdays he and Herzliya's sixteen other Haganah recruits learned how to load and shoot weapons, take out snipers, toss grenades, and obey orders without arguing. For target practice, they descended into an ancient Roman tunnel that served as the Herzliya *slik* and firing range. The boys blasted away, and no one up above heard a thing. Chaim was lucky—his group was trained by Yisrael Amir, a charismatic leader who had been active in Haganah from the start and rose rapidly through the ranks. In 1935, Amir would set up two secret factories to produce grenades and mortars for Haganah, and in 1942 he would found and head up the Haganah intelligence branch, known initially as Shai, that later morphed into Mossad and Shin Bet, Israel's intelligence and internal security services. After independence he became the first commander of the Israeli air force.

When Amir's training course was over, Chaim and his comrades were rewarded with a hiking trip through the backcountry. It was July and the heat and drought of summer had scorched the land. Still, Chaim embraced the return to the mountains and valleys he had come to love in his first years in Palestine.

It was good Chaim had gotten away when he did. A month after the hiking trip, there was another round of anti-Zionist violence—far worse than the outbreaks of 1920 and 1921. No one used the word *pogrom* for what started in the summer of 1929. This time it was more like the opening battle in a civil war.

That summer in New York all anybody talked about was the stock market. Or so Sam told his brothers after making the rounds of their accounts. Everywhere he went, Sam heard about how rich other people were getting off their investments. It wasn't just the businessmen and salesmen either. The shoe-shine boy, the barber, the grocer, the guy delivering milk—all of them were trading stock tips, cashing in, moving up. Even if you didn't have a dime, a broker would front you. You couldn't lose. Sam worried that they were missing out on the greatest run-up in history. "We have more brains than any one of these people I meet," he told his brothers. "Yet we just sit here and let opportunities pass us by." Sam proposed to Harry and Hyman that they take the company's excess cash and sock it away in the market.

Hyman was against it. They hadn't gotten where they were by taking foolish risks, he told Sam. They'd be better off investing in the growth of their business. The market was going up now, but it couldn't last forever. Hyman got Harry to take his side—two against one.

Sam kept hammering away at them. By August the city was sweltering and the market was sizzling. Headlines blazed with reports of equity shares hitting new records. "Stock prices have reached what looks like a permanently high plateau," declared one prominent economist. The brothers had always pulled together—all for one and one for all. But if Harry and Hyman refused to budge, Sam would go it alone.

The fighting began on August 15, 1929, at the Western Wall in Jerusalem. There was no place on earth more sacred to Jews—or more contested by their enemies. The Romans had destroyed the temple that rose atop this massive retaining wall in 70 C.E., laid waste to Jerusalem, and cast the Jews from its ruins—but for two thousand years the pious had found a way to come back and pray beside the slabs of stone. Muslim Arabs conquered the Holy Land after the fall of Rome, and in the seventh century they crowned the platform that the Wall supported—the Temple Mount—with two splendid mosques, the Dome of the Rock and the Al-Aqsa Mosque. Ottoman Turks supplanted the Arabs in 1517 and made Jerusalem an outpost of their vast empire. Still the Wall endured in substance and even more in the imaginations of Diaspora Jews; a trickle of the faithful always came to worship and to mourn in its shadow.

As long as the Jews remained small in number and docile in demeanor, the rulers of Jerusalem let them daven and weep by the Wall. But the Jews who massed here on August 15, 1929, had not come to pray. Their demeanor was anything but docile. Militant young followers of Haganah commander Ze'ev Jabotinsky had organized a youth movement called Betar, and on August 15, Betar members gathered by the Wall to stage a large, noisy anti-Arab demonstration. Brandishing the blue-and-white Jewish national flag, the Jabotinskyites sang the anthem "Hatikvah" and shouted, "The Wall is ours!" That was all it took to light the fuse. Arabs demonstrated the following day and fighting flared; there followed five days of wild rumors, random attacks, extreme tension—and killing. Seventeen Jews were dead at the hands of Arab rioters in Jerusalem by August 24. More died in Hebron, an ancient city north and west of Jerusalem, where a long-established Orthodox Jewish community had lived peacefully for decades with the majority Arab population. Earlier in the week, the Hebron Jewish community, convinced that their Arab friends would keep them safe, had turned down an offer from Haganah to protect them or assist with evacuation. It was a terrible mistake. On August 23 and 24, sixty-seven Jews died in the violence at Hebron—stoned, stabbed, shot by Arab mobs. The victims included yeshiva students, women, and children under the age of three. One observer insisted that "not a Jewish soul" would have survived in Hebron "if it had not been for some Arab families" who took pity on their Jewish neighbors and, risking their lives, hid them in their homes.

Eighteen Jews later died in Safed, the ancient city in the Galilee where pious Volozhiners had supported a religious colony in the nineteenth century, and there were also killings in Tel Aviv. As wildly exaggerated rumors of Arab casualties flew from cities to the countryside, attacks began to flare up in the agricultural settlements as well. Here the conflict was more traumatic because the scale was so intimate—neighbors attacking neighbors in adjoining fields. At Kfar Uria, a cooperative farming village between Tel Aviv and Jerusalem where the writer A. D. Gordon had lived for a time, settlers were saved because a local village sheik took them in and gave them shelter. The Jews watched, however, as Arabs from a nearby village looted and torched their homes and farms. The settlement was completely destroyed and abandoned.

Chaim was lucky: the fighting did not spread to Herzliya, no doubt because local Arabs and Bedouins observed Haganah recruits manning the colony's observation posts around the clock. Drilling was stepped up, but there was no call to use the light arms and grenades hidden in the Roman tunnel.

Haganah units in Tel Aviv, Haifa, and Jerusalem managed to repel some attacks, and friendly Arabs kept the Jewish death toll down. But the Jews were outraged at how little British forces did to protect them and how late they were to respond. Zionists also bitterly resented the fact that the official British reports characterized the riots as "disturbances" or "conflicts" or "loss of life," suggesting that the attacks were mutual, when in fact

Arabs struck and Jews tried to defend themselves—or perished helplessly. The casualties on both sides were heavy: 133 Jews dead and 339 wounded; 116 Arabs dead and 232 wounded. But there was this critical difference: nearly all the Jewish blood was spilled by Arabs, whereas nearly all the Arab casualties were inflicted by British security forces attempting to restore order.

August 1929 was the end of a Zionist era and the beginning of a new and far more troubled one. What little trust and cooperation there had been between Jews and Arabs crusted over. In the aftermath of the riots, there was no reconciliation, no easing of the trauma. Self-defense now occupied a central place in the Zionist mission, as essential to survival as the conquest of labor. Haganah embarked on a rapid and intense expansion, transforming itself from a ragtag collection of cells to a regional fighting force with a steady supply of weapons imported from Europe. The training program that Chaim had completed was broadened in scope, seriousness, and membership. At Herzliya, they bulked up the *slik* with new weapons stashed handily in the workers' houses.

The violence finally ceased. A tense fragile peace returned. The dead were buried. Inquiries were held by the British authorities. Official "white papers" were handed down from London. Chaim went on working in the citrus groves. But the mood had shifted. The idea of peaceful coexistence and gradual accommodation was finished; now came the era of resistance.

Chaim had been little more than a boy when he arrived in the Kinneret in 1924, a teenager buoyed by boundless hope and idealism. Idealism alters when it has to wear a sidearm. The tragedy of twentieth-century Palestine was that farmers like Chaim had to learn to beat their plowshares into swords.

Sam had had enough. In the middle of October, he called a stockbroker and put in an order for Consolidated Gas Company (the forerunner of Consolidated Edison). In Hyman's recollection, Sam's buy was thirteen shares at $135 a share—a total of $1,755 (a hefty sum when you consider that Itel's initial $4,000 investment in Enid Frocks was just about all the money she and William had). Sam was superstitious. He never should have bought that odd lot of thirteen. On October 28—Black Monday—the stock market crashed, losing 13 percent of its value between the opening and closing bells. The next day it plunged another 12 percent. In five hours, 10 billion dollars in stock value was wiped away. Sam hadn't even taken possession of his stock and already it was in the toilet. Harry and Hyman agreed to bail out their brother. They let Sam transfer ownership of the stock to the business so the company would absorb the loss. Though of course they would never let him live it down.

Itel, Harry, Sam, Hyman, their parents and siblings, aunts and uncles had done well for themselves in America. They arrived all but penniless in a flood of penniless immigrants and now a couple of decades later they had houses, cars, businesses, money in the bank, children in private schools, servants, security. Not that any of it had come easily. America was the land of opportunity, but it was also a land of xenophobes, bigots, nativists, anti-Semites, and racists. The decade just coming to an end had been a banner time for mass discrimination against any group perceived as foreign or un-American. New laws enacted in 1921 and 1924 all but barred the golden door. The Ku Klux Klan came roaring back to life. Red-baiting politicians blamed Jews for the Russian Revolution and the looming Soviet threat. In Germany, the rising Nazi Party said exactly the same thing.

Still, in 1929, there was no better place to be a Jew than the United States. Some four and a half million strong, America's Jewish community was emerging as the world's largest, wealthiest, and most powerful. To the Cohen family, America, not Palestine, looked like the true promised land of the twentieth century.

And then in two calamitous days in October, the bottom fell out. In the Great Depression that followed the crash, all the world's major economies toppled—but the countries hit hardest were the United States and Germany.

Sam got off fairly easily. His Consolidated Gas shares tanked but at least he had family to bail him out. Business was cyclical, all the big shots kept saying. In a couple of months they'd look back and see the crash was just a dip. Things would come roaring back—just wait. Sam, for all his bluster when making a sale, was not an optimist, but he tried to believe it.

CHAPTER TEN

THE DEPRESSION

Who would buy a bra if she couldn't afford to eat? Itel wondered about Maiden Form's prospects as 1929 slid into 1930 and the nation, and then the world, plunged into the worst economic depression in modern history. Sales of all the products that had buoyed the great boom of the 1920s slumped rapidly in 1930. Unemployment more than doubled its 1929 level, from 1.5 million to 4.3 million. Some 26,300 businesses went belly up that year, including 1,372 banks. Life savings evaporated; salaries for those lucky enough to hold on to their jobs declined. Itel looked on in disbelief as one big dress house after another closed its doors. Had she followed her brothers' advice that would have been her fate. Somehow, Maiden Form not only stayed in business but sales continued to grow. Evidently a lot of women still had a few dollars to spare on beauty.

Itel's company survived the first year of the Depression, but her family did not. When he was sixteen years old, Lewis had contracted pneumonia. Still, bright and handsome, he seemed to have recovered and he went on to live a normal life, graduating from Columbia College and then enrolling in Columbia Law School. But his body had never rid itself of the abscess—the pus-filled cavity—that had formed in his lung. At some point an infected clot broke off from the lung and traveled through the aorta into the vessels supplying Lewis's brain, where the clot embedded itself in the soft tissue of the right parietal lobe and festered. By the spring of 1930, the brain abscess had become life threatening, and Itel and William rushed Lewis to Germany, which then had the most highly skilled brain surgeons in the world. In June, the German doctors performed a craniotomy—the surgical removal of a piece of the skull in order to reach and drain the abscess—but the procedure failed. The Rosenthals brought their son back to New York and on June 23 they had him admitted to the Neurological Institute of New York. The doctors did their best to keep Lewis comfortable—another operation was out of the question. The infection spread to the meninges, the membranes that sheathe the brain and the spinal cord. Lewis died in the Neurological Institute at 1:30 in the morning on Monday, August 4, 1930, six days shy of his twenty-third birthday.

The family gathered for the service at eleven o'clock the following morning at the Riverside Memorial Chapel on West Seventy-sixth Street. Itel and William had never been observant Jews. They had not circumcised their son at birth, nor had Lewis ever learned Hebrew, attended synagogue, or celebrated his bar mitzvah. Instead of Judaism, the Rosenthals belonged to the Ethical Culture Society, a quasi-religious group that advocated morality without theology, personal fulfillment through education and philanthropy, and the interdependence of self-reform and social reform. Nonetheless, when Lewis died, Itel and William chose a Jewish funeral home for the burial—no doubt out of respect for Abraham and Sarah.

Whatever depths of grief Itel felt over losing her only son—by all accounts a promising young man who was expected to take over the company one day—she did not share it with her siblings or parents. Itel was a fiercely private, supremely disciplined person. Devastated, she forced herself to get back to work. Only on rare occasions did her feelings show. Years later, at a family Hanukkah party, she sat grim-faced while a tactless relative rattled on, not without a twist of envy, about how lucky she was. She lived in a mansion, drove to work in a chauffeured limousine, always flew first class, had hundreds of employees to obey her every command. "So lucky!" Itel replied, bursting into tears. "I'd give up all of it to have Lewis back."

Sarah, a canny businesswoman in Russia, had become in America a timid, invisible wife who rarely left the tight circuit of house, market, and shul. Hyman was surprised, then, when his mother showed up unannounced at the Broadway showroom of A. Cohen & Sons one day. She had taken the trolley and subway down from the Bronx by herself; she had braved the transfers and the beggars, the apple carts and shoe-shine stands manned by former business executives and factory workers, the lines snaking outside soup kitchens. Sarah made her way through the arched granite portal at 584 Broadway, slipped into the A. Cohen & Sons office, murmured a few words in her halting, accented English to the receptionist, and found her son. She told Hyman that she wanted to have a word with him—without his secretary present. Sarah summoned up negotiating skills she had not used in two decades. She reminded her son of what terrible shape the city was in—unemployed men everywhere, no jobs to be had, no sign that this horrible depression had run its course. Hyman knew full well that his wife Anna's brother Harry Raskin had lost his job. Where on earth was he going to find another one? "Hyman, you are in a fortunate economic position," said Sarah, "but you cannot live for yourself alone. I want you to make room for Harry." There—she had said her piece. She knew she had no business meddling in her son's affairs, but she could not in good conscience remain silent.

"Stop worrying," Hyman replied without hesitation. "Go home; be happy. Harry can start working just as soon as he can get here."

It was not written into the bylaws, but A. Cohen had an unofficial policy of hiring any family member in need of work—in-laws too. Never had this policy been more welcome than during the Depression. They were not all promoted or highly compensated; some spent their entire careers wrapping parcels in the mail room or punching numbers into an adding machine at a bookkeeper's desk; occasionally, though rarely, one had to be fired. But no family member was turned away, even when the business was struggling to stay alive.

And the business was indeed struggling. At the end of 1930, Isidor Boguslav, a Brooklyn public accountant, did the A. Cohen & Sons audit and revealed that the company had earned a pretty skimpy profit that year. Though sales had netted $1,091,974.05, the brothers had to write off

$32,332.77 in bad debts. After subtracting salaries, rent, office expenses, insurance, taxes, the cost of the merchandise, and all the other odds and ends of running a business, they ended up netting $7,778.36. In other words, they were in the black—but just barely. Somewhere hidden in those columns of numbers was the loss that Sam had taken on his Consolidated Gas stock.

Nobody got rich off A. Cohen & Sons that year, but everyone in the family who wanted a job had one, including Harry Raskin.

Itel had always been more hard-nosed than her brothers when it came to the bottom line. If a relative showed promise, she'd find a place, but she had zero tolerance for deadwood, no matter where it grew on the family tree. Though Maiden Form had a raft of Rosenthals and eventually a couple of Cohen cousins and nephews on the payroll, the company never adopted A. Cohen's open-door policy for family.

Once the Depression hit, relatives had an even tougher time getting hired at Maiden Form, because they had to compete with huge numbers of unemployed strangers. William's brother Moe, the manager of the Bayonne factory, could barely get through supper without someone knocking on his door "crying that they needed a job to feed their children." Their sister Masha was besieged by job seekers whenever she went outside. "They used to push presents into my hands," Masha said, "I should give them a job. I never took the presents but would ask them to please come to the factory. Sometimes we would have hundreds of people, sitting and waiting for jobs at Eighteenth Street. Moe used to pick out some people, and I would pick out some of them, and we would interview them and hire them."

The family firms were fortunate. The year 1930 was bad but 1931 was worse. Nationwide, unemployment nearly doubled again from 4.3 million in 1930 to 8 million in 1931, more than five times what it had been just two years earlier. Stocks continued to sink, with sharp drops from the late winter into spring and again in September and December. That summer, drought decimated grain crops in the Plains states, killing the livelihood of tens of thousands of farmers, while European bank failures led to the collapse of the German and Austrian economies. By year's end, New York City soup kitchens were serving some eighty-five thousand free meals every day.

In October 1931, about 40 percent of Chicago's workers were unemployed; in Boston the figure hovered around 30 percent; in Detroit it reached 50 percent. There was no relief and no end in sight.

On the last day of the terrible year of 1931, Abraham and Sarah gathered their family, friends, neighbors, and business associates—some 175 guests in all—to celebrate their golden wedding anniversary in the Bronx. The Cohens rented out the ballroom of Burnside Manor, a big fancy function hall with crystal chandeliers and brocaded drapes. Women arrived in full-length gowns and a few had furs wrapped around their shoulders against the winter chill; the men were clean shaven and sleek in their tuxedoes and slicked-back hair—except for Abraham and half a dozen *frum* (observant) fellows from the shul who covered their heads and left their beards untrimmed as the law prescribed. On the dais, Abraham and Sarah held the place of honor at the center of the table, with their offspring arrayed by age around them: Itel in a low-cut black dress sat beside her father; Ethel pinned to a huge trailing corsage sat beside her mother; then Harry and Sallie; Sam and Gladys; Hyman and Anna; Lillie and her husband Joe. They dined on gefilte fish and consommé, sweetbreads, roast chicken, and candied sweet potatoes. At midnight they cheered and toasted the patriarch and matriarch—not with champagne (Prohibition would not be repealed for two more years) but with celery tonic and Appolinaris sparkling water. The photographer hired to commemorate the event must have told the guests to look dignified because in the official photo nearly every face is wary and mirthless. William frowns fixedly at the tablecloth: Itel, sporting a long strand of pearls, seems about to cry; Sarah, standing behind her white tiered cake, gazes off anxiously to the side, as if scanning the doors for gate-crashers.

A week earlier a little boy had approached Abraham in the street, tugged at his sleeve, and asked for a present. "Can I have a new toy gun, please?" The same thing happened every December: because of the long white beard, they took him for Santa Claus or pretended they did. Abraham smiled and shook his finger at the child. "Vuz you good?" he asked, playing along. Maybe kids in the Bronx thought Santa had a Yiddish accent. Abraham laughed it off but Sarah worried. Who knows what the goyim said to their children about the rich Jew with the beard and the business named after him? The scribe and his family had done well for themselves in their two decades in America—maybe too well. Back in Russia a Jew with money either left or lost it or had it taken by the government. Times were hard—if things got worse, the same thing could happen here.

The party broke up after midnight and the guests returned to their apartments and row houses. The next morning they all awoke to a new year—1932—the year that 12 million Americans, nearly a quarter of the labor pool, would be out of work. It was the year that the Great Depression hit its nadir. Even Maiden Form sales declined.

That summer in New York, the Dow Jones industrial average bottomed out at forty-one points, nearly 90 percent below its high of three years earlier. Some 34 million Americans had no source of income—over a quarter of the nation's population subsisted on handouts, or starved. Never had the extended family been so grateful to Itel, Harry, Sam, and Hyman for having the foresight and stamina to operate two successful, or at least solvent, businesses. Mrs. Bissett had retired from Maiden Form due to poor health and Joe had been more or less squeezed to the sidelines. The company was Itel and William's to run as they pleased. Itel kept her eye on the bottom line and dealt with the bankers; William cranked out one new patent after another—nursing bra, maternity bra, full-fashion bra "made with a knitted cup shaped on a form without a single seam," scooped out demi-bra to wear with low-cut dresses, formal bra contoured around low-backed evening gowns. To keep growing they pushed into overseas markets—Europe, Latin America, Hong Kong, the Philippines, Malaya, Singapore, Egypt, India. Women all over the globe had breasts, and Itel made sure they found out how much better their breasts felt with a little uplift. Back when she first started selling bras, Itel had offered her customers a money-back guarantee: go home, slip it on, and ask your husband what he thinks. If he turned up his nose, you could bring the bra back and collect your refund. Itel, of course, won that bet. There was no need for gimmicks or money-back guarantees anymore. Sales were a bit off in 1932, but Itel wasn't worried. She had become a shrewd businesswoman—one of the first and one of the best. She knew that this depression wouldn't last forever. Instead of hunkering down, she concentrated on expanding markets and maintaining quality.

"You've got nothing to worry about as long as we have back orders," Moe kept telling the operators on the Bayonne factory floor. As a sign of their financial solidity, Itel and William moved the corporate showroom uptown to 200 Madison Avenue and added a second factory in Perth Amboy, New Jersey. Maiden Form was in it for the long haul.

In the mad rush of legislation with which he kicked off his first one hundred days in office, FDR pushed through the National Industrial Recovery Act—a bill that significantly bolstered the heft of labor unions by granting them the right to collective bargaining. Plutocrats howled that the newly empowered unions would put them out of business, but the act was popular with workers, including workers at the Maiden Form factory in Bayonne.

On October 14, 1933, the city of Bayonne turned out for the biggest parade in its history—the National Recovery Act parade mounted in support of the new National Recovery Agency. Sixty marching bands led twenty-five thousand working people up Bayonne's main artery and into the City Park Stadium. Every major Bayonne business from the A&P to Sears Roebuck did their bit with a flag or a poster or a special sale ($3.60 tires at Sears; 99-cent hats at W. T. Grant), and Maiden Form was no exception. The operators had whipped up an enormous brassiere and mounted it on poles like a banner; the prettiest girls in the company were enlisted to carry it up Broadway in the parade. It was a mild sunny Saturday afternoon, and the crowd cheered wildly when the breeze came up and the giant brassiere filled like a sail. Men standing on the sidewalks tossed coins into the swelling fluttering cups.

Itel and William would have plenty of labor trouble at the Bayonne plant in the years ahead. But not that day. Labor and management were all smiles for the National Recovery Act parade as the giant Maiden Form bra sailed up Broadway jingling with change.

CHAPTER ELEVEN

"WE WILL BE GLAD TO TAKE YOU BACK"

Shalom Tvi's youngest daughter, Sonia, was eighteen years old when she introduced herself to Ze'ev Jabotinsky, the fiery right-wing Zionist leader who advocated aggressive, maximal Zionist expansion in Palestine. Jabotinsky was speaking at a conference in Warsaw, and, after much badgering, Sonia persuaded her parents to let her attend. Though she was still a girl, black haired, slender waisted, moody, she was a girl who had made up her mind. Jabotinsky was her man. Betar, the militant youth movement that rallied round Jabotinsky, was her party. "You can't buy a country—you have to pay in blood!" Jabotinsky declaimed when he toured Poland to drum up support for his Revisionist Party. Sonia believed it was the truth. She didn't care that Jabotinsky was known as the Jewish Mussolini because he favored solemn parades and armed, uniformed foot soldiers. Sonia liked the swagger. She wore the brown shirt, she learned the drills, she supported the fastest possible expansion of Jewish territory, with violence if need be. In Warsaw, when she saw the great man in the crowd at the convention, Sonia went up and introduced herself. She stood before the comrade of Joseph Trumpeldor and proudly informed him that she was a Kohen from Rakov, a Zionist and a loyal member of Betar. One day soon she would make aliyah and fight the good fight in Eretz Israel.

Sonia never said what Jabotinsky replied to her—but he must have been impressed. Strong willed and beautiful, warm, confident, single-minded, Sonia was the female soul of Zionism. Who wouldn't want her marching in their army? Though she was the baby of the family—seven years younger than her married sister, Doba, forever quarreling with the skinny, brittle middle sister Etl—Sonia was no baby. She knew exactly what she wanted. Like her cousin Chaim, she had attended the Tarbut school in Vilna. She had no desire, however, for Doba's comfortable life in Vilna with a husband and baby. If she stayed in Rakov she knew she would get sucked into the never-ending fuss over finding a match for Etl and the never-ending worry over the leather business. She had no stomach for such things. Sonia was a good daughter to Beyle and Shalom Tvi. She tried to be an observant Jew like her parents, but it would kill her to spend her days selling belts and harnesses to Belarusian peasants and her Shabbats gossiping in the women's section at shul. She endured life in exile only because she knew it would end. The economic crash of 1929 blew past her—Rakov was hit especially hard since the Soviets had sealed the border to Minsk and put an end to the lucrative smuggling operations. Sonia, however, was not thinking about the economy. The only news that mattered to her was about the unrest in the Land. Lots of other pretty young girls in Rakov called themselves Zionists—they sang "Hatikva" and danced the hora in the parlor of the haberdasher's house on Zaslavi Street and flirted with the Zionist boys. Sonia was not flirting. She spoke perfect Hebrew. She had met Jabotinsky and gotten his blessing. She devoured the letters that Chaim sent the family from Herzliya. Where one cousin led, the other would follow.

But first she had to convince her parents to let her go.

For all the fine Zionist rhetoric about absolute equality between men and women, a daughter was still a daughter. Chaim had departed for Palestine to a chorus of Hebrew folk songs and a flourish of handkerchiefs. When Sonia's time came there would be tears.

Sonia turned twenty-two the spring of 1932—old enough to decide her own fate. *Maybe too old to be a fresh wife*, the yentas whispered behind her back—though in truth she had never been more beautiful. Her step was light, her body supple, her skin clear and glowing, her smile, on the rare occasions she allowed herself to smile, warm and inviting. She was a graduate of the Tarbut Gymnasium in Vilna. She spoke Hebrew with her Zionist friends, Yiddish at home, Polish in the shops. She read Tolstoy, Chekov, and Turgenev in Russian. But now she was through with Yiddish and Russian. She was through with Poland. She was through with servants, coffeehouses, forests, rivers, mushrooms, snow, cemeteries shrouded in pine shadow, forbidden churches with their icons and stained glass. Sonia had made up her mind to go to Palestine. But she couldn't leave without her family's blessing.

Shalom Tvi and Beyle had no problem with their daughter's Zionist views, at least in theory. Shalom Tvi shared her enthusiasm for Jabotinsky's Revisionist Party and often spoke of making aliyah himself one day. But it was one thing to let her go to meetings, sing the folk songs, dance the hora, wear the shirt—and another to let her risk her life alone and unprotected in the wilds of Palestine. They were a family of worriers. How could they take this calmly? Shalom Tvi worried about how a girl with no skills or experience could support herself over there. Etl, competitive and envious, worried that she'd end up an old maid in dreary Rakov while her younger sister played under the palm trees. Soft-hearted teary Doba worried that she'd never see her again. Her mother worried about everything else—what she would wear, what she would eat, whether she would be happy so far from home, how she would survive the malaria, the cholera, the heat, the Arabs. Their life was comfortable in Rakov. Did Sonia have any idea how much she would suffer in Palestine?

Sonia knew the path she had chosen was the right one; she had perfect faith in herself; there was nothing else she wanted out of life. Wasn't that enough? When a son made aliyah, he packed his bags, promised to write, and set off. For a daughter it was a never-ending opera of hand-wringing and second-guessing.

Toward the end there were raised voices and slammed doors. A terrible row blew up between Etl and Sonia that would haunt them both forever. The parents withdrew into sighs and tears. There was endless bureaucratic delay and confusion about securing a visa. In the wake of the 1929 riots, the British had begun to backpedal on their liberal policy toward

Jewish immigration to Palestine and by 1932 the visa process had become a nightmare. But the family was worse than any bureaucrat. Every time Sonia raised the subject, they came up with another reason to delay—or cancel. Guilt flowed in a torrent. How could she leave her aging mother? How would Etl find a husband when she had to spend all her time looking after the house and tending to the business? And what about Doba? Had Sonia forgotten that her sister was pregnant with her second child? Why not put off the trip until the next year so she could attend the bris of her new nephew? Her mother would die of grief. Her father would bankrupt himself sending her money. She'd have to turn right around and run home. She was being irrational. She'd regret it forever. She had no idea what she was letting herself in for.

"I was twenty one and a half when I left home in Rakov," Sonia told her children many years later (in fact, she was a year older). "I behaved like a grown-up and did not take a cent from my parents. I did not want to, saying that I would work hard, that I would do laundry for money. I did many loads of laundry in Herzliya as well as Kfar Vitkin—I did not mind."

And so with her own money and her own fierce will, Sonia finally made it happen. Since the entry visa proved to be impossible to obtain, Sonia figured out a way to duck under the red tape by pretending to travel as a tourist. She and four friends bought round-trip tickets with a tour company called Totzeret HaAretz (Produce in the Land) for 500 zlotys (the Polish currency) each (a considerable sum at a time when the average Polish worker earned 125z a month). Their plan was to use the tour company to get into the Middle East and then, in effect, jump ship. Sonia went to Vilna in the first days of August 1932 to spend a few days with Doba before setting out. "Difficult mood," Etl wrote of the departure from home. Doba's husband, Shepseleh, had agreed to accompany Sonia to Warsaw and put her and her companions on a train bound for the Romanian port of Constanta (the same port that Chaim had sailed from). But Sonia was sulky and tense the whole time and Shepseleh's feelings were hurt. He could not understand the foul humor. At the Warsaw train station, Sonia shrugged him off, boarded the Romanian-bound train with her friends, stowed her luggage, and tried to ignore her racing heart. Her brother-in-law's long, pale, mournful face appeared at the window before slipping away behind her. After Warsaw petered out, the green Polish countryside swallowed them up. The girls made a point of conversing in Hebrew.

At Constanta one of the fathers was on hand to see them from the train station to the port and get them settled on a steamer bound for Lebanon. Sonia's spirits lifted as soon as she boarded. It was August 9, high summer on the Black Sea, and the ship's deck was full of ruddy sailors and dashing young fellows in fedoras. The girls posed for snapshots clutching armfuls of exotic fruit—bananas, grapes, lemons, something spherical that might be a melon. A first taste of the Mediterranean. When the ship docked in Beirut, the captain reminded the tour-group passengers of the standard terms: they had been required to prepay for the round-trip, but not a single groszy of the five-hundred-zloty fare would be refunded for unused return tickets. So they had a choice: go back to Poland after their visit to Palestine or lose their money. It was not the first time nor would it be the last that a Jew was bilked for the privilege of immigrating to the Promised Land. The girls disembarked on the Beirut pier and disappeared into the crowd.

Somehow they found a driver who agreed to take them down the coast to Haifa. The tourist visas sufficed to get them into the British Protectorate at Rosh HaNikra, a settlement in the extreme northwest corner of Palestine—and once they were across the border, no one bothered about their status. As soon as they were safely past the checkpoint, the driver pulled over and told the girls to get out of the car. They must have a look at the most spectacular view in the world. White chalk cliffs tumbled into the sea below; before them, the land relaxed in a wide fertile plain that paralleled the coast on one side and rose on the other side into low hazy mountains that veiled the mysterious east; to the south, where their journey led, beckoned the long blue arc of Haifa Bay. When they had stood long enough to gaze their fill and shed tears and embrace each other and murmur about the homeland, the friends returned to the taxi and continued on to Haifa. The road was appalling, the houses and people and animals outside the car windows unbelievably strange and alarming, the air blowing in intolerably hot. Finally the driver stopped in the center of Haifa and the five of them and a small mountain of their luggage tumbled out. A taxi was maybe not the most glorious way to make aliyah—but they had done it.

Sonia's cousin Ruth, one of the girls in the group, had a relative in Haifa named Hinda, who would put them up, but Ruth had no idea where Hinda lived. She and Sonia wandered around in the heat and glare hoping to bump into her. Palm trees, whitewashed houses, strands of riotous bougainvillea, Jews in shorts and sandals, Arabs driving mule carts and camels, British soldiers hanging from their jeeps—all the clamorous life of the port revolved around them in a dizzying montage. Finally they screwed up their courage and approached a woman pushing a baby carriage; Ruth asked her in Yiddish if she happened to know her cousin Hinda—a recent arrival from Poland with six children. Haifa's Jewish community was not so large in those days. The woman not only knew Hinda but also offered to bring them to her house. Sonia thanked God that she would not be spending her first night in the Land sleeping on a park bench. Hinda welcomed them, gave them tea, and found them a room in a seaside hotel, since there was not an inch to spare in her own house. Sonia filled a few days with sightseeing, sunbathing, and writing letters to Rakov and Vilna. She had ascended to the Land; now she had to find a way to live there.

Rakov, September 4, 1932

Dear Sonia,

Yesterday we received your letter and we were very disappointed. We did not expect such a letter from you. You traveled the world, you saw various towns and many new things. You have been in Eretz Israel a week already, and yet you still were not in the mood to write and describe anything to us. Not a hair of joy in your letter. In every one else who arrives in the Eretz, one detects a spark of joy, but in your letters one does not see any eagerness or happiness and we regret that we had let you go. I understand that you feel depressed. I saw on the page of the letter that you tried to write to me in Polish but changed your mind. Next time write to me separately. Write about everything, good or bad.

Your letter has saddened us a great deal. How did you spend the time on Shabbat? Write about your impressions. Travel to meet with your acquaintances and take care of yourself. Father is also writing.

Your sister, Etl

My dear daughter Sonia!

According to your letter, nothing interesting is happening to you, while others who have come to the Land write with awe and elation. Don't worry. Look at everything and see where you want to settle, whether a village or a town. If it does not work, don't worry about expenses. You can spend a month there and then come back home. We will be glad to take you back.

You have not written to us how you felt being alone and where you were on Shabbat.

Do not lose your spirit.

Your loving father

CHAPTER TWELVE

IN LOVE
IN THE LAND

Nothing was as Sonia had imagined. Haifa was hot and beautiful but it was far from the agricultural settlements and the harbor was full of noise from the British dredging project. The people went about their business like people everywhere—not like blessed dwellers in the Promised Land. Where was the fire and passion that Jabotinsky had spoken of? Where were the Hebrew foot soldiers poised to claim the soil from Dan to Beersheba? Jabotinsky said you had to pay for the homeland with blood, but all she saw in Haifa were industrious citizens trying to make a living. Sonia paid for her room and left the hotel in Haifa, she said good-bye to her cousin Ruth and Hinda and the six children, she took the bus to Herzliya, where Chaim had been living and working for the past three years. She knew her family would be furious when they learned that she had separated from Ruth, but Sonia was prepared to brave their wrath. She had not come to the Eretz to live in a city. In Herzliya there were *halutzim* and *halutzot* working the land, bringing life where there had been only waste and desolation. She had to go and see this new thing for herself.

She got out of the bus at the side of the sun-bleached Haifa-to-Tel-Aviv road and walked the rest of the way through the dunes to Herzliya. The place looked to her like the ends of the earth—sandy, desolate, with no shade. The parched fields and orchards and naked housing blocks withered in the sun. Chaim was nowhere to be found. The other settlers gave her a funny look when she asked for him. Did he have a girlfriend? Was he secretly married? Sonia explained that she was his cousin, fresh off the boat from Poland, as if that weren't obvious. They gave her a room for the night; it was stifling hot inside so she threw open the windows and collapsed into bed. "I had no idea that there were a lot of mosquitoes," she said later. "When I woke up the next morning, I was unrecognizable, swollen from being covered with mosquito bites and with a very high fever. It was terrible!" In her delirium Sonia heard one woman cluck to another in Yiddish, "How am I going to write a letter to her parents in Rakov to tell them their daughter just arrived and is no longer with us?"

Sonia did not die. Chaim turned up and welcomed her properly to Eretz Israel. Sonia had a letter for him—really just a few words that her father wanted her to pass along.

Greetings to my dear nephew, Chaim Binie.

I would like to ask you to write to us about Sonia and her future. We wonder if she will she be able to get along there, although she is not talented working with her hands.

Your uncle Shalom Tvi Kaganovich

Not exactly a vote of confidence from the folks back home.

Chaim had been eighteen, Sonia fourteen when they last saw each other. Now, eight years later, in the full glare of Palestine's summer sun, they sized each other up awkwardly—cousins, fellow Zionists, but semi-strangers. Sonia felt like a child next to this brown muscular *halutz*. He knew how to farm, shoot a gun, fix a broken irrigation pipe, and coax a wheezy engine to life; he had friends, comrades in Haganah, and no doubt a girlfriend—maybe several. She could tell from the way he looked at her that he was surprised, but she couldn't tell by what. That she was now almost as tall as he was? That she had become a dark graceful beauty? That her parents had allowed her to make aliyah even though she had no talent with her hands? Maybe he was wondering what he was going to do with her. As a cousin he would feel obliged to look after her, make sure she didn't get into trouble, help her find work, keep the comrades off her. Maybe he didn't think she would be worth the effort. Maybe Chaim, like her father, was wondering if she would be "able to get along there."

Sonia had used up her own money to get to Palestine. Now that she was here in Herzliya, how was she going to support herself? Asking her family was out of the question. She would never go begging, especially after the letters they were writing. *We regret that we had let you go. If it does not work, spend a month there and then come back home.* She'd sooner die. But how was she going to live?

She considered enrolling in the First Agricultural School for Women that feminist-Zionist Chana Meisel had founded a few years earlier at Nahalal in the Jezreel Valley. Meisel took shtetl girls like Sonia, turned them into real *halutzot*, and helped them find places on collective farms. If she stayed on at Herzliya, she'd be stuck in the kitchen and the laundry. Sonia had eyes—she saw how it was: men working in the fields, women chopping onions and scrubbing shirts. Forget what they said back in Poland about equality between *halutzim* and *halutzot*. Here in the Land, when it came down to dividing the work and the glory, the *halutz* was the hero and the *halutza* was the cook, the maid, the laundress, and, once she married, Comrade So-and-so's wife and the mother of his kids. If Sonia wanted to plow and plant and reap and harvest, the other women told her, she should go to Nahalal and take Chana Meisel's course. Otherwise she'd better get herself a few more aprons and a pair of rubber gloves.

Sonia was torn. It bothered her how the bitter women in the kitchen slapped the plates down in front of the male farmworkers and glared at them when they fell on their food. Sonia liked to see a hungry man eat a big meal. Though she chafed to be out working the land herself, she didn't feel demeaned by cooking or doing laundry. It was not in her nature to resent or put herself forward. She was not a complainer. She had come to the Land to work—and if they had her doing women's work, so be it. She didn't expect to have it easy. She didn't *want* to have it easy. Sonia didn't need to plow and sweat beside the men to feel like a pioneer. She was strong—her respect came from within.

Sonia was not always happy in Palestine, but from the moment she set foot there she felt at home. If she missed her parents and sisters, if she suffered in the climate, if she was bored by the endless loads of laundry, if she pined for the life outside the Land, she kept it to herself.

And so in the end she decided not to enroll in Chana Meisel's First Agricultural School for Women. Besides, if she left Herzliya, she wouldn't see much of Chaim anymore.

———

Rakov, Rosh Hashanah [September 30], 1932
Leshanah Tovah Tikateivu

To my dear daughter Mistress Sonia,

Write to us about where you live and how much it costs and about the food, too. Are you renting a room with meals or are you cooking for yourself? Will you settle in a village or a town? Write about whether you are getting used to the weather, to the life and to the food in the Eretz. Our only pleasure now is to hear good things from you, and may be the hope that one day we shall all be together.

Write to the family in America to let them know where you are.

May your wishes come true.

Your father, Shalom Tvi Kaganovich

To my dear nephew, Chaim B.

I thank you for the help and care you have extended to Sonia. We are grateful from afar. May be, some day we shall live near you and then will repay you. See to it that she settles in a village or a town, whichever she prefers.

Shalom Tvi Kaganovich

After Rosh Hashanah, a month went by with no letter from Rakov. Not even a postcard. By the third week, Sonia was starting to imagine disasters. Finally, in the first week of November, a letter from Etl arrived explaining everything.

In August, soon after Sonia left, Shepseleh had brought his four-year-old son Shimon—Shimonkeh, they always called him—to Rakov for a long visit with the family there. Since Doba was close to term in her second pregnancy and in no condition to travel, she remained in Vilna by herself. It seemed like a good arrangement for everyone: Doba would get a rest before the new baby was born, and Shimonkeh and his father would walk in the woods, breathe the clean air, dabble their feet in the lake, and go to shul with Shalom Tvi. Shepseleh filled the idle hours playing chess—he was a renowned chess master and he taught anyone who was interested how to play, even the priest from the Polish church. Shepseleh returned to Vilna before Rosh Hashanah, leaving the boy behind in Rakov for a little more spoiling by his grandparents. And spoil him they did. Every morning Shimonkeh woke up shouting, "Savtah [grandmother], give me latkes!" and even though latkes were typically served only on Hanukkah, Beyle complied. On Shabbat Beyle had to explain that there would be no latkes that day since it was forbidden to cook on the Sabbath. The next morning, Sunday, the boy told his grandmother solemnly: "Savtah, make a lot of latkes so there will be enough for tomorrow in case it will be Shabbat again." Beyle and Shalom Tvi laughed till the tears ran. Shalom Tvi recounted the whole thing in a letter to Doba and she wept with laughter too. "What can I say," Doba wrote Sonia from Vilna, "Shimonkeh, may he be healthy, is the greatest joy of my life."

On Erev Yom Kippur, the boy fell seriously ill with scarlet fever and the house went into an uproar. Beyle had never forgiven herself for the death of Feigele—her youngest daughter, who had come down with scarlet fever during the war and poisoned herself by swallowing down all her medicine at once—and now she had another sick four-year-old on her hands. The same age—the same disease. Not, she prayed fervently to God, the same outcome. Beyle decreed that her grandson must be watched day and night.

On November 6, Etl sat down and described the whole ordeal in a letter to Sonia:

Shimonkeh's condition deteriorated quickly and his temperature went up to more than 40 degrees (C) [104 degrees Fahrenheit]. We wrote to Shepseleh immediately, but he could not come because of Doba and to her we said nothing.

The ailment had affected the child's heart, and when he worsened, we asked a doctor from Vilna to come. The doctor came here on the first day of Succot [October 15], and Shimonkeh's condition did not please him. You cannot imagine how much we had suffered. We did not think about the Holiday, we forgot to eat and to sleep. We did not think we could make it through. There was simply a panic in the little town. Our house had turned into a quarantine. No one could come inside except for the family. For two weeks I did not take off my clothes and did not sleep at night.

The child was "already 99 percent in the world to come" but he lived, "thank God," Etl continued. "While I am writing to you, he is sitting in bed, playing and singing his songs. He is so weak that he cannot stand on his own. He needs to be kept and watched for six more weeks and when he is well I will take him to Vilna." Etl, who had a bit of a sour streak, could not help adding, "In the future I will not take care of a child who is not mine."

Etl saved the good news for last. On October 28, Doba had given birth to her baby—another son whom they named Wolf, after Shepseleh's grandfather. The family had a weakness for diminutives, and Wolf inevitably became Velveleh or Volinkeh. He was fretful but very beautiful, with black hair and a round cherubic face.

November 20, 1932

My dear daughter Sonia!

Let us hope that your decision will turn out well and that you will not lose your courage. In any case, if things are not as successful as you hope, you can always come back to your own room, you are certainly not superfluous here.

Even if you do not find work quickly, don't worry about spending a few dollars—you need to gird yourself with patience—it is not so terrible. I remember that even in America, a few months passed before they were able to find work.

It is autumn here now and the weather is damp. Maybe business will start to improve. The gentiles scream about how expensive leather goods are and how they have to part with a whole cow for a single pair of boots. But what can one do?

Be healthy and with the help of God may you be happy.

Your father, Shalom Tvi Kaganovich

Doba "cried and laughed from happiness" when Etl returned her firstborn to her early in January 1933. "At first I did not recognize him he had grown up so much," Doba wrote to Sonia. "His language and mind are like that of a mature man." Shimonkeh quizzed his parents about the tiny howling black-haired stranger who had been acquired during his absence. *You should have bought a larger size*, the boy told his mother, *because this one cries too much at night.* "He asked me how much I had paid for the baby. I said, '120 gulden.' He said it was too much, I should only have paid 30 gulden." Winter gripped the north, and Etl wrote to complain of the endless boring nights. "No one to go see, and nothing to do. . . . The season is dead. . . . I am sick of this way of life. . . . Rakov, literally, is fading from day to day." It was frigid but no snow fell. Twice a week friends came to play lotto, but the company barely made a dent in the frozen boredom. Bitter that she had yet to find a husband at the age of twenty-five, Etl pined for a match but "the situation" never came to a head. "It is hard to choose," she lamented. "When you look into the depths of each one separately, it seems that they are all lost." As winter dragged on, Etl pointedly reminded Sonia of how lucky she was to be in sunny Palestine: "I simply envy you that you enjoy life more than I do. What can one see here in Rakov? Whereas there [in Palestine] for a few coins you can go to town or to a settlement, meet with friends, meet new people and generally see what goes on in God's world. Here, even if you want to spend a little money, there is nothing to buy." Etl was furious to learn that the friend who was supposed to deliver some nice sausage and kishkes that they had made for Sonia had eaten them all herself. "Of course it was utter rudeness."

From Vilna, Doba also complained, but in a fond maternal way, of the mischief and noise that the boys raised. They had taken to calling Velveleh, the younger boy, "Bandit" because he was such a little outlaw. Still, the baby was "one of the best" and Shimonkeh, now fully recovered, was showing great talent in music. "He is the best singer in kindergarten and knows all the songs." Shalom Tvi wrote to remind his daughter to follow the traditions and observances of her people: "We are asking you, my dear daughter, not to stray from the ways of behavior that you learned at home. Rest on holy days and on Shabbat. Keep the Pessach rituals as you have done at home. Be careful to eat kosher food, and avoid whoever transgresses in any of these things. Thus you shall be loved by God and by people, and everyone will esteem you more for it and you can be proud."

Each one of them repeatedly urged Sonia to tell the "whole truth" when she wrote them individually, even if she might varnish things a bit when she wrote to the others. Yet all of them carefully varnished the situation in Poland. They wrote about their daily joys and trials—children, holidays, clothing, gifts, money, gossip, weather, the foibles of their neighbors and friends—but almost nothing about what was happening outside their kitchens and bedrooms. Shepseleh mentioned that he was looking for better work or more work; Shalom Tvi vaguely let drop that "business worsens" because "the situation is bad." Rakov was "getting even smaller" as young people left for Russia, for Palestine, for anyplace else where they might make a better living. But the letters from Vilna and Rakov were entirely silent about the growing anti-Semitism of Polish newspapers and politicians, the mounting calls for Jews to get out of Poland, the attacks on Jewish culture, Jewish institutions, even on the use of Yiddish. It was impossible to travel without seeing the slogans "Poland for the Poles" and "Ours to Ours" plastered on buildings and walls, but no one spoke of this in a letter to Sonia. "Remember that it's not good to save on food," Etl wrote on January 31, 1933. "Keep your health. We do not play lotto any more. People are confused and they do not get together." Not a word about the fact that Adolf Hitler had been appointed Reich chancellor the previous day in Berlin. "People say that Feytzeh [one of the girls Sonia had traveled to Palestine with] has a fiancé and will marry soon," Etl ends the letter. "Tell me if it is true."

Rakov was emptying steadily of Jews, and the Polish authorities were glad to be rid of them. In fact, it was becoming state policy: Jews were not Poles and never could be; they had brought down the economy through their stranglehold on Polish business; they should self-deport voluntarily. Neither Shalom Tvi nor Shepseleh spoke of these matters in their letters to Sonia, but they both felt the sting. Shepseleh dropped wistful hints about moving to the Land one day. He could learn Hebrew and a little English and set up as an accountant or small businessman. What did Sonia think? "We are waiting for Etl's lottery ticket to win at least a few thousand dollars," Shalom Tvi wrote to his daughter on February 2, "and then we shall all get out and come to you. Write to us and tell us how much land for cultivation costs. It may suit us to buy a parcel somewhere over there and then we could all live together."

Six months earlier they had bitterly opposed her decision to make aliyah. Now they were dreaming—idly dreaming—of joining her.

Spring came to Herzliya and Sonia breathed the perfume of orange blossoms for the first time. She had made up her mind to stay on in the settlement and was now working in the citrus groves. Her days were pruning, irrigating, weeding, spraying; her nights were singing with the other young people or collapsing in exhaustion. She had gotten a room of her own—a spotless cubicle decorated with linens embroidered by Etl and a red tablecloth that her mother had lovingly packed and shipped to her. She was happy and glowing with health. Sonia fit in well at Herzliya, even though the flagrant irreverence of the *halutzim* offended her. The guys around her were godless, anti-kosher, horny, tough, and entitled—she was forever fighting them off. Luckily, she had Chaim to look out for her. "It seems that of all our young women, you have succeeded the most," Etl wrote her on March 20, "and all is thanks to Chaim."

In fact, Sonia and Chaim had fallen in love. It must have started at a dance. Handsome Chaim danced her off her feet, then tried to dance between her legs. Sonia was four years younger and a decade less experienced, but she was old enough to know that Chaim was the one. She liked his brusque brazen manner and his way of overwhelming her with his need. She liked how competent and cocky he was. She liked how his brown chest showed at his open shirt and how he grinned at her when he'd had a few beers. Sonia was not a drinker. Her idea of a good time was a walk through the orchards and a big meal prepared by her. She was conservative by nature, maybe a little frightened of too much freedom. Having broken with everything familiar, she now craved stability. She never really strayed from the Judaism she was raised with. Chaim was not religious but that didn't matter. He was part of her past; it felt right they should make a future together. Talk of Chaim's old girlfriend stopped. If anyone thought it was strange for first cousins to have a romance, they kept it to themselves. The family was overjoyed, if a bit mystified, at how quickly they had reached an agreement. "I believe that this is your free will and that you are not forcing yourself," Etl, ever skeptical, wrote soon after Purim (March 12 that year). "Chaim is one of us, we know where he comes from, we've heard so much about him and everybody praises him. With someone like that you can peacefully build your life. We on our side will help you build your house, which, with time, will also be ours."

The house Etl wrote of was not just a fantasy. After nine years in Palestine working on land that belonged to others, Chaim had found a place of his own. In a sense this was another family endeavor—only the family involved were not blood relatives but comrades, fellow *halutzim*. Four years earlier, a group of twenty-one Labor Zionists (nineteen bachelors and one married couple) had been allocated land by the Jewish National Fund for a new cooperative farming village—a moshav—up the coast from Herzliya. They named the settlement Kfar (village) Vitkin, after early Zionist visionary Josef Vitkin who had preached "the conquest of labor through the conquest of the soil." Kfar Vitkin was the perfect next step for Chaim. One of the founders was a comrade from the Volozhin HeHalutz, and friends from the Kinneret and Herzliya were relocating there.

The moshav's balance of the communal and the individual also appealed to Chaim. On a kibbutz, he would have surrendered all autonomy to the group: he would work on rotating shifts assigned by committee, eat his meals in a group dining hall, have his kids raised communally. On an individual farm, he'd be totally on his own—no backup, no safety net, no protection against raids, no hedge against market fluctuations. But a moshav like Kfar Vitkin combined the best of both worlds. Chaim would have his own plot of land (identical in size and quality to those of the other moshavniks); he'd live in his own house, grow his own crops, bring up his children under his own roof. The personal was private at Kfar Vitkin, but the economic was communal. Whatever was needed to run the farms—fertilizer, feed, seed, water—the moshavniks purchased collectively; what they produced, they sold collectively. When someone got sick, members pitched in to help out the family. When a new baby was born, women covered for each other. When the founding generation died, the land would pass undivided to one member of the next generation. New moshavniks were accepted when a parcel fell empty—but under no circumstances could land be transferred to an Arab. The arrangement suited Chaim ideally. The question was whether it would suit Sonia.

Sonia had come to Palestine not as a Labor Zionist *halutzah* but as a Jabotinskyite bent on rapid, armed expansion of Jewish territory in Palestine. Chaim and Sonia may have been first cousins, but politically they belonged to different "families." This was no small matter in interwar Palestine, where ideology and affection were so tightly intertwined that they fused into a single thread binding every aspect of life. Sonia obeyed her father's injunction to observe the Sabbath and keep to "the ways of behavior that you learned at home"; it bothered her even to be in the presence of nonkosher food. Chaim never went to synagogue if he could avoid it, ate what he pleased, and celebrated not with fasting and prayer but with carousing all night with friends and girlfriends. Sonia had had little experience with men. Etl warned her sister pointedly to hold fast to her modesty, "because there are plenty of evil guys [over there]. Stay away from unfit elements. Don't 'fly' too much because it is not too late for your wedding." The family in Rakov clearly had no idea of all the flying Chaim had done. When Etl got an inkling of how irreligious and "licentious" most of the *halutzim* were, she suffered a "crisis of faith regarding Eretz Israel." "They live there almost like in Russia," she wrote Sonia in disgust, "but are covered with the national mask." In other words, beneath the appearance of working for the Jewish homeland, the socialist Zionists were no better than Bolsheviks in their promiscuity and atheism. Etl may not have realized that she was describing Chaim to a *T*, but Sonia did.

Was it a love match? Sonia had left home in anger, having quarreled with Etl and defied her parents. She had not quite burned her bridges, but she was far too proud ever to return to Rakov with her tail between her legs. The life in Palestine, much as she loved the Land, was not what she had expected. How long would she have been able to fend off the "evil guys" if Chaim hadn't been there?

Sonia was a dreamer, but she was also a survivor. "She was very beautiful," her daughter Leah said many years later when asked whether her parents' marriage was a happy one. "And she and Chaim fell in love. There was not time to be happy—they worked so hard, they lived in such bad conditions. Our mother was very strong."

Sonia and Chaim came to an agreement in the spring of 1933. Chaim had already bought in at Kfar Vitkin and there was much talk about the house he would build there—*our* house. "But," as Shalom Tvi wrote to Sonia at the end of April, "the obvious problem is the money."

September 21, 1933
Rosh Hashanah Eve, Rakov

My dear daughter!

It is hard to believe that we have not seen you for over a year. We need to believe that everything will settle, that we all will be healthy and will hear good things from you all. Doba and the children are in our house now and it makes us happier. Volinkeh, the little one, is a good boy, very active, and Shimonkeh is already a young man.

Be healthy. From your mother Beyle.

Dear Aunt Sonia,

I wish you Shanah Tova, be healthy and eat many cakes and sweets.

Shimonkeh

In 1933, Yom Kippur fell on the last day of September, a Saturday, and Abraham as usual had spent the day in shul with his son Sam and his son-in-law Sam Epstein, Ethel's husband. The men didn't talk business on their way to shul—the sons knew better than to raise the subject on the holiest day of the year—but they all thanked God silently that business was a little better. Franklin Delano Roosevelt had taken office in March and everybody said the new president was going to turn the country around. Abraham heard what everybody said but privately he had his doubts. The scourge would end when Hashem, not man, decreed.

A few days after Yom Kippur a letter from Rakov arrived for Abraham— a letter from Shalom Tvi. Though the brothers had not seen each other for twenty-four years, a letter was always a big deal—something to study line by line and pass from hand to hand and talk about until they had savored and digested every precious morsel. This letter was particularly juicy. It seemed that the niece and nephew who had moved to the Land were going to be married. Cousins marrying cousins—it was not forbidden in the law, and Shalom Tvi had given his blessing. Now he wanted his brother's blessing as well, the blessing of the patriarch. Chaim already had a plot of land to cultivate—the boy had become skilled at farming and had chosen his land carefully. But before he could bring his bride there, he needed to build a house, and to build a house required money. Shalom Tvi had asked Sonia and Chaim to write a letter requesting Abraham's assistance, but in case the young people were too shy, Shalom Tvi was taking the task on himself. Could a brother help this niece and nephew in the Land? It would be a mitzvah if he sent two hundred dollars so Chaim and Sonia could build their house at Kfar Vitkin.

Abraham took up his pen and wrote back to his brother right away. *Tell the children to write me everything about their land, their house, when they intend to plant. Do not worry, I will send them the money.* He found his checkbook and wrote out a check for two hundred dollars—worth more than three thousand dollars today—and sent it to Chaim in Palestine.

October 3, 1933

My dear daughter Sonia! Leshannah Tova Tikateivu.

We have received your letter and we are glad that you are content. With God's help may you live in the Land all your life, glad and content.

Now I will write about us. Business is still getting worse and we have also lost dollars from Etl's dowry. Even when we receive a few dollars from America, they have lost a third of their value by the time they get here. I wrote to America and requested a large check, but it seems to me that they will not send it. They need to leave some money in the bank for themselves. The head is splitting with thoughts of what to do.

As for Shepseleh, his business is not successful. There is nothing for him and Doba to do in Vilna. He is searching for ways to go to Eretz Israel.

I have a question for you. Each settlement must have shop keepers, right? Since you are building a new settlement, maybe we could come and start a store there. Think about all of this and weigh it carefully. We are counting the days until we can be together.

Be healthy. I wish you a happy new year.

From me, your father Shalom Tvi Kaganovich

On December 7, 1933, eight years to the day before the Japanese attacked Pearl Harbor, Sonia and Chaim stood side by side under the chuppah (bridal canopy) while their *ketubah* (Jewish nuptial document) was read aloud. The vows were exchanged, the glass was smashed underfoot, the wine was drunk, the feast consumed, and the guests split into circles to dance the pulse-quickening Zionist folk dances of love and hope and solidarity. The first cousins were now husband and wife.

Shalom Tvi had urged his new son-in-law to build a house with an extra room so he and Beyle and Etl could stay with them if they came to Palestine, but Chaim did not have the means to take this advice. Even with the two hundred American dollars sent by his uncle Abraham in

New York, he had only enough money for a kitchen, a bathroom, and a bedroom, all made of cinder block covered with stucco. But there was space to expand—someday. Chaim situated the house at the top of the property, near the road, with a porch at the back overlooking the chicken coop, the toolshed, a couple of acres of fields, and beyond that, a blue slice of the sea. The plot of land he had been assigned by the moshav committee—a long narrow parcel that dropped off gradually from front to back—was near the village center and across the street from the site of the future synagogue. In fifteen minutes he and Sonia could walk over the dunes and be on the beach. From the still unpaved street their neighborhood looked almost like a working-class suburban subdivision—houses and shacks set close together, each with its bit of front garden—but every house had a farm field behind it and there were larger tracts set aside around the margins for orchards and citrus groves. Chaim and Sonia planted two olive trees on either side of their front yard, a symbol of peace and a pledge to the future. All the moshavniks did the same. One day the olive boughs would knit together in a continuous band of silvery green, living proof that the land was truly and forever theirs.

Chaim and Sonia had missed out on the precarious first three years, when the moshav barely clung to life, but their neighbors told stories. Back in the autumn of 1929, when the first settlers had led a convoy of borrowed horses, carts, and plows onto the fields, Bedouin Arab sharecroppers from the surrounding lands of Wadi al-Hawarith rushed out waving sticks and shouting at them to leave. All work came to a halt. The settlers went out the next day and tried a different section, but the same thing happened. "We went back to Hadera in a somber mood to await further instructions," one of the men wrote in his diary. "We were there mainly to reinforce the fact that the land had been bought by Jews and was Jewish land."

Jews may have bought the land for Kfar Vitkin, but the Bedouin farmers refused to concede that it was now "Jewish land." In fact, this parcel had been plagued with tension for decades, and the arrival of Zionist pioneers only exacerbated it. In 1870, a prosperous Lebanese Maronite named Anton Bishara Tayan purchased the 30,000 dunams (7,500 acres) of Wadi al-Hawarith and ran it as a tenant farm. Tayan built a large square lime-stone farmhouse, dug a well, planted an orchard, and hired local Bedouins to farm and graze some of the acreage. But Tayan's tenancy was not peaceful. When the Bedouin tenants felt that their rents were too high, they clogged Tayan's well and uprooted his trees; on one occasion a Bedouin woman struck the landlord and drove him off when he came to collect his share of the harvest. By some accounts, Tayan ceased to collect his tithe regularly because the amount was so trivial and the tenants so intractable. By the 1920s, Tayan's heirs, now scattered over three continents and saddled with their father's considerable debts, were compelled to mortgage the land. When the Nablus District Court ordered Wadi al-Hawarith to be sold at public auction in 1928, the Jewish National Fund (the arm of the Zionist Organization in charge of land purchases) moved quickly—and perhaps unscrupulously—to snap it up. The land was especially desirable to the JNF because it was the first sizable chunk of the northern coastal plain to become available for Jewish settlement: its purchase gave the Jews a strategic foothold on the coast.

The tenant farmers fought the sale of Wadi al-Hawarith not only with sticks and shouts but in court. The crux of the legal dispute involved two laws intended to protect the rights of the indigenous people who worked and lived off the land: one was the right of first purchase under Ottoman law (still for the most part "the basis of justice" in Mandate Palestine), which should have given the Bedouins an opportunity to buy the land before it was put on the public market; the second was the Protection of Cultivators Ordinance of 1929 (amended in 1931), which sheltered tenant farmers from immediate dispossession and required them to be compensated "on their receiving valid notice" to leave. Since the JNF had purchased the land "directly through the courts," these rights were annulled. The Bedouins countered that this was a bit of legal chicanery that trampled on their long-standing tribal practices. The Mandate government offered to help relocate the Bedouins to another parcel fifty miles away and the Zionists tried to strike a compromise whereby the tenants could lease back some of the land on a temporary basis, but the Bedouins categorically rejected these offers: their livelihood, their culture, their identity depended on *this* piece of land. It was Wadi al-Hawarith or nothing. The two sides were deadlocked, and they have remained deadlocked over these same issues ever since.

When the tenant farmers persisted in their refusal to leave, the JNF

Shimon Dov, a Torah scribe in the yeshiva town of Volozhin in the second half of the nineteenth century, who was the son, father, and grandfather of scribes.

מצבה כו שבט תרס ד תנצבה

Beyle, Shimon Dov's wife and the mother of his six children, who supported the family on the proceeds of her small grocery store.

A contemporary view of the Volozhin yeshiva, Europe's most esteemed and influential center of Torah study for much of the nineteenth century.

A composite portrait, assembled from three different photos, of Abraham Cohen and family. From left to right: Lillie, Abraham, Sarah, Anna; Hyman (inserted from a different photo) at the center; then Sam (in bow tie), Harry (seated), Ethel, William (seated with his son, Lewis, on his lap), and Itel.

Hyman, the youngest of Abraham and Sarah's three sons, at the time of his bar mitzvah in Rakov in 1905.

Brothers Harry (seated) and Hyman, who apprenticed together in 1906 at a clock-making shop in Smargon, Russia.

Though the boys ran the business, Abraham kept the boys from killing one another. His portrait was always prominently displayed in the showroom.

From left to right: brothers Sam, Harry, and Hyman outside the original A. Cohen & Sons office at 126 East Broadway on New York City's Lower East Side.

Chaim, the first of Shimon Dov's descendants to make aliyah, just prior to departing Volozhin for Palestine in 1924 at the age of eighteen.

Hyman, who was drafted to fight in the Great War at age twenty-five and saw heavy action with the First Infantry Division of the U.S. Army at Cantigny and Soissons during the spring and summer of 1918.

Abraham and Sarah's fiftieth wedding anniversary celebration, December 31, 1931, Burnside Manor, the Bronx.

Itel and William vacationing in Miami Beach with their daughter, Beatrice, in the late 1920s.

A 1932 studio portrait of Beyle and Shalom Tvi seated in front of their daughters Sonia (at right) and Etl (at left), their son-in-law Shepseleh, and their firstborn grandson, Shimonkeh.

Etl and her nephew Shimonkeh in 1932, the year he fell ill with scarlet fever.

Sonia, who left her family in Rakov in August 1932 to move to the Promised Land—"I behaved like a grown-up," she declared, "and did not take a cent from my parents."

Sonia and Chaim at Herzliya in 1932, shortly after Sonia made aliyah.

הרצליה רחוב ברוקס בן-נעמן 3

Workers' housing at Herzliya in the 1930s.

Chaim and Sonia on their
wedding day, December 7, 1933.

A studio portrait of Shepseleh, Doba, and their two sons, Shimonkeh and Velveleh, taken in Vilna
around 1933 or 1934.

From left to right: Beyle, Doba, Velveleh, Shepseleh, and Shimonkeh relaxing in the woods by their dacha outside Vilna, about 1935.

From left to right: William, Itel, Bert sitting on his mother Anna's lap, Hyman, and Barbara (Hyman and Anna's daughter), vacationing by the shore, possibly in Florida, around 1935. Vicki, the terrier, belonged to Itel and William.

Etl, her daughter Mireleh, and her husband, Khost, around 1937.

Shimonkeh, circa 1937, at the family's dacha.

Brothers Shimonkeh (left) and Velveleh playing chess in the country outside Vilna while their father, Shepseleh, supervises.

Brothers Shalom Tvi (right) and Avram Akiva [Abraham], separated for three decades, reunited in the summer of 1939, when Shalom Tvi left Poland to come to New York.

Beyle and Doba in Vilna, February 19, 1941. Despite the war and her poor health, Beyle had made the trip from Rakov to attend her grandson Shimonkeh's bar mitzvah.

Red Army officials surveying the charred remains of the pyres of logs and corpses at the Klooga slave labor camp in Estonia on September 24, 1944.

Itel, who by the early 1940s was presiding over one of the largest family businesses in the world, with Maidenform's bra and girdle sales topping $4.5 million annually.

The first ad in Maidenform's "dream" campaign, launched in 1949, which became an advertising legend—and sent company profits skyrocketing after the war.

I dreamed I went shopping in my *maidenform bra*

Wake me quick...this dream's too lovely! Designer hats...millions of them...peacock-bright, moon-dark, sun-spangled. What could be lovelier? Only my figure...so pretty in my Maidenform bra! I never dreamed that I could be so curve-sure, so secure, 'til I discovered Maidenform! Maybe you've dreamed of a bra with letter-perfect fit like this! Shown, Maidenform's Allo-ette® in white rayon satin. Just one of a vast and varied collection of styles, fabrics and colors.   There is a *Maiden Form,* for every type of figure secured an eviction order, which the Bedouins appealed. A protracted and bitter legal battle ensued. The Bedouins' first appeal was rejected, and in September 1930, 1,200 of them were forcibly evicted from their farms and ended up camped out at the side of the highway. The case dragged on for three more years and for a time it became a cause célèbre in the Arab press. The Wadi al-Hawarith Bedouins, poor and marginal though they were, showed remarkable solidarity and tenacity in their struggle to hold on to the land and maintain their tribal society. But in the end, the JNF prevailed in court and the Zionist pioneers prevailed on the ground, with their sweat and seed and water.

The sale of Wadi al-Hawarith was one of the first instances of Zionist ambition uprooting a large traditional Arab agrarian community. What made it particularly significant—and galling to the Arabs—was the size of the parcel involved: it ranked as the third-largest land deal in Palestine during the British Mandate.

While the fate of their colony was being litigated, Kfar Vitkin's original group of twenty-one lived together in Anton Tayan's big stone farmhouse. When the stone house filled to bursting, new settlers moved into portable wooden cabins clustered in a tight compound around the old farmyard. It was a bleak but inspiring spot. Beyond some irrigated orchards and fields near the house, the landscape was featureless scrub for miles in all directions—so empty and uninterrupted that the settlers could look from the Mediterranean to the mountains of the Jordan, Palestine's west and east margins, with a turn of the head. In most places in the world, a battle over 7,500 acres would be a strictly local concern, but in this pinched bottleneck of a country, it became a flash point for violent regional conflict that still rages today.

In the spring of 1930, Kfar Vitkin's one married couple had a baby daughter, a sign from God that this enterprise might thrive after all. The settlers celebrated their first Passover seder in the stone house. Since there was no electricity, some of the men went to Hadera to borrow lamps and lay in ingredients for the feast. On their return, they dressed themselves in boots and Russian shirts (the height of Zionist fashion at the time) and waited for the guests—young single women from Hadera and a nearby kibbutz—to arrive. Night fell with no sign of the girls. Since it was dangerous to travel the roads after dark, some of the men went down to the nearby British military camp and enlisted four soldiers to escort them in a troop transport. When they got to Hadera, the Jewish-British scouting party found the young women waiting impatiently in the street. The moshavniks piled them into the transport, drove on to the kibbutz to pick up more girls, and returned to the stone house. Finally the Passover seder could begin. "Everyone gathered together—even the British soldiers were invited to join," one of the settlers recalled. "We read the Haggadah. The food was plenty and sumptuous. Later we played the gramophone and danced until morning. We continued to celebrate after dawn, riding horses to the beach and bathing in the sea. Only toward evening did we drive the girls back home."

All the improvised magic and hope and sexiness of the Zionist endeavor were present that night—and so were the fear and constraint that shadowed every Jewish celebration in the Land. The tragedy of modern Palestine was that one oppressed, thwarted people had come to settle among, and inevitably to displace, another oppressed, thwarted people. Since they didn't find a way to live together, they lived separately until one was large and strong and determined enough to oppress the other. It is the nature of human society, at least human society in the Holy Land, that the bliss of one people dancing all night and racing horses into the sea at dawn would lead directly to the other people's sorrow, bitterness, hatred, and revenge.

When Chaim bought into Kfar Vitkin during the spring of 1933, the moshav was in its second stage. Having evicted the last of the Wadi al-Hawarith Bedouins and divided all the acreage into individual lots, the moshavniks finally felt secure and numerous enough to leave the compound by the stone farmhouse and live on their own land. One by one, the portable cabins of the founding families were mounted on wheels and dragged by tractor out to their designated parcels. But still nearly half of the plots stood empty, waiting for new families to arrive and join the community.

Sonia and Chaim were among those new families. They moved into their house before Passover 1934 and got to work. More money was needed for tools and farm equipment, so they borrowed. They lacked a pot large enough for making jam, so Sonia asked her parents to send one. She had toughened to the rigors of farmwork during her year and a half in

Palestine. It was a good thing, because the labor of getting a small farm up and running was herculean and never ending. Side by side, she and Chaim planted citrus and avocado trees, plowed up the field behind their house to grow feed for cattle, and hammered and nailed together sheds and out-buildings. Tomatoes were Kfar Vitkin's prize summer crop and Sonia and Chaim set aside a patch of their land for the sprawling, pungent vines that bore fruit from June through September. Day after cloudless hot day they watched the fruit swell and darken from pale green to milky jade to glori-ous ruby red—day after summer day they fretted over mildew, viruses, too much or too little water. On summer mornings they were up at 4 A.M. to get a jump on the work before the sun was too punishing. A couple of seasons in, when Kfar Vitkin had reached its capacity of 150 families and the fields were pumping out quantities of produce all summer long, Chaim signed on to become the moshav's truck driver. The dexterity at loading a hay wagon that he had acquired in the Kinneret came in handy now as he packed the Kfar Vitkin truck with canisters of milk and crates of eggs and rattled up to Haifa to deliver the produce to the Tnuva food cooperative. When Chaim came home late in the evening, Sonia always had a meal waiting for him. Actually "meal" does not do justice to the breadth and depth of Sonia's cooking. For all her Zionist austerity, Sonia was a real *ima Polania* (Polish mother) who took pride in heaping her table with gefilte fish, kreplach, chicken soup, potatoes cooked in oil, and a pearly brown gelatinous deli-cacy made from rendered calves' hooves and known as *p'tcha*. It took some maneuvering to get her hands on calves' hooves in Kfar Vitkin back in the 1930s, but Sonia was equal to the task. She would have died of shame if anyone, most especially her husband, rose from her table less than stuffed to bursting.

Between her twenty-second and twenty-third birthdays Sonia had changed everything: her country, her marital status, even the language she spoke every day. Though she and Chaim had learned to speak Hebrew back in Poland, it was not their mother tongue (Yiddish was their first language, Russian and Polish their second and third, respectively). Indeed Hebrew was no one's mother tongue back then except for the sabras—the children born in the Land. It would have been soothing for Sonia and Chaim to lapse into Yiddish in the privacy of their home, but they made the effort to speak only Hebrew, even with each other, as a point of pride and loyalty to the cause. "It is necessary that we have a language to hold us together," Ben Yehuda, the Russian-born father of modern Hebrew, declared—and he took it upon himself to fill that need by recasting biblical Hebrew (which had not been spoken except in prayer during the centuries of the Diaspora) into a modern living language suited to "the business of life." Ben Yehuda's heroic campaign to get Hebrew adopted throughout Jewish Palestine was one of the Zionists' proudest accomplishments: it was a rare instance of a language being willed back to life by zeal and discipline alone. Among settlers on the kibbutzim and moshavim, speaking Hebrew became a badge of honor, a sign that they had put the shtetl mind-set of the Diaspora behind them for good. Children picked up the language effortlessly, but for adult immigrants like Sonia and Chaim the shift of idiom required ceaseless, sometimes excruciating internal warfare. No matter how drained they were by their work, no matter how excited or worried or eager they felt to share some bit of news or simply to relax with a chat in Yiddish, they swallowed the words that came naturally to their lips and willed themselves to converse in Hebrew. Their children remember hearing Yiddish spoken when their parents wanted to hide something, share a dirty joke, or chat with old friends. But the children grew up with only one tongue.

In America Itel and Hyman worked hard to erase their Yiddish accents: it embarrassed them to say "vell" and "vuz" and "dis" and "dat" in front of gentile business associates. Sonia and Chaim erased Yiddish not out of embarrassment but out of pride. They believed it was their duty to ensure that the Jewish homeland was not tainted by the language of the ghetto.

Behind the cinder-block walls of their tiny, spartan house, the cousins worked out the economy of their marriage. Sonia did the laundry (outside, under the burning sun, in a wringer washer that she filled with a pail, stirred with a paddle, and cranked by hand); Chaim drove the truck and changed the oil. Sonia baked bread in an oven whose design dated back to biblical times. Chaim laid irrigation pipes and built an incubator for the chicks. Sonia raised the chickens, tended the vegetable garden, butchered, cooked, cleaned. She was a bright young woman, well educated, well-read in several languages—she could have spent her days reading, teaching, writing, arguing about politics or books in city cafés. She could have run a business. She could have opened a shop. But she had come to the Land to be a farm-wife. Sonia had a stubborn rebellious streak—she never would have made it out of Rakov without one—but in her depths she was dutiful, generous, maternal, and long-suffering. She never resented being Comrade Kagano-vich's wife—on the contrary, it was a source of pride. "She worked just as hard as Chaim," says Galit Weiser, the oldest of her granddaughters, who knew her well in the last years of her life, "and did not see her role as any less than what Chaim did. Sonia accepted her role. If she had any feminist qualms about it, she did not project them outwardly."

At Kfar Vitkin, Sonia always considered herself wealthier than her sis-ters or cousins. On the moshav, she had food, freedom, love, camaraderie, and the satisfaction of living her ideals. As it took root and flourished, Kfar Vitkin became not only Sonia's home but also her homeland. Far from being a second-class citizen, she was the mistress of her own tiny but boun-teous kingdom. Relatives who counted their blessings in coins or comforts were to be pitied. To ripen a tomato or fill a bucket with milk in the holy land of Kfar Vitkin was Sonia's fortune.

They had staked everything they had—and whatever they could borrow—on Kfar Vitkin, but in the first summer, Sonia and Chaim risked losing all of it by getting involved in an illegal smuggling operation. They were not smuggling merchandise but people—their fellow Jews. It was a sign of the times that smuggling clandestine Jewish immigrants (*ma'apilim* in Hebrew) into Palestine had become necessary by 1934. The portal through which Chaim had strolled in 1924 and around which Sonia slipped eight years later was closing fast. It was closing precisely because so many were now pressed against it. After Hitler came to power in 1933, the numbers of Jews seeking entry into Palestine from Europe spiked: Sonia was one of 12,533 who made aliyah in 1932, but the following year the figure tripled to 37,337 and it would double again in 1935 to an interwar peak of 66,472. Horrified at the Jewish influx, Arabs began pressuring the British to restrict the flow, and the British complied. Hence, the *ma'apilim*. To Zionists, immigration to Palestine was the lifeblood of their movement; for German Jews in 1934, it was becoming the only hope. The Jewish community took matters into its own hands by organizing a secret human smuggling campaign under the name "Aliyah Bet."

Chaim and Sonia joined the network. In the summer of 1934, the couple was called to action. The first *ma'apilim* ship, the SS *Vallos*, chartered in Europe by members of HeHalutz, was due to arrive off the coast near Kfar Vitkin on August 25 with 350 passengers. Haganah had arranged to meet the ship and get the passengers safely to shore and then slip them into Palestine. Under cover of night, Chaim and his fellow Haganah recruits gathered on the beach and waited for a signal from the *Vallos*. Then they rowed out, off-loaded a few *ma'apilim* into their small boats, and rowed them to shore. The operation went on for several nights until all 350 passengers were off the ship. Sonia welcomed groups of *ma'apilim* into her home with food and hot baths and provided them with clothing in which they could pass for Jewish settlers.

If they had been caught by the British military police, Sonia and Chaim would have been arrested and imprisoned, but they were willing to take the risk and to live with the anxiety.

The anxiety was all the more intense because Sonia was four months pregnant.

Leah, Sonia and Chaim's first child, was born on January 27, 1935. The baby's arrival in the winter was a stroke of luck—or careful timing—since farmwork was relatively light during the rainy season. The miracle of having a beautiful rosy dark-eyed baby girl—a sabra—sleeping and squalling under their roof somehow seemed even more miraculous in the Land. Sonia chatted and sang and soothed and shushed the baby in Hebrew; and, another miracle, when Leah began to speak, Hebrew words came bubbling out of her mouth. Another tie with Europe severed, another stake planted in the sandy soil of Palestine.

Leah was two months past her first birthday when anti-Zionist violence shook Palestine once again. As with the riots of 1929, the trigger in 1936 was a seemingly isolated incident—in April, some Arab thugs boarded a bus and attacked and killed two of its Jewish passengers. A spiral of revenge and escalating reprisals ensued. With incredible speed fueled by rage, the initial rounds of random killings and uprooting of crops coalesced into a disciplined, prolonged, unified national uprising. Arab leaders urged the people to quit paying taxes to the British after May 15, and then attempted to shut down Palestine's economy through a nationwide strike. Arab workers walked off their jobs en masse and Arab business owners shuttered their shops and offices. Though it halted public transportation and snarled government, the strike actually proved to be a boon to the Jewish economy. Jewish immigrants who had long complained of being shut out by low-wage Arab workers were finally getting hired in the citrus groves and vineyards. Urban markets, deprived of cheap Arab produce, had no choice but to stock fruits and vegetables grown on the kibbutzim and moshavim. But the economic benefits of the seven-month shutdown were more than offset by the violence that swept the region. Arab guerrilla bands, swelled by thousands of volunteers from neighboring countries, struck at outlying Jewish settlements. Under cover of night, the insurgents slaughtered livestock, burned crops, cut down thousands of trees that Jewish settlers had lovingly planted, and picked off the unlucky and unwary. Most of the attacks were fleeting and furtive—a lone farmworker shot in a field, a grenade thrown from a train window, a couple of Jewish nurses killed in a Jaffa hospital.

Kfar Vitkin was not spared. One of the moshavniks was on his way back from the beach with a cartload of building soil when an Arab gunned him down. Now every time a jackal screamed in the night Sonia stopped to listen and wonder.

When the general strike was called off on October 11, 1936, the death toll stood at 305—80 Jews, 197 Arabs, 28 British (many of the Arabs and British troops died fighting one another). But even though Arabs returned to work and reopened their shops, the killing was far from over. As fighting spread and intensified the following year, the Jews were forced to reckon with the fact that they were facing an Arab nationalist movement akin to Zionism in its ferocity, pride, and determination. This was civil war—one people hurling against another in the same land. And there was a new element: this time the Arabs were fighting with the active support and encouragement of the Nazis.

The violence at first sickened Palestine's Jews and then goaded them to unify and take furious action—a familiar pattern. Haganah emerged from the shadows and began to launch retaliatory raids, with the tacit complicity of the British. Working together, Jewish and British forces organized highly effective "Special Night Squads" that emulated Arab guerrilla tactics and occasionally crossed the borders to strike at guerrilla bases in neighboring states. A new spirit of resolve and faith in their mission spread through Jewish Palestine—a feeling, as one young Jewish writer put it, that "their roots had gone deeper and that a time of organic growth had come." Part of it was numbers—a critical mass of Jewish immigrants had begun to tip the scale. Part of it was desperation. With violence abroad in the Land, Jews developed a new technique of rapid-fire homesteading reminiscent of the American West: in the course of a single day, a convoy of young settlers would rumble into a remote piece of arable land, erect a prefabricated watchtower and a block of houses, string up barbed wire, and post guards. By nightfall a new Jewish dot had appeared on the map of Palestine: another bit of contested soil that Jews vowed never to abandon or surrender. Zionists had their eye on the prize of Jewish nationhood. The more land they effectively controlled, the wider the boundaries of the future Jewish state.

In the dozen years Chaim had been in Palestine, the character of Zionist pioneering had altered almost beyond recognition. The joyous nights of song and dance in the hills of Galilee had given way to the barbed wire of the instantaneous "stockade and tower" settlements.

"We are fated to live in a state of constant battle with the Arabs and there is no escape from sacrifice of life. If we wish to continue our work in this country, against the wishes of the Arabs, we must take such sacrifices into account." It sounds like Jabotinsky, but in fact these are the words of Arthur Ruppin, the peace-loving Zionist leader who had devoted his early career to the planting of collective farms like the Degania Kibbutz and the Kinneret Colony where Chaim had worked. After the Arab uprising of 1936, even Ruppin was resigned to bloodshed without end.

As the violence escalated in 1937 and 1938, the British first sent reinforcements—and then bureaucrats to study and reflect on the situation.

British soldiers finally retook Jerusalem's Old City in the summer of 1938, but the bureaucrats came and went without finding even a remotely tenable political solution. The Peel Report, issued in the summer of 1937, dangled the possibility of partitioning the region into Jewish and Arab states, but only at the price of a serious curtailment of Jewish land purchases and the scaling back of Jewish immigration to twelve thousand a year. Even that meager offer did not remain on the table for long. In the face of stiffening Arab opposition, subsequent British commissions radically pared back the land area of the proposed Jewish state and insisted on yoking Jewish and Arab political entities together in a clearly unworkable economic union. The deteriorating world situation worked against Zionist interests and the Arabs knew it. As Hitler grew more threatening, the British vacillated, appeased, and caved. In the event of war, it was clear that Britain would sacrifice the Jews rather than run the risk of alienating the Arabs and losing their oil. But even without war, the British no longer seemed inclined to invest much political capital in the idea of a Jewish state.

On March 12, 1938, at the height of the Arab uprising, the Nazis overran Austria and took the crisis in Europe to another level. In the grand imperial boulevards of Vienna, Jews were spat at, robbed, beaten, and taunted with shouts of "Jude verrecke"—death to the Jews. Two days later, rapturous crowds filled the Austrian capital to welcome Hitler back to the land of his birth. In the days that followed, Jewish houses were ransacked; Jewish shops and businesses were shut down or appropriated by Aryan employees; Jewish government workers, teachers, lawyers, actors, and musicians lost their jobs. The Gestapo moved in to arrest Jewish journalists, political leaders, and intellectuals. Mass deportations to Dachau began.

Hitler had spent five years gradually and systematically stripping Germany's Jews of their civil and human rights; those who were not in prison camps in the spring of 1938 lived in miserable poverty. Austria's Jews were broken in a matter of weeks.

Aliyah Bet was stepped up, but the number of immigrants that Sonia and Chaim and their comrades were able to smuggle in was minuscule in comparison to those left behind and barred.

In August 1938, while Hitler was maneuvering to seize the industrialized western fringe of Czechoslovakia known as the Sudetenland, Sonia somehow found the money and cleared the red tape to book passage back to Poland for herself and three-and-a-half-year-old Leah. Sonia could not explain the source of her impulse, but suddenly she was desperate to return to Europe to see her family.

CHAPTER THIRTEEN

RETURN TO RAKOV

It was Itel's idea to switch Maiden Form over to piecework—compensation based on the number of pieces produced rather than the number of hours clocked—and like most of her ideas it paid off handsomely. Sales picked up again after the brief stumble in 1932—"we really took off during the Depression years and kept growing and growing," said one of the early salesmen. If the company was going to capitalize on the uptick, it had to find a way to keep pace with demand. The new piecework pay scale did the trick. Machine operators who had been earning fourteen dollars a week were initially reluctant to make the switch—Itel spent six months charming union bosses—but the grumbling stopped when they realized how much more money they were pulling down by working more efficiently. "The sky's the limit," Moe told the workers on the factory floor. "Make as much as possible and do a good job." Production tripled and company profits soared. Itel and William became very wealthy indeed during the 1930s.

Monetizing industrial engineering came naturally to Itel—she was born to be a tycoon—but William had the soul of an artist. For him, satin and lace and cotton mesh were just another medium, though a particularly profitable one. He had always loved making beautiful things with his hands. When he went to the beach in the summer, he pushed wet sand into reliefs of voluptuous naked women. At home he had a studio where he sculpted the torsos of laborers in clay and crafted molds for bronze busts.

Like many an artist, William in middle age felt the urge to return to his roots. He was fifty-six years old in 1937—three decades had passed since he had last seen the town of his birth, the scenes of his youthful romance with Itel, the cemetery where his ancestors were buried. Unlike most artists, William in middle age had the means to satisfy his curiosity. The same year piecework revolutionized production at Maiden Form, he crossed the Atlantic alone and journeyed back to Rakov.

This is what he wrote after the visit:

In 1937, I visited my hometown and found it to be quite different from what I had left: A border town, under the Polish authorities, separated from Minsk and the large estates which surrounded it. I found it in utter poverty, expecting charity from relatives in America. I stayed there for some time and observed the poverty of the people, how some of them were, literally, down to their last piece of bread. But it must be said, that in spite of this dark picture, the social-cultural life was as effervescent as ever: the bank, the community institutions, the Hebrew school, and the Youth Movements—they were all full of bustle, energy, and many activities. All of these made one hopeful, and were the basis for the belief that somehow the town would overcome the material crisis.

William did not write about his family, but he must have passed many hours sipping tea and schnapps with assorted Kaganoviches, Botwiniks, and Rosenthals. For all his fame and fortune, William was never one to put on airs or lord it over anyone. Shalom Tvi and Beyle received him gladly and graciously (they were connected on both sides—Itel was Shalom Tvi's niece and William's mother was related to Beyle). Before he left, William met with Rakov's rabbi, Israel Helprin, and agreed to make a substantial donation toward the construction of a large new religious school. He might belong to the Ethical Culture Society in America, but back in Rakov he didn't forget he was a Jew. He distributed some American dollars to each of the family members. They all parted on good terms. Shalom Tvi hoped that one day he and William would meet again in New York.

Sonia returned to Rakov the year after William's visit. She had been away only for six years, but she was just as stunned as William by the changes. Maybe more so. The poverty she was prepared for—the town had been suffering before she left and she knew from her father's letters that business was weak and the economy depressed. But it was the atmosphere of naked contempt that she found new and intolerably oppressive. When had it become a crime to be Jewish in Poland? In Kfar Vitkin, Sonia lived freely as a Jew among Jews. If a neighbor's cow strayed into her vegetable patch, she could yell about it without being called a dirty Yid. When she and Chaim went to Haifa or Tel Aviv they could sit in a café or barter in a shop without being muttered at behind their backs. But after six years in Jewish Palestine, Sonia found it difficult to breathe in Poland. She opened a newspaper and saw Jews branded as the "internal enemy." "The Jewish influence on morals is fatal," Poland's Roman Catholic primate Cardinal August Hlond wrote in a widely published pastoral letter. "One does well to prefer one's own kind in commercial dealings and to avoid Jewish stores and Jewish stalls in the markets."

The Polish government held the same views and endorsed a boycott of Jewish businesses. Market day in Rakov brought threats and attacks. Anti-Semitic placards were everywhere. Gentile shop owners now displayed signs guaranteeing their "Aryan" purity while the stalls of Jewish merchants were vandalized or wrecked. In Warsaw, gentile gymnasium students circulated a pamphlet advocating violent attacks on Jews and Communists: "Remember if you have a Jew or a Communist in a lonely spot, hit him with an iron bar in the teeth. Do not be afraid and do not feel sorry for him." At the universities Jews were being forced to sit apart on "ghetto benches." Members of the fascist anti-Semitic ONR Party (the "Polish Hitlerites") had taken to proclaiming "Jewless days" at Polish universities—and soon "Jewless weeks." Jewish students were routinely attacked by ONR thugs and several were murdered.

This was the Poland Sonia returned to in August 1938. Why had her family failed to mention any of this in their letters?

It quickly became obvious that the subject was off-limits. Compared with what was going on in Germany and Austria, they were lucky, so best not to talk about it. To draw attention to trouble was to court it. The safe path was to ignore what couldn't be changed. She had come home to enjoy herself, so why ruin it? It was high summer. The fields around Rakov were golden; Beyle's garden was bursting with cucumbers and beets; the little wooden houses—so much more cheerful and cozy than the cinder-block hovels of the Jewish settlements in Palestine—looked like toys painted by children. Sonia should relax, have a holiday, let her mother and sister spoil her. Everyone wanted to know about life in the Land, squeeze her muscular arms, admire her brown complexion. Everyone wanted to hear Leahleh speak Hebrew—such a prodigy! Only three years old and already she spoke better Hebrew than Rabbi Helprin! After a couple of days of prattling on command for rapt strangers, Leah burst into tears and clammed up altogether. Did they think she was a performing poodle?

They put politics aside and wrapped themselves in the big tattered quilt of family affairs and town gossip. For years Etl had worried that she was doomed to drag out her days as a "traveling maiden," but she had finally found a match and gotten married. The husband was a teacher at the Polish school named Khost Goldstein, a trim natty young man with wavy fair hair and a shy shifty smile. Sonia had read all about the courtship and marriage in the family letters, but they repeated the whole story nonetheless—how Khost used to come to the house with other young folks to play cards and one thing led to another until Etl, nearly thirty years old, became a bride. On a schoolteacher's salary Khost would never be rich—to economize they lived with Shalom Tvi and Beyle—but at least he had a steady source of income, unlike poor Shepseleh in Vilna, who was still trying his hand at this and that and not making a living at any of it. So now all three Kaganovich sisters were married, and all three were mothers. Etl and Khost's daughter, Miriam—Mireleh—was two years old that summer, the spitting image of Shirley Temple, with soft brown curls and a tiny rosebud of a mouth. Etl, another wizard with needle and thread, whipped up adorable matching frocks for herself and the child—though in truth with her angular, small-breasted figure she looked less like Mireleh's mother than her maiden aunt. No matter. Being a wife and mother had softened some of Etl's sharp edges. She was still hypersensitive and judgmental, but she had quit feeling sorry for herself and envying Sonia. Although the fight that had stained Sonia's departure to Palestine was not forgotten, the two sisters put the past behind them. It helped that their daughters took to each other. The two little girls slept in the same room and every night they went to bed crooning Hebrew songs. *Nachas*—pride in the happiness and success of one's offspring—flowed thick and fast. Shalom Tvi and Beyle went around misty eyed with joy.

A big family wedding was celebrated during Sonia's stay in Rakov—no one recalls who married whom—and relatives from far and wide gathered to eat and pray and gossip and toast the newlyweds. Tsipora Alperovich, one of the little cousins from Vilna on Beyle's side, had come without a proper dress to wear, and Etl stitched together something lovely for her in a single day. Tsipora was ten years old at the time but she never forgot it. Beyle, meanwhile, made sure there were enough tasty dishes to feed all the poor of the shtetl.

"It was a tremendous effort to get back to Poland," Sonia told her children long afterward, "but it was very important to me to visit." Given the difficulties and cost of travel, a short stay made no sense. Three months was barely enough time to fit in all she wanted to do. Her pace was rapid, even hectic. She must see everyone, go everywhere, show Leahleh off to every last aunt and uncle and cousin. From Rakov she went to Volozhin to visit with Chaim's branch of the family—his mother and stepfather, his sister Chana, his older brother Yishayahu. Yishayahu, the sibling Chaim was closest to, was much loved and admired in the old yeshiva town. Though he earned a living running an imported fruit shop with Chana's husband Meir Finger, Yishayahu's heart and soul belonged to Zionism. He was one of the founding teachers of Volozhin's Tarbut (Hebrew language) school, and his forceful, levelheaded manner was an inspiration to all who studied with him. Yishayahu was the one adult who didn't make a fuss over Leahleh's Hebrew. He assured Sonia that it was only a matter of time before he made aliyah with his wife, Henia, and their daughter, another Leah. Meanwhile, he and every other relative in Volozhin had packages for Sonia to schlep back to the Land.

By coincidence, an aunt and uncle from America—Beyle's brother Hayim Yehoshua Botwinik and his wife, Esther—were visiting Rakov at the same time as Sonia, and the family threw a big party to celebrate the coming together of the three branches. After the food and drink had been cleared away, they all posed for a photo: two dozen grinning young people dressed to the nines and standing in rows behind their proud round parents, aunts, and uncles. Shalom Tvi, with his bald head uncovered, looks distinguished in a stylish dark suit; Sonia, beautiful in a plain black dress with her hair parted in the middle and pulled back fashionably, smiles with her mouth but her eyes are tense and strained; Etl, in a tailored brown suit jacket, has her head cocked as if trying to catch the punch line of a joke. The joke must have been good because all the young glossy-haired men and rouged, lipsticked women in the back are laughing openly.

Uncle Hayim Yehoshua made good money in America with his New Haven machine tool business, and he left everyone in the Rakov family with a check for twenty-five dollars.

Sonia and Leahleh spent their final weeks in Vilna with Doba and Shepseleh and their sons. Sonia knew Vilna well—she had attended the Tarbut school there as a teenager and had stayed in the city for a few days in 1932 right before departing for Palestine (in a black mood). Even though Leah was too young to notice or appreciate much, Sonia wanted to show her daughter the sights. How could she be in Poland and miss Vilna? There was no city in Europe prouder of its Jewish heritage and culture than the "Jerusalem of Lithuania," as local Jews never tired of calling their home. Three Yiddish theaters, six Jewish dailies, twenty Jewish schools, 105 synagogues including the Great Synagogue, where the revered Gaon of Vilna had discoursed on the Talmud at the age of six. Vilna was also the birthplace of the Bund and home of YIVO—the Yiddish Scientific Institute, which in a mere thirteen years had become the essential archive of Jewish history. Nowhere in Europe did Jews live with more beauty and history. The old town was cobbled, pastel, graced by a noble university, splashed with courtyard gardens. Vilna had something of the elegance and refinement of prerevolutionary St. Petersburg, though on a more comfortable human scale. But unlike in St. Petersburg, Vilna's Jews accounted for a substantial percentage of the population—more than a third at the time of Sonia's visit.

Doba and Shepseleh lived well amid all this splendor and loveliness, though they rarely dipped a toe in the great river of culture. A few years earlier they had moved from their flat across from the chemistry faculty to a more stately apartment on Pivno Street, a wide thoroughfare of three-story apartment buildings with grillwork balconies and high skinny windows vaguely reminiscent of Paris. Though far from grand, the new flat was airy, plush, and richly furnished—a berth in the solid middle of the middle class. Doba had a maid who kept everything clean and orderly—you'd never know two little boys had the run of the place. The flat was just a block from the city's holiest Christian shrine—the Gate of Dawn, an arched portal into the Old City that housed the wonder-working icon of the Ostra Brama, the Black Madonna, in a chapel above the gate. The narrow street beneath the shrine was choked all day long with beggars and kneeling worshippers. Whenever a Jewish man approached, the gentiles demanded that he uncover his head, which of course Jewish law forbade. Orthodox Jews went out of their way to avoid it; Jewish children secretly spat on the paving stones beneath the arch and ran. Shepseleh and Doba could afford to roll their eyes about such primitive superstitions. The lives they led were thoroughly modern and secular. Though they kept kosher and attended Taharat Hakodesh, the ornate Moorish-style Orthodox choral synagogue a few blocks from their apartment, it was more out of duty than piety. Shepseleh wouldn't dream of going out without a fresh shave and nice tie. Doba and Shepseleh kept up the Jewish traditions because their parents expected it, but their true religion was the happiness of their children.

Sonia and Doba spoke endlessly about the boys. Did Sonia think Shimonkeh was too skinny? Doba was concerned that he had never fully recovered from his bout of scarlet fever. His legs were sticks, his chest like a bird's—you could see every knob and rib. But he thundered up and down the hall day and night, he insisted on cropping his blond hair close to his head like a soldier, and though he was only ten, he had learned to ride a bicycle. He took after his father—tall, thin, serious with a bit of sly mischief. As for Velveleh—what was there to say? Six years old and already a dreamboat. Who could resist those big, dark, shining eyes of his? (*May the evil eye be averted*, Doba was careful to add whenever she ladled out even a teaspoon of praise on her children.) Could there be anything sweeter than the way the boys held Leahleh's hand when they crossed the street or how they laughed at her Hebrew (Leah was speaking again, but only with other children)? Doba didn't like to boast, but Shimonkeh promised to be a brilliant student—musical too. Maybe if he stopped, for a minute, tumbling on the floor with his brother he'd sing something nice for his aunt Sonia.

When the children went to bed their parents discussed the future. Everybody had said Sonia was crazy for leaving Rakov for the wastes of Palestine, but with Poland the way it was now, she looked like the sane one and they should have their heads examined. Sonia had a house and a farm, Chaim made a decent living driving Kfar Vitkin's truck. Shepseleh was forty-two years old and still no steady paying job in sight. He was trained as an accountant, and he *looked* like an accountant with his slicked-back hair, high-waisted trousers, and prominent ears; but for him employment was one long tale of woe. For a couple of winters he sold wood and coal, but the profits were meager and storage an issue. Then there was the friend in Tel Aviv—the rich son of a Vilna rabbi and a distant relative through Abraham's wife, Sarah—who might be able to wangle him a toehold in the Land. If he learned Hebrew and a little English, he told Sonia for the twentieth time, maybe he could get something in Tel Aviv as a bookkeeper or small merchant? Shepseleh was always writing letters, dropping hints, visiting consulates and agencies. In the end here he was in Vilna, still looking, still hoping. Sonia listened, advised, sympathized, and finally lost patience. For years this brother-in-law had been singing the same song. Why didn't he do something about it? Though she would never breathe a word to Doba, Sonia was starting to think of Shepseleh as a superfluous man out of Turgenev or Chekhov—always dreaming, never deciding. She was mystified how he and Doba managed to afford the lovely flat, the stylish clothes, the dacha on the banks of the Vilnia River. Maybe Shepseleh's family had money? He was brainy and cultured, a doting father, a sweet husband, but Sonia could not imagine him driving a truckload of tomatoes on the dusty road to Haifa or grafting shoots onto a thorny orange tree. One day in the sun at Kfar Vitkin and he'd wilt like a lettuce leaf.

As the end of the visit approached, Etl traveled to Vilna from Rakov—without her husband or child—so the three sisters could be together. There is no record of the date but it was probably well into the autumn—maybe the beginning of November.

Before starting the arduous journey back to the Land, Sonia took Doba aside and handed her the twenty-five-dollar check that Uncle Hayim had given her in Rakov. Doba protested—she had a check of her own from Hayim—Sonia should keep the money and buy something nice when she returned to Kfar Vitkin. "She did not want to take the money," Sonia told her children, "but I told her, 'Dobka, we lack for nothing in Eretz Yisrael. We have a garden and a cow and plenty of food. Here the situation is not so good so maybe you will need this.' For years afterward, I was so happy that she took the $25."

December 7, 1938
Pivno Street 6/8
Vilna

Dear Sonia,

You cannot imagine what we have gone through since you left. Everything seems like a dream, something sweet that cannot come back. We were so emotional and confused at the end. You probably remember that even before you left, our mood had not been so good, and your leaving has devastated us. Etl did not go back home that day, because we wanted to be together at that moment.

What state was the house in when you returned? How did Chaim look after everything while he was alone for so long? How is Leahleh feeling? Does she mention us? Volinkeh says now that she could have stayed a little longer because Mireleh will not come here to us.

Warm regards to Chaim and thanks for the cards. Kisses for Leahleh.

From your sister Doba

Doba made no mention of Kristallnacht. Why should she? Enough weighed on their hearts already without piling on insanity. Anyway, Sonia had still been in Poland when the madness broke and she had seen the newspaper accounts herself.

The Nazis had been looking for an excuse for a mass pogrom and they found it in Paris on November 7, when a seventeen-year-old Polish Jew named Herschel Grynszpan took a loaded revolver to the German embassy and shot German diplomat Ernst vom Rath. Supposedly, Grynszpan decided on the assassination when he learned of the summary expulsion from Germany of thousands of Polish Jews, including his parents and sister, and their internment in a refugee camp on the Polish-German border. But another, more shadowy motive may have been at play: vom Rath, a notorious homosexual, and Grynszpan had been lovers, and by some accounts Grynszpan was driven to violence by an intimate grievance or betrayal.

When word reached Berlin on November 9 that vom Rath had died of wounds inflicted by a teenage Jew, Nazi propaganda minister Joseph Goebbels unleashed gangs of SA storm troopers throughout Germany and Austria with instructions to torch synagogues, smash Jewish store windows, destroy Jewish property, and haul young Jewish men off to prison. Ninety-one Jews died in the violence; some thirty thousand were sent to concentration camps. Jews were beaten to death before the eyes of their neighbors and families. Nearly every synagogue in Germany and Austria was either destroyed or damaged that night, Jewish cemeteries were torn up and desecrated, Torah scrolls and prayer books were burned. Scores of Jews committed suicide while the pogrom raged.

Kristallnacht—the night of broken glass—signaled the Nazis' transition from economic and social oppression to physical violence and murder, though they continued to extract as much money as they could from the remaining Jews. In the aftermath, the German government decreed that German Jews must atone for the assassination of vom Rath by paying a collective fine of 1 billion reichs marks—roughly 5.5 billion dollars in current currency. They extracted the money by confiscating 20 percent of all Jewish property. In a final stroke of diabolical "justice," all the insurance money owed to Jews for losses on their property and businesses was seized by the government to cover "damages to the German Nation."

Doba did not mention Kristallnacht in her letter of December 7, but Sonia could read between the lines. She already knew how frightened and desperate her sister was. While she was still in Poland, Sonia had heard Doba beg Uncle Hayim Yehoshua to take her and her husband and sons back with him to the United States. Doba swore she would repay every penny of the cost. It wasn't so easy anymore, Uncle Hayim Yehoshua explained; you needed family sponsors, visas, certificates of good conduct, bank records, all of it submitted in multiple copies. It required time and money. He promised he would do what he could when he got back to New Haven.

———

February 10, 1939

Sonika! I don't know where to start. I have so much to write about, but when I take the pen in my hand I get confused.

First our situation has completely changed. Hayim Yehoshua and Sarah Leah [Hayim's sister] have written from America and they want us to come to them. They have even hired an attorney. They want all of us to come together. The plan is that father and mother will come to you [i.e., to Palestine]. The problem is that one cannot take money out of here, and we do not know what will happen. The parents and Etl are in Rakov, and it is hard for me to think of parting from them. We have to brace ourselves with patience. Everything will clear up with time.

Father has written to Avram Akiva and to William Rosenthal about the goings-on here, so everyone is taking part and we hope that something will come of it.

Your sister Doba

But nothing did come of it. Some link in the chain broke. Winter dragged on, and Doba and Shepseleh and the boys remained in Vilna; Shalom Tvi and Beyle, Etl and Khost and their daughter, Mireleh, in Rakov. Some unpleasantness had bubbled up between Etl and her husband, but its nature and cause have also vanished. Doba told Sonia, "In every letter I ask [Etl] what is going on with her, and she answers me that the situation has not improved. I can imagine what she is going through." Had Khost betrayed his wife with another woman? Squandered her dowry? Insulted her parents? "He [Khost] had planned to come to Vilna and enjoy himself a little,"

Doba wrote in disgust, "but I have not responded because I don't want him to come to me and I cannot look at him."

Winter ended, the sweet season of lilacs and peonies commenced, Shepseleh looked for work, Khost taught school, was forgiven or tolerated for whatever offense he was guilty of. Nothing changed in their private lives. Whatever changes took place around them, they ignored or refused to speak of.

But change did come finally, suddenly, irrevocably. Early in the summer, Shalom Tvi and Beyle sold their leather business in exchange for promissory notes payable in September. They retained some merchandise—hides, leather garments—to sell, just in case, but everything else was liquidated. Free of the business they had run together for forty years, husband and wife traveled to Vilna, leaving Etl and Khost behind with Mireleh to look after things in Rakov. Shalom Tvi and Beyle visited with Doba's family, prayed at the Taharat Hakodesh synagogue, took in the sights and pleasures of the city. On the last day of June, Shalom Tvi hugged and kissed his two grandsons, embraced his oldest daughter, shed tears in the arms of his beloved wife. They parted at the Vilna rail station. Beyle went back home to Rakov. Shalom Tvi and Shepseleh caught a train for Gdynia, a port city on the Baltic a few miles west of Gdansk. The next day, July 1, Shepseleh accompanied his father-in-law to the harbor and saw him safely aboard the HMS *Piłsudski*, a resplendent new two-funneled steamer run by the Gdynia-America Line. Shalom Tvi was sailing alone to America.

CHAPTER FOURTEEN

"THE WORLD OF TOMORROW"

The *Piłsudski*, named for Poland's recently deceased leader, arrived in New York harbor shortly after dawn on July 11, 1939, the final summer of a low dishonest decade. Shalom Tvi stood on deck with the other passengers to see the fabled skyscrapers shimmering in the white sky; he saluted the Statue of Liberty; he watched as the ship approached Ellis Island. The engines shuddered and died, and now he was close enough to make out his family waving from the pier. Abraham and Sarah (Avram Akiva and Gishe Sore they would always be to Shalom Tvi), as well as his brother-in-law Hayim Yehoshua and sister-in-law Esther were there to welcome him to America. Already the first- and second-class passengers were streaming off the ship, and now the crew was lining up the third-class passengers and ordering them to have their documents ready for inspection. Shalom Tvi handed his papers to a man in a blue coat and waited. Other third-class passengers were being waved through on either side. But him they detained. A "special inquiry" had been deemed necessary, so instead of disembarking, Shalom Tvi had to stay on board the ship. Even through the Yiddish interpreter, it made no sense. His brother was ready to vouch for him; he had money in his pocket, documents in hand, a place to stay—what was the problem? "Special inquiry," the interpreter repeated. It meant they were not letting him in.

For two days Shalom Tvi stayed on the empty creaking *Piłsudski* with a handful of other detainees. Then at 9:40 on the morning of July 13, Inspector Kaba summoned him for the special inquiry. Through an interpreter Kaba swore him in, after which he fired away with his questions: full name, age, country of residence, race, marital status, occupation in Poland, who paid for his passage, purpose of his visit to the United States.

The alien was dimissed, and Inspector Kaba turned to his colleagues Inspector Magee and Miss Cozzolina. In Kaba's opinion the case was routine. The alien was traveling on a tourist visa; he had failed to obtain an immigration visa, which would have entitled him to remain in the States and look for work; he claimed he had come to visit his family—but Kaba was dubious. That's what all the Jews were saying these days, but most of them really intended to stay indefinitely. Kaba moved that the alien be required to file a bond of fifty dollars guaranteeing his departure after three months. The vote was unanimous in favor.

At 12:35 P.M., Shalom Tvi was summoned back and Kaba delivered the verdict through the interpreter: "Bond has been furnished on your behalf to guarantee your departure from the U.S. within three months. You must so depart; otherwise you will be here in violation of the law, subject to arrest and deportation and forfeiture of the collateral on the bond, and while in this country you should not accept any gainful employment or engage in any business, for then too you will incur the same penalties. Do you understand?"

Shalom Tvi replied "Yes" but in truth he did not understand. When his brother came to America three decades earlier, he had waltzed through Ellis Island. Now just to visit he needed a passport, favorable report from the local police, doctor's certification of good health and absence of "physical handicap which might make him a public charge," birth and marriage certificates, detailed bank statements indicating assets and income, affidavit filed by the sponsoring family indicating their assets and their ability to support the newcomer—all of the documents properly authenticated and valid simultaneously. Shalom Tvi had applied, filed, stamped, duplicated, and paid. Still it wasn't enough. Now they wanted fifty dollars as a guarantee that he would go home in three months.

Inspector Kaba was correct when he wrote "doubtful" on Shalom Tvi's file. Shalom Tvi himself was doubtful about the purpose of his trip. Strictly speaking, he had come to America neither as an immigrant nor as a visitor but as a kind of scout. In a world without forms, he would have looked around, talked to the relatives, scoped out the job prospects for himself and Shepseleh, borrowed money to help get the rest of his family out of Poland. But in 1939, forms were absolute.

In the end, early in the afternoon of July 13, the officials in blue uniforms let Shalom Tvi off the *Piłsudski* with the understanding that the fifty-dollar bond would be refunded when he boarded a ship bound back to Poland on or before October 13.

———

July 16, 1939

Dear children Sonia and Hayim,

May you have much nachas from your dear daughter Leahleh.

Today is my fifth day in America. I arrived on the boat at eight o'clock in the morning on July 11 and everybody had come to welcome me, relatives from my family and from mother's. Unfortunately, they were not allowed to come close to me, and they detained me and other people for a few days. They asked me many questions, and it went on for two and a half days. On the crossing, I had had a few bad days and I almost regretted going on the trip. But now, thank God, I feel well and all the members of the family are here and healthy. We all gathered in the house of Avram Akiva, kissed each other and celebrated. With God's help we shall all continue to celebrate.

Mother and Doba are now in Druskininkai [a spa town in Lithuania]. I wrote to mother that it would be beneficial for her to go and rest, because she is sad without me. She is not used to being away from me for such a long time. Mother had wanted to come with me [to America], but from the beginning I had not wanted to draw such a large sum, and she is in poor health. But it seems that they wouldn't have given her a visa, because there had been instances even with wealthier people when they did not give the wife a visa to America. Perhaps it is better that she has not come. The journey was very difficult and it's not at all like Rakov and Vilna here. You can't go anywhere by yourself—you have to drive everywhere and there is no one to drive you. Everyone here is very busy.

Write to me what is going on with you in the Eretz, I want to know everything.

Be healthy.

Wishing all of you well, your father Shalom Tvi Kaganovich

The Americans were determined to show him a good time in the land of plenty, and Shalom Tvi complied. He couldn't drive, he spoke no English, he found the scale and pace of New York overwhelming—so he let himself be wined and dined and taken around like a tourist. After a couple of weeks in the Bronx, he went to stay with Hayim Yehoshua, in New Haven. The brother-in-law, married to Beyle's sister Esther, had a cottage on Long Island Sound, so Shalom Tvi got to swim in salt water and relax on the beach. Then it was back to his brother in the Bronx and up to the Catskills to the *cuchalain* (bungalow with a kitchen) that Abraham rented—Shalom Tvi called it a dacha in his letters home. "We are having a good time here," he wrote Sonia. "We bathe in the river and tan in the American sun."

The 1939 World's Fair was going full blast that summer in Flushing Meadows. No one came to New York and missed it. Shalom Tvi sat in one of their cars, got driven out to the former ash pit in central Queens, paid his seventy-five cents admission, and spent a summer day being dazzled by "the world of tomorrow." Television! Color photography! Nylon! Fluorescent lights! Air-conditioning! Automatic dishwashers! All of these wonders were up and running at the fair. Soon lucky consumers would be able to install them in their living rooms, bedrooms, and kitchens. Shalom Tvi rode the world's longest escalator up into the Perisphere—the eighteen-story high globe that occupied the center of the fairgrounds alongside the seven hundred-foot-tall Trylon needle—and took his place on the revolving observation platform. Though he didn't understand a word of the piped-in English sound track, one of the relatives explained that they were looking down on "Democracity," a model of the coming American utopia with a high-rise commercial-cultural core ringed by residential Pleasantvilles, light-industrial Millvilles, and an outer greenbelt of tidy parks and productive farmland—all of it looped through by superhighways. He walked past the endless line inching toward the entrance of General Motors' fabled Futurama—a narrated ride in a comfy cushioned chair through a maniacally detailed diorama of the America of 1960: Bubble-shaped cars! Sprawling suburbs! Superhighways with nary a traffic jam! But Shalom Tvi declined to join the queue. The futuristic razzle-dazzle concocted by the wizards of Broadway, Madison Avenue, city hall, and corporate industrial-design departments would have been lost on the alien from Rakov. Nor was he interested in the time capsule that would preserve Camel cigarettes, a Kewpie doll, a Mickey Mouse watch, and the words of Albert Einstein and Thomas Mann until the year 6939. He bypassed Vermeer's *The Milkmaid*, on loan from the Rijksmuseum in Amsterdam and the speech synthesizer installed by Bell Labs. What grabbed Shalom Tvi at the fair was not art or science or the magic of modern appliances or the promise of the sunny streamlined world to come. It was the reflection of the politics of the day. He wrote Sonia that he had spent three hours examining the Jewish Palestine pavilion, "the smallest one" in the fair, with a copper relief sculpture of "The Scholar, the Laborer, and the Toiler of the Soil" on its façade. He was also bowled over by the Russian pavilion—"They wanted to show the world that they are 'hopping and dancing' and they have done it extraordinarily well. They have brought everything from Russia and erected a glorious pavilion, and they say that afterward they will send it back to Russia and turn it into a museum. There are other pavilions from other countries, but the cursed Germans did not get a spot here."

There was more "hopping and dancing" going on at the Aquacade synchronized swim spectacular and the girlie show bizarrely staged inside a replica of an eighteenth-century Manchurian Lama Temple, but Shalom Tvi skipped those too. He did *not*, however, miss the seventy neon signs flashing Maiden Form ads at strategic points by the fairground entrances. If ever Shalom Tvi harbored doubts about how well the family was making out in America, here was graphic proof in tubes of colored light. The last time he had seen Itel she was a frizzy-haired teenager decrying the tsar in the Rakov market and inflicting no end of *tsouris* on her parents. Now his brother told him that she and William drove to work in a chauffeured limousine and lived in a swanky apartment on Central Park West; William was not only rich but also generous, a donor to Jewish causes—Rakov's beautiful new religious school, just completed that month, had been largely financed by him. Evidently the wealth of the American family was like an iceberg with the bulk of it invisibly submerged. His brother Abraham lived modestly in the upper floor of a house he shared with his son and daughter and their families, but their business had been thriving for twenty-seven years now; they all had cars; their wives had mink coats and diamond rings; in the winter they vacationed in Florida.

There was no doubt in Shalom Tvi's mind that the American relatives had the means to help his family get out of Poland. The question was, could he motivate them to use it? And would he? Shalom Tvi was a quiet, reserved man—it wasn't in his nature to ask, even from his brothers and sister.

He may have come to the States as a scout, but his mission seems to have drifted after a couple of weeks. Or perhaps he realized the mission was futile. He had only just managed to secure a three-month visa for himself—he had no reason to believe that his wife or daughters would do any better. Like it or not, he had to return to Poland by October 13, so he decided to relax and enjoy himself and make the most of his time in America. He went to the Metropolitan Museum of Art ("I walked and looked for a few hours but saw only a small part") and the circus ("not like the circus in Vilna and certainly not like Tel Aviv"). He slept on a folding bed in the living room of Abraham's flat—every morning he put the bed away and stowed his clothes neatly behind the sofa. On Saturday he went to shul with his brother. He put up with Sarah's cooking and politely ate everything they put in front of him except corn on the cob, which he indignantly refused as fit only for animals. He accepted every invitation to eat downstairs with his nephew Sam's family, since Gladys was a wonderful cook and served all the dishes he was accustomed to at home.

Everyone was sweet, helpful, generous, accommodating—but the truth was that after the first few weeks, America left him cold. The brassy New York of 1939 made his head spin. Everything moved so fast; everyone was in a hurry; everywhere he looked there was something for sale. All anyone ever talked about was how the economy was finally bouncing back. A. Cohen & Sons was in the process of making yet another move uptown—this time to 27 West Twenty-third Street, half a block from the Flatiron Building, and the nephews schlepped him down there so he could admire the forty-eight thousand square feet of office space being fitted out in the latest contemporary showroom style by a rising young architect. Except for his brother, the family here felt like strangers. They talked about business incessantly—every meal, every drive, every walk to shul. A. Cohen was expanding, Maiden Form already had sales in the millions and its products were on the shelves of 95 percent of the nation's department stores: this is what mattered to the American family. Not the boycott of Jewish businesses in Poland. Not Sonia and Chaim's struggle to eke out a living at Kfar Vitkin. Not the sporadic violence that continued in Palestine. These expensively dressed middle-aged executives were his flesh and blood; the nephews had been bar mitzvahed in the Rakov shul; the nieces had worked in their mother's store and run dresses and coats through their sewing machines just like his daughter Etl. They all used to sit together at holidays and sing the same songs and pound the table and raise a glass to the patriarch, Shimon Dov. They used to tell the same jokes and laugh and cry together in Yiddish. But America had turned their heads. They had forgotten what life was like in Rakov. For a Jew there was no hope of assimilating in Poland—the goyim made it impossible. But in America it was all but impossible *not* to assimilate. To live here you had to give up your past, your customs, your traditions, your identity. His brother and sister-in-law kept to the old ways, but the nieces and nephews were Americanized—and the children of the nieces and nephews were fully American. What did it mean that they were family when they spoke different languages, bore different names, lived such different lives?

"I went to the World's Fair and I saw everything," Shalom Tvi wrote to Sonia and Chaim. "I saw everything but you, my dear children. You, I could not find there. To tell the truth, I already miss home. But I feel that I'm obligated to spend the time here."

In the last week of August, Shalom Tvi went to the shipping company in Manhattan to inquire about his return passage. He was booked on a ship due to sail back to Poland on October 1, but the clerk told him that if war broke out before that he must apply to the Immigration and Naturalization Service for an extension of his visa. "I am confused," Shalom Tvi wrote Sonia. "I don't know what God may bring or whether he plans to sweeten our lives with any pleasure."

Just before the start of September he traveled up to Stamford, Connecticut, to stay with his youngest brother, Herman, for a few days before continuing on to Hayim Yehoshua's place in New Haven. On the last day of August, he sat down to write to Sonia and Chaim from New Haven about how worried he was about the danger of war. "First, because we have separated from each other in such uncertain times and second, who knows what will happen to Shepseleh and Khost."

Shalom Tvi was right to be worried. By the time he went to bed that night, German tanks and troops were crossing the border into Poland and hundreds of Luftwaffe planes were dropping bombs on Poland's major cities. Hayim Yehoshua kept a radio in his living room, and on the morning of September 1, the whole family stood and stared at the floor while the crackling voice of the announcer shrilled at them. *The Wehrmacht is on the move, Poland is in flames, but the Polish army has been mobilized and resistance is expected to be stiff.*

To my dear and beloved wife Beyle and to my dear children Etl, Khost and Mireleh:

Be healthy and may God shield you from all calamities.

I am writing to you with a broken heart from the disaster that has happened to the world and especially to us. I am left severed from you and I cannot even send letters. I will try to send this through Eretz Israel, and maybe it will arrive.

I don't know what will happen to you. Will all of you be in Vilna or stay in Rakov? I hope that you will live together, my dear and beloved ones. I had hoped that we could see each other soon, but now only God knows when this will happen.

May all of you be together and healthy and may Khost and Shepseleh not be taken from you. I am going around crushed by a weight of anxiety. Everyone here sits by the radio all day long.

May this letter reach you. This is my only comfort. Everyone here prays to God that He will defeat the dog Hitler.

From me, your husband and father, Shalom Tvi

CHAPTER FIFTEEN

SECOND WORLD WAR

Doba was still a young woman—only thirty-seven years old—in 1939, but she was emotional and high-strung and a bit of a hypochondriac. Motherhood, her greatest joy, was also the source of endless upset, which no doubt contributed to her attacks of nerves and ill health. If Shimonkeh or Velveleh so much as skinned a knee, Doba flew into a passion; when Shimonkeh nearly died of scarlet fever the summer Sonia made aliyah, no one could breathe a word to pregnant Doba, lest she become unhinged. With so much angst flutter-ing her heart, Doba was forever craving rest and relaxation. When her in-laws offered her and Shepseleh and the boys use of a cottage that they had rented in the spa town of Druskininkai that summer, Doba jumped at it. Druskininkai's mineral baths were renowned; the country air would do all of them good; there was a hammock stretched between two trees where they could take turns snoozing on warm afternoons. Doba decided that she would spend the entire summer there and, after some cajoling, she pre-vailed on her mother to join her. After all, Shalom Tvi was in America and the leather business had been sold, so for the first time in her life Beyle was free to leave Rakov and do what she wanted. What better occasion for a nice long stay in the country?

Beyle joined Doba's family at the spa right after Shalom Tvi's departure at the start of July and stuck it out at Druskininkai for as long as she could stand it. She took the waters; she tried to sleep in the hammock; she sat in the shade; she watched Shimonkeh, now eleven years old, ride his bike and Velveleh, seven, sit with his father and move wooden pieces around the chessboard. She wrote letters to her husband and bustled around the kitchen. She went to shul on Saturday with Doba. But five weeks in, Beyle decided that she had had enough. After more than forty years of hard work, idleness did not come easily. She wanted to be home. It was arranged that Beyle would depart and that Etl, Khost, and Mireleh would take her place in the Druskininkai cottage for a few weeks' vacation. By August 21, Beyle was back in Rakov writing to Sonia and Chaim about how healthy she felt after taking the waters and how glad she was that Etl's family had a chance to relax at the spa before Khost started another busy year teaching school.

It was only because Khost was away in Druskininkai that he avoided being called up by the Polish army when the Germans attacked on the morning of September 1.

With the outbreak of war, there was no question that they must leave Druskininkai immediately—but where should they go? The two couples sized up the situation anxiously. Clearly, Etl and Khost would return to Rakov—Mother could not be left alone and Khost had a job there. But what about Doba, Shepseleh, and the boys? Wouldn't it be better for them to come to Rakov too so the family could all be together? They didn't have long to debate it—they must get out before the roads became impassable and the rail lines were bombed. In the event, they decided that their two families should separate, reasoning that if they were in different places they would have a better chance of keeping some line of communication open with Sonia in Palestine and Father in America.

The little rail station outside of Druskininkai was pandemonium, but somehow the two couples shoved their children and luggage onto separate trains and somehow the trains got through to Vilna and to Olechnowicze, the station closest to Rakov. Thank God, they thought, that Rakov and Vilna were in the east of Poland, far from the Nazi invaders. (Rakov and Vilna had been incorporated into the newly formed Polish state in the 1920s, so when the war broke out, the members of both families were Polish citizens.) Thank God that on September 3, Britain and France declared war on Germany. Thank God that Poland had an army, an air force, tanks, modern weapons, the will to fight. Doba wept with joy when they opened the door to their flat near the Dawn Gate and saw that all was exactly as they had left it in June.

Then came the first German bombing raids. Sirens wailing in the street—screams and shouts in the hallway—the pounding of shoes on the stairs as the neighbors fled to the cellar. Doba and Shepseleh leapt out of bed, woke the boys, and fled downstairs with the others. They cowered in the dark and strained their ears for the thud of explosions. They huddled together trembling until the all-clear sounded. When they returned to their flat, their hearts were racing, sleep impossible. In the morning, Doba and Shepseleh dragged themselves out of bed hollow-eyed and desperate for news.

It came thick and fast in those September days and none of it was good. Britain and France were technically at war with Germany but they did nothing to help Poland. The Polish retreat from the western border had turned into a rout. The Wehrmacht seemed to be everywhere and unstoppable. The Luftwaffe dominated the skies. By September 14, Poland's air force had been effectively disabled. Sixty German divisions were converging on Warsaw, and German planes, unchallenged, were bombing every major city in the country. In the general mobilization, Khost was called up for service with the Polish army. (Shepseleh, though subject to the draft as a citizen of Poland, was spared.) Etl had no idea where her husband was being sent or when he would return. The news that arrived on September 17 baffled all of them: the Russians were now attacking Poland from the east. Evidently, the Nazis and the Soviets were allies in this new war—it made no sense, but that's how it was. Only later did it emerge that Hitler and Stalin, by the terms of a secret nonaggression pact worked out by their foreign ministers, Ribbentrop and Molotov, at the end of August, had agreed to carve up Poland between them. Hitler took the west, including Warsaw, Lodz, Cracow, and Lublin; Stalin got the east, with Lithuania thrown in as a "Soviet zone of interest." In this new division of Poland, Rakov was Russian once again; and Vilna, which had flown God knows how many flags in the past twenty years, became Russian again too, at least for the time being.

EASTERN EUROPE DIVIDED BY
GERMANY AND USSR, SEPTEMBER 1939

Gulf of Finland

LENINGRAD
(ST. PETERSBURG)

TALINN

(Estonia)

(Russia)

Baltic Sea

(Latvia)

RIGA

(Lithuania)

VILNA

where Doba and Shepselah
lived under alternating Soviet
and Lithuanian control

RAKOV

where Beyle, Etl, Khost,
and their daughters lived

VOLOZHIN   MINSK

(Poland)

(Belarus)

WARSAW

GERMAN-CONTROLLED
TERRITORY

SOVIET-CONTROLLED
TERRITORY

(Ukraine)

Vilna, Rakov, and Volozhin were absorbed by the Soviet Union after Stalin and Hitler divided
Poland between them at the start of the Second World War, September 1939. (Current borders are
indicated with — · — · — · — ; names of current nations are in parentheses.)

As quickly as it started, the war seemed to be over. The bombing stopped in Vilna. Blackout curtains were removed; street lamps were lit again at night. Shimonkeh and Velveleh slept all night in their own beds. Polish troops started to trickle back, many passing through Vilna on their way home. "I cried when we saw soldiers returning and Khost was not among them," Doba wrote her father. She and Shepseleh feared the worst, but God was merciful.

November 28, 1939

Dear Father,

I have much to tell you, but it is hard to do in a single letter. I have written to you before that Khost had been drafted to the Army. Now I can tell you that he has come back—first to Vilna and from here he returned to Rakov. You cannot imagine how happy we were when we saw him.

He was lucky. He was with us at Druskininkai and therefore reported for duty a bit later. That changed the whole situation. Shepseleh worried that if "the big ones" [i.e., the Russians] had not come, his fate would have been the same. The fact that we can joke about it is a good sign. So you don't have to worry about our men, or the rest of us. We were very glad to see the "big ones" because we had been weary of staying days and nights with the children in the basement.

The real problem now is that there is not enough money. Zloties [the Polish currency] are worth nothing. Shepleseh does not have work. The office has shrunk. Only a few workers were left and it is hard to find work. The big firms are no more. Everything has changed suddenly.

Who could imagine that such a situation could ever happen? Briefly, dear father, we are left with no means of livelihood. What I have written is only a drop in the sea. What you read in the papers is nothing in comparison to what has happened here in only three weeks.

I envy the Americans their peaceful life. They cannot fathom what is happening here and in the rest of the world.

Love, Doba

The situation in Vilna remained volatile. The Soviets had seized the city on September 19, two days after they invaded Poland, but they agreed to turn it over to Lithuania at the end of October on the condition that 20,000 Red Army troops be permitted to remain in Soviet bases on Lithuanian soil. In the final days of the Soviet occupation, civic life collapsed. The *Forward* reported that "Vilna is congested with refugees and its population suffers hunger and privation; economic life has come to a halt and many Jews wander the streets begging for a piece of bread." The Soviet pullout triggered a three-day pogrom. Vilna's Polish and Lithuanian population beat Jews in the street, wounding 200 and killing 1; scores of Jewish shops were vandalized; a policeman was killed. A typhus epidemic broke out and hospitals overflowed (Lithuanians claimed that disgruntled Poles had triggered the epidemic by cutting the city's water supply, while Poles insisted that *Volksdeutsche*—German nationals residing in Vilna—had connected sewer pipes to the municipal water supply). Meanwhile, 14,000 Jewish refugees from Poland's German-occupied sector streamed in—among them "the spiritual elite of Polish Jewry" including 2,000 *halutzim*, 2,440 rabbinical students, 171 rabbis, and assorted Bundists, teachers, journalists, and scientists whom the Nazis had expelled. The refugees survived on charity distributed by the American Jewish Joint Distribution Committee ("the Joint"), but Vilna's non-refugee Jewish residents were on their own. "The food supply is being rapidly depleted," wrote one resident. "One must brace oneself to acquire a little butter and some eggs. The queue for these items is enormous. . . . It is pointless to join the queue at 6 A.M., for by that time thousands wait at the door." White-collar workers who had been accustomed to conducting business in Polish, Russian, and Yiddish were laid off in droves because they could not speak Lithuanian, the new official language. Shepseleh, now forty-two years old, joined the ghosts who haunted the streets looking for work.

My dear Father-in-law Shalom Tvi,

   The big problem is that it is hard these days to find work. I traveled to Kovno [the Yiddish name for Kaunas, Lithuania's second-largest city and the temporary capital during the interwar period] to see if I could find something. I spent money for the trip but found nothing. All the big companies have lost everything, and there is no one to turn to. Of course, the idleness causes the money to dwindle away and the cost of living has gone up. We still have food and do not suffer, but when I think of the future, I feel like my brain is exploding. To stay sane and healthy, it is better to not think too much. Who knew that the situation would deteriorate so fast?

You know, father, that I am not one to make life difficult, so if I allow myself to write to you like this, it shows that I am totally broken. Though truthfully, others have bigger problems. There are people who were well-to-do in the past who have no roofs over their heads. There are those who have lost a relative. So we should be satisfied with our lot and not complain.

Father, please write to us in detail about yourself, about Reb Avram Akiva and his family and about Hayim Yehoshua and his family. If you have not yet received our letter, I am reminding you that the money you sent has arrived and we thank you and uncle from the bottom of our hearts. Write to us what is happening with the visa. We can no longer take care of it from here. Maybe you can handle it.

Your son-in-law Shepseleh

For the family, there was one ray of light that dark season: on November 28, Sonia gave birth to a son. They named him Arie, for Chaim's late father, though they called him Areleh as a baby and Arik when he was older. As he grew, no one could understand where the child had come by his looks—bronze, athletic, chiseled, a lanky golden boy in a short dark family. It was as if some warrior gene, after skipping many generations, had surfaced under the fierce Mediterranean sun.

"Mazal Tov, Mazal Tov, with God's will may the tender born son bring luck, blessing and peace to the world," Shalom Tvi wrote his daughter and son-in-law from New York. "May you raise him easily and may he merit a long life." Shalom Tvi sent Sonia not only blessings and prayers but a steady stream of packages—hand-me-down clothing from the rich American relatives ("here one wears clothes a few times and then they discover a new fashion, discard the garment and buy something new"), money, even the occasional brooch or necklace. Sonia's insistence that she had no need for jewelry puzzled her father. "Is it forbidden to wear jewelry there?" he demanded. "Surely women in the big cities wear jewelry even in Palestine." Jewelry was the last thing on Sonia's mind in those days. She had a toddler, not yet five, and a newborn but no refrigerator; their cow ate voraciously but provided only a trickle of milk; she worried about Arab attacks every night when Chaim drove the truck and was late getting home. *We'll come when it's quiet*, her mother and sisters used to reply when Sonia urged them to join her in Kfar Vitkin—*quiet* was their euphemism for peaceful, free of violence—but it was never quiet in the Land. Now Europe wasn't quiet either. For as long as this war lasted, Sonia knew there was no hope of getting her mother or sisters out of Poland and into Palestine. She was on her own with two small children, a stingy cow, a tiny house baking in the sun, meat and cheese spoiling in the heat, an antiquated wringer washer, hostile Arabs over the next dune, and the cowardly British government that valued oil more than human life.

So no, Sonia was not thinking about jewelry when Areleh was born in the dwindling days of 1939.

Many years later, when she had children of her own, Leah asked her mother why she had spaced her children at such long intervals. Nearly five years separated Leah and Arik, another five and a half years passed before a third child was born, and yet another five years before the last one—four children in all spread out over sixteen years. "We waited because we were poor and there was so much work to do," Sonia told her daughter.

"We met some wise people who are aware that we are sitting on the mouth of a volcano," Doba wrote her father as winter closed in on Vilna. "Anyone with means has already escaped from here. Dear father, we must do something so that we can all come to you [in New York]—Mother, Etl, Khost, Mireleh. We are not interested in going to Eretz Israel, as you suggested. It is not quiet there. We simply don't have the strength to go through a third war."

Doba saw what was going on in Vilna—the refugees lining up for bread at the Joint; prominent lawyers, wealthy businessmen, distinguished congregants from Warsaw in rags, subsisting on handouts; men like her husband broken and despairing. Escape to New York now seemed like the only hope. "We have a joke about the refugee situation," she wrote. "Everyone is laughing and saying that it pays to become a refugee, because at least someone takes care of *them*." Doba was high-strung and hyperbolic—but she wasn't foolish. She knew what was burning inside the volcano. She had a friend named Marisha whose husband had been taken by the German army at the start of the war and had not been heard from since. Four months without a letter—who knew whether he was still alive? Doba heard the rumors that the refugees brought with them—about the seizure and burning of Jewish homes and businesses in Warsaw and Lodz; about the sudden disappearance of able-bodied Jewish men. The Germans moved in and the next day the men were gone: rounded up, imprisoned, deported, God knows what. Doba wouldn't talk about it, but she knew how close it was.

Winter came and the weather turned savagely cold. For days on end Doba refused to set foot outside the apartment. The boys quit going to school on the coldest days and stayed in bed under their feather quilts—it was cheaper than paying for extra coal. Velveleh was still jumpy from the German bombing raids. If a door slammed or a book fell he startled and trembled. Shimonkeh, a year away from celebrating his bar mitzvah, was growing tall and serious. What kind of future could she give them? Doba watched the luckier neighbors pack up and leave, and she envied them. Someone had sent for them. Someone had paid their way. Someone had arranged their papers. Why not her family?

Doba was tenderhearted. It was not in her nature to heap scorn, to recriminate or lash out. But as the first winter of the war dragged on, she began to seethe. It made her crazy to see others heedlessly enjoying what she and her children lacked. No one she knew enjoyed more than the American relatives. They became the focus of her fury. She blamed them for being rich while she and her family were poor, for being comfortable while they were suffering, for not doing more to help them.

Every week, Doba wrote to her sister in Palestine and her father in New York. Every week, her letters grew more bitter:

January 17, 1940

Dear Father,

It is good that you are not here. If you were home you would have suffered.

Who could have imagined that so horrible a war had begun? You were able to see Warsaw [before leaving for America], but now Warsaw is all in ruins. Tens of thousands were killed and woe to the few Jews who remained. What we didn't see in the previous war we are going through in this war.

January [date missing], 1940

Dear Sonia,

The truth is that father's stay in the USA is a big deal for us. He sees to it that the family sends money and help to us. But we are such egotists that it does not satisfy us.

I do not understand to what extent the family [in the United States] wants to bring us to them. If they wanted us, they would begin to arrange the papers because it takes a long time, but when one does not work on it nothing will happen. Why doesn't Rosenthal make an effort? Everyone who has even a distant relative in America does all they can to get them out of here. But we have a wealthy family, and they prefer to send money instead of inviting us. Write me what you think about this.

You know that my heart is bitter. I am angry with the family and cannot understand why they have not sent all of us an invitation to come to them.

January 25, 1940

Dear Father,

I wish at least that William Rosenthal would be interested in us and help us survive in these hard times. A person needs hope. We received some money for food, but that is all the money we have. The Joint helps the refugees in Vilna but we have a family who can help us. Rakov is already barred and we can't get any money from them. God forbid that we should be refugees. Doesn't the family over there want us? Why do they remain indifferent in these hard times? They are waiting and this is a great mistake.

February 12, 1940

Dear Sonia,

Father said that a family like ours needs $50 to $60 a week [to live in America]. It will be hard to make a living [in New York] because Shepseleh does not know the language. We are still young and we can learn the language if we have to. Of course, it will be hard at first, but it will be very good for us. But they don't care so it will never happen. In my opinion, if it were not for father, we would never have received even this money.

February 19, 1940

Dear Sonia,

Father allowed me to understand that they will never invite us. Too much of a burden for them. I don't want to ask. It is enough that father needs to ask them for money to help us. It is very cold and the children spend the whole winter in bed. Thus we pass the days, while in America when it gets too cold for them they go to Florida.

March 15, 1940

Dear Sonia,

  As the holiday [Passover] nears I see how our family is torn. There are moments when my heart goes to pieces from pain for them [the family in Rakov]. Mother writes in every letter that she wants father to stay there [in New York] and bring her there. Father writes me now that they will not let him stay in the U.S. permanently. When he went to HIAS [Hebrew Immigrant Aid Society] they did not accept his application. Sonika, father should be happy to be there and not in Rakov, because in Rakov the situation is not good.

March 26, 1940

Dear Sonia,

  Hayim Yehoshua [Beyle's brother] has written from Florida—just one letter during this entire time. He writes that we need not worry. They are taking good care of father. He devotes not a single word to our situation, does not ask if we need anything, and God forbid, he does not mention anything at all about whether we could come to America. He writes calmly, as if nothing has ever happened in the world. Nothing has happened to him, because it is quiet over there and they think only about having a good time. I am angry that none of the family we have there is the least bit interested in inviting us to come to them. We know that moving to a new country one does not lick honey, but we think about our children. It would be good to take them out of here once and for all, so they at least could live peacefully during the years of their childhood and youth.

  People are leaving here and going to America and to Palestine. Thousands are fleeing from here—refugees and people from Vilna. They get their travel permits by cable—everything is settled very quickly. Naturally we ask why our family, who are people of means, cannot

*receive us and the family from Rakov? This question has cost me my
health.*

In fact, nothing was settled quickly nor did many succeed in leaving. Once
the war started, international travel became difficult to arrange. Vilna's
travel agents arbitrarily stopped booking tickets for anyone older than
eighteen or younger than fifty. Berths on transatlantic ships were scarce
due to wartime demand. Even if Doba and Shepseleh had somehow been
able to book passage out, it would not have been easy to get in. The U.S.
government had not altered its immigration policy after the outbreak of
war, but the State Department began enforcing the law more stringently
and snarling its red tape more impenetrably. State Department officials jus-
tified the squeeze by claiming they were trying to keep out potential spies
and saboteurs. But this was a smoke screen for entrenched isolationism,
xenophobia, and anti-Semitism. Public opinion was solidly on their side.
The majority of Americans had no desire to open the doors to the likes
of Doba and Shepseleh. Even after Hitler invaded Poland, the country
remained overwhelmingly opposed to easing immigration restrictions. A
bill introduced by New York's senator Robert Wagner to admit twenty
thousand German refugee children died in committee in 1939 due to opposition from the powerful anti-immigration bloc and President Roosevelt's
failure to get behind it. The truth is that from September 1939 forward,
Vilna's Jewish residents and refugees had little hope of securing sanctuary
in the United States or anywhere else in the world. The ranks of those who
succeeded were tiny: according to one report, as of April 1940, a total of 137
Vilna Jews had immigrated to all countries excluding Palestine; of these, 41
were admitted to the United States. The Joint managed to get some into
Shanghai or Siberia. South America was a haven for a handful. But very few
went from Vilna to America.

Doba blamed the American relatives for refusing to "invite" them (i.e.,
file the necessary sponsorship affidavits) and there is no evidence that the
relatives tried. But even had they done so, it's unlikely they would have succeeded.

"I walk around confused and ponder how everyone could have been envious of me for going to America," Shalom Tvi wrote to Sonia after the war started. "Maybe in America I could have done something for my children—but then suddenly came such calamity. I have been separated from everyone and only God knows for how long." The weeks dragged on, he renewed his tourist visa for another three months, letters from Doba and Etl and Beyle trickled in, but otherwise nothing changed. There were no more trips to the museum or the World's Fair. The sycamores and maples shed their leaves; the sky over the Bronx turned leaden gray. With nothing to do but ask for handouts and worry about his wife and children, Shalom Tvi became despondent. He came to depend more and more on his brother for support and guidance. Abraham found him a job at A. Cohen & Sons packing jewelry into boxes in the shipping room. It was menial, repetitive work but Shalom Tvi was happy to get it—anything to help pass the time. "I go to work a little at my brother's store and earn a little because I don't want to stay idle," he wrote Sonia. "When one does nothing the mood is much worse."

Shalom Tvi and Abraham had been close in Rakov thirty years earlier. In New York the brothers became close once more. Shalom Tvi was not as strictly observant as his older brother, but they were cut from the same traditional cloth and it was a solace for both of them to be together in old age. Shalom Tvi fell in with his brother's weekday routine: first thing in the morning they went to shul to pray, then they returned home for a bowl of cereal and two hard-boiled eggs, then Abraham had a short rest on the sofa, and then at ten o'clock they left together for work. The brothers rode home together in the evening chatting in Yiddish in the back of Sam's car. Shalom Tvi shared a single bathroom with the other family members—eight of them under one roof including Ethel and her husband, Sam Epstein, and their three children, ages twenty-one, eighteen, and twelve.

The Americans called Shalom Tvi the Uncle, and behind his back they joked fondly about his "greenness." On his first Saturday in America, the Uncle had taken out a piece of paper with an address in Texas written on it and asked one of the nephews to walk there with him. He was incredulous when they told him it was impossible. When a new baby daughter was born, the Uncle made a little sachet with salt inside, tied it with a red ribbon, and tucked it under the cushion of her carriage. Once the Uncle wandered into the living room when one of his pretty young nieces was in the arms of her fiancé engaged in what used to be called heavy petting. "Oh, I see you're playing cards," he murmured in Yiddish and left them to it. The younger relatives thought of the Uncle as a benign phantom from the Old World—polite, tidy, quiet, unassuming, wrapped in a cloud of sadness and incomprehensible Yiddish.

What Shalom Tvi thought of the Americans he never said, not even in letters to his wife and daughters. The only one he singled out for special mention was his oldest brother. In America, no one seemed to have much respect for anything or anyone, but all of them respected Abraham. Not only the family, not only the members of the Hebrew Institute of University Heights, not only his fellow Jews. Christian clerics sought him out for his wisdom about the Talmud. The Chevrah Mishnayos—Mishna study class—he founded at the shul was always full of eager students young and old. Though Abraham lived modestly, he was clearly a man of substance— substance grounded in security and law, not like in Poland where every decade a war or pogrom blew all you owned into the whirlwind. A truly religious person, Abraham was tolerant of the beliefs of others and bent to the customs of his adopted country. He let his grandchildren hang a stocking on Christmas Eve and secretly filled it with candy. When one of the granddaughters landed a job that required her to work half a day on Saturdays, Sarah hit the ceiling but Abraham said, "She is an American girl— she's lucky to have a job—let her work." Abraham was the patriarch and his word was law, but he laid down the law gently and with humility. "I had two heroes growing up," said one of his grandsons. "Grandpa and FDR." Though he had long since given up the work of the scribe, Abraham still loved to make things with his hands; his grandchildren remember him sitting outside in the summer whittling them toys and whistles with their names carved in Hebrew letters. "Mr. Cohen's patriarchal appearance distinguished him from all the people in the congregation," wrote one of the members of his shul. "He was the leader of the older generation and lived the way of life which brought respect and admiration even from people unaccustomed to it and unwilling to subscribe to it."

Shalom Tvi would have been lost in America without his brother. His niece Itel was rich but intimidating. Even her generosity was imperious—at Hanukkah Itel always made a point of giving twice as much gelt (money) to the nieces and nephews as the other aunts and uncles. William was more approachable, but he was so busy with Maiden Form that they rarely saw him. His nephew Sam downstairs was happy to chat and joke in Yiddish, yet most of the time Sam was too consumed by fighting with his brothers over the business to pay his uncle much attention. Shalom Tvi dropped hints about his family. He complained about how much money he had lost as a result of the devaluation of the Polish zloty. The Americans listened, shook their heads, and told him to keep his spirits up. No one talked about the fate of Poland. The name Hitler was a curse that they refused to utter. Abraham sent money; the others were kind but vague.

The visa extension that Shalom Tvi had been granted after the outbreak of war was due to expire on April 13, 1940. As the date approached he sized up his situation. "They will either give me a few more months, or I will have to go back to Rakov," he wrote Sonia on April 1. "In the meantime I don't have another place to go. May there be peace! I need papers to go anywhere, and if I don't have them I will have to go back to Rakov—this is surely not good." His latest idea—bringing Beyle to America and then traveling with her to Palestine after the war—was dashed when he went to the HIAS office to inquire about the paperwork. The one hope now, Shalom Tvi wrote his youngest daughter, was that "God would bring quiet to the world and we could all come to you together."

England and France were technically at war with Germany, but Europe had been eerily quiet since the carving up of Poland the previous September. The six-month lull—which came to be known as the phony war—was punctured on April 9, 1940, when the Nazis launched an air and sea attack against Norway and Denmark. Britain and France sent troops to Norway on April 18, but the Allies bungled the defense, and by the end of the month the Germans had pushed them back sufficiently to consolidate a three-hundred-mile line connecting Oslo and Trondheim. Denmark surrendered at once. The swastika now flew over Norway, Denmark, Austria, Czechoslovakia, and half of Poland.

The Cohen family wasn't paying much attention to the world situation that spring. They had troubles of their own to worry about—business trouble. After weeks of fruitless negotiations over a new contract, Local 65, the CIO-affiliated chapter of the United Wholesale and Warehouse Employees Union, went out on strike against A. Cohen & Sons. Abraham had always considered the warehouse workers at A. Cohen & Sons his friends, practically his family. He took it as a personal betrayal when picketers shouted at him in the street and jostled him as he tried to get inside the new West Twenty-third Street office. Hyman, who had played a reluctant part in the failed negotiations, became irate. It was bad enough that the union guys yelled at his father, but this was the sloppiest picket line he'd ever seen. Hyman had drilled with the First Division in France! He wasn't going to stand by and watch while these Bolshevik deadbeats slouched around at the entrance to his office. Hyman grabbed a placard from one of the strikers, rested it on his shoulder like a rifle, and, with back straight and chest thrust out, marched a few steps back and forth on the sidewalk—just to show them how it was done. "If you're going to picket—picket!" he shouted. Everybody laughed and it broke the tension. But it was a bitter day for Abraham.

The workers picketed for three days, after which the mediation board intervened and brought the two parties together. "The strike upset Father," Hyman wrote later. "He just could not believe that people, friends whom he helped in time of need, would picket against him. Actually they were picketing against the Company. He was badly hurt psychologically and never the same after the strike."

For Orthodox Jews, the weekend starts at sundown on Friday and ends at sundown on Saturday. Sundays are a workday like any other—which explains why Abraham was at the office when he collapsed on Sunday, April 28. One of the sons heard the old man fall and rushed in to find him conscious but weak. The brothers conferred and quickly decided that their father would be better off at home than in the hospital. They got him into Sam's car and tried to make him comfortable. Sam, a terrible driver under the best of circumstances, somehow managed to keep the car on the road between Manhattan and the Bronx. When they reached the house, they moved Abraham into a chair and the men carried him up the stairs and got him into bed. Dr. Fred Glucksman, who lived a few doors down on Andrews Avenue, was summoned to do an exam. The doctor broke the news to the family that Abraham had suffered a heart attack. Hyman believed that the warehouse workers' strike was responsible, but that seems unlikely. Abraham was in his late seventies; the family had a history of high blood pressure and hardening of the arteries; the strike had been settled for some time when he collapsed.

The heart attack had been fairly mild and Dr. Glucksman said that the patient should be okay in a few days if they kept him in bed and made sure he was quiet. But on May 6, a Monday, he took a turn for the worse. By the time Dr. Glucksman arrived at his bedside, Abraham was in a coma. He had suffered a serious stroke. "Pray that he does not recover," the doctor told the family. "If he does he will be a helpless invalid."

At dawn on May 10, the Germans terminated the phony war once and for all with a coordinated surprise attack on Luxembourg, Belgium, and the Netherlands—a swift deathblow that was being called a blitzkrieg—lightning war. At eight o'clock that night, Abraham died at his home in the Bronx. Since it was a Friday and after sundown, Shabbat had begun and the body could not be moved. A man from the synagogue came to sit by the bedside of the deceased and pray through the night. The family arranged a funeral service for 1 P.M. on Sunday at the Riverside Memorial Chapel, the same chapel that had handled the funeral of Itel and William's son, Lewis, a decade earlier, but the leaders of the shul wanted to do something more. They asked to have the pine coffin of the patriarch placed in the sanctuary of the synagogue he had helped to found fifteen years earlier—an honor bestowed only on rabbis and esteemed religious scholars.

University Avenue is a major six-lane thoroughfare slicing north/south through the Bronx, parallel to the East River, but on the day of the funeral the police closed the avenue to traffic on the block of the Hebrew Institute. The synagogue staff set up loudspeakers outside so the crowd that overflowed into the street could hear the prayers. The ancient poetry of the mourner's kaddish drifted into the soft air of spring.

Yit'gadal v'yit'kadash sh'mei raba
May His great name be exalted and sanctified

Yit'barakh v'yish'tabach v'yit'pa'ar v'yit'romam v'yit'nasei
v'yit'hadar v'yit'aleh v'yit'halal sh'mei d'kud'sha
Blessed, praised, glorified, exalted, extolled, mighty, upraised, and lauded
be the Name of the Holy One

B'rikh hu.
Blessed is He.

Abraham's grandfather had been alive at the time of Chaim the Volozhiner, the beloved student of the Gaon of Vilna. His father, Shimon Dov, had died while the last war raged. Now every hour brought word of fresh disasters from Europe.

Two thousand people turned out that day to pay their respects. It was the end of an era not only for the family but also for Jewish New York. The old guard was passing on and there was no one to take its place. The patriarch had died; there would be no patriarch after him.

While they were sitting shiva, Shalom Tvi approached his nephew Harry. As the oldest son of the oldest son, Harry was now by rights the head of the family. Shalom Tvi took him aside and told him quietly that, because his brother was dead, he must return to Poland. He had found a ship that was due to embark shortly and he was going to buy a ticket. Why should Ethel and Sam Epstein continue to put him up? It was one thing to live with a brother—but a niece and her husband had no obligation.

Ever gracious, Harry sat with the Uncle until he talked him out of it. Ethel and Sam would never throw him out no matter what happened. Europe was burning; the Atlantic was swarming with German submarines; how could he even think of sailing back? Here in the States he had a job and a place to live with people who loved him. He must remain until the war was over and he could be reunited with his own family.

Finally, Shalom Tvi bowed his head and agreed to do as Harry said.

According to family lore, the ship on which he had been planning to sail back to Poland was torpedoed and sunk.

Brussels fell to the Germans on May 17, a week after Abraham's death. By May 21, German soldiers were on the shores of the channel gazing across toward England. At Dunkirk, what Winston Churchill called the "whole root and core and brain of the British Army" was cut off by the Wehrmacht and had to be evacuated between May 26 and June 3. The Germans entered Paris a week later. The enfeebled French government sued for peace and a French-German armistice was signed on June 22. The Battle of Britain began soon after.

"The big ones make plans which are impossible for our heads to grasp," Shalom Tvi wrote to Sonia. "God knows how this will end."

———

July 15, 1940

Dear Sonia,

Soon it will be Rosh Hashanah, but this year the world has turned on its face. A year ago, when I arrived here, my heart was glad. Today there is mourning. Etteh [Beyle's sister] passed away. Here, my beloved brother Avram Akiva passed away. In New Haven there is also mourning. Hayim Yehoshua, our beloved brother-in-law, has died. Mourning at everybody's. The air is full of mourning—the pain and the sadness are great.

From your father who kisses all of you,
Shalom Tvi Kaganovich

CHAPTER SIXTEEN

UNDER THE BIG ONES

Etl, as the middle sister, five years younger than Doba, three years older than Sonia, had spent her life in the shadows. Doba was the acknowledged family beauty and her marriage had brought her all the pleasures and diversions of Vilna. Sonia, the family rebel, was a pioneer in the Land, the mother of sabras! Etl was the sister who had never left home. Pinched, irritable, sharp-tongued, she had married late after a score of failed matches; she was pushing thirty by the time her first child was born; she was thin and sickly and prone to digestive trouble. While Doba browsed the fashionable shops of Vilna and Sonia made the desert bloom, Etl toiled away through the years in Rakov at the family leather business, kept house for her elderly mother, nursed sick nephews, bent over a sewing machine in the failing light of dusk, and harbored grudges against spoiled relatives.

But Etl came into her own during the war. Although Khost had been pressed into the Polish army soon after the German invasion, his service was brief and relatively painless. Other fellows from Rakov had disappeared without a trace—killed, captured by the Germans, imprisoned in Soviet labor camps, never to be heard from again. But Khost had come home unscathed after a few weeks and resumed his teaching post in the Rakov school. When the Red Army marched into Rakov at the end of

September 1939, the local Communists welcomed them as liberators, and all others held their breath to see what would happen. Teachers like Khost soon exhaled. Factories, banks, and large estates were nationalized or confiscated; in the market, shops and stalls were quickly depleted of their merchandise and then closed down as government-controlled shops took over; anyone branded a capitalist, industrialist, or speculator was arrested and sent to Siberia. But the schools remained open; Jewish teachers were welcomed, even promoted; Jewish students who showed promise had a chance of winning a place in a Soviet university, with no ghetto bench.

Young Jews and the Jewish "working intelligentsia" were "really happy," wrote one contemporary, "as if awakened to a new life. New and unheard-of opportunities for work were opened up before them." The Russians were no angels and they wasted no time in outlawing Rakov's Jewish institutions—the Zionist youth groups, the Bund, the Jewish community council (kehilla), even the mikveh (ritual bath). The faithful trembled when word came that the revered Volozhin yeshiva had been converted into a cheap restaurant where gentiles gathered to wash down greasy pork with shots of vodka (supposedly the ghosts of yeshiva boys could be heard singing and praying within the walls at night). This was a tragedy. But at least pious Jews could still go to shul to pray and hope, even if, under the Big Ones, their prayers "had lost their Jewish essence and flavor." As long as a Jew wasn't too rich, too loud, too critical of Stalin, too religious, too inquisitive, too flashy, too stubborn, or too fastidious to grease the palms of Soviet officials, he could live and be well under the new regime. Khost qualified on all counts. Every month he brought home a good paycheck, and whatever Beyle needed for the household expenses, he gave. The Rakov family had enough left over to send money to Doba and Shepseleh. Despite the devaluation of the zloty and the disastrous sale of the family leather business in Rakov, they were fine. More than fine. They still had their garden of summer vegetables. They could still get milk and eggs and every now and then a chicken. No one went hungry. They listened to the stories of the refugees who had fled the Germans and felt blessed. "For most people, life appeared normal and safe," a shtetl Jew said of the Soviet period. "Nobody thought about war."

Etl felt blessed with her daughter too. Nearly four years old, Mireleh had turned from a pink-cheeked, ringleted cherub into a funny, chatty, lanky little girl. Her grandmother swooned whenever the child opened her mouth. "My only comfort is Mireleh," Beyle wrote to Shalom Tvi. "She will be a wonder girl, with her brains and the excellent way she speaks. I love how she sings and dances. She is tall and beautiful and it is a pleasure to talk to her." Etl risked the evil eye by singing her own child's praises. She wrote Sonia proudly that Mireleh was now old enough to wear trousers and run around all day on her long legs. Mireleh still remembered her cousin Leahleh in Palestine, or said she did, even though nearly two years had passed since Sonia's visit. Like Doba, Etl spoke of moving to the Land one day, but for her it was a vague, rosy dream born of longing, not desperation. Never shy about complaining, Etl evidently had nothing to complain about in the spring of 1940. Her family had the proper flour to make matzo for Passover. Thanks to Khost, they had cash to pay for food in the market, and thanks to Shalom Tvi they had a few leather hides left over from the sale of the business to barter for vegetables and chickens with the peasants. It pained Etl that her parents were separated by the war and that another visit from Sonia was out of the question, but otherwise life was good—better in some ways than before the war, because now she and her husband were the family anchor. "We need nothing," she wrote in every letter to her father and Sonia.

Whatever marital trouble there had been between Etl and Khost was long past. They were thinking about having another child.

At the start of June, Shalom Tvi went to talk to a man in New York about the logistics of traveling from the United States to Palestine. The man evidently had an official role with a Jewish immigration agency. After the meeting, Shalom Tvi went back to the Bronx apartment and wrote in great exhilaration to Sonia. All he needed was proof that he had a thousand pounds (Palestinian pounds, which had a slightly different value from British pounds) to be issued an immigration certificate as a "capitalist," thus bypassing the 1939 white paper quota. "It is so easy after all," he wrote. "I don't understand why I had been afraid before. I felt great happiness in my heart, that it will be easy to come to you." The only blot on his joy was that the family in Rakov and Vilna could not come too—"the times do not allow this. The situation is bad with mother and it will be difficult to bring them [to Palestine] from there. They say that they do not let people leave."

He mentioned the certificate and the thousand pounds in a subsequent letter, but with less excitement and more uncertainty, and then he lost his nerve. "You ask me in your own name and in the names of mother and Doba why I am not arranging a certificate to come to you," he wrote Sonia later in June. "The reason is that we cannot anticipate what will happen there, so I have decided that I should not move anywhere until there is peace in the world, until God has mercy on us and on all of Israel." Apparently, the New York relatives had talked him out of it: the crossing would be too perilous, they said, the situation in Palestine was uncertain, better to play it safe and stay put in a nation at peace. Shalom Tvi remained in the Bronx, mourning his brother and packing boxes at his brother's business. Sonia toiled on the farm at Kfar Vitkin with Chaim and their two children. Doba tore her hair out in Vilna. Shepseleh found a bit of merchandise to trade (or sell on the black market), while gratefully accepting gifts of twenty-five, fifty, sometimes one hundred dollars from the family. Etl and Khost looked forward to the end of the school year and the long lingering days of summer.

The Big Ones make plans that are impossible for our heads to grasp. God knows how this will end.

In the same month, the Big Ones made plans for the Baltic states. Alarmed by the Nazi conquest of most of Western Europe, the Soviet Union decided to raise its geopolitical profile by absorbing Lithuania, Latvia, and Estonia. The pace of regime change was particularly dizzying for Vilna: since September 1939, the city had been Polish, Soviet, Lithuanian, and now, as of June 1940, Soviet once more. The Big Ones lost no time in dismantling Vilna's institutions and economy and recasting them in the Soviet mold: large companies, banks, and factories were nationalized; capitalists were arrested and deported; "class enemies" were hounded out; and the leadership of any organization considered a threat to the Soviet Union was eliminated. Jews were tolerated as individuals, but because the Soviets aimed to erase Jewish identity and assimilate Jews into the Stalinist masses, every pillar of Jewish cultural and political life was toppled. The city's once thriving Zionist groups, religious societies, the Bund, and the Yiddish newspapers were immediately banned. Centuries of Jewish culture, consciousness, and nationalism disappeared or went underground. Overnight, the Jerusalem of Lithuania was stripped of its aura of holiness.

For Doba and Shepseleh the Soviet takeover was a crisis, not a catastrophe. Shalom Tvi quit sending money from America for fear that the Bolsheviks would appropriate it—but under the new regime, there was less need for handouts. Since Shepseleh was out of work anyway, the economic shake-up hardly made a difference. Neither he nor Doba was especially religious or politically involved, so the shutdown of Jewish institutions didn't affect them much. A Yiddish newspaper soon began to appear again, though it adhered to a strict Communist line. A Jewish labor leader became the city's vice mayor. The Joint was permitted to continue distributing charity to refugees. The city's synagogues remained open, though attendance fell off dramatically. Doba, perhaps fearing that her letters would be read by the authorities, was careful not to criticize the new regime. But in fact, the change of government had its advantages. Anyone who had been a resident in Vilna on September 1, 1939, automatically became a Soviet citizen, which meant that Doba and Shepseleh were now citizens of the same nation as Beyle, Etl, and Khost. For the first time since the war broke out, the two branches of the family could visit each other. "I miss everyone like a little girl," Doba wrote Sonia. "Imagine my joy when I can finally see them again. Etl writes that mother has aged and weakened from yearning."

It was hot and eerily tranquil that summer in Rakov. When school let out, Etl and Khost took Mireleh for walks in the woods and they bathed in the lake. At the end of June, Etl discovered that she was pregnant, though she kept it a secret for the time being. Beyle, suffering in the heat, pined over her scorched garden. Ready-made bread had disappeared from the stores, so Beyle had to send grain to the mill to be ground and baked in an oven fueled by wood that she carried herself. Though milk and meat were scarce, no one went hungry. Etl refused all of her father's offers of money, insisting they needed nothing. "What a wonderful country," Shalom Tvi wrote sarcastically of Sovietized Poland. "They have nothing but they need nothing."

As summer wore on, the pace of political arrests by the NKVD (the Soviet security police) accelerated. Bundists and Trotskyites were purged.

Zionist leaders were given an eight-year jail sentence. "Nonproductive elements" disappeared from the shtetlach and the cities. Had the family held on to the leather business, they might have been at risk, but NKVD agents were not interested in an old woman and a young mother supported by a schoolteacher. Most of the family's money had evaporated when the Zloty was abolished on January 1, 1940, a fate they shared with many. As one journalist wrote, "Within an hour, in one stroke everybody became poor: he who owned a million Zloty and he whose entire property did not exceed a few Zloty." Still, most found a way to get by with a side job, a bit of foreign currency, some dabbling in the black market, and bartering with local peasants. The Rakov family was lucky compared with their cousins in Volozhin. Chaim's brother Yishayahu and his brother-in-law, Meir Finger, lost their imported fruit business after the Soviet takeover and both of them remained out of work for months. Yishayahu, down to his last coins, still hoped to move to Palestine. Chaim's sister Chana fared no better. The Soviets appropriated her house in Volozhin and subdivided it: Chana and her family were left with one small room and the kitchen, and were forced to pay rent for the privilege. Grumbling about it was ill-advised—NKVD agents were only too happy to round up malcontents and ship them off to Siberia.

The Volozhin relatives also kept their mouths shut when the town's new chief Soviet administrator ordered that the central marketplace be made over into a "people's park." This was part of an official Soviet policy of razing the old commercial hearts of the shtetlach and moving businesses into large state-owned buildings. Workmen got busy demolishing the shops, pulling up the paving stones, planting trees and flower beds, and installing benches. One day an enormous crate arrived from the Soviet Union containing the pieces of a statue. A local Jew named Mendl Goldshmid described what happened:

We assembled the pieces, and a tall statue grew up. Stalin wearing a military dress dominated the square, extending his hand westward. But a grave problem yet arose. Close to the statue stood a huge Catholic cast iron cross. The communist secular authorities considered the presence of a cross beside the "Sun of the Nations" as an unbelievable sacrilege. They decided to demolish the cross. On a Saturday evening a unit

*of soldiers encircled the site. A demolition charge was set, and the cross
was blown up. I was ordered to take away the broken fragments.*

*The Gentiles accused me of being responsible for the destruction of
the holy cross. They waited for the revenge time.*

Under the Soviets, everything was political. When the new school year
began in September, Khost was appointed principal. With the promotion,
however, came constant scrutiny by NKVD agents for "ideological fidelity."
Schools were the ideal environment for political indoctrination, and the
pressure on Khost to enforce the party line was enormous. If any teacher
deviated, Khost would be held accountable. Hebrew was banned and Yiddish took its place; classics of (politically acceptable) Yiddish literature
could be taught, but anything that promoted religion or the religious
impulse had to be rigorously excluded from the curriculum. Jewish history,
any mention of the Bible, and anything that smacked of Jewish nationalism
were banned. (In Volozhin, a friend of Yishayahu quit teaching in protest
when Yiddish was substituted for Hebrew at the Tarbut school.) The Jewish
library was emptied of objectionable books—that is, most of its contents.
Khost was ordered to introduce special classes on Marxism and Leninism
into the curriculum; he traded his tailored suits for coarse open-necked
shirts and high boots (de rigueur under the Soviets); he had to work on
Shabbat. His mother-in-law still attended shul, but it would have been
politically risky for the school principal to be seen wearing a yarmulke.
Khost was aware that Mireleh would grow up with little or no Jewish education, and perhaps only the vestige of a Jewish identity. But that was a price
he and Etl were willing to pay. The alternative was the Nazis.

Vilna was still crowded with refugees, but otherwise life had improved
so much under the Soviets that Doba quit raging about escape and shifted
the lens of her anxiety to her parents. "Father is suffering," she wrote Sonia
in October. "He is alone, broken and has to live in the same house with
good Gishe Sore. He sounds sad and worried. He always asks: When will I
see you children? I cry and wonder when mother and father will be together
again. She wrote to me that she misses father with every step she takes."
Doba let drop in the same letter that Shepseleh was finally working and
bringing home four hundred litai (the Lithuanian currency) a month.

By the start of the new year, Chaim's brother and brother-in-law had found work in Volozhin as well. It didn't hurt that Kestlikh, the chief administrator who had ordered the marketplace cleared for the people's park, was himself a Jew. There was no question that Jews were rising under the new regime. Jewish school principals, Jewish mayors, Jewish officers commanding squads in the Red Army, Jews getting jobs while Poles were being packed off to Siberia. *Where would it end?* the local gentiles muttered through gritted teeth.

———

Vilna, January 20, 1941

Dear Sonia,

I have good news for you. A dear guest has arrived here—Mother!— may she stay well. I have not dared to imagine that this would happen. They kept promising to come but only now have the authorities allowed them. At long last we see each other. Mother has aged since we had last seen her. Soninka, I cannot tell you how glad I was to see her.

Mother has already been with us for two weeks, and I want her to stay a few more weeks, until after the Bar Mitzvah of Shimonkeh on February 11. But Mother does not want to stay that long because Etl is due to give birth. She suggests that she would stay if Etl and Mireleh could be persuaded to come here to Vilna and Etl could give birth here. I would be so happy finally to see them all.

Love, Doba

Beyle remained with Doba and Shepseleh and the boys for a month—long enough to celebrate Shimonkeh's bar mitzvah on February 11, 1941. "It was a fabulous visit and I enjoyed it very much," she wrote her husband. "Doba came with Shimonkeh to meet me at the train station, and we both cried from happiness." She couldn't stop marveling over her grandsons. Velveleh was a model child, sensitive, artistic; he played the violin, he drew beautifully, his teacher praised him as the best student in class. Shimonkeh, thin, pale, and serious, was growing up to be a true Jewish scholar. He chanted his haftarah portion perfectly at his bar mitzvah service; he dutifully laid tefillin and prayed every day. Doba was proud to see her firstborn become a man, but she couldn't help worrying about what kind of future he would have under the godless new regime. When the talk turned to politics, they spoke in code and euphemisms. Hitler was referred to as Haman, the evil Persian councilor in the Book of Esther who plotted to kill the Jews, or "your stepfather." *Do you think your stepfather will try to invade Palestine?* they asked when discussing the news of Rommel's German Afrika Korps massing against the British in North Africa. They hoped the boys did not understand. Doba and Beyle shed many tears over the interminable separation from Shalom Tvi. As always they talked about moving to Palestine or New York, or joining the families together in Rakov. But it was just talk and they knew it. The Big Ones weren't letting people out, and the English and the Americans weren't letting people in. *After the war, after the war*, they said again and again. God willing Haman would be defeated, his bones broken and scattered.

Beyle returned to Rakov in the middle of February. Etl had her baby two weeks later—another girl, born at home on March 1, 1941. The birth was easy, the baby was healthy, Etl was up and around in a couple of weeks. They agonized over the name and finally chose Doba Beyle, honoring sister, mother, and grandmother.

Their letters moved (slowly) around a three-noded circuit through winter and into the spring. It took weeks, sometimes months, for a letter to arrive, but that didn't deter them from pouring out their hearts to each other. They were a close, anxious, communicative family. The same letter sometimes made the complete circuit so that those in Vilna, Rakov, Kfar Vitkin, and New York could all enjoy it.

Etl chastised Sonia for failing to send any greetings to Khost in her last letter: "I wonder about it and am angry. Absolutely unpleasant to receive such a letter. Possibly you wrote without thinking. Next time think about it. Khost has said nothing, but it was very strange."

But by the next letter, Etl had forgotten all about it. Five days before Passover, she snatched a few minutes to write to Sonia about the children and their preparations for the holiday: "Doba'leh [five weeks old] develops well and it seems that she will be a pretty girl. She already knows how to scream. Mireleh is very happy with her sister, and watches that no one will take her. On Monday night it will be Pessach Eve. We have already baked matzot and we have good chickens. The weather is poor, cold and wet."

Beyle added her own brief message at the end. She was suffering from a heart condition and was unable to get the fresh fruit that her doctor had prescribed. Her spirits were low; the weather depressed her; she could barely summon the strength to write even a few lines: "Sonikah, be careful about your health. I did not have enough wisdom to guard my health, and now I am sorry. I sit at home and can do nothing and the situation is difficult. When father was with me, he watched over me but those were different times. That is how it is. Everything is from God and from providence. I am asking God to make the weather warmer and then I will feel better. I want to unite with father and come to you, as we had planned. Yours, Mother."

That letter was dated April 7, 1941.

On May 30, 1941, Doba sent Sonia a postcard from Vilna:

I want to go home for a few days and bring mother.
Have you heard from father? Mercy on him.
So alone in his old age. May there be peace and then
we could see each other.

And then the circuit was broken.

The Nazis entered Vilna on June 24, Volozhin on June 25, and Rakov on June 26. There were no more letters from Europe after that.

CHAPTER SEVENTEEN

"THEY SNATCH WHOLE STREETS"

The summer solstice fell on Shabbat in 1941, which meant that in Volozhin devout Jews had to wait until nearly ten o'clock at night before they could kindle a spark or flip a switch. Reuven Rogovin was such a Jew, and on Saturday, June 21, 1941, he duly sat through the long silent gloaming before turning on his radio. It was worth the wait. Louis Aragon, the celebrated French Communist writer, was visiting Moscow and a concert in his honor was broadcast from the Soviet capital that night. The reception in Volozhin was spotty, but good enough for Reuven to enjoy the music as brightness slowly drained from the sky. After the concert, the announcer read the news as usual—nothing of note. Reuven went to bed. The next morning, he didn't bother with the radio—nothing ever happened on Sunday. But bad news came the old-fashioned way, spread from mouth to mouth: Fayve Yosef Simernicki, a local socialist activist, had died of old age. Reuven joined the small procession to the old Jewish cemetery on a knobby hillside behind the yeshiva-turned-restaurant. It was on the way to the funeral that a friend shared with Reuven another piece of bad news, more startling than the death of an old man. "Molotov [the Soviet minister of foreign affairs] spoke on the radio," the friend confided nervously. "The Germans attacked Russia. Their planes bombed Minsk, Kiev, Harkov, and other Soviet towns."

When the funeral was over, Reuven hurried to the people's park in the former Volozhin marketplace. A great crowd had gathered.

I saw many of the Volozhin Jews crowded together. They argued in loud voices. They formed two camps: one was pro-Soviet and the other pro-German. Workers and artisans were sure that the Soviets would overcome the Germans swiftly. Merchants and dealers, to the contrary, were convinced that the Germans would win. They refused to listen to any of the refugees' tales about the German atrocities and their blood-curdling deeds against Jews. They considered the accounts of horrors as Soviet propaganda. Many Volozhin inhabitants witnessed the German 1918 invasion. They assumed that the 1941 Germans would not be in any great measure different from those in 1918. During the occupation of the First World War they [the Germans] did not hurt any Jews. So they said, "It is not reasonable that this cultivated and organized nation could change during one generation. Why would they hurt us now? The people working for the Bolsheviks, and in love with them, they should be afraid now, but not the common Jews."

Similar conversations were taking place in Rakov and Vilna and every shtetl, town, and city in Russian-occupied Poland. Nobody, not even Stalin, had had an inkling that Hitler was planning to break his pact with the Soviet Union and launch one of the most massive invasions in history. No Polish or Lithuanian Jews went to bed on the night of Saturday, June 21, thinking that they had observed their last Shabbat in freedom. Etl sang Mireleh a song, bid her mother good night, gave baby Dobaleh a late feeding in the hope that she would sleep longer. Then she got in bed beside her husband. At 3:30 A.M. on Sunday, while they slept, 3 million Nazi soldiers and two thousand Luftwaffe bombers sprang at them out of the west.

When the crisis came, the Soviet authorities proved to be useless. Scrambling to save their own necks, they left the local population utterly on their own in "bewilderment and panic." In Volozhin there was a hasty conscription of able-bodied men under the age of fifty. A thousand reported for duty, but the Soviets could only process fifty men—and those were dispersed when a Luftwaffe squadron passed overhead while they mustered.

"The authorities were busy trying to evacuate the important persons to safe places deep inside Russia," wrote Reuven Rogovin. "The Soviets did not tell us what to do, whether we should stay in our town with the German enemy approaching rapidly or whether we should escape to Russia. Each person had to decide for himself."

Chaim's brother Yishayahu debated this question heatedly with his good friend Benjamin Shishka. Benjamin said he was going to evacuate with the Russians; Yishayahu tried to talk him out of it. Yishayahu was convinced he had nothing to fear from the Nazis: he was a Zionist, not a Bolshevik—let the Germans send him to Palestine if they didn't want him. Benjamin fled east with the Soviets. Yishayahu went home to his wife and children and waited.

Rakov, twenty-five miles east of Volozhin, had one more day to wait. The Soviets organized a hasty evacuation of the schoolteachers along with a handful of intellectuals and a dozen young men who had been conscripted into the Red Army. After bidding farewell to Etl, Beyle, and the children, Khost left with this group. They were headed to Minsk—east, away from the Germans.

Doba had been sixteen years old in the last months of the Great War when the Germans marched into Rakov. She remembered it perfectly. They were all afraid when the Germans entered the town, but it quickly became apparent that they had nothing to fear. The Germans stole nothing, burned nothing, insulted no one. They sang while they marched.

The German soldiers who entered Vilna on June 24, 1941, neither marched nor sang.

There had been bombing raids on the city on Sunday and again on Monday—but by dusk the droning of aircraft receded. As night fell, Lithuanians took to the streets and Jews shut themselves in their apartments. Doba and Shepseleh's front windows gave on Pivno Street, a major thoroughfare, and they stood looking out from behind the curtains at their Lithuanian neighbors milling around below. In the street, the sound of distant engines rose in a whining crescendo—the motorcycles of the German vanguard. The soldiers rode two to a bike—one driving, the other training a machine gun at the windows of the buildings. Next came tanks decorated like parade floats, with huge red banners stamped with black swastikas at the center, and then the artillery and finally an endless stream of trucks crammed with soldiers. The bystanders cheered and waved white cloths and shouted "*Valia, valia!*" (Long live). The Lithuanians joyously welcomed their Nazi "liberators."

Pivno Street was silent and deserted when Doba, Shepseleh, and the boys awoke on Tuesday, June 24. The shopwindows were shuttered; even the arch under the Ostra Brama was empty. Everyone who had the will and the means to escape was heading east with the retreating Red Army. Everyone who remained in Vilna was now a subject—or prisoner—of the Third Reich.

"I don't know and cannot imagine what has happened with them," Shalom Tvi wrote Sonia frantically. "Have they stayed where they were or have they escaped to Russia? Only one thing is clear to me, that wherever they are it is not good. May God allow that they be healthy and alive. For mother it would be better to remain in Rakov, also for Etl with the children and Doba with the children it would be better to remain, because whatever happens, they would be in their own beds, and they would not be starving. But for Shepseleh and Khost it would be better in Russia."

Even half a world away, they knew each other's thoughts and anticipated each other's decisions. Doba and her children stayed put and slept in their own beds. Etl and her daughters did the same. Khost fled for the Soviet Union. Or tried to. In the event, the party of Rakov teachers and intellectuals was too slow, and the Germans caught up to them outside Minsk. Khost and the others were taken prisoner and marched into Minsk with the entering Wehrmacht. He was the first of the family to disappear.

The Nazis had had two years of experience in the gutting of Jewish communities, and by the summer of 1941 they had gotten it down to a science. First they removed the leaders. A couple of random public killings instilled fear and enforced submission. Next the able-bodied men were targeted. The cowed survivors fell quickly into line.

But there was always room for improvement. Vilna, with its combustible mix of cultured Jews, anti-Semitic Lithuanians, and stateless Poles, became a kind of laboratory for Nazi terror and mass murder.

Shepseleh's job, whatever it had been under the Soviets, ended the day the Germans took control. Overnight, he joined the huge ranks of the Jewish unemployed: Jews who were fired from Vilna's hospitals, universities, and public offices; Jews whose businesses were shut down or appropriated or "Aryanized"; Jews who were replaced by Lithuanians. Shepseleh stayed inside with the boys—already Jewish men were being attacked or grabbed off the streets. On June 28, a dead body was found near their home on Pivno Street. Doba left the apartment only when they needed food. Jews were now forbidden to walk on the sidewalks, to converse with a gentile or set foot in a gentile home, or to appear on the city's major thoroughfares. Doba took her place in line outside the food shop, but the Lithuanian neighbors shoved her to the back. Gentile women who a week ago had smiled at her and stopped to ask after her sons now turned their backs. The Nazis had quickly set up a Lithuanian police force to do their dirty work, and Lithuanians signed on enthusiastically. The next time Doba went out for food, the Lithuanian police were on hand to divide shoppers into two lines—one for Aryans, one for Jews. Doba spent the morning of July 4 sewing: starting that day every Jew in Vilna had to wear two badges—one on the chest, one on the back—of yellow circles set in a square of white cloth, with the letter *J* stitched like a barbed hook at the center. Four days later the orders changed and they had to replace the patches with yellow armbands. So Doba had to sew four of those.

Or by that time, maybe only three.

Herman Kruk was a Warsaw-born journalist, library director, and bibliophile, who kept a meticulous diary of his experience in the war. Soon after the Nazis took Warsaw, Kruk escaped and made his way to Vilna, where he continued to write faithfully in the diary. Actually, what Kruk composed was less a diary than a modernist collage, a kind of verbal newsreel of official orders, newspaper headlines, rumors, overheard dialogue, eyewitness accounts of arrests, evacuations, random violence, orchestrated violence, vital statistics, laments, surrealist street theater, and intimate cries of grief and fear. Kruk went prospecting in the mud of occupied Vilna and whatever he hauled out he wrote down. The diary survived and remains one of the most vividly textured accounts of daily life under Nazi occupation.

On July 3, 1941, Kruk wrote:

They Snatch Whole Streets

In the past two days, the snatching assumed a mass character. It is dangerous to leave your home.

PEOPLE ARE DRIVEN OUT OF THEIR APARTMENTS

Most recent events: they come at night, drive the whole family out of the apartment, take the men away, and the rest remain with their belongings in the open courtyards. The apartment is sealed. And there isn't anybody to protest to.

At some point, very likely early in July, Shepseleh was snatched. The exact circumstances will never be known but the range of possibilities was narrow. The Nazis were ingenious but repetitive: the same scenario with only minor variations was executed thousands of times in those weeks. It could have happened in the courtyard of the Pivno Street apartment building in the middle of the night or in broad daylight on a city street. Shepseleh might have been hurrying down an alley with some precious object that he intended to trade for food or simply standing by the window when he was spotted and reported. The vise of a hand closed on his arm, the snout of a gun tapped at the small of his back, a shoulder shoved his shoulder, and they had him. Already there was a Yiddish word for them: *hapunes*—snatchers.

Shepseleh was forty-four years old that summer, thin, refined, healthy but not robust. What he wanted most in the world was to support his family. As the *hapunes* led him away they told him that they were taking him to work. "To work, to work," they kept shouting, never saying where or at what. *Work was good*—or better than nothing; work was life for Doba and the boys. Shepseleh was put in a sealed courtyard or a holding pen at

Lukiszki Prison with an ample platoon of "co-workers"—fifty or sixty men in their twenties, thirties, forties, and fifties, many, like him, wearing suits and ties, some carrying small suitcases or little leather kits for their razor, toothbrush, and comb. So they could stay tidy while they worked. They were marched out of Vilna to the south into the fields that pressed up close to the city. It was infernally hot and dry in Lithuania that summer, and in no time the men's shirts and the armpits of their jackets were wet through with sweat. Shepseleh was accustomed to spending summer afternoons sitting in the shade outside a dacha playing chess with Shimonkeh and Velveleh. It had been years, decades, since he had walked so far under the blazing sun. Finally the fields gave way to woods of pine, oak, and maple. The sun was broken by needles and leaves into flecks of gold. Birds trilled liquidly. Some of the men asked for water but the guards hurried them along. Shepseleh could make out the occasional peaked cottage roof between the tree trunks: they were in dacha country. Paneriai the Lithuanians called this forested summer colony—Ponery in Polish, Ponar in Yiddish. Shepseleh's family had never vacationed here but he had heard of it. *Halutzim* used to come to picnic amid the wildflowers. Ponar meant rest, quiet, trees echoing with birdsong. Why on earth were they being taken to work *here*?

From the diary of Herman Kruk:

What is happening in Ponar?

On the tenth of this month [July], a rumor came to the Judenrat that people were shot in Ponar. The Judenrat didn't want to hear anything and considered it an unfounded rumor.

Ponar was a gift that the Soviets had unwittingly left behind for the Germans. In the last months of their occupation, the Soviets had started work on a massive fuel-storage facility adjacent to the existing rail line at Ponar. The plan was to excavate a series of pits in which to sink fuel tanks, but the Germans arrived before the project was completed. Nonetheless, one pit measuring sixty feet across and twenty feet deep was in place, a second sixty-foot pit had been partially dug out, and five satellite pits had been started. One of the pits had a twenty-foot-deep trench going halfway around its perimeter. The Nazis understood at once that these immense empty cavities in the earth could be used for something other than fuel storage. The business of mass slaughter was just ramping up in the summer of 1941. Later it would become routine, but in the early days the planners and designers were still making it up as they went along. Ponar was an inspired bit of improvisation.

Hitler and his henchmen deemed the business of genocide too vast, complex, and important to be handled by the Wehrmacht—the regular army. Instead, the SS (Schutzstaffel—"defense echelon"), a paramilitary police force that reported directly to Hitler, was tapped to set up an elite unit called the Einsatzgruppen ("special duty groups" is the rough literal translation—"mobile death squads" captures their function). Tough Nazi loyalists were recruited to be Einsatzgruppen foot soldiers; its officers included a large proportion of lawyers, doctors, doctorates, even a few pastors. The four Einsatzgruppen (lettered A through D) were further broken down into subunits of Einsatzkommandos and Sonderkommandos. Since the manpower of the entire Einsatzgruppen was only about 3,000 (each of the four main groups had between 600 and 1,000 men), efficiency and ingenuity were essential.

Einsatzkommando 9, a subunit of Einsatzgruppe B with about 160 men at its disposal, was assigned the task of "cleansing" Vilna, a city with 60,000 Jewish residents and an additional 20,000 Jewish refugees. It was a daunting task but Einsatzkommando 9's leader, SS-Obersturmbannführer Dr. Alfred Filbert, a lawyer from Darmstadt, set about it energetically. Filbert put together an auxiliary force of 150 men cherry-picked from the Lithuanian political police to assist with the work; he had lists drawn up of Vilna's Jews, with a separate category for wealthy families, intellectuals, and political activists; he ordered "snatchers" to target the leaders and able-bodied men first so as to leave the women, children, and elderly defenseless. And he had the good fortune of inheriting a ready-made mass murder site at Ponar. "The executions are to take place away from cities, villages, and traffic routes," SS commander Heinrich Himmler specified. "The graves are to be leveled to prevent them from becoming places of pilgrimage. . . . Executions and places of burial are not to be made public." Ponar was perfect on every score.

Ponar was supposed to be a secret but there were witnesses to what happened there that July. In the first week of the month, a couple of Wehrmacht drivers and a clerk saw a column of prisoners marching on the road and they followed them to the site. They noted that the men moving the column along with their carbines were not Nazis but Lithuanian civilians wearing armbands. The clerk reported that all the prisoners were men "between about twenty and fifty. . . . These prisoners were really quite well-dressed and most of them were carrying hand luggage such as small suitcases." When they reached the site, the prisoners were marched around the perimeter and into the semicircular trench that ringed one of the partially excavated pits. They were ordered to stand silently in the twenty-foot-deep trench, but not all complied. According to one of the drivers, "An elderly man stopped in front of the entrance for a moment and said in good German, 'What do you want from me? I'm only a poor composer.' The two civilians standing at the entrance started pummeling him with blows so that he literally flew into the pit."

Shepseleh was not one for making trouble. He took his place with the others in the trench. He waited for his pick and shovel to be issued. But no work tools were in evidence. Instead the men with the carbines ordered all of them to take off their shoes, jackets, and shirts. Jackets and shoes were to be piled on the side of the trench. Shirts were to be wrapped around their heads and faces. Anyone who was slow or reluctant got slammed with a truncheon or the butt of a rifle. The orders were loud, clear, quick but incomprehensible. Shepseleh was told to grasp the naked waist of the man in front of him. A pair of wet trembling hands grasped his waist from behind. Shepseleh and nine other men were marched like that out of the trench. The ten of them stood in a blind human chain at the lip of a pit intended for fuel tanks. The air exploded, bullets ripped into flesh, and Shepseleh fell into the pit. The witnesses differ on exactly how the firing was done. One said there were ten Lithuanian auxiliaries armed with rifles or handguns—one for each victim in the batch. Another swore the killing was done by one man with a light machine gun. When Shepseleh's body fell into the pit, it landed on a pile of warm bodies. Some of them were still alive. A guard stationed above the pit used his pistol to finish off anyone who was moving.

"We stayed there for about one hour," one of the witnesses said later, "and during this time some four to five groups were executed, so I myself watched the killing of about forty to fifty Jews." The witnesses made no move to stop or protest what they saw, but their consciences were not entirely defunct. "We all said to one another what on earth would happen if we lost the war and had to pay for all this?"

By the end of the day, Shepseleh's corpse was embedded in a layer of four hundred fresh corpses. Before calling it a night, the guards sprinkled them with a thin coating of sand and lime so the pit would be ready for the next day's slaughter. Witnesses recalled seeing the sand shift and heave for hours afterward.

Still, they all died eventually. By September, twenty thousand Jews— most of them men, like Shepseleh, in the prime of their lives—were missing from Vilna.

CHAPTER EIGHTEEN

"AKTION"

July 11, 1941

Dear Sonia and Chaim,

Thank God that we are all healthy and that it is quiet at your place. May God grant that it is always quiet there. Now, dear children, things have changed. Even though you write you received letters from mother and from Doba and that they are well—now only God knows what is happening to them. They are in the line of fire. May God protect them, that they should stay alive. I am very worried about them. I am sure they suffer hunger, but the most important thing is that they survive.

Live in goodness.

Your father,
Shalom Tvi Kaganovich

A man who fled east with the group of Rakov schoolteachers said that Khost was imprisoned in a German camp near Minsk. It might have been Stalag

342, the notorious prison in Maladzyechna where some thirty thousand Soviet citizens and soldiers died in the course of the war. According to his comrade, Khost escaped but was recaptured and killed by the Nazis. Date unknown.

July 27, 1941

Dear Children,

The atrocities described in the newspapers grip me with fear. There are nights in which I cannot fall asleep—I am troubled by such difficult thoughts. But I quickly change them to happier thoughts. I imagine the good and happy times when you came to visit us with Leahleh. Ah! How sweet and happy that time had been. And so I expel my thoughts and brace myself with hope for the good.

Your father who blesses and kisses you,
Shalom Tvi Kaganovich

July 28, 1941

Operational Situation Report USSR No. 36
Einsatzgruppe B:
Location: Minsk

1. *Police Activity*

Until further notice, about 200 persons are being liquidated daily in Minsk. . . . Actions were further carried out in Rakov, about 40 km from Minsk, and in the forest region north of the Minsk-Borissov-Krupka line. 58 Jews, Communist officials, and agents as well as soldiers in plain clothes suspected of having contact with partisan groups, were liquidated. In addition, 12 Jewesses who were proven to be agents for the KP during the Polish campaign were shot.

Etl was alone with her aged, ailing mother, a four-month-old baby, and a bright, curly haired, fatherless five-year-old when the first *Aktion*—roundup and slaughter—was carried out in Rakov.

In the initial weeks, the occupiers were careful to give reasons for why they killed. There were laws and they were simply enforcing them. If your patch was too small or the *J* was off center, if you set foot on the sidewalk, if you refused to hand over instantly whatever they demanded, you had broken the law and the penalty was death. If a German died, ten Jews must pay with their lives—or better yet a hundred. It was always the victims' fault—even the war itself was laid at the feet of the Jews. The Germans were not murderers; they had their reasons as to why the death penalty was necessary for every infraction of their law.

The "reason" given for the first *Aktion* in Rakov was that the local Jews had aided a group of Russian prisoners. The Germans had taken so many prisoners from the retreating Red Army that they had to press one of the Rakov synagogues into service as a military prison. The prisoners, according to one account, were "close to death when they arrived—starving, naked, barefoot, beaten and abused." They were so hungry that they ate the grass and flowers in the synagogue courtyard and stripped the bark off trees. Rakov Jews saw an opportunity to help while earning a bit of desperately needed money. Women cooked and baked and then smuggled the food into the synagogue compound and sold it to the prisoners. Security must have been lax, because with the help of the local Jews all the prisoners managed to escape and melt into the surrounding peasant villages. This was the pretext for the Nazi *Aktion*. Operatives of Einsatzgruppe B rounded up fifty-five Rakov Jews (the exact number varies in different accounts), including women, children, and the elderly, took them into the forest about twenty-five miles from town, shot them, and dumped the bodies in a shallow grave.

A Rakov Jew named Moshe Pogolensky wrote about the aftermath:

> At first, we did not know where to find them since we were not allowed to walk in the streets. A few days passed and some of the Christians said that they saw the bodies inside a hole in the ground. As soon as the rumors spread in the shtetl, three members of Chevra Kadisha,

the Jewish burial society, immediately volunteered to give them a proper burial, despite the perils involved in doing such a mitzvah. Among them, Israel Yitzhak, the smith, Hirshska, the ingle, and Yakov Cholsky, volunteered to bring them to Jewish burial. They secretly went to the killing field, removed the cover of the hole in which the bodies were thrown, quietly took all the victims they found, and put them on buggies and took them to the Jewish cemetery for burial. Sadly, the Germans found out about this, discovering the three men. They immediately took the men away and executed them and their remains were never found.

Fear and darkness spread amongst the Jewish population in town. Each person tried to find a hiding place until the terrors would pass. Not one Jew was seen outside. Everyone closed himself in his home with his shutters shut and there was a deathly quiet surrounding the town.

Etl sealed up the house on Kashalna Street and took charge of her family. She knew how to sew; she was experienced in buying and selling from years of working in her parents' leather business; she was smart and resourceful and desperate. She was sure—they all were sure—that "the terrors would pass." She just had to keep her family alive long enough to greet that day. She probably had some leather hides or garments stashed away that she could sell or barter. There might have been a bit of cash. Many Jewish women were forced to work for the German occupiers, cleaning their homes, washing and sewing their clothes, scrubbing the streets, pushing papers in their offices, and Etl may have been among them. She did whatever it took to survive. Etl was, or had been, on good terms with the gentile neighbors, and she was fortunate that the gentiles in Rakov were mostly Belarusians, not Lithuanians. The Nazis brought out the worst in everyone, but the Lithuanians were among the more eager collaborators, and their worst was worse than the Belarusians'.

Etl and her mother and children spent the scorching summer of 1941 shuttered in their house near the Catholic church. What happened outside seeped in through the cracks like a foul odor. The Nazis set up a Judenrat—the council that mediated between the occupiers and the prisoners. Though no one wanted to serve, the Germans threatened more killings if four men did not step forward. An unwilling council was formed. Their main task was serving as bagmen for the plunder that the Germans demanded—clothing, jewelry, money, even eggs and chickens. The Jews were filthy vermin but evidently their possessions escaped the taint. One day the Germans announced that the bodies that had been retrieved by the slain members of the Chevra Kadisha could be buried in the Jewish cemetery after all: graves were dug amid the stunted pines, prayers were chanted hastily, the dead were consigned to the hands of the Almighty. Then fourteen more Jews disappeared, murdered and dumped where no one would ever find them. There were stories of "good" Germans who turned a blind eye and sadistic Germans who went out of their way to humiliate, torture, draw blood. Some of the tortures could have been concocted only by madmen. Devout old Jewish men were lined up in the marketplace and forced to yank out each other's beards. The inmates of insane asylums were turned loose in synagogues to taunt and beat and crush the bones of observant Jews. The Judenrat of a nearby shtetl was given twenty minutes to come up with ten thousand cigarettes. There was no logic, no motive, no apparent pattern, except that more and more Jews died.

Still Etl heard nothing from her father and sisters, nor they from her.

In Vilna, your fate depended on what symbol was inked on your documents. A certificate typed in German and stamped with a swastika, proof that you worked for the Nazis, was usually enough to persuade a snatcher to let you go. The horse stamp used by the Lithuanian administration had less authority. The various rubber stamps applied by private employers permitted you to work but rarely to escape if a snatcher grabbed you. People were "driven out of their minds" trying to figure out which stamp was the safest and how to get their hands on the "iron document" issued by the Nazis. But often it made no difference. Plenty of snatchers ripped up your documents no matter what stamp they bore, threw the scraps in your face, and hauled you off to Ponar. Without a stamp you starved. With a stamp—horse, swastika, whatever—you worked and you prayed for luck.

Doba, widowed, though she would never know how or when, had no certificate of any sort. No job. No source of income. No shred of security.

What she and the boys lived on is a mystery—probably they eked out the crumbs of the handouts that used to come from America.

Doba would never let her children starve but there was nothing she could do to keep their childhood alive. Shimonkeh and Velveleh's days of riding bikes in the country and playing chess with their father were over. Velveleh was not yet ten years old, still an innocent—but Shimonkeh was already a man. Hadn't they all told him so over and over again six months earlier, when they celebrated his bar mitzvah at the Taharat Hakodesh synagogue (now the Germans' medical warehouse)? But what did it mean to be a man, a Jewish man, in Vilna in the summer of 1941? Most of the men had been snatched—those who remained clung to life by the filament of work. Some boys no older than Shimonkeh lied about their age and got themselves hired in the peat bogs outside the city. They toiled half naked all day, every day, from dawn to dark, but when they returned home at night they had a few coins and sometimes vegetables or eggs they had bought in the villages. Some boys put on their father's work clothes and hired out as painters, carpenters, electricians: they knew nothing of such trades, but they learned as they went. Shimonkeh was not a strong boy. His frame was awkward, his limbs long and scrawny; his ears belled out on either side of a narrow face; his sandy hair was barely longer than stubble; his hearing may have been permanently impaired by his childhood bout with scarlet fever. But intelligence can be a kind of strength. In the shuttered city, Shimonkeh registered whatever passed before him with the fierce, abashed regard of a thirteen-year-old prisoner. "The children did not complain," wrote one Vilna father of that season. "They understood they had to stay inside. . . . They did not ask questions or demand an explanation. The opposite happened—they protected and guarded us, the grown-ups."

Shimonkeh heard his mother's sobs. He heard the screaming in the courtyards at night. He was forbidden to go outside but the agony of the city reached him through the walls. His father had disappeared. He was the man of the family now. Did that mean he would disappear next?

Shimonkeh was born a year before Anne Frank and a year after Yitzhak Rudashevski, a Vilna boy who kept a diary of the German occupation. If Shimonkeh wrote down what he saw and felt that summer, the pages have been lost. But the imprisoned children had a kind of mute underground. On the spot they invented their own codes, accommodations, wild fantasies, and invisible, infinitesimal survival strategies. Had he been able to read Anne Frank's diary, Shimonkeh would have understood implicitly:

Who has inflicted this upon us? Who has made us Jews different from all other people? Who has allowed us to suffer so terribly up till now? It is God that has made us as we are, but it will be God, too, who will raise us up again. If we bear all this suffering and if there are still Jews left, when it is over, then Jews, instead of being doomed, will be held up as an example.

CHAPTER NINETEEN

VILNA GHETTO

For the parents, every new Nazi decree or personnel shuffle rekindled hope. The children, instinctively, knew better. At the end of July, Vilna got a new administration—district commissioner Hans Hingst and his deputy for Jewish affairs Franz Murer. Murer, a barber in his former life, had graduated from Hitler Youth to become a die-hard Nazi. Soon they were calling him Mem—the Angel of Death. The Angel wasted no time. On August 6 he told the Judenrat that they had twenty-four hours to deliver 5 million rubles into his hands—with the usual *or else*. But Murer was a small-time chiseler compared with his boss. Hingst had big plans that required time and finesse to bring to fruition. On the last day of August, he judged that conditions were ripe for what became known as the Great Provocation. In the afternoon, two armed Lithuanians entered a building on Glezer Street in the old Jewish section; outside, the street was crowded with German soldiers queuing up for a movie. The Lithuanian intruders fired off a couple of rounds and then dashed into the street, hollering to the soldiers that there were Jews inside the apartment building shooting at them. This was Hingst's pretext for a mass *Aktion*. On Monday, September 1, "The city seethed all day," wrote Kruk. Rumors swirled that in the ancient Jewish quarter, the residents of every building were being "driven out." Not just the men—everyone. "Lines of people march on both sides of the street," wrote Kruk, "winding behind one another—all with yellow patches. . . . Those who saw it describe dreadful scenes. The wailing reached the sky. The young were leading the old. They were dragging sick people and children. There were dozens of well-known and distinguished Vilna Jews in the groups. Those who saw it wept with them." In the course of two days Hingst evicted some 3,700 Jews from the congested heart of Jewish Vilna and crammed them into Lukiszki Prison. From there, they were dispatched in groups to Ponar—men on foot, women in trucks. The Einsatzgruppen report broke down the numbers by gender and age—864 men, 2,019 women, 817 Jewish children. By Friday, September 5, wild new rumors congealed around a single word. *Ghetto!* The purpose of the Great Provocation became clear: the old Jewish quarter had been emptied so that Jews from other parts of the city could be confined there. Vilna's 40,000 remaining Jews had a single day to relocate. The Germans had deliberately fixed on Shabbat as the moving day so as to inflict maximum pain.

Kruk, September 5, 1941:

Better stop thinking. But how?

It is 11:30 at night. Everyone is awake. My house borders the district of the Fourth Precinct. I listen to the nocturnal silence. Maybe I'll hear something. Neighbors go from door to door and don't know what to do with themselves.

Maybe pack? Pack what?

In the street, I hear shots.

My friends, where are you? What's happening to you now? Will I ever see you again?

The hours drag on like years!

Doba, like every other Jew still alive in Vilna, had a few hours to sort and bundle up the fragments of her life. On the morning of Saturday, September 6, she dressed herself and the boys in as many layers as she could zip and button around them so there would be less to drag with them through the streets. A column of Lithuanian police and civilian guards stormed their building, forcing open doors, shouting at the residents to be quick, beating and herding them. The halls and stairwells filled with screams and sobs and the shuffle of shoes on stone. Doba, Shimonkeh, and Velveleh staggered under their burdens—Doba knew that every shirt, every dish, every piece of silverware meant another loaf of bread so she tried to haul away as much as possible. The boys blinked and squinted when they emerged into the sunlight they had barely seen since June. The streets were "a picture of the Middle Ages," wrote one of the herded, "a gray black mass of people . . . harnessed to large bundles." Lithuanian guards stood by to hustle and club them; bystanders heckled and jeered and robbed the unwary. "A bundle was suddenly stolen from a neighbor," wrote fourteen-year-old Yitzhak Rudashevski, who went to the ghetto that day with the rest of them. "The woman stands in despair among her bundles and does not know how to cope with them, weeps and wrings her hands. Suddenly everything around me begins to weep. Everything weeps."

The Germans had ordered the gentile populace not to assist the Jews in any way—but a few kind souls endangered their own lives by lifting a pack onto the back of a tottering old woman or hiding the valuables of a neighbor. Doba and her sons took their places in the black parade. "The Lithuanians drive us on, do not let us rest," wrote Rudashevski. "I think of nothing: not what I am losing, not what I have just lost, not what is in store for me. I do not see the streets before me, the people passing by. I only feel that I am terribly weary, I feel that an insult, a hurt is burning inside me. Here is the ghetto gate. I feel that I have been robbed, my freedom is being robbed from me, my home, and the familiar Vilna streets I love so much. I have been cut off from all that is dear and precious to me." Doba and the boys marched without knowing where they were going; they had no idea that ahead of them the stream was being forced into three channels: one drained into the tiny crabbed precinct of the old Jewish quarter, abutting the Great Synagogue; one into the half dozen dismal blocks anchored by the Judenrat headquarters on Strashuno Street; the overflow filled Lukiszki Prison. Doba and her two boys ended up in the Strashuno Street ghetto—the Large Ghetto, as it became known. They were comparatively lucky. Anyone who could not be crammed into the Large Ghetto spent Saturday night penned outside on Lidski Lane; on Sunday they were all carted off to Lukiszki Prison and from there to Ponar.

Those who got in first, or had the muscle or gumption, seized the better flats and barred the doors. Doba was in no shape to hustle or grab. She and the boys may have spent the first night sleeping in a courtyard or in the gutter—many did. The black parade continued long after dark; the angry rustle of voices and the crack of rubber and wood on bone never stopped. Doba and her sons trudged up and down a thousand filthy steps, knocked on a hundred doors, shoved their way into other shoving bodies. At some point, after God knows what epic ordeal, they ended up at Strashuno 15, a few doors down from the Judenrat on the main street of the Large Ghetto. It was a building of three floors, maybe three apartments to a floor. Eventually, Doba, Shimonkeh, Velveleh, Doba's brother-in-law Yitzchak Senitski, and 437 other Jews lived in that one small building.

"What can I say," Doba had written Sonia in happier times, "Shimonkeh is the greatest joy of my life." In the ghetto, the dregs of that joy turned, like poison gas, into torment.

CHAPTER TWENTY

YOM KIPPUR, 1941

tel had entered her queenly phase. She was fifty-five years old in 1941, rich, polished, tireless, infallible. Her business had never been more successful, her appearance more striking, her manner more imposing. She dressed and groomed with exquisite taste. Her pearls were large and numerous. Her life was full. Her happiness apparently secure. Maiden Form, now one of the largest family businesses in the world, employed 1,450 people; yearly sales of bras and girdles topped 4.5 million. The Bayonne plant produced more bras than any other manufacturing facility anywhere on the globe. Bea, a graduate of Barnard College, had married a tall manly doctor two years earlier and was working her way up in the company. It pleased Itel no end that Maiden Form would remain under family control, a female dynasty, passed from mother to daughter. In regal fashion, Itel kept strict guard over her privacy while tossing the press glamorous tidbits about her tastes and temperament. She was a voracious reader; she and William were regulars at the theater and the opera. She loved to dance—at corporate bashes, the tuxedoed young execs jockeyed to partner her. Her travels, of course, had been trimmed back because of the war, but she still made the most of every hour on the road. "She could romance a customer out of his shoes and socks," remarked one of the company's rising young men. "In market week, she would float around the showrooms very gracefully. . . . She made it her business to say hello to every single person who came in." Itel herself was a little more blunt about it: "I warm up sales. Then I let the salesman take the order."

With a kingdom so large and prosperous, it was time to move to a palace. Itel and William bought an eighteen-room mansion on a private beach in a swanky enclave on Long Island's North Shore. The previous owner, a wealthy Broadway impresario, had been terrified of a house fire, so there was lots of bright shiny tile everywhere. Salvatore, the Italian gardener, kept the grounds immaculate, tended the flower beds, and rolled the clay tennis court. A Norwegian cook named Anna prepared their meals. There was a ballroom, a library, a studio where William could sculpt, servants' quarters, a boathouse. Every workday Vincent, the chauffeur, drove Itel and William into Manhattan. In the summer, William fished from his own jetty. The Rosenthals were not invited to the parties of their rich WASP neighbors, but they had plenty of society of their own. Though Itel had never been especially family minded, except with her own immediate family, she saw that every relative got at least one invitation to Bayville. The mansion on the Sound hosted many a sweet sixteen, wedding, birthday bash, boating weekend, and bridge evening.

Had she cared to, Itel could have stepped in as head of the family after Abraham's death the previous year. She was the oldest, the richest, the most worldly, the most respected of the siblings. But the role of matriarch was not in her repertoire. She once told an interviewer who asked about her background that her father was "a wonderful man, intellectually gifted, wrapped up in his dogma. My mother was very short, a good business-woman." So much for family heritage. Without a leader, without strong ties to the past, without Judaism to bind them together (only Sam and Ethel among the six siblings had an appetite for the faith of their father), the American family splintered. Itel and Harry grew closer, and Harry and William spent a lot of time together as well. Both were members of the Jewish Club—an uptown venue for chess, cards, cigar smoking, and high-minded lectures founded by well-heeled Eastern European Jewish men who had been excluded from the echt German Jewish Harmonie Club (Hyman joined later in the decade). Ethel and Sam, still upstairs-downstairs neighbors in the same tight little house in the Bronx, held the fort and kept the faith. They attended their father's shul every Shabbat, their kitchens were kosher, they celebrated all the major holidays, but under their breath they both muttered about being second-class citizens. Ethel still shared the upstairs apartment with her mother and Shalom Tvi, who still slept on the foldout bed in the living room.

Two years had passed since Shalom Tvi had come to the United States to visit his brother. Now the brother was dead, Shalom Tvi's country no longer existed, his family was in the hands of mass murderers, and he was a lost soul sojourning in a strange land.

Itel and William had never been frequent visitors to the Bronx, and with Abraham gone the treks to Andrews Avenue tapered off. Shalom Tvi couldn't drive and wouldn't travel on Shabbat so he rarely made it out to Bayville. Still, there was some contact between uncle and niece during these years. William had spent time with Shalom Tvi and his family during his visit to Rakov in 1937, and William's name—and wealth—were invoked frequently in the letters Doba and Shalom Tvi exchanged during the early months of the war. Much hope was pinned on the Rosenthals' money and power. They did in fact give generously and at one point consulted with an attorney about helping family members emigrate. But once the Nazis took Rakov and Vilna, what more could they do? What could anyone do? Itel and William kept abreast of the news in both English and Yiddish, so they saw the first accounts of the atrocities and mass murders that appeared in the Yiddish dailies that summer. They were regular *New York Times* readers as well, but what little the *Times* saw fit to publish about the Nazi killings was buried, downplayed, or treated with skepticism. Itel knew that her uncle's family was in peril—they all knew—but they all kept silent about it. What was there to say? After the death of Lewis, Itel had locked the door on her inner life: anyone who dared even to knock was dismissed with silent rage. She and the rest of the family accorded Shalom Tvi the same severe respect. His situation was unbearable—why make it worse by intruding? "We never talked about the Nazis," recalled one of Sam's sons. "We never talked about the plight of Uncle's family." They might have imagined but they didn't discuss the anguish he was pouring out in his letters to Sonia—the sleepless nights, the numbed bewilderment, the hollow prayers, the ray of hope he refused to extinguish. Shalom Tvi lived among them like the shadow of death. They loved him and they took care of him and they honored him and treated him with dignity, but they could not bear to look him in the eyes and ask him what was in his heart. They drove him to and from work. They took him to the shore in the summer so he could swim in the ocean. They gave him clothes and cast-off toys to send to Sonia. They read the news. But like the editors of the American papers, they couldn't or wouldn't face or believe the enormity of what was happening to his loved ones.

In Vilna, a few souls survived the hail of bullets and the cascade of corpses at Ponar and dragged themselves, bloody and wild eyed, back to the ghetto. When they told what had happened, no one believed. In New York in September of 1941, no one had even heard of Ponar.

At 8:50 in the morning on September 30, William's brother Moe stopped what he was doing at the Maiden Form plant in Bayonne and bent his ears to a strange sound. Instead of the soothing motorized hum of needles punching thread through satin and lace, Moe heard the ceiling groan with the scrape of chairs and the clatter of shoes—thousands of shoes pounding on the floor above and thundering down the stairwell. He immediately switched on the public-address system in his office and began bellowing at the top of his voice: "I'M NOT GOING TO TELL YOU WHAT TO DO. MY PLEA IS FOR INFORMATION. I WANT TO KNOW WHAT THIS IS ALL ABOUT." But it was already too late. The factory's 1,100 workers— nearly all of them female—were piling into the street, blocking traffic, laughing, shouting slogans, and singing for all they were worth: "Moe, Moe, a thousand times no." "Gaiety and abandon rare in labor circles" filled the air outside the factory. The police were summoned to open a lane for traffic. But the women didn't care. They were giddy, irrepressible. The fact that it was the eve of Yom Kippur made no difference. Most of them were Polish or Italian anyway. They had had enough—enough of management from Moe Rosenthal down, enough of the International Ladies' Garment Workers' Union that had ceased to represent their interests. They were going out on strike, 1,100 strong, against the Rosenthals, against ILGWU president David Dubinsky, against union dues that they paid in but never saw any benefit from, against the spiraling cost of living that chipped away at their wages, against the chintzy piecework pay scale and the long hours and piddling vacations. The strikers decided to sever ties with the ILGWU and start their own breakaway union, the Brassiere Workers Union. "[Ours] is a fight by 1,100 average Americans of Bayonne, against oppressive, out-of-town dictators," declared Michael Vatalaro, president of the new ad hoc union.

"The strike is not authorized and is absolutely an outlaw strike, started by some Communists," shot back ILGWU representative Israel Horowitz.

Outlaw or not, the strike shut down the Bayonne factory and spread to the Maiden Form plants at Jersey City and Perth Amboy. Five weeks passed before the two sides came together—a fiscal eternity that gouged a chasm into the company balance sheet, not to mention the household budgets of struggling workers. There had been strikes before at Maiden Form but never one so rancorous, so prolonged and difficult to settle. In the end, after the usual rounds of threats, bluffs, offers, huffy refusals, and a stormy meeting in Bayonne's Knights of Columbus hall, at which seven hundred indignant Maiden Form employees booed Dubinsky off the stage, an agreement was reached. Clippers and operators working on the piecework scale received a guaranteed minimum increase of one dollar and fifty cents a week; those being paid by the hour got a raise of two dollars a week, with a third dollar dangled after four months "subject to negotiations and arbitration."

Neither Itel's nor William's name appeared in any of the newspaper stories about the strike, but of course they were intimately involved in everything. Strikes always flummoxed them—as old Bundists they felt they should be immune from labor unrest, but somehow the clippers and operators didn't see it that way. The breakaway Brassiere Workers Union issued a broadside laying out the sins of management in enraged uppercase type: "NO WAGE INCREASE AT MAIDEN FORM WAS EVER WON WITHOUT THE THREAT OF A STRIKE! AND FOR FOUR YEARS A GREAT MANY OF THE WORKERS HAVE HAD NO INCREASE AT ALL." The Rosenthals may have voted for Eugene Debs, but when it came to their own company it was business as usual.

Itel and William had long since ceased to practice Judaism, but the fact that this agonizing five-week strike had started on the eve of Yom Kippur was not lost on them. No Jew, no matter how lapsed, passes the Day of

Atonement without a twinge. Itel and William had both grown up in Orthodox households. As children they had attended services in the Rakov synagogue with their parents and many siblings. On Kol Nidre night, the eve of Yom Kippur, they had seen their fathers stand before the ark when the Torah scrolls were removed and raised before the congregation. They had listened to the cantor chant the ancient Aramaic text of the Kol Nidre that sounds like a sobbing, heartbreaking aria but is in fact a declaration of legal obligations.

> And all the congregation of the children of Israel shall be forgiven, and the stranger that sojourneth among them; for all the people were in error. . . . O pardon the iniquities of this people, according to Thy abundant mercy, just as Thou forgave this people ever since they left Egypt.

That was how Yom Kippur began every year of Itel and William's childhoods in Rakov, and that was how it began every year since the two of them had fled Rakov for America, one after the other, in 1905. But Yom Kippur of 1941 was different. There was no prayer or chanting on the last Day of Atonement in Rakov that year. There was iniquity but no mercy. Whether there was pardon for what happened in Rakov on October 1, 1941, only God knows.

In a family of visionaries, rebels, pioneers, paranoids, sages, sighers, egotists, and dreamers, Etl was a pragmatist. Before the match with Khost, her health had been poor, her tongue sharp, her temper short—but marriage and motherhood sweetened her disposition and strengthened her constitution. She had never moved away from the place where she was born, but she felt no urge to leave. After Shalom Tvi went to New York, she took charge of the house, the family's money, and her ailing mother without a whisper of complaint. Even the war did not faze her. They still had their house, their bit of land. Revolution had toppled the hated tsar; the Kaiser's army had come and gone during the last war; the Poles had come and gone after the war; the Soviets had come and gone during the present war. One day this war would end and the Nazis would go too. And when that day came, Etl and her family would still be in Rakov to observe the Sabbath, to bake matzo at Passover, to welcome the New Year joyously and atone for their sins on Yom Kippur.

Yom Kippur of 1941 put an end to such hopes. That Yom Kippur, Etl and her mother and daughters did not go to shul to murmur Hebrew prayers through the drowsy hungry afternoon and gossip with the other women. Instead they were hounded from their home and herded to the Rakov marketplace. A survivor named Uri Finkel left an account of what they were forced to endure that day:

> On Yom Kippur of 1941 the fascist murderers drove the entire Jewish population of Rakov to the marketplace. They made them bring all the books, Jewish, Hebrew, religious and worldly, along with the sefer-toyres [Torah scrolls], and burned them. For an entire day the Jewish cultural treasures of the shtetl burned. The Jews had to stand over the bonfire, dance, jump and sing; those who could not do this were shot on the spot.
>
> The fire and smoke from the burning were visible far from the shtetl. In one day no fewer than 16,000 books burned and a couple of hundred sefer-toyres, among them neviim [writings of the prophets] and megilles [scrolls with the Purim story]. . . . In the auto-da-fe of Jewish books were also burned two Jewish men and a Jewish woman, whom the fascists and the police threw into the fire.

Another survivor named Moshe Pogolensky wrote that "the Germans caught the son-in-law of Puchinsky and threw him in the flames, where he was burned alive before the eyes of the entire community. . . . The Jewish victims stood shaking as they watched. . . . The SS men ordered everyone to dance around the pyre and sing 'Hatikva' ["the hope"—the song became the Israeli national anthem]. This torture did not satisfy the Germans. As soon as the fire was extinguished they ordered everyone to give them their hidden money."

After the burning and the stealing came the killing in earnest. The SS selected thirty-one sturdy-looking Jews from those assembled in the market and marched them to the Jewish cemetery—a five-minute walk past wooden houses and garden plots brimming with autumn's bounty. Inside the cemetery walls they handed out shovels and ordered the thirty-one to dig a "huge, deep hole." Meanwhile, those who remained in the marketplace were divided by gender into two groups. When word came that the hole was ready, 112 men were culled from the market and sent to the cemetery. The Germans and their Lithuanian accomplices were ready for them. The thirty-one diggers were ordered to lie flat and motionless on the ground: with their faces in the earth, they couldn't see what was happening, but they heard the shots and the moans and the thud of bodies falling into the bottom of the pit and then falling on top of other bodies. When all 112 men were dead and piled in the pit, the thirty-one grave diggers were ordered to get up and take their shovels and cover the dead—their relatives, their neighbors, their friends, their enemies, their fellow Jews.

Sonia had been prophetic when she walked through this cemetery as a child and shuddered at its aura of "total destruction, poverty and the feeling of exile."

At some point during that Yom Kippur, Beyle got sucked into the vortex of violence and disappeared forever. Accounts of what happened to her are cloudy, their provenance unknown. Years later, Sonia wrote that her mother was "murdered on Yom Kippur eve in 1941 in Rakov at the hands of her Christian neighbors," but Sonia's children think that Beyle may have died on Yom Kippur itself. The grandchildren speculate that some Rakov gentiles, under cover of the carnival of killing, targeted Jews they believed had money or merchandise to steal. It was common knowledge that Beyle had operated a leather shop and factory for years, so the neighbors must have assumed she had a cache of money or hides. Very likely they broke into the house and demanded all of her money and shot her or clubbed her or beat her to death when she was slow or unwilling to hand it over. Beyle was sixty-six years old, thin, frail, and suffering from a weak heart. It wouldn't have taken much to kill her. Her body was never found. She has no grave. Her beloved husband in New York, her beloved daughter in Kfar Vitkin, her other beloved daughter in the Vilna ghetto had no idea she was dead. But Etl knew—very likely Etl watched and screamed with a screaming baby in her arms and a screaming toddler by her side while her mother was killed before her.

"It is very hard for me to describe the fear and the depression that spread within the remnants of the Jewish population that survived," wrote Pogolensky. "Most of the men at that point were annihilated and the few who survived tried to hide. Almost every home suffered a victim and each and every family was in mourning. The words, 'today it was them, tomorrow it will be the rest of us,' were heard in every conversation. It was as if this sentence was constantly hovering over the community and the ambiance was bleaker than a most grave depression. No hope for survival or renewal spread to every home."

At dawn the following day the survivors of the Yom Kippur massacre were ordered to leave their homes and move into a cluster of houses and *batei-medroshim* (prayer houses) around the synagogue compound: 950 Jews, most of them women and children and the elderly, crammed into nine homes and four prayer houses. This was the Rakov ghetto. Etl, holding seven-month-old Dobeleh in one arm and clutching the hand of five-year-old Mireleh with the other, took her place in the procession of prisoners. SS and Polish police lined the route and clubbed them along with batons. The walk from the Kaganovich family home to shul took ten, maybe fifteen minutes. Etl had come this way a thousand times before on Shabbat, on holidays, for bar mitzvahs and funerals. But on that day terror made the familiar strange. Etl walked with every nerve ending flayed, every instinct alert, offended, primed for action. Yet action was out of the question. She was a sensitive reed of a woman, thirty-four years old. She endured what she had to in silence so she could live for her daughters. Etl was devout so she may have prayed to God, silently, under her breath. Or maybe instead of praying she cursed God for taking her husband and her mother, for separating her from her father and sisters, for burdening her with two doomed helpless children.

———

October 26, 1941

Dear Sonia,

You write about sending letters through the Red Cross but this is in vain because where our family members are the Red Cross doesn't serve them. We ask at the post office but they know nothing about it. They said to ask in another place. I asked them [the American relatives] to ask about it since this is New York and everything is so far and you have to drive and you need time to get to places. They promised me that they would ask about it.

I read here in the papers that they count all the refugees from Poland but there is nobody from our area. From Vilna there are three [refugees]. I am always looking in the papers to see what they write about it.

> *Your father,*
> *Shalom Tvi Kaganovich*

Sonia and Chaim had both made aliyah by ship, sailing from Constanta to Istanbul, around the blue-gray mountains that rim the spectacular Turkish coast and across the eastern basin of the Mediterranean to Palestine. Once the war began, these storied waters became a Jewish death pit like Ponar. Jews without papers were forbidden to cross from Europe to Palestine, and many who tried died in the attempt. The British adopted a strict policy of turning back, hunting down, and firing "at or into" ships carrying illegal immigrants, a policy they enforced with obsessive viciousness. Hundreds died on board unsanitary, unseaworthy, or sabotaged ships. Those who tried to disembark without proper documents were deported to the island of Mauritius, in the Indian Ocean, where they rotted in packed detention camps for the duration of the war.

In November 1940, the *Patria*, carrying 1,700 illegal Jewish immigrants, was blown up in Haifa harbor in a Haganah plot gone awry (the bomb that was intended to cripple the ship, and thus keep it in port, accidentally sank it). Two hundred fifty people were killed. The Sea of Marmara swallowed the 230 refugees on board the *Salvator* in December 1940. Some 770 Romanian Jews went down with the *Sturma* in the Black Sea in February 1942: the ship was in dire condition and dangerously overcrowded, but when it docked in Istanbul for two months, the Turks refused to permit entry to any of the passengers and the British would not bend to the pleas of the Jewish Agency to grant them Palestine visas. Finally, the Turks ordered the ship to be off and it sank in the Black Sea a mile off the Turkish coast. Seventy children died; 250 women drowned; one passenger survived. In the aftermath of the *Sturma* disaster, posters branded with the word *MURDER* and the photograph of the British high commissioner fluttered on the walls of Palestine's cities: "Sir Harold MacMichael ... wanted for the murder by drowning of 800 refugees on board the *Sturma*."

British intransigence inflamed Jewish resistance. The first round of terrorist bombings and assassinations in Mandate Palestine were a direct result of the brutality and inhumanity that the British displayed toward Jewish refugees during the war.

Sonia read the newspaper, read her father's letters, exchanged news with her fellow moshavniks, and went slowly out of her mind. The words *hope* and *God* and *future* appeared in nearly every letter her father wrote, but after the *Patria* and the *Salvator* and the *Sturma*, Sonia could hope no longer. Even if by some miracle Etl and Doba and their children could be extracted from the ghettos of Rakov and Vilna, the British would never let them set foot in Palestine. The war had snapped shut a perfect trap. The Jews of Palestine despised their British governors, but they were utterly dependent on British power. Without the British military, Rommel's Panzer divisions would sweep in from the west and they would be prisoners of the Reich just like their relatives in Europe (an Einsatzgruppe unit was stationed in Greece, ready to descend on Palestine and begin liquidating the Jewish population when the time came). With the British in control, though, they were powerless to help their brethren trapped in Europe. Sonia and Chaim could do nothing but work their land, raise their children, and wait.

With every passing month of war, Sonia set her heart more fiercely on bringing her father to Palestine. But this too was maddeningly impossible.

The Nazi-appointed Judenrate—literally, "Jewish councils"—were not councils at all but instruments of more efficient oppression and murder. When the masters wanted to enumerate, rob, transport, or kill the slaves, the Judenrat was charged with making the numbers come out right—enough money, enough bodies. If they failed, they died first. If they succeeded, they died anyway—maybe a few hours later, a few weeks, a month, but they died nonetheless. So it was no honor and no guarantee of safety that Chaim's brother Yishayahu was forced to serve on Volozhin's Judenrat. The local SS probably tapped him because he had been a teacher.

The holy city of Volozhin was cursed with an especially sadistic bunch of Nazi occupiers. Their greatest pleasure was torturing little girls to death. When one Jewish girl was caught taking a bottle of milk from a Christian woman, the Nazis made her crawl up a hill on her hands and knees gathering potatoes until she was bloody and exhausted. "The tortures lasted for hours until her powers ceased, then they killed her," recounted one witness. The Nazis grabbed two Jewish girls and marched them to the top of Priest's Mountain along with two dogs. "On the mountain they shot the girls and beheaded the dogs to mix Jewish with animal blood. Those who passed away naturally were considered lucky."

On October 28, 1941, Yishayahu and the other members of the Volozhin Judenrat were summoned by the local head of the Gestapo—a thug by the name of Moka. Moka told them to come up with a heap of boot soles—why or for what he did not specify. The Judenrat, figuring it was just another random act of Nazi madness, complied, but the madness did not end there. Moka returned to the Judenrat later that day with a couple of SS officers. This time he ordered the council members to assemble the entire population of the ghetto for "an interesting lecture" on work ethics. Again, Yishayahu and his fellow councilors spread the word through the ghetto. A survivor described what ensued: "When a large number had assembled, Moka sent most of them back to the ghetto. He imprisoned the rest in the cinema hall. From there he took groups of ten people at one time, conducted them to the neighboring sports ground and killed them." Two hundred Volozhin residents died in this action, including Jacob Garber, the Judenrat head. After the shootings, Belarusian police were called in to despoil the bodies: "[They] stripped the clothes off the corpses, took away any rings and jewelry and pulled their gold teeth out of their mouths. Then a group of Jews was brought and ordered to bury the dead." Yishayahu may have been among the victims—able-bodied men were targeted first and he was not yet forty. Like Beyle, like Shepseleh, like Khost, Yishayahu Kaganovich had no grave. His name appeared just once in the records of Volozhin as a member of the Judenrat, then vanished. He left a wife, a daughter, and a two-year-old son.

"Life in the Ghetto grew harder and harder," wrote a survivor. "One day several SS men entered the house which served as a House of Prayer. They took a Torah Scroll, spread it out on the ground, made several dozen Jews lie down on the sheets and killed them." Perhaps this was one of the scrolls inked by the soft skilled hand of the patriarch Shimon Dov HaKohen—grandfather of Yishayahu and Chaim; Doba, Etl, and Sonia; Itel, Harry, Sam, and Hyman.

Sam's oldest daughter, Dorothy, had always been strange—shrill, irrational, obsessive, hypersensitive, suspicious of others. Today she would probably be diagnosed as borderline schizophrenic or bipolar, but in 1941 she was written off as peculiar. Her siblings joked that Dorothy had a radio with its own unique frequency, which explained why she knew about news events and weather conditions that no one else had ever heard of. When Dorothy emerged from her bedroom on the afternoon of Sunday, December 7, 1941, shouting that Japanese planes had bombed the U.S. battleship fleet in Pearl Harbor, no one in the family believed her. *Where the hell was Pearl Harbor, anyway?*

But for once, Dorothy's radio had gotten it right. In the course of the surprise attack, four U.S. naval battleships were sunk, four others were damaged, 2,402 Americans died, and 1,282 were wounded. The following day Congress declared war on Japan, and the declaration of war on Germany came three days later.

Chance, fate, and ambition had divided the family of the scribe. War reunited them.

CHAPTER TWENTY-ONE

WONDER GIRL

Word seeped into the Rakov ghetto that America had entered the war, but the Germans saw to it that the news raised no hope or unrest. Nazi officers convinced the Rakov Judenrat that the United States and Britain intended to make peace with Germany and that when the fighting stopped the Nazis were going to transport the Jews to Palestine. "Many such shameful and worn-out lies guided the activity of the Judenrat," wrote one Rakov Jew. "Rich storekeepers and factory owners, people with initiative who handled their difficulty with gelt . . . were in the Judenrat. They exacted a harsh price from the population. No one can say that the gelt did not help them. Meanwhile hundreds of children, women, old people and weak and sick men were living in great hunger and need." Etl and her daughters were among those.

The day after the United States declared war on Japan, the first killings by poison gas took place at the Chelmno extermination camp in Poland. The murderers mounted an elaborate charade, telling the victims that they must have a medical exam and shower—and then shoving them naked into the back of a paneled truck in batches of fifty to seventy and asphyxiating them with carbon monoxide. Murder by gas would be perfected over the next few months and a gas called Zyklon B, far more efficient than carbon monoxide, would be used to kill on an industrial scale at the extermination camps at Auschwitz-Birkenau, Treblinka, Belzec, Majdanek, and Sachsenhausen. But gas was not necessary for mass murder. Plenty, like Shepseleh, were shot over pits; murdered, like Beyle, by greedy neighbors; captured and imprisoned and executed like Khost. Disease, exhaustion, and malnutrition claimed many more. In the six months between June and December 1941, the Nazis slaughtered a million Jews in the territory they had seized from the Soviets—most of them killed by bullets and fire, the preferred weapons of the Einsatzgruppen.

By the end of 1941, Hitler had made it clear that the elimination of Jews from Nazi-occupied territory was now his top priority. Accordingly, on January 20, 1942, SS general Reinhard Heydrich convened a conference in the Berlin suburb of Wannsee to inform key governmental and military personnel of how the "Final Solution" of European Jewry would be effected. Heydrich announced that the Reich's goal was the elimination of some 11 million Jews not only from the countries at war in Europe but also from the United Kingdom and neutral nations including Switzerland, Sweden, Spain, and the European sector of Turkey. Able-bodied Jews would be worked to death; the remnant would be "dealt with appropriately."

The Jews of Rakov were among the first to be "dealt with" under the blueprint of the Final Solution.

They were torn from sleep at dawn on Wednesday, February 4, 1942. *To Minsk, to Minsk*, adult voices muttered. Mireleh was only six but she knew what Minsk meant. Minsk was where her father had gone. Minsk was the city. Shops. Crowded sidewalks. Cakes and sweets and stores crammed with delicious food. If they were going to Minsk maybe she'd get to see her daddy again. Maybe her mother would smile.

The snow was still shadowy blue outside, but inside everything was in an uproar. Her mother was frantically pulling clothes into bundles. Dobaleh was hungry—Mireleh was hungry too but she knew better than to whine about it. *To Minsk, to Minsk*. They must pack only what they could carry in their arms. Mireleh was big enough to carry a bundle of her own, but Dobaleh was still a baby. What did Dobaleh know? She had spent half her life in the ghetto, her father had disappeared before she could say "Daddy," she couldn't even walk properly. In one month it would be Dobaleh's first birthday—but Mireleh doubted that there would be cake.

Fists were pounding on the walls and then the door flew open and men's voices shouted at them to get moving. Everyone who had been stuffed into this tiny house since Yom Kippur grabbed what they could and then all of them tumbled outside into the snow.

Even in the feeble dawn light Mireleh could see the ring of armed men in uniforms. The voices kept shouting commands that she couldn't understand. The women screamed as the men with guns grabbed their bags and shoved them along. *No need for bags where you're going.* Anyone who tried to resist or turn back got cracked on the head with a rifle butt. A few fell to the ground bleeding. Mireleh clung to her mother's hand and they moved with the surging crowd. Cries and curses echoed over her head. *They are not taking us to Minsk. They are taking us to death.* One or two broke off from the mass and began to run. Fire from the machine guns dropped the bodies onto the trampled snow. The sound of pain was deafening.

The noise subsided a little when they were all assembled in the courtyard of the three synagogues: the old shul, the new shul, and the small *shtible* where the Hasidim used to dance until their black clothes flapped in the air like crows' wings. They were low and humble, these three beloved shuls. Their roofs were shingled; their wooden walls were darkened and ridged by time; inside they were bare and dim but for the jeweled light that shone from the Torah scrolls. Still, they were the glory of Rakov. But why were they at shul today? It wasn't Shabbat and it was much too early. Mireleh pressed close to her mother and baby sister in the courtyard as the ring of men tightened. They were all being squeezed toward the entrance of the old shul, and one by one they disappeared inside. The bony ends of knees and elbows jabbed at Mireleh from every side. The breath was crushed from her body. And then it was their turn to take their place with the others in God's house.

Nachum Greenholtz, a Rakov Jew, had been warned of what was coming that day and managed to hide inside a "field bathroom." He wrote: "From the cracks in the wall we could see the Germans searching and checking and surrounding the town. Later we saw the flames coming from the ghetto and we instantly understood what was happening. We heard the sound of the screams."

A group of six witnesses reported: "Crying children were pierced by rifle bayonets and thrown over the crowded heads. The synagogue doors and windows were blocked with nailed planks. The murderers spilled gasoline on the walls and set the building on fire."

Others said that a few managed to get out of the synagogue and run for their lives, but the guards shot them down.

Moshe Pogolensky gave a different account:

> At dawn . . . the ghetto was surrounded and the entire Jewish community, nine hundred and fifty souls, was put in the yard of the synagogue. They took ten of the healthiest people and separated them. The rest were taken group by group to the entrance of the synagogue, where they were shot and killed by automatic machine guns. The ten separated people were ordered to throw the individual bodies in the synagogue. As soon as the last of the people were thrown in the synagogue, the ten people were pushed inside without shooting them. They shot the building and set it afire and everyone was burned to death.

"She will be a wonder girl, with her brains and the excellent way she speaks," Beyle had written Shalom Tvi of their granddaughter Mireleh a few months earlier. "I love how she sings and dances." The wonder girl died at the age of six with her mother and baby sister. Whether fire, bullets, or bayonet blade killed them, whether they were shot at the entrance to the synagogue or incinerated alive inside, it will never be known. Fire consumed what remained.

"We sat there as if we were frozen and had lost touch with ourselves," Nachum Greenholtz wrote of himself and a fellow survivor after the fire. "We did not speak the entire day. The night was very dark and very cold. We kept walking, two lonely broken-hearted Jews who tried to save their souls and left behind them everyone they knew and loved—all that were now annihilated."

BREAKDOWNS

Sonia and Shalom Tvi were both in terrible shape that February. Neither of them knew about the conflagration in Rakov; they received no news or letters from the handful of survivors (those would come later), not a word appeared in the press. But at some unconscious, visceral level they intuited what had occurred and collapsed.

Shalom Tvi was at shul one Thursday morning around the time of the fire when he was suddenly stricken with a "huge headache." He stripped off the tefillin, folded his tallith, and "fled home with great pain." The doctor called in by the Epsteins prescribed some pills and told him to apply an ice pack to the headache. A few days later Shalom Tvi took a turn for the worse and the doctor was summoned back. When a second round of pills had no effect, the doctor recommended that he be hospitalized, but there was a problem finding an empty bed. The Epsteins "immediately called the whole family," Shalom Tvi wrote Sonia, "and since [William] Rosenthal is a director of a hospital, he said that he must have a room for his uncle, and through him they secured a hospital room and right away they sent an ambulance and took me on a stretcher since I was not allowed to sit up." Shalom Tvi was exaggerating a bit—William was not a director but he did sit on the board of the Bronx Hospital (he went on to serve as its vice president after the war and he was among the founders of the Albert Einstein College of

Medicine at Yeshiva University). A team of doctors was called in, X-rays were taken, and eventually Shalom Tvi was diagnosed with hardening of the arteries in the head. When he was well enough, he wrote Sonia in detail about his recovery:

> *They ordered me to lie in bed for three weeks and not to sit up. They gave me medications several times a day, and two doctors came to see me every day—not doctors from the hospital but private ones for me. My family has insisted on doing everything possible to save me, and thanks to God and thanks to my family who helped me so much, after three weeks they brought me home. It cost several hundred dollars for a private room here in the hospitals and for the doctors, and they [the American relatives] paid it all. May God keep them all healthy and see that they never know illness.*

At the same time, Sonia was suffering a kind of nervous breakdown. In the decade since she made aliyah, pioneering had lost its shine. She was thirty-four years old, a farmwife and mother with two young children to raise and no female relatives to help out or kvetch to. Seven-year-old Leahleh was a sweet studious schoolgirl, but at three and a half Areleh was a handful—obstinate, rambunctious, headstrong, impossible to manage. Sonia worried he was becoming a *julik*—Russian for wise guy or crook. Life at Kfar Vitkin in time of war was precarious and suffocating. She and Chaim were still struggling with the farm; the cows failed to thrive, their calves were puny; the harvests were often disappointing; the work was relentless; the summers punishing. When Chaim was away driving the truck, Sonia was left alone with the children, the cows, and the chickens. Reading had always been her great solace, but it was when she picked up the newspapers that she fell apart. There was nothing about Rakov—what shattered her were the accounts of what was happening elsewhere. Though Sonia's letters have not survived, it's clear from her father's responses that at the start of February she had reached the breaking point. Shalom Tvi wrote her in frantic anxiety:

> *I can tell you, my beloved daughter, that your recent letters broke me so much that I could not sleep the whole week and I am going around*

confused. The last letter has actually made me ill and gives me too much heartache. The tragedies reported in the newspaper I avoid read-ing. I don't want to burden myself with much worry since the doctors have cautioned me to stay calm. You too need to remain calm. We can-not help them in anything. We can expect the worst and hope for the best. I believe you should see a nerve doctor—your nerves are too stretched. My situation is worse than yours. You are, thank God, in your nest, in your own house, in your bed, your husband, your chil-dren, thank God all of you are together, may all of you be healthy, and live whole and peaceful lives together. But I am an old man, alone with-out anybody. It is certainly good that I have such a family.

Shalom Tvi recovered his health and went back to work at A. Cohen & Sons. Sonia wept, poured out her heart in letters to her father, and dragged herself through the motions of life. It's unlikely a "nerve doctor" practiced anywhere near Kfar Vitkin, and in any case, Sonia was too proud and too busy to seek out psychiatric treatment. She carried on by force of will.

The United States had been at war for only three months, but already the American family was feeling it. Ethel, Harry, and Sam all had draft-age sons; Itel had a draft-age son-in-law; and two cousins—the sons of Uncle Herman—were also of draft age. Twenty years separated Abraham and Herman, the oldest and youngest of Shimon Dov's six children, and their first children, though technically in the same generation, were born thirty-one years apart: Itel in 1886 and Leonard in 1917. Itel and Leonard were first cousins, even though Itel was old enough to be his mother. In the American branch of the family, Len Cohn (his father, Herman, had broken ranks and dropped the "e") was the one who saw the most action in the Second World War.

Handsome, blue eyed, and compact, Len entered Yale at the age of sixteen—no mean feat for a Jew in the 1930s—and graduated with the class of 1937. In his sophomore year he had signed on with ROTC, an odd choice for a self-described left-leaning pacifist, but he thought it would give him a chance to improve his horseback-riding skills. Two years out of Yale, he was approached by an army officer and pressured to join the reserves. "I was torn," he recalls. "On the one hand I was a pacifist because of what had happened in the First World War—but on other hand it was 1939 and the horrors going on in Germany made me feel I should go." Len shelved the pacifism and entered the reserves. On April 4, 1941, at the age of twenty-four, he was called up to active duty and sent to Fort Devens, outside of Boston. He was appointed second lieutenant—a "shavetail" in army slang, the lowest-ranking commissioned officer—with the First Engineer Combat Battalion of the Army's First Infantry Division. It was the same division— the Big Red One—that his cousin Hyman had served with during the Great War.

Eight months later came Pearl Harbor and "the whole world changed for us." The division began intensive training in amphibious landings in preparation for storming the German-held beachheads of North Africa and Europe. On the night of August 1, 1942, the Big Red One, sixteen thousand strong, shipped out of New York harbor.

Forty years after his father Herman had come to America in steerage, twenty-four years after his cousin Private Hyman Cohen had been packed into the lower deck of a British troop ship bound for the trenches, Lieutenant Leonard Cohn crossed the Atlantic with the First Division officer corps in a first-class stateroom on the *Queen Mary*. By November, he was fighting in the British-American invasion of North Africa.

Chaim never learned when or how his brother Yishayahu, his sister Chana, and their families in Volozhin died (their mother, Leah, had passed away before the war). They could have been killed in the stadium *Aktion* of October 1941—or they may have endured six more months of misery and wretchedness before being shot and burned to death in the *Aktion* of May 10, 1942. Two thousand Volozhin Jews died that stifling spring day— dragged out of the ghetto, marched to a smithy behind the synagogue, imprisoned in the blacksmith's house, and slaughtered. Mendel Wolkowitch, a Volozhin Jew who managed to hide in an attic during the roundup, recounted that the killing was done in a leisurely, almost sporting fashion by a drunken troop of SS officers and local Polish and Belarusian policemen. The gunmen set up a table stocked "with all kinds of liquor" and they fired off machine-gun rounds "between one drink and the next. [T]hey shot into the building in order to silence the weeping of the children and the outcry of adults." Two rabbis imprisoned in the stifling house argued about resistance: one urged his fellow Jews to "take a brick, a stone, or an iron bar . . . and attack the murderers," but the other, quoting some sacred text, cautioned that "even when a sharp sword is pressed against a man's throat, let him not cease to hope for mercy." Some prisoners did manage to bash a hole in the roof of the house and get away. Wolkowitch said that when the shooting was over, "they set the house on fire and the Jews of Volozhin went up to heaven in flames." Strays who had hidden in the ghetto were ferretted out, shot, and buried in pits along with "dead cats, dead dogs and all kinds of rubbish" that their gentile neighbors flung after them. "Father in Heaven, I thank Thee for having purified us of this Jewish filth!" one devout Christian woman cried out when day was done.

There was one final *Aktion* in August 1942, when three hundred Volozhin Jews were killed in the streambed of the Volozhinka. The eighty or so survivors fled, some to join the partisan bands in the forest. The town that had been revered for its yeshiva for 140 years was now *Judenfrei*. A single relic remained: the chaste white yeshiva building survived the incineration of its community.

Yishayahu and his wife, Henia, had two children, a girl and a boy; Chaim's sister Chana and her husband, Meir Finger (Yishayahu's business partner), also had a son and a daughter. Four cousins of Leahleh and Areleh, two aunts and two uncles—gone forever without a grave, a prayer, a coffin, a date of death. Only the cause of their deaths can be surmised: bullets or fire, like their relatives in Rakov. Though in truth, bullets and fire were but the agents of death. The cause must be hunted elsewhere.

May 1942 was when Maiden Form switched over to "war production mode." In addition to bras, the factories were now churning out pants, coats, shirts, and undershorts for the military, along with mattress covers, parachutes, pup tents, and mosquito netting. There was many a hoot of laughter when GIs spotted the Maiden Form Brassiere Company logo stamped on their army-issue briefs—but it kept the name in broad circulation. Not that bra production slackened off. "Women workers who wore an uplift were less fatigued," claimed Itel—and the War Department bought it.

Itel managed to secure a "declaration of essentiality" from the government that gave Maiden Form priority in receiving scarce materials. God only knows how the war would have gone if American women did not have the proper support. Since rubber, elastic, and metal hooks and eyes were impossible to come by, William and his design team made some adjustments. Gingham plaid had to be substituted for imported lace—less sexy, but eminently practical for all those hardworking Wacs, Waves, and nurses.

Itel, as usual, was miles ahead of the rest of the pack. Though a third of the company's resources went into war production, bras continued to sell briskly on the home front. The "Variation" line set a company record in 1943 when sales hit 2 million. Itel kept pouring money into advertising even though everyone told her she was crazy and all the competition was retrenching. She knew that this war wouldn't last forever. When it was over, women would still be wearing bras; thanks to Itel's campaign to "safeguard the value and goodwill of Maiden Form's name," more women than ever would be wearing Maiden Form bras. The United States had only just begun to fight, but Itel already had her eye on the big money waiting to be made when peace returned.

The war forced Sam to change his job. Before the war, A. Cohen & Sons' bread and butter had been cheap consumer goods made of chromium, steel, copper, cast iron, and silver, but these materials were declared "strategic metals" after the attack on Pearl Harbor. The product lines dried up overnight. Unlike Itel, the boys were not able to persuade the War Department that chromium-backed hairbrushes, stainless steel flatware, waffle irons, pewter cocktail shakers, and oxidized copper radio lamps were essential for the war effort. The company was hit with a merchandising crisis. After thirty years in the field as a salesman, Sam was brought "inside" to help find suitable stuff for the company to sell.

It was a bittersweet moment. Being inside put Sam on a par with Harry and Hyman, but selling had always been his forte. He was good at schmoozing, wheedling, pressuring, persuading. Good with people. Now he had an executive role in an impossible business climate. Sam beat the bushes and came up with "fringe" lines of products made of glass, ceramic, and cloth.

Gold, though restricted, was still available so the company edged into the jewelry business. The brothers caught a break when they managed to secure some semiprecious German stones that had been seized by the Alien Property Custodian. Woodrow Wilson had originated this office during the First World War to appropriate enemy assets held in the United States—and President Roosevelt resuscitated it by executive order in March 1942. German and Japanese merchandise, real estate, business, and intellectual property in the United States now belonged to the U.S. government. When the Alien Property Custodian put the lot of semiprecious German stones up for auction, A. Cohen & Sons scored a big chunk, and the brothers cut some lucrative deals with leading jewelry manufacturers. "The purchase of the stones put us solidly in the jewelry business," Hyman remarked later. Even with business barely limping along, the brothers were scrupulous about abiding by quotas and adhering to government price regulations. They also promised the union that all employees "fighting to preserve our American Way of Life" would be able to resume their former positions after the war.

It went without saying that the jobs of family members in uniform were safe. All three of Sam's sons were in the military—Sidney was with the 82nd Airborne Division; Lester had been drafted by the navy (he trained briefly at Annapolis and shipped out, but he had a nervous breakdown while home on leave and, after a stint in a military mental hospital, got an easy berth on a submarine hunter based in Florida); Marvin, the third son, was stationed in the Pacific. With Leona, the youngest child, away in college, only Dorothy remained at home with Sam and Gladys. Even in the best of times, Dorothy grated on everyone's nerves; with the anxiety of three brothers in the service, she became unbearable.

Sam and Gladys no longer saw Shalom Tvi every day, because they had moved out of the Andrews Avenue duplex into a place of their own a few blocks away, on the corner of Andrews and West 179th Street. They weren't greenhorns anymore—why should they all live crammed together in one small house? Harry and Hyman had apartments in Manhattan, and Itel had her own private palace on Long Island Sound. It was time for Sam and Gladys to spread out a little. Even with wartime shortages and austerity, they could afford it.

Sam remained loyal to his father's shul and he davened there with

Shalom Tvi every Friday night and Saturday morning. Sam had no memories of his cousins in Palestine—Chaim had been a toddler and Sonia not even born when he left Rakov—but Shalom Tvi showed him pictures: two sunburned pioneers in shorts and sundress, a cinder-block farmhouse, a citrus grove, two adorable sabra children. As for Doba and Etl and their husbands and children, Shalom Tvi didn't bring them up and Sam didn't ask.

Shalom Tvi was in the habit of strolling over to his sister Leah Golda's house every Shabbat, so inevitably he saw a good deal of Rose, the younger daughter of Leah Golda and the late Shmuel Rubenstein. Twenty-three years old in 1942, Rose was a pretty, articulate, thoroughly Americanized girl who lived at home with her mother and kept a diary during the war. Rose recounted gathering around the radio every night to listen to "Hitler's raucous, roaring voice, Roosevelt's paternalistic, calming voice, and Churchill's literary, pedantic tones." She wrote about installing blackout shades in the windows of their Bronx home, about cars driving at night with no headlights through eerily dark city streets in which "a cigarette light showed for miles." The air-raid siren was tested every Thursday at 11 A.M. In the summer, her family went to Swan Lake in the Catskills, and occasionally Itel and William sent their chauffeured car around to take Rose to the Saturday night shows at the President Hotel (a Borscht Belt fixture). "We were the poor relations. Itel and William never wanted to see my brother Louis—he reminded them of their lost son, Lewis."

At the start of the war, Rose had been working for A. Cohen & Sons (six days a week, 9 A.M. to 6 P.M. for fourteen dollars a week—a two-dollar premium over the normal wage because she was family), but when her uncle Abraham died she decided to quit and take a job with a rich enterprising refugee. She was eager to strike out on her own. After her sister, Betty, got married and her brother Sol was drafted, Rose was left alone with her mother. She didn't like to complain, but it was hard to be stuck in the Bronx caring for an ailing widow while New York was "teeming with servicemen of every allied nation."

Rose's diary has a photo of her uncle Shalom Tvi taken at Betty's wedding, in 1942. He sits with his hands clasped, wearing a *kippah* and tie, handsome, dignified; his mouth curves up slightly in a dim smile, a smile of obligation. Rose wrote under the photo, "Shalom Tvi came here for a visit and couldn't go back because of the war." Nothing else.

But there was something else. Seventy years later, when pressed to speak about the war years, Rose came out with a memory that she had long kept to herself: "Shalom Tvi walked over to our house every Saturday. One Saturday when he came, my mother was bedridden and I was alone with him. He got very amorous and grabbed me on his lap and felt me all over. I had to fight him off." Rose couldn't recall exactly when this happened but she was sure it was after Shalom Tvi's family had been killed by the Nazis. It had never happened before and, since Rose told her family, her brothers made sure it never happened again. As soon as she disclosed the incident, Rose regretted it. "He was a nice man but he had this terribly devastating event in his life. I shouldn't have said anything."

CHAPTER TWENTY-THREE

DESPAIRING PEOPLE

The killing had stopped. The old, sick, and disabled, the strong, healthy, and male—and plenty of others besides—were already dead. The small ghetto had been disposed of at Ponar the previous October (1941) and another nine thousand souls had been slaughtered in the Gelbschein *Aktion* of November 3, 1941. A few minor roundups continued into December and then, at the start of 1942, the killing in Vilna stopped. Vilna ghetto was now classified a "working ghetto," a euphemism for labor prison barracks—and why would the Germans kill off their workers when the wages were so low and the incentives to work so powerful? Yellow permits ("the blood-drenched delusion," one ghetto prisoner called them) were handed out to the fortunate, the well connected, the determined and resourceful: permit holders left the ghetto every day at dawn and returned at dark, sometimes with a bit of food they had scrounged. Doba had no permit. "They had nothing, nothing," said Tsipora Alperovich, a cousin (on Beyle's side) who lived in the ghetto with her mother. "Doba was very poor. Sometimes my mother gave her some soup. Doba had to battle every day for her life." Tsipora was one of the lucky ones: though she was only fourteen, she had a job at a factory making German military uniforms. She and her mother survived on beans and horse meat.

Doba and the boys would have starved were it not for Shepseleh's older brother Yitzchak Senitski. Before the war, Yitzchak, a prominent educator, had run Vilna's Dinezon School and directed sports programs and field trips for the city's Jewish youth. After Shepseleh disappeared, Yitzchak took Doba and her sons under his wing. He was a good man, a confirmed bachelor in his late forties, brave, kindhearted, respected in the community—the ideal uncle. According to the May 1942 census of 15,507 ghetto prisoners, Doba, her two sons, and Yitzchak lived together at Strashuno 15—an address they shared with 437 other people. Tsipora, who lived in a different building in the ghetto, recalled that the four of them divided a small room with another family: the average "living space" in Vilna ghetto was about eighteen square feet per person. Yitzchak kept the family going on what he earned as a teacher in the ghetto school.

Yes, there were schools in the ghetto. After the initial days of tumult and murder, schools were opened. Yitzchak played an active role as organizer and chair of the Teachers' Association. Shimonkeh was fourteen in 1942; Velveleh was ten. Going to school was the most wonderful thing that had happened since they were shut in the ghetto the previous September.

"The opening of the ghetto school was fantastic for us," recalls Tsipora. "We sat on the floor to write. We had a club. We sang. We put on plays. The Song of the Partisans became our anthem—*As the hour that we longed for is so near, Our steps beat out the message—'We are here!'* For us school was just life." Tsipora and Shimonkeh, who were the exact same age, sat on the floor in the same classroom. They sang the same songs, wandered through the same crowded courtyards, looked at the sky over the same thirty-foot-high wooden walls. Seventy years later, Tsipora would remember Shimonkeh as a tall skinny boy, nice-looking, quiet. She remembered him playing with a yoyo. She remembered that he suffered serious hearing loss.

No memories survive of Velveleh. In the last photos taken before the Nazi occupation he was lengthening out, shedding his baby fat, and losing the angelic roundness of his face. The bombing at the start of the war made him nervous. He was musical. No one in the family ever breathed a word of complaint about him. Tsipora can bring back nothing about him, and what she recalls of Shimonkeh—the yoyo, the deafness, the long bony physique—reveals nothing of his inner life. The mind and spirit of a fatherless youth on the cusp of adolescence can only be surmised from fragments left by other prisoners.

This much is clear. At fourteen, Shimonkeh was old enough to bristle at the sight of the leather-jacketed Jewish police that the Nazis appointed to cow and club and rob their own kind. He was old enough to burn with desire, to fall in love, to ache for beauty and dream of violent, heroic revenge. He was old enough to take part in the culture of his city and to feel proud that, as one writer put it, "the insanely wild conditions of life did not break the Jewish creative spirit." A few doors down the street was the ghetto library—always thronged. Librarian Herman Kruk (the escaped Warsaw journalist and diarist) threw a party for the community when the one thousandth book circulated. "The book unites us with the future, the book unites us with the world," wrote Yitzhak Rudashevski, the teenage ghetto diarist, on the day of the celebration. Bundists protested "No theater in a graveyard!" when a ghetto theater was organized early in 1942, but soon the variety shows, musicals, and satirical sketches were playing to full houses. Shimonkeh had learned to play chess from his father—maybe he played in one of the ghetto chess competitions; maybe he won. A nearby courtyard (everything was nearby) served as a cramped sports stadium. A youth group collected ghetto folklore—"dozens of sayings, ghetto curses and ghetto blessings are created before our eyes . . . the ghetto folklore is . . . cultivated in blood," wrote Yitzhak Rudashevski in his diary. His youth club organized a committee to record the history of Courtyard Shavler 4: they interviewed residents, analyzed the responses, and concluded that "everywhere [there was] the same sad ghetto song: property, certificates, hide-outs, the abandonment of things, the abandonment of relatives." Shimonkeh was old enough to feel the agony of abandonment; old enough to mourn the death of a beloved teacher, to see the poetry in snow drifting against ruined walls, to breathe the melancholy of autumn nights when workers hurried through the streets with their shoulders hunched and the child vendors stood over trays of moldy potatoes and a couple of cigarettes scrounged from God knows where. "Frozen, carrying the little stands on their backs, they push toward the tiny corner that is lit up," wrote Rudashevski of the child vendors. "They stand thus until they hear the whistle and then they disappear with their trays into the black little ghetto streets."

Maybe Shimonkeh stood by a tray in the cold to sell whatever his mother had left.

There were Bundists and Zionists in Shimonkeh's family. At fourteen his uncle Chaim had already been enrolled in HeHalutz. His aunt Itel had been inhaling revolutionary literature. His aunt Sonia had been dreaming of making aliyah. Perhaps Shimonkeh too had the soul of a revolutionary. Maybe someone smuggled him a copy of "The First Call," the fiery manifesto that twenty-three-year-old Zionist Abba Kovner delivered to the delegates of Vilna's Jewish Youth Movement on the night of December 31, 1941:

> Let us not go like sheep to the slaughter, Jewish youth! Do not believe those who are deceiving you. Out of 80,000 Jews of the Jerusalem of Lithuania, only 20,000 remain. In front of your eyes our parents, our brothers and our sisters are being torn away from us. Where are the hundreds of men who were snatched away for labor by the Lithuanian kidnappers? Where are those naked women who were taken away on the horror-night of the provocation? Where are those Jews of the Day of Atonement? And where are our brothers of the second ghetto? Anyone who is taken out through the gates of the ghetto, will never return. All roads of the ghetto lead to Ponary, and Ponary means death. Oh, despairing people, tear this deception away from your eyes. Your children, your husbands, your wives—are no longer alive—Ponary is not a labor camp. Everyone there is shot. . . . It is true that we are weak, lacking protection, but the only reply to a murderer is resistance. Brothers, it is better to die as free fighters than to live at the mercy of killers. Resist, resist, to our last breath.

Shimonkeh must have known that Abba Kovner and Itzhak Wittenberg were recruiting Vilna's young Zionists and Communists into an underground resistance movement called the FPO (Fareynegte Partizaner Organizatsye—United Partisan Organization). He must have known that Judenrat chief Jacob Gens, a former officer in the Lithuanian army, carried a pistol and that he had gotten the Nazis to arm his Jewish ghetto police with guns, rubber sticks, and brass knuckles. The FPO was amassing arms as well. When the "actions" started again, they would be ready.

News of the war seeped through the walls. The prisoners smiled and winked at each other when they learned that the Red Army had fought the Germans to a standstill at Stalingrad in the autumn of 1942. They knew all about the Anglo-American attack on German forces in North Africa that November. "An American incursion has landed," Rudashevski wrote in his diary on November 12. "The Germans are suffering dreadful blows. . . . When the English [and Americans] finish in Africa, it is expected that a second front will be opened in Europe and then . . . we can still manage to leave the ghetto. We become encouraged hearing that the battle is proceeding, that our spark of hope still flickers."

If Rudashevski was aware of this at the age of fifteen, then fourteen-year-old Shimon Senitski must have been aware too. Shimonkeh knew that his mother had relatives in America. He knew that the relatives had sons. It was no great stretch for a boy with imagination to picture these sons marching into battle against the Germans.

Still, it's unlikely that Shimonkeh imagined the truth: that in November 1942, his mother's first cousin, Len Cohn, was among the American forces dealing "dreadful blows" to the Germans in North Africa. A spark of hope flickered across the globe unseen from cousin to cousin.

The First Division, Len Cohn among them, landed in Oran in Algeria on November 8, 1942. The Vichy French forces defending Algeria put up little resistance, and after three or four days of fighting the Americans secured the area. Len, an adjutant on the battalion staff, bivouacked with his unit near Oran and stayed put for a couple of months. Then in February 1943, they were ordered east to stop the forces that Rommel was massing in Tunisia. What followed was the costly, bloody Battle of Kasserine Pass, fought in a gap in the rugged Atlas Mountains that rim Africa's northwestern coast. It was the war's first major engagement between American and German forces, and it did not go well. Americans suffered heavy casualties and significant loss of tanks and antiaircraft batteries before finally forcing Rommel's Afrika Korps back and reoccupying the pass on February 24.

Seventy years later, Len remembered his involvement in the battle like this:

> *At some point I was out in a jeep with a work party. I don't remember all the details, but we were working on a road. It was open country with the Atlas Mountains rising on one side and railroad tracks on the other. There had been snow in the mountains in January, but that day was mild. At some point I noticed a column of smoke rising half a mile away. I got out of the jeep and told the driver to turn the vehicle around and be prepared to go back to base. I walked toward the railway embankment—trying to figure out what this smoke was about—when suddenly I was shot at. I dove to the ground and took cover in a tank track a few inches deep. I got my pistol out of its holster and thought I better wait there until dark. Then I heard Germans come up from behind me—I heard them talking—they were close enough for me to know they were speaking German. I froze where I was, realizing that I had somehow gotten behind German lines. I was absolutely aware of how the Germans would have treated me if they captured me. An American officer named Cohn. I'd heard the stories of what happened to Jewish POWs taken by the Germans.*
>
> *In the event, I stayed where I was and waited them out. When it got dark, I climbed up to the train tracks and followed them back to our base. When the sentry heard me, he yelled out Jimmy and I yelled back Dolittle. That was the password sign and countersign that night.*

After Kasserine Pass came brutal, costly battles at El Guettar, Beja, and Mateur, but by the middle of May, Tunisia belonged to the Allies. American forces were now poised to open the "second front" in Europe that the teenage Rudashevski dreamed of.

But by then, the killing had resumed in Vilna. "It has begun again," Rudashevski wrote in his diary on Monday, April 5. "Today the terrible news reached us: 85 railroad cars of Jews, around 5,000 persons, were not taken to Kovno [a city near Vilna] as promised but transported by train to Ponar where they were shot to death. . . . The ghetto was deeply shaken, as though struck by thunder. The atmosphere of slaughter has gripped the people." The following day, Rudashevski closed his diary entry with the words: "We may be fated for the worst." It was the final entry.

Vilna ghetto lacked the stomach and unity for the kind of uprising that raged in the Warsaw ghetto that April and May. The calls for armed resistance issued by Yitzhak Wittenberg, the charismatic leader of the FPO, fell largely on deaf ears. Jacob Gens, now de facto governor of the ghetto since the Judenrat had been dismissed, ruled with ruthless pragmatism. To fight, warned Gens, was suicidal—better to temporize, compromise, cooperate, play along, run out the clock. "Work for life" was his watchword. Gens vowed to keep as many people alive as possible, as long as they obeyed him. Wittenberg countered that life was not worth living as the slaves of murderers. Between them, Gens and Wittenberg divided the soul of Vilna ghetto, though Gens took the lion's share. A showdown was inevitable.

On the night of July 9–10, the First Division, Len Cohn among them, took part in a massive Allied air and sea attack on the Sicilian coast near the town of Gela. Much was disastrously bungled in the initial assault and German resistance was ferocious. Still, the Allies had breached the perimeter of Nazi Europe. The news reached Vilna ghetto immediately, but there were no winks or smiles of celebration. "Many of us would have drunk a toast yesterday," Herman Kruk wrote in his diary on July 10, "if there weren't recently such an air of death in the ghetto. A question mark hangs over the ghetto. The air grows thicker."

The question concerned the fate of resistance leader Yitzhak Wittenberg. Tipped off by a traitor in the ranks of the FPO, the Gestapo had demanded that Wittenberg be turned over to them alive. Gens, though by some accounts he secretly supported, funded, and armed the FPO, agreed to do what he could to arrange the capture. On July 15, he set up a meeting with Wittenberg, in the course of which he betrayed Wittenberg to the police (sources differ on whether the Jewish or the Lithuanian police made the arrest). However, an FPO contingent succeeded in freeing Wittenberg and hiding him in the ghetto. "The chase after Wittenberg went on for hours," wrote one resident. "The whole ghetto felt involved." Hidden in an attic, disguised as a woman, Wittenberg issued the call for an immediate uprising. But the Gestapo outwitted him. An ultimatum was issued that put

Jewish Vilna in an impossible bind: either Wittenberg be turned over to the Gestapo alive or they would kill every last Jew in the ghetto. Gens coined a slogan that was shouted in the streets: "1 or 20,000." The ghetto erupted. A throng of "underworld characters and Jewish police, masses of ghetto Jews" descended on FPO headquarters screaming "We want to live!" In the end, with the ghetto on the brink of a civil war of Jew versus Jew, FPO members persuaded their leader to surrender. "Look, Jews are standing in the street," Abba Kovner told Wittenberg. "We shall have to fight them in order to reach the enemy, and he will probably stand there and laugh. Are you prepared for this?" Wittenberg entered Gestapo headquarters with a hidden capsule of cyanide (some believe Gens slipped it to him). He committed suicide in his cell.

July 16, 1943—a day of shame that became known as Wittenberg Day—signaled the beginning of the end. Three weeks later, on August 6, a thousand Jewish workers were pulled off their jobs at Vilna's Porobanek Airfield, herded into a railway yard, and forced onto cattle cars. Many tried to run, assuming they were bound for Ponar, and were shot down. But this roundup was something new. With their armies being pounded and pushed back in Russia, Sicily, and North Africa, the Germans were desperate for weapons, ammunition, concrete blocks for bunkers, tanks, uniforms, fur coats, machine parts. The workers seized at the airfield on August 6 were not being sent to die at Ponar but to live and work as slaves in Estonia, where the Nazis were amassing huge concentration camps—not extermination camps like Treblinka and Sobibor but war-industry work camps. If the slaves worked themselves to death, so be it—fewer to kill in the end. By Wittenberg Day, Vilna ghetto, like all of Europe's ghettos, had already been assigned an expiration date and a liquidation program. The fit prisoners would go to Estonia. The "unnecessary" would be disposed of.

Vilna, in fact, was the first place where the Nazis began to murder Jews on a methodical, industrial scale. It was also the site of their greatest success. Of the eighty thousand Jews living in Vilna when the Germans seized the city in June 1941, only two to three thousand survived the war. At Ponar alone, some seventy-two thousand Jews from Vilna and the surrounding region were shot and buried. "No other Jewish community in Nazi-occupied Europe was so comprehensively destroyed."

After the August 6 deportations, a second round took place on August 24. Eight days later a new Gestapo chief named Bruno Kittel took over to oversee the third cull. The fourth—and final—round began on September 23. By then Jacob Gens was dead—shot by Kittel's orders in the courtyard of the Gestapo headquarters on the evening of September 14. The liquidation of Vilna ghetto proceeded without its king.

According to the last ghetto census conducted on May 29, 1942, Doba was living with her two sons and her brother-in-law at Strashuno 15. At some point in 1943, Doba "vanished"—her cousin Tsipora's word. Tsipora has no recollection of the particulars. After the May 1942 census, there is no trace of Doba; no document with her name in it; no survivor who can attest to her disappearance. Only these two facts have surfaced: on May 29, 1942, Doba and her sons were alive. In 1943, she vanished.

This is probably how it happened.

At seven o'clock on the morning of September 23, Ukrainian soldiers broke into their room and at gunpoint ordered Doba, Yitzchak, and the boys to vacate the building. "Screaming obscenities, [the soldiers] demanded our so-called jewelry," recorded one prisoner. "There was very little left, mostly watches." Doba grabbed whatever of value remained and hid it in an inner pocket or the seam of a coat, and then she and Yitzchak and the boys joined the mass of people in the courtyard. They walked the two blocks to the main ghetto gate on Rudnicka Street, they passed the sign on the gate that warned of typhoid danger—"Entry is strictly forbidden for non-Jews"—they entered the streets of the city, the gentile city. "As soon as we passed the gate, we were surrounded by other Ukrainians who stood ready for us with outstretched rifles," wrote a survivor. "Instinctively we closed ranks a little more and kept walking." The streets were eerily deserted—no jeering bystanders, just troops armed with rifles and clubs and a long dark river of prisoners.

Doba's reply had been "none" when the ghetto census-taker asked her profession. Her sole occupation had always been daughter, wife, and mother. Wife had been taken from her when Shepseleh died at Ponar two years earlier, but she had clung to mother. Doba was not a saint. Her heart was large but fragile and selfish. It must have driven her mad to share half a room with two miserable boys for two years, to listen to them cough and bicker, to see their childhoods wither. No one emerges from a ghetto ennobled. "It is naïve, absurd, and historically false to believe that an infernal system such as National Socialism sanctifies its victims," Primo Levi wrote. "On the contrary, it degrades them, it makes them resemble itself." Doba's humanity was assaulted mercilessly by the agents of National Socialism. Maybe they succeeded in degrading her. Maybe she broke down and turned on her family. Maybe she grabbed food for herself and let them starve. Maybe she came to hate the sons she had once loved more than life. There is no way of knowing what was in her heart. But the facts speak for themselves. She was a widow without a work permit imprisoned in a ghetto, and yet she kept two boys alive.

At the outskirts of the city, streets gave way to hills and gardens. At a bend in the road, the slender twin baroque towers of the Missionaries Church of the Assumption came into view above the walls of the Rossa Monastery. Chaos descended as Doba and her family approached this place of worship. "Germans tore into our columns," wrote one prisoner. "We were pushed in all directions. We could not see anything but felt that something terrible was taking place." Families were being split up—men to one side, women and children to the other. What were Shimonkeh and Velveleh—children or men? Velveleh had a month to go until he turned eleven. After two years in the ghetto he would have been stunted and emaciated, so he probably looked closer to seven or eight. A child. He went with Doba into the monastery courtyard. Shimonkeh, fifteen and tall for his age, was judged to be a man. With the crack of a rifle butt, Doba lost her firstborn son. Shimonkeh and his uncle Yitzchak disappeared into the crowd.

Soldiers with rifles and clubs forced Doba and Velveleh toward Rossa Square, an immense enclosure in the monastery complex. At the entrance "there were two rows of Gestapo facing each other for about 200 feet." The air reverberated with the sounds of people inflicting and enduring pain. "I don't know how to describe the sound and the smell of death that reigned around us," remembered one prisoner. "By this time, most of the women ... were walking aimlessly in a daze with desolate looks on their faces as if they had already lost their minds. There were small children crying, looking for their parents." At the far end of the square there was an opening, an exit into a narrow corridor, and in front of this opening the naked bodies of two young men and a young woman dangled from poles—FPO partisans who had been caught trying to escape through the city sewers and killed by Kittel's orders. One witness wrote that the men were dead but the woman had enough life to croak out, "No, they won't do this to you." Tsipora, who was present in Rossa Square that day, remembers only two bodies, a man and a woman; she believes that they had been strangled for putting up a sign that said, "Jews go right." It was always the same when the Germans did a "selection"—right meant life, left was death.

All around Doba, women were pinching their cheeks so they could color up and look younger. Anyone who had lipstick smeared her mouth with bright red. The crowd shoved Doba and Velveleh toward the hanging bodies at the far side of the square where the "selection" would determine their fates.

It rained the night of September 23 and the Jewish women and children in Rossa Square got soaked. "Ukrainian guards walked among the half-sleeping people, robbed and beat them," wrote Kruk. The final selection of the 8,000 ghetto survivors was completed on September 24. An estimated 1,400 to 1,700 young women went right—to the Kaiserwold concentration camp in Latvia. Between 4,000 and 4,500 women and children went left—to the gas chambers at Sobibor. A few hundred were deemed so weak, sick, or old that they were not worth transporting to a gas chamber and instead were taken to Ponar and shot over the brimming pits.

Kaiserwold, Sobibor, or Ponar: those were Doba's options. It seems unlikely that she and Velveleh were selected for Ponar—only a small number of the weakest were sent to the death pits. Kaiserwold, a labor camp, would have bought Doba a few more months of life, assuming she survived the rigors of slave labor. But that also seems unlikely. Tsipora's thirty-four-year-old mother was with her in Rossa Square on those two days, and when the moment of their selection came, the mother went left and Tsipora went right. "At thirty-four my mother was considered too old for work," Tsipora says. Doba was nearly forty-one.

That leaves Sobibor.

The gas used at Sobibor was carbon monoxide piped from a large gasoline engine into sealed chambers measuring about 270 square feet each. It took half an hour for the gas to asphyxiate Doba. There were so many women in the death chamber with her that she didn't lean or fall as her life ebbed away. She died standing up, wet with perspiration and excrement, her naked body and shorn head pressed tight into the naked bodies and heads of the women around her.

Four days before the liquidation of Vilna ghetto, Shalom Tvi went to Montreal, Canada. Although the Hudson and Champlain valleys were ablaze with fall color, this was not a journey made for pleasure. It was a journey of bureaucratic necessity. Shalom Tvi had now been living in the United States for four years on a tourist visa that he renewed and extended every six months. In order to upgrade the tourist visa to an immigration visa that would enable him to remain indefinitely, he had to leave the country, file an application at an American foreign consulate, and reenter the United States with new documents reflecting his altered status. Since Montreal was the site of the American foreign consulate nearest the Bronx, Shalom Tvi duly made the trip to Canada, filed the "Application for Immigration Visa (Quota)" on September 20, 1943, and presented the newly approved and stamped immigration visa, No. 436, when he crossed back into New York State at Rouses Point.

On the visa application form, he indicated that he was seventy years old, gray haired, blue eyed, five feet four inches tall, and that his "purpose in going to the United States" was "to reside, and I intend to remain permanently." In the space for nearest living relative he wrote, "Mrs. Bella Kahanowicz, whose relationship is wife and whose address is Rakov, Poland."

Four days later, Vilna was finished; Volozhin was already finished; Rakov had been finished nearly eight months earlier—and still Shalom Tvi believed, or hoped, that he had a wife whose address was Rakov, Poland.

"Perhaps you hear about our area," Shalom Tvi wrote Sonia after his return from Montreal. "Here we know nothing. My only consolation is getting frequent letters from you."

CHAPTER TWENTY-FOUR

KLOOGA

They put the men in rows of ten and ticked them off a row at a time. Gestapo Chief Kittel did the counting himself: "10, 20, 30, 40, 50, 60, 70—right! 10, 20, 30, 40, 50, 60, 70—left!" Two trains were waiting on two separate tracks. The squads filled the empty freight cars in alternating waves—seventy men to a car. Each car was identically bare: no seats, no toilet, a single window crisscrossed with barbed wire high up in the corner. When a car was full, a guard stuck his head in and shouted that if one man went missing, all would be punished. Then the sliding door was slammed and locked and the next car was filled.

In one of those freight cars, packed in the stifling dark with sixty-nine other men, stood Shimonkeh. His uncle Yitzchak may have stood next to him. There had been no selection for the males of the Vilna ghetto. One hundred of the old and feeble were weeded out and shot—but the rest were crammed indiscriminately onto the trains. Smooth-faced teenagers, arthritic middle-aged shopkeepers, once-famous musicians, laborers with callused hands, teachers, librarians, electricians, attorneys, pharmacists, chemists, hospital directors, yeshiva students—the Germans needed the bodies. Had there been a selection, Shimonkeh might have been sent left like his mother and brother. He was a tall lank scarecrow with spindly arms and narrow shoulders; knobs of bone rippled from the base of his skull down his back; he could barely hear. But the Germans didn't care. Shimon was swept onto the train with the rest. He had ceased to be Shimonkeh when his mother and brother disappeared in Rossa Square. Now he was Shimon Senitski—an emaciated fifteen-year-old boy standing in the dark and wondering when the train would move and where it would go.

It was night by the time the engine shuddered to life. The air already reeked of excrement. Ten minutes outside the city, a wild cry tore through the car: they had taken the track to the right—they were going to Ponar. "People started to cry," said Saul Slocki, who was on the train that night. "Some started to say good-bye to each other. Others prayed." Then, after a few agonizing minutes, the train ground to a halt, idled, and reversed until it was back on the main track. Bound to Estonia—not Ponar. This was the Nazis' idea of a joke. "Why not?" wrote Slocki. "If they couldn't have the pleasure of murdering us, this little joke was something for them to enjoy."

Shimon was on that train for three days. In some cars the men got bread, water, and sausage—in some cars they got nothing. When he needed to relieve himself, he had to squat over the pail in front of the others. The men put the pail next to the door to minimize the stench, but when a guard came to inspect them he kicked it over and a slick of urine-soaked shit spread through the car. "On the train, no one spoke," said one survivor. "I cannot describe the horror. We were not human anymore. It was like we were made of death." Some men died on the train; by the end of the third day all of them thought they would be dead before the journey ended.

Shimon was still alive when the train halted at Klooga, in northern Estonia, on Wednesday, September 29, the eve of Rosh Hashanah, 5704. "Klooga aedlinn" the sign said—the garden town of Klooga. Shimon got out of the train and sank his feet into the sandy soil; there was a tang of salt in the air—a few miles away the Baltic laved a beautiful white sand beach where Estonians came on holiday. Through the scrub pines he could see the gate and a signpost with the words "O.T. Betriebe Klooga." Next to the gate, block letters snarled the same message in German, Russian, and Estonian— "Stop! You will be shot without warning." The guards shoved Shimon into a line of prisoners and marched him through the gate. "Inside the gate they lined us up," recalled a survivor who went by the name Michael Turner after the war. "I heard someone being killed. Through loudspeakers a voice said 'If you are hiding gold you will be killed.' There was a big box to put in jewelry, watches and money." After that the guards stripped Shimon naked, shaved a swath through his hair from forehead to nape, and gave him a prisoner's striped jacket, shirt, pair of trousers, pair of wooden clogs. The jacket bore a Star of David with the number 641 sewn onto it. He had ceased to be Shimonkeh when they took his mother. He ceased to be Shimon when they took his clothes and half his hair. He was prisoner #641, a slave belonging to Albert Speer. They put him in a huge light-flooded barracks with rows of bunks and little stoves at either end. The next morning they gave him a cup of chestnut coffee, lined him up in the camp yard with the others, made him stand rigidly still while they called the numbers of every prisoner. Anyone who moved got clubbed over the head by an SS guard. Roll call took an hour, then he went to work.

His first job was to string barbed wire around the perimeter of the camp so no one could escape (some escaped anyway and were tortured and killed when caught). Then he got assigned to Klooga's specialty: the production of underwater signal mines made of reinforced concrete and hundred-pound concrete blocks used for bunkers. Shimon, who probably barely weighed a hundred pounds himself, had to make fifteen of these concrete blocks a day, every day. That was at the start. Gradually the daily quotas were raised to nineteen, thirty, and thirty-five, until they stabilized at forty. The skin flayed off his arms; his limbs ached and swelled. Exhaustion haunted his every step. "I was in six different camps in Estonia," says Ben Anolik, a survivor. "Klooga was the worst." "Nights I did not sleep," says Michael Turner. "I am a man. I am supposed to be the strong one. You got used to being hungry, dirty. We were alive."

Shimon's life varied only with the seasons, the temperament of the camp guards, and the disposition of the "strong ones"—the tough enterprising slaves who controlled the flow of food. "Everywhere [the strong ones] are the first ones, everywhere they get the best deal, and everywhere people owe them change," wrote Kruk, who continued his diary at Klooga. In winter Shimon froze and shivered through the night in his bunk; in summer he burned. Roll call became a daily torment—"sadistic exercises of brutality and cruelty," wrote one inmate. "They would use the roll call to punish 'offenders' by strapping them to a specially designed bench and beating them to a pulp while we all stood and watched in horror. At times they would have us sit for an hour or two with our hands up for no apparent reason in spite of the freezing weather." When Kurt Stacher, "a man the size of a fat bear with a large bloodhound at his side," was camp commander, Shimon cowered. Stacher's particular pleasure was to turn his dog loose and look on while it savaged prisoners. Michael Turner watched SS guards whip his father to death: "The concrete blocks were dried in little warehouses. One day they did not dry because my father was on duty and he had fallen asleep before the blocks dried. The chief of the Gestapo whipped him and he died of the lashes."

There was a women's camp adjoining, even more crowded than the men's camp. Same work; same food. "The hunger was unbelievable," recalls a survivor named Tola Urbach. The midday meal was a bowl of soup ("dirty dishwater soup with a few grains of barley swimming in it") eaten from an empty sardine can; dinner was bread and margarine—though the margarine was so foul smelling that many could not choke it down. To squeeze out a few more calories prisoners picked potato peels out of the garbage and salvaged the grounds from fake coffee. The food ration was "neither enough to live nor to die on," wrote Kruk. "Hunger knows no restraints. A hungry person is ready for anything except for stifling the worm inside you, which gnaws and gnaws. . . . Everyone followed his animal instinct, forgetting that he arrived here in the image of man—the crown of creation, the most beautiful of all creatures!" Tola Urbach: "My sister's friend went insane. In Vilna she had been a talented pianist. She became totally lost. One day they took her out and gave her an injection that killed her." Life became briefly more tolerable when a humane Dutch *Lagerführer* (commandant) was in charge. "He was exceptional," said one of the women. "He did not act like an SS man." One day during the summer of 1944 he took the women to the beach. "It was a long march to get there," says Tola. "It was the only time we were out of the camp." The Dutch *Lagerführer* was soon transferred—too kind for Klooga.

Shimon turned sixteen on February 5, 1944. Three years earlier he had stood beneath the golden hands—the hands of the Kohanim—that adorned the ark of the Torah at Temple Taharat Hakodesh and chanted his Bible portion in Hebrew. A bar mitzvah boy. His mother and grandmother wept with pride. Did Shimon remember it was his birthday? Did he still believe in God? Occasionally the slaves sang Hebrew songs—songs "filled with nostalgia, hope, and desire for life." Did Shimon join in? Some of the men smuggled prayer shawls and tefillin into camp, God knows how or at what cost, and observed the prescribed prayer rituals every morning and every evening. A few written traces of Shimon's imprisonment at Klooga survive, but the documents shed no light on the state of his soul. On a card labeled: Häftl. Nr [prisoner number.]: a clerk typed in 641, SENIZKI, Schimon. Another card indicates that he was born in Vilna in 1928, that his occupation was Arbeiter (worker), and that he was working in a Sonderkommando—"special unit." In extermination camps like Auschwitz, the Sonderkommando was the task force that collected the corpses from the gas chambers and transported them to the crematoria—the worst job of all. But there were no gas chambers or crematoria at Klooga—the Sonderkommando that Shimon worked in may have had something to do with the clinic. A card indicates that at some point he was assigned to a construction crew that built signal boxes for the railroad. His name and number appear on a list headed "Transport": possibly a group sent to work off-site. Six numbers and names appear under the Transport heading: 211 Rudnizki, 217 Gordon, 679 Chodonk, 4439 Kaplan, 6255 Bellizkes, 641 Senizki. Then there's a line, a different heading—illegible—and another column of names.

Some of the prisoners died of disease. Some starved to death. Some were killed when they were found with a second shirt. Some dropped dead of heart attacks. Some were beaten to death. One hundred were shot after three prisoners succeeded in escaping. If a prisoner became too infirm to walk, he "had to depart for the next world," in the words of the sadistic alcoholic infirmary chief, Wilhelm Genth. In June 1944, Klooga had 2,122 prisoners, the largest number of any camp in Estonia.

It appears that Shimon was still among these prisoners. He must have had someone to look out for him. There were more women than men at Klooga, and the sexes, though segregated, found ways to mingle. Maybe a friend of Doba's took pity on the boy. Someone did. Without an ally, a frail, cerebral, gently brought-up sixteen-year-old did not stand a chance. Shimon survived. He became a skeleton but he survived.

Klooga was sealed off from the world by barbed wire, dogs, and SS guards. But news of the world filtered in. Tola Urbach recalls that there was a barracks in the women's camp full of "misfits and homosexuals" pulled out of the German army. One of these men had a radio and he passed on news of the war to the Jewish prisoners. "We knew the Russian armies were advancing," says Tola. "We raced around the camp rejoicing at news of Russian victories. We knew the advance of the Russian army was our only hope of salvation."

Word of the Allied landing at Normandy on June 6, 1944, reached the prisoners. Shimon's cousin Sidney Cohen, Sam's oldest son, was a paratrooper serving with the 82nd Airborne Division, but he was invalided out on D-day due to a case of dysentery; his unit parachuted onto the Normandy beaches without him.

In July, the Red Army took Minsk and Vilna.

The prisoners at Klooga heard the news and waited for their turn. "Everything is being liberated, even Warsaw (!!!), everything except us," wrote Kruk at the end of July. "We are so upset, our nerves choke us. . . . We count not just the days, but the hours and minutes: any minute we may get out of hell."

Itel was also doing her bit to help the Allies win the war in the summer of 1944. Maiden Form had already filled the largest order for bras and garter belts ever placed by the U.S. government. Now the War Department tapped the company to pitch in on another front—this one involving not breasts but birds—pigeons, to be precise. Despite advances in technology, homing pigeons remained in widespread use for battlefield communication during the Second World War. Pigeons had a number of obvious advantages. They could fly at speeds of a mile a minute over short distances with a range approaching a thousand miles. They could navigate terrain impenetrable to earthbound messengers. In tiny capsules attached to their legs, pigeons could carry not only messages but also maps, microfilm, mini cameras, and blood samples. Unlike wireless signals, they did not reveal their sender's position when intercepted. The U.S. military even set up a Pigeon Service to groom avian couriers and their human handlers. Hundreds of troops went into action on D-day with pigeons tucked under their coats, but this was clearly awkward for infantry and impossible for paratroopers. The U.S. Army Signal Corps drafted Maiden Form to come up with a better way of transporting homing pigeons safely and securely behind enemy lines. "You people ought to know about designing something to hold a live, curved object," the army rep told Itel. In July 1944, William and his designers submitted final drawings for the pigeon vest—a cloth pouch that got wrapped around a pigeon's body and wings and then attached to a paratrooper by a long buckled strap. In braspeak, the pigeon vest had "just enough shirring to accommodate the wings"; the material was porous mesh that enabled the bird to breathe; and the "cup" was adjustable since pigeons, like breasts, are not all the same size. On an outside flap, each vest had a label with the words: IMPORTANT DO NOT RETAIN PIGEON IN VEST IN EXCESS OF SIX HOURS.

The Signal Corps placed an initial order for 28,500 vests at $0.716 each.

Itel knew she had a dream of a PR opportunity—*Maiden Form Outfits U.S. Paratroopers! Bras for Birds!*—once the war was over and the top-secret project could be disclosed.

At sundown on Friday in the summer of 1944, Sonia placed the Shabbat candles on her table at Kfar Vitkin, covered her eyes as her mother had done, said the prayers, and then fled in tears. Something about the guttering of the flames above the columns of melting wax twisted her heart. She ran from the house, from her family, and, as she told her father, from herself.

Shalom Tvi wrote back to chide her.

> *My dear daughter, this is not the right way to behave. Children must not be left with lit candles without supervision. You should be at home with your husband and children and thank God that our fate has taken us out of there. How could we help if our fate were the same as theirs? Perhaps someone has survived and we could help them.*
>
> *I suggest you go to a nerve doctor [psychiatrist] and ask him for something to calm you down. You have to be a "mensch." You have to be a healthy mother for your children. Heed my advice, my dear daughter.*

Shalom Tvi also counseled Sonia to have more children. "This will be good for you and good for the Eretz. It may be hard at first, but in older age it will be much easier."

Depressed though she was, Sonia heeded her father. Areleh would turn five that November. Leahleh was already nine. They had no first cousins, no aunts or uncles. Their family had shrunk almost to nothing. Sonia felt it was her duty to bring another life into the world.

At Klooga the slaves had a new greeting for each other: "May we be liberated as soon as possible." The front was approaching. By the first week of August "mighty explosions and bombardments" were audible in the camp day and night. Everyone was scrutinizing the guards for signs of a change of mood, a shift in their intentions. The Germans seemed anxious, and some tried to make peace with the prisoners. "Soon you will be liberated," they told the Jews. "And our lot is bad. They will slaughter us with no mercy." The male prisoners were taken to the beach. The midday soup became thicker.

What did it mean?

They endlessly debated this question. The optimists said it was obvious: the Nazis were losing the war, the Red Army was closing in, soon they would go free. The pragmatists said it was unlikely the Germans would simply walk away and leave them. There were rumors of mass evacuations from Tallinn, the Estonian capital. Maybe the prisoners would be moved west with the retreating German army? Maybe they would be relocated to another camp? The pessimists said that the Germans always destroyed the evidence and covered their tracks. Klooga would be no different.

And so the summer of 1944 drained away. Kruk wrote on August 29, "You can sense the front. . . . All around us is noise, pilots are being shot at and do not relent, day or night." But still the work details went out every morning and returned exhausted every night. Five hundred prisoners were shuffled from Klooga to Lagedi, a more primitive camp near Tallinn. Rumors flew that these prisoners were going to be transferred to Danzig, that they would end up at the Stutthof concentration camp, that they had already been shot in the forest or drowned in the Baltic. "May we be liberated," they kept saying at Klooga—a talisman, a prayer. If they could only hold out another day, another hour.

On September 19, the prisoners were routed out of the barracks as usual at five in the morning and assembled in the plaza where the roll was called. The devout among them remarked that it was the second day of Rosh Hashanah: by the Jewish calendar, it was exactly a year since they had been imprisoned here. They all noticed the armed guards. Usually four guards stood by while the roll was called: now there was a platoon of men with weapons.

They were lined up and counted, but they were not given their fake coffee and they were not sent to work. Instead they were told that their evacuation to Germany was imminent. They would be traveling by ship to East Prussia. At seven o'clock an order was issued for 301 strong healthy men to leave the plaza. Ten Estonians escorted them out of the camp. Those who remained were ordered to cross their legs under them and then sit on their legs. In a few minutes their muscles went numb. The plaza was filled with two thousand temporarily paralyzed prisoners.

Everyone thought the same thing: evacuation to Germany meant *life*. They had made it this far. The war would be over soon. The Allies would march on Germany, Hitler would fall, they would be liberated. Shimon would join his aunt and uncle in Palestine. Or his cousins in New York. He was sixteen years old. His body would heal; the wounds would crust over; he would cease to be prisoner #641 and become a human being again—the crown of creation!

The 301 healthy men who had been pulled from the ranks were told they were being sent back to work. They must finish the job that remained undone from the previous day. In fact they did go to work, but not on any tasks they had done before. The guards took them to train cars stacked with logs and ordered them to unload the logs and carry them into the forest. When all the logs had been moved, the guards ordered them to build four platforms, spread out in the clearing. The instructions were precise: they must lay four large logs on their sides to form a square and then build a kind of floor inside the square out of split crosspieces and shorter logs. At the center of each square they erected four upright poles about a foot apart.

It looked like the start of a compound of summer cottages: four log platforms, thirty-foot square, each one fitted out with the framework for a central chimney.

The work was going smoothly until one of the workers ran from the forest back to the camp plaza and shouted, "Jews, save yourselves, they are killing us!" An SS officer silenced his voice with a bullet. The assembled prisoners, paralyzed from sitting on their legs, could do nothing but stare at each other in horror.

In midmorning, twenty-five men dressed in black boots and peaked caps arrived in the camp—"special commando," some said, which everyone knew was a euphemism for death squad. At 11 o'clock the twenty-five disappeared into the dining room. The lunch was brief; the kitchen staff remarked on their rude manners.

The prisoners were fed at noon. A big hearty meal. One remembered it as pork, another as flounder, another as "an unusually rich soup." "Why all of a sudden this big meal?" one woman wondered. "We smelled a rat."

Around 2:30 they heard the first shots—a burst of fire, a pause, another burst. "At first people said it was military maneuvers," Tola Urbach remembers. "But after it happened repeatedly we can no longer deny that it's the end. People became hysterical." The women started screaming; men and women got to their feet and pushed their way to the perimeter of the wire. Then the special commando began the cull. Armed guards entered the plaza, counted off a group of men—some said it was twenty-five, others said fifty to a hundred—and marched them into the forest. The remaining prisoners huddled on the ground; the women hugged each other. They strained their ears to the forest. In a few minutes they heard the shots—a volley of automatic fire followed by the pops of single bullets. Then silence. Then the guards were back for the next load. Only men.

At four o'clock, five young men were called out and taken away. Thirty minutes later they were back. "We managed to find out that the five men had pulled a car loaded with two drums of gasoline to the forest," wrote one of the prisoners.

Another group of men was removed from the camp and marched into the forest. And another. The male prisoners dwindled away.

When the men got to the clearing, they understood. The log platforms were the foundation—or rather the first layer. The next layer was made of human beings, rows of men lying facedown on top of the logs. Each man had a hole at the back of his head next to his ear. But the structure was not yet finished. The new batch of prisoners had to build the next layer. First they stacked split logs on top of the bodies, then they were ordered to lie down, heads facing out, on top of the logs. Then came the bullet to the brain, though not every shot was accurate. Some of the shots missed altogether; some merely clipped off a wound; some entered the head but failed to kill.

Then the guards went to fetch the next layer.

As evening fell, about a hundred prisoners made a break for it. In the fading light they slipped past the wire and dashed into the barracks. One enterprising soul cut the power line. The rest scattered, hiding under beds and in cupboards, racing upstairs to the second floor. SS guards stormed the barracks and opened fire with machine guns; eighty-seven prisoners were killed on the ground floor. But the SS left the second floor alone. It was getting dark. Maybe they were tired. Or scared.

The shooting in the forest went on into the night. When all the men were gone the women got their turn; last were the patients and staff of the infirmary.

After the shooting stopped there was a long interval of silence and then the sky exploded. "From the upstairs of the barracks we saw yellow and red flames," said one of the men hiding on the second floor. "We did not know what was going on. We lay there and we heard whispering in the corners. We looked out on yellow and red flames." "A wall of fire spread over the area," wrote another. "Over the noise of the crackling fire we heard the impatient calls of the Germans shouting again, over and over, 'Schnell, schnell!'" (quickly, quickly). While the flames roared into the night sky, the Germans fled.

The pyres of logs and bodies were still smoldering when the Red Army liberated the camp five days later. The Germans had not destroyed the evidence after all. The pyres were standing, blackened but intact. Many of the bodies were barely singed, though others were charred to stumps. Of the estimated 2,000 prisoners killed at Klooga on September 19, 1944, 491 could be identified. Only 108 survived.

Prisoner 641 was not among them.

Shimon Senitski, the great-grandson and namesake of the priest and scribe Shimon Dov HaKohen, was the last of his family to live and die in Europe. Two branches remained, but the third and oldest branch of Shimon Dov's family ended in a pyre of logs and corpses in the Estonian woods.

CHAPTER TWENTY-FIVE

POSTWAR

FOR FUTURE GENERATIONS

Neighbors in Camp Klooga often ask me
Why do you write in such hard times?—
Why and for whom? . . .
. . . For we won't live to see it anyway.

I know I am condemned and awaiting my turn,
Although deep inside me burrows a hope for a miracle.
Drunk on the pen trembling in my hand,
I record everything for future generations:
A day will come when someone will find
The leaves of horror I write and record.
People will tear their hair in anguish,
Eyes will plunge into the sky
Unwilling to believe the horror of our times.

—**HERMAN KRUK**

The truth came slowly and in fragments.

One of the relatives in New York remembers a group from Rakov coming to the house on Andrews Avenue with a list of names of landsmen who had been killed and asking Shalom Tvi whether he could identify any of them. But there is no mention of this visit in the letters

Shalom Tvi wrote faithfully, fanatically to Sonia every week in 1944 and 1945. From these letters it is clear that he never received definitive confirmation of the deaths, the synagogue fire, the actions at Volozhin, the liquidation of the Vilna ghetto, the pyres at Klooga in which his grandson perished. In the absence of news, he was left alone to conclude the worst.

A relative in the Bronx, when asked many years later how Shalom Tvi dealt with his gaping loss and uncertainty, replied, "He took it with a grain of salt."

This was a façade. He did not take any of it with a grain of salt.

On July 6, 1945, two months after Hitler committed suicide (April 30, 1945) and the Germans surrendered to the Allies (May 8, 1945), Shalom Tvi wrote Sonia and Chaim begging them to secure a certificate that would allow him to immigrate to Palestine:

Dear Children, try any way with those who manage the certificate affairs, don't leave them in peace. Apply every day and tell them about my tragedy and about what has happened to our family. Here in America I have also lost everyone [Gishe Sore, his sister-in-law, had died on February 16, 1945; his sister Leah Golda, Rose's mother, died on June 19]. My dear sister had been my only consolation. I had spent all the Shabbats and holidays with her, and now I am left by myself. I don't even have a person to whom I can open my heart and cry. Dear children, make an effort for me and knock on all the doors in every possible place and maybe you will succeed in stirring some feelings of pity. I am sitting here on embers.

It had been four years since Sonia received a letter postmarked Rakov. The envelope trembled in her hand. The handwriting was unfamiliar. The name of the sender—Hillel Eidelman—rang a faint bell. The letter was dated June 23, 1945—and given how erratic the mail was in those days, it probably arrived at Kfar Vitkin at around the same time as her father's letter of July 6.

Greetings, Beyle's Sonia!

Our fate is very bad.

None of us survived, no one from your family or from ours. I'm as alone as a solitary stone. . . . I am writing to tell you that the entire village was burned with everyone burned alive. . . . [They] were pushed into the synagogue, kerosene poured in there, then hand grenades thrown in and burned them. Mercy on them! There were mothers with their children there. May God preserve the martyrs of Rakov. They didn't stop until everyone was burned up. Now we see nothing more than little pieces here and there.

Write to me. I would continue my letter but I'm sitting here, crying, with trembling hands. It is very difficult to write you such news.

So now Sonia—and Shalom Tvi—knew the truth, at least about the Rakov family.

On July 31, 1945, ten months after her nephew Shimon was shot and burned at Klooga, Sonia gave birth to her third child—another son. She and Chaim named the child Shimon.

On August 23, Shalom Tvi wrote Sonia to congratulate her on the birth of the son. "I think that [the new baby] will truly be fortunate, because right after his birth I received the certificate [for entry to Palestine]. The child has brought you luck, and with the help of God our good luck will also begin and I shall deserve to see you." He promised to bring many beautiful presents with him when he came, though the date of his departure could not be fixed until he received a new Polish passport, which could not happen until Poland's new government opened its consulate in New York. More red tape. More waiting.

At the end of the letter he mentioned in passing that a big parade had filled the streets of Manhattan after the news of the Japanese surrender was broadcast on August 14.

Shalom Tvi never forgot the old man with the cane who had blessed him when he was a little child in Volozhin. "May you have light your entire life," the old man had said after Shalom Tvi led him home by the light of his lantern one autumn night. "May you have light throughout your journey." Shalom Tvi told Sonia that he always believed that this blessing spared his life.

The Polish passport was finally issued on October 28, 1946. Shalom Tvi booked the first available passage on board the SS *Marine Carp* and sailed out of New York. On the Application for Reentry Permit filed with the U.S. Immigration and Naturalization Service, he indicated that his reason for going abroad was to visit family, that he intended to be absent from the States for "less than one year," and that his temporary address overseas would be Kfar Vitkin, Palestine. Only the last of these assertions was strictly true.

Shalom Tvi arrived at Haifa harbor on February 2, 1947, a tumultuous time in the Land. The Jews in Palestine, enraged by Britain's continued adherence to a strict immigration quota and their punitive treatment of illegal Jewish immigrants, were embarked on a terrorist campaign aimed at forcing the British out. When the Zionist paramilitary group Irgun blew up a wing of the King David Hotel in Jerusalem on July 22, 1946, the British acknowledged that their continued presence was untenable. The newly formed United Nations was enlisted to resolve the matter. On the night of November 29, 1947, Sonia, Chaim, Shalom Tvi, and the children gathered around the radio that Shalom Tvi had brought with him from New York. They were listening to the broadcast of the United Nations General Assembly vote on Resolution 181, which called for the end of the British Mandate and the partition of Palestine into separate Jewish and Arab states. Shimon was only two years old, but he heard the story repeated so many times that it became a memory of his own. When the last vote was cast and the numbers were tallied—thirty-three nations in favor, thirteen opposed, ten abstentions (including the British)—Kfar Vitkin went crazy. "We ran in our pajamas to the moshav center," recalls Shimon, "and we all danced together. Everyone was banging pot lids together. They opened the market and gave sweets to the children. It was a night of joy." Shimon also remembers that the moshavniks went to the British army base near Kfar Vitkin and shouted to the illegal immigrants detained there that they were now free.

The joy ended in violence. On the official termination of the British Mandate, on May 15, 1948, the Arab states mounted a full-scale war aimed at driving the Jews from the region. The fighting was particularly bitter around Jerusalem. Arab forces overran the Jewish quarter in the Old City in the first days of the war. On May 28, the Old City's Jewish community surrendered and some 1,500 Jewish residents were evacuated. Jewish West Jerusalem was surrounded and virtually cut off. In desperation Israeli forces opened a bypass route, dubbed Burma Road, to supply the besieged residents. Chaim, an experienced truck driver, was pressed into service to drive an armored supply truck stocked with food and medicine. When the fighting was intense, he spent the night—or several nights—in West Jerusalem. Eight Israelis died on Burma Road in a Jordanian attack on June 8. Sonia was frantic whenever Chaim stayed over. Shimon remembers that one time after an agonizing absence, his father drove the truck back to Kfar Vitkin with ice cream for the children, but it had all melted by the time he arrived.

In the course of the war, hundreds of thousands of Arabs fled their villages in Israeli territory, settling in miserable refugee camps that still exist today. The Arabs who had remained at Wadi al-Hawarith, the Bedouin farmlands from which Kfar Vitkin had been carved in 1929, abandoned their homes—the village was "ethnically cleansed," as the Palestinians put it—after May 15, 1948. In 1998, an estimated 15,672 refugees traced their ancestry to Wadi al-Hawarith—and the figure is certainly far larger now. In six months of fighting, the Israelis repulsed attacks from Egypt, Jordan, Syria, Lebanon, and Iraq and then pushed into territory beyond the boundaries drawn by the UN partition plan of 1947. A broad swath in the center of the country, from the Galilee south to Beersheba, along with a chunk of the western Negev was now part of the State of Israel. On January 7, 1949, a cease-fire went into effect that both sides, finally, observed. A state of "neither war nor peace" ensued. Sixty years later this remains more or less the status quo in the region. Within a year of the cease-fire, the Jewish population of Israel almost doubled, from six hundred thousand to 1 million.

For Sonia and Chaim, 1949 was memorable as the year when Shimon, then four, was kicked in the head by a horse. The injuries to his face and nose were serious enough to keep him in the hospital for six months. When word reached the family in the States, they put together a huge box of toys and art supplies. "We were very poor in those days," recalls Shimon. "Everyone at Kfar Vitkin was struggling. When that box arrived, we were the only kids in Kfar Vitkin with toys. All the kids of the moshav came to see the miracle of the toys! I was King Creole."

Maiden Form launched its famous Dream Campaign that same year. Itel had always been aggressive and adventurous about advertising, but even she hesitated before signing off on this new and risqué series of print ads crafted by Mary Fillius at the Weintraub ad agency. The ads depicted beautiful young women doing fun, zany, strenuous, absurd, or ordinary things out in public places while clad from the waist up in nothing but their Maidenform (as the company now styled itself) bras. The kickoff ad featured a glamorous beauty in biceps-length black gloves, a chic black hat, billowing white satiny skirt, lace-up sandals, and, slung between her willowy bare midriff and her delicate bare shoulders, a very pointy satin Allo-Ette bra. She leans on a table of gewgaws in some elegant boutique and gazes at herself rapturously in a hand mirror. The copy line reads simply: "I dreamed I went shopping in my Maidenform bra." Subsequent Maidenform dreamers included a female Tarzan ("I dreamed I had a swinging time . . ."), gunslinger ("I dreamed I was WANTED . . ."), firefighter ("I dreamed I went to blazes . . ."), political candidate ("I dreamed I won the election . . ."), and housepainter ("I dreamed I painted the town red . . .").

It was one of the most celebrated, successful, and (briefly) scandalous ad campaigns in marketing history. The likes of Irving Penn and Richard Avedon were brought in to do the photography. The tagline was so catchy that Bing Crosby and Louis Armstrong referenced it in their song "Dardanella" ("She looks so dreamy in her Maidenform bra"). Prudes tutted that the ads were obscene, but American women—amused, flattered, defiant, newly assertive, flush with cash, and hip to the Freudian suggestiveness—voted with their pocketbooks. *Fortune* reported in 1950 that Maidenform sales now stood at 14 million dollars a year, accounting for a tenth of all bras sold in the United States.

Itel and William could afford to be generous. In December 1949, they brought over a relative named Zelig Kost, who had been living at the Foeh-renwald displaced-persons camp near Munich since the end of the war. Foehrenwald, one of the largest and longest-lasting DP camps in Europe, housed between three and five thousand Jewish survivors from 1945 to 1957. Zelig Kost, a relative on Sarah's side, had a particularly moving story. A strapping, good-looking man—"movie-star handsome," according to females in the family—Zelig had run a dairy shop in Ivenets (a shtetl near Rakov) before the war. He was married and the father of a daughter named Esther. When the Nazis seized eastern Poland in 1941, Zelig's family was imprisoned in the Nowogrod ghetto but he managed to escape. He went to look for some kind of hiding place for the family, but when he returned, he discovered that in his absence the ghetto had been liquidated, his wife and baby daughter shot and burned. Zelig fled into the woods and joined a group of partisans. For the duration of the war, he took part in sabotage attacks on Nazi convoys and rail shipments. Zelig and his comrades stayed alive by making raids on local villages: they demanded food at gunpoint; peasants who refused were shot.

Zelig went to Rakov after it was liberated in the summer of 1944. He left this account of what remained:

The edge of Vilna Street stayed intact. There I found Hillel Eidelman [who had written to Sonia describing Rakov's destruction] with a few other wretched, miserable fellows who had reached the shtetl ahead of me. Their appearance, and the sight of the destruction, filled my heart with depressing sadness. A few minutes passed, and none of us uttered a word. We just sat on the ground mourning silently and let our tears flow uninterrupted.

We walked together to the market square. Here was the town's cen-ter and its commercial hub. Generations upon generations had made their livelihood here. We stood in the middle of the market square. For a second we forgot everything and wondered why was it dead silent here? For a short moment we imagined that the stores and the shops would be opened soon, that the Gentiles would jam the place with their wagons and then it would be filled with the hustle-bustle of a market place. . . . And as much as the years in the forests had hardened us we could not hold back our tears.

We reached the "Shul-Hoif" and were jolted. Here stood the synagogues—the "Old" and the "New." Their walls absorbed the prayers of generations of Jews and their pleas to God in Heaven. Within their walls Jews poured their tears during Fast Days and during the Days of Awe. . . . Now—a mountain of ashes. We were standing among the ruins of this sacred place where there was no sign of all those who filled it with their prayers and with their studies of God's Torah. This was the site of the slaughter! Its air still carried the horrifying screams and moaning of those who had been led to their death. Here was the valley of manslaughter. Here was the last act of the bloody tragedy of the Jews of Rakov. Some charred bones could still be seen over here, and over there—the remains of a child's shoe, which, for some reason, was not consumed by the fire and which did not rot during the two years that had passed since that day. We stood silently, remembering the souls of our saintly dear ones. I turned and faced East, and said "Kaddish" in memory of my sister and her family, who died here with the rest of the martyrs of our town.

Homeless and despairing, Zelig made his way to Foehrenwald. There he met and married a fellow partisan named Shoshanna Buckerman, a dressmaker from the Belarusian shtetl of Horod'k.

In December 1949, Zelig and Shoshanna set sail for New York on board the *General Stuart*. On the ship's manifest, they listed their destination in the United States as Quanacut Drive, Bayville, New York—Itel and William's Long Island mansion. Itel got them both hired at Maidenform and the couple moved to Bayonne, New Jersey, and had a daughter named Estelle.

"They were not happy people," Estelle said recently. "Dad was a bright and caring man, but he did not have much left after the war. He suffered from depression all his life and had numerous electric shock treatments. He worked as a mechanic on the sewing machines at Maidenform—it was just a job, not what he wanted to do with his life. There were many days when he could not get out of bed. The culture of my household was very secretive. My mother did not talk at all about the war—she was very jealous of dad's first wife and child whom he loved a great deal. He was a broken man."

Captain Leonard E. Cohn returned from the war with a Bronze Star Medal awarded for "meritorious achievement" in North Africa. Len and all of his American cousins in uniform survived the war unharmed. They had fought and won the good war; they had brought down Hitler; their comrades had liberated the death camps—but none of them thought or talked much about the connection between their military service and the fate of their cousins in Vilna, Rakov, and Volozhin. "I never knew they were killed," said Sol Rubenstein, Leah Golda's son and Doba and Etl's first cousin, who was stationed in the Aleutian Islands with the navy. "We had no idea."

In the memoir he self-published in the 1960s, Hyman includes one paragraph about Shalom Tvi and one sentence about the death of his family: "His family perished when the town Synagogue, in which they were herded was sealed, and set afire." The use of the passive voice is telling. *We never talked about. We never knew. It never came up. No one mentioned it.* Every American cousin said more or less the same thing when asked about the fate of their relatives. "I never knew we had relatives who died in concentration camps," one cousin remarked—but of the seventeen family members who perished in the Shoah, only two likely died in a gas chamber. The others were shot over pits, lined up and machine-gunned, murdered by gentile neighbors, burned alive, worked almost to death, and then shot and incinerated. "Auschwitz," writes Yale historian Timothy Snyder, "generally taken to be an adequate or even a final symbol of the evil of mass killings, is in fact only the beginning of knowledge, a hint of the true reckoning of the past still to come."

But the two surviving branches of the family grew closer. Thanks to the many modern appliances that the American family had given Shalom Tvi to take to Kfar Vitkin, Sonia and Chaim were doing better. Benny, their fourth child, was born in February 1951. Leah turned sixteen that year; Areleh—now called Arik—was eleven. Shimon, who was six, shared a room with his grandfather. "He was always very good with his hands," Shimon recalls of Shalom Tvi. "Always fixing things. He didn't talk much and he didn't eat much. He loved to go to the beach—he carried a black umbrella when he walked there. He was always trying to find ways to help Sonia around the house." Shalom Tvi prayed daily at the synagogue across the street from their house. Sonia was also devout. "It was her way of honoring her father and her dead mother and the relatives killed in the Holocaust," says Shimon.

In 1952, Itel and William bought a Ferguson twenty-eight-horsepower kerosene-fueled tractor and had it sent to Kfar Vitkin. Shimon recalls proudly, "It was something very special. We had the second tractor in the moshav—everyone else was still using horses." Chaim built a shed to house it next to the poultry incubator. Itel and William also contributed generously to a clinic, named in honor of William, in the Israeli city of Ashkelon.

A. Cohen & Sons prospered during the postwar years, though not as spectacularly as Maidenform. As promised, all war veterans were able to resume their jobs. Though the three brothers were still nominally in charge of the business—Harry as chairman of the board, Sam as vice president, Hyman as president and CEO—their sons and sons-in-law were shouldering more responsibility. Harry's older son, Melvin, appointed secretary in 1949, was being groomed to take over after his father retired. The company added new product lines—Corning Ware, Rado watches—and opened offices in Atlanta and Los Angeles. The younger generation got married, moved to the suburbs, filled their big comfortable homes with children, squabbled and griped about each other as their fathers had done.

In 1958, William died of a heart attack at the age of seventy-six in the Bayville mansion. Itel sold the house and moved into a small, elegant apartment on lower Fifth Avenue, near Washington Square Park. Harry died the following year, at the age of seventy, after a series of heart attacks. At the next A. Cohen & Sons board of directors meeting, the slate of officers was reshuffled: Hyman took over as chairman and Harry's son Melvin became president. Sam's youngest son, Marvin, was named vice president and Sam's son-in-law Meyer Laskin (married to Sam's younger daughter, Leona) secretary.

In 1959, Chaim suffered a serious stroke at Kfar Vitkin. Chaim had always embodied the spirit of the *halutz*. He was a singer and a dancer; he loved to hike through the mountains and valleys of Israel; every vacation, he piled the children of Kfar Vitkin into his delivery truck and drove them to remote corners of the country for camping trips. Nothing made him happier than hanging out with friends, drinking, and smoking Eden brand cigarettes into the night. Every year he returned to his beloved Kinneret to take the waters at the Tiberias hot springs. He had friends in Tel Aviv, Jerusalem, and Haifa, and he took pleasure in sharing the bounty of Kfar Vitkin with them. "Chaim was a professional class salad-maker," wrote his youngest son Benny, "and every Shabbat morning he would prepare a super finely diced green salad. His favorite songs were 'Ein Gedi' and 'Evening Has Come.' Many times he danced all night until his shirt was in shreds."

The singing and dancing stopped after the stroke. Chaim was only fifty-three but he was a "broken man" in Benny's words. It rankled Chaim that Shalom Tvi—his father-in-law and uncle—was still spry and active in his eighties while he was partially paralyzed in what should have been the prime of his life. The children remember tension between their father and grandfather. Sonia was caught in the middle. She and Chaim and Shalom Tvi lived together in a small house with four children. It was impossible for Sonia to honor her father without angering her husband. With Chaim disabled, more of the farmwork fell to the others. Shalom Tvi's contributions only made Chaim more bitter. All of them suffered. Chaim eventually found a small apartment in Jerusalem and spent much of his time away from the family.

In the spring of 1963, Itel and Hyman and Hyman's wife, Anna, came to visit the family at Kfar Vitkin. The farm was actually the last stop on their Israeli trip. First they got the grand tour of the young nation's major sights and institutions, with special guides befitting a visitor of Itel's stature and generosity. In Jerusalem they had an audience with Zalman Shazar, Israel's third president, a native of Belarus who had made aliyah the same year as Sonia.

Shimon, eighteen at the time of the visit, remembers that Sonia told Chaim to put on his "fancy pants" to receive his famous cousin from New York, but Chaim refused. "I'll go as usual," he told his wife. The cousins sat together on the covered verandah at the back of the house overlooking the tractor shed and the chicken house and an azure strip of the Mediterranean. They spoke Yiddish. Hyman was stunned to see Shalom Tvi, now ninety-one years old, feeding the chickens. "He was happy to be in Israel," Hyman wrote of his uncle, "but not too pleased with the life. The illness of his son-in-law who had suffered a stroke made life rather unpleasant. He saw his daughter working very hard, taking care of the farm."

Shalom Tvi died at Kfar Vitkin on September 18, 1964, a month shy of his ninety-second birthday. Chaim died the following year, at the age of fifty-nine. Chaim had always dreamed of being buried at the tiny beautiful cemetery by the Sea of Galilee where he had lived and worked as a youth. The poet Ra'hel is buried there along with many early Labor Zionist leaders. But it was not to be. The officers in charge of the cemetery denied the family's request. Chaim is buried instead in the Kfar Vitkin cemetery in a rustling grove of ficus, grevillea, and casuarina trees on a hill overlooking the moshav.

Itel turned eighty in January of 1966, but she refused to retire. She always said she didn't have time to stop working. "First, I can't afford it," she once told an interviewer. "Second, I like it here. And the second reason is the truth." She still spent about half her time on the road. "Quality we give them," she told the *Time* magazine reporter who profiled her in 1960. "Delivery we give them. I add personality." Her company was now taking in upward of 35 million dollars a year.

Itel was on a business trip in Milwaukee in 1966 when she suffered a stroke that left her seriously impaired. She was conscious and mobile afterward, but much of her mind was gone and she rarely left her chair. Relatives recall seeing her sit for hours on end stroking a small dog in her lap—the only thing that brought her comfort. She died in New York on March 29, 1973, at the age of eighty-seven.

The Maidenform dynasty Itel founded endured for only three generations. The company declared bankruptcy in 1997, and the trademark and management of the business passed from the family. People lost their pensions. There was—and is—bad blood.

"With God's will may the new born bring luck, blessing and peace to the world," Shalom Tvi had written to Sonia when she gave birth to her first son, Arie, in November 1939. "May you raise him easily and may he merit a long life." None of these wishes came to pass.

Arie—Areleh—Arik—had always been a golden boy—taller, more athletic, more handsome than anyone else in the family. Sonia fretted to her father that the boy was rough and rambunctious, but Shalom Tvi countered that rowdiness was a sign of intelligence and spirit. This grandson, he assured Sonia, was destined to be another Bar Kochba—the hero of a Jewish uprising against the Romans. As a youth Arik played basketball and broke girls' hearts. He had a square jaw, tousled brown hair, his mother's brown eyes, a fine mind, and an intense work ethic. Arik won a place at the Technion in Haifa, Israel's MIT, and did well in his studies. He married and fathered two daughters, all the while serving as an officer in the tank corps of the Israeli Defense Forces.

When a coalition of Arab states mounted a surprise attack on Israeli positions in the Sinai and the Golan Heights on October 6, 1973—the Yom Kippur War—Arik, now a major, was hastily called up in the general mobilization. His tank corps unit was deployed to the Golan. On October 12, a Syrian missile scored a direct hit on the tank Arik was operating and he was instantly killed. His death came a month before his thirty-fourth birthday. Arik is buried in the Kfar Vitkin cemetery in a section set aside for those who have fallen in Israel's many wars.

Benny said that after Arik's death his mother shut herself in the house at Kfar Vitkin to be "alone with the tragedy." War had already killed her mother, her sisters, her brothers-in-law, all of her nieces and nephews. Now, like her cousin Itel, she had lost her oldest son as well. "Arik's death cut flesh wounds that never healed," said Benny.

In the 1960s, Sam and Gladys began making yearly trips to Israel. Sam had always been the most observant of the Cohen brothers, and in Israel he felt a deep sense of connection to his roots, his faith, his heritage, and most of all his family. Sam and Gladys and Sonia, though virtually strangers, forged an immediate bond when they gathered in Israel. Their shared affinities ran deep. After Sam retired, the Israel trips grew to several months in duration.

Sam was ailing when he and Gladys departed for Israel in February of 1974, but he decided to go ahead with the trip. Gary Cohen, a grandson who was at the airport to see them off, remembers Sam saying he was going to Israel to die. "He didn't say it in a sad way, more a factual way."

Sam and Gladys spent a few weeks at a beachside hotel in Netanya, a short drive from Kfar Vitkin, and then moved to Tiberias, the ancient city overlooking the Sea of Galilee where Chaim had come for yearly spa treatments. In Tiberias, Sam suffered a massive heart attack and was rushed to the Poriya Medical Center. He died in Israel at the age of eighty-four.

Hyman, the last of the Cohen brothers, died in his sleep of a heart attack in 1980 at the age of eighty-eight. Thirteen years before his death, Hyman wrote and self-published a memoir called *As I Recall* about "the three-quarters of a century of my life." Since "I never kept diaries," as he stated in the preface, the book was based on "recollections from memory." Despite some errors of fact and a bit of self-serving spin, the book is the best—in fact the only—account of the Cohen brothers' childhood in Rakov, their early struggles on the Lower East Side, the founding and decades-long flourishing of A. Cohen & Sons. That chapter of family history came to an end in 1978, when financier Ronald Perelman took control of Cohen-Hatfield Industries (as the company was called after its 1968 merger with Hatfield Enterprises) with a 1.9-million-dollar loan guaranteed by his wife. Perelman proceeded to liquidate the company's holdings and fire nearly all of its employees, including family members. With proceeds from the liquidation of Cohen-Hatfield, Perelman trained his sights on McAndrews & Forbes Company, a licorice extract importer and producer. Perelman tapped Sam's son-in-law Meyer Laskin, one of the few family members he had retained, to run McAndrews & Forbes. It was some consolation to out-of-work Cohens that the share price of the company stock, which had been limping along for years in the single digits, was valued at $58.50 when Perelman bought up the outstanding shares in order to take the company private. The sons and daughters of the three founding brothers—at least those who had held on to their stock—made out handsomely. And Sam's son-in-law Meyer embarked on a new career in the international licorice trade.

Sonia secluded herself for a year after Arik's death, but her family drew her back into the world. "Despite her tragedies, Sonia regained her peace of mind," says Benny. "All the children, grandchildren and great-grandchildren were always happy to come to see her. Our mother had great patience, which she probably received from her father. Her face was always bright and happy." Sonia also found consolation in memorializing her family's history. Yad Vashem, the Holocaust memorial museum and archive in Jerusalem, had launched a massive project to assemble the names and stories of victims of the Shoah, and Sonia filled in cards with what she knew about the deaths of her mother, sisters, brothers-in-law, cousins, nieces, and nephews and sent them in. Each year, she observed Holocaust Remembrance Day—the twenty-seventh day of Nisan in the Jewish calendar, the day the Warsaw ghetto uprising began—with families from Rakov and Volozhin.

On Holocaust Remembrance Day of 1992, Sonia sat down with Benny and Benny's oldest son, Rotem, to tell the story of her life—her girlhood in Rakov with Doba and Etl, the death of their sister Feigele during the Great War, her decision to make aliyah and the trip to Palestine in 1932, her romance and marriage with Chaim, their struggles together during the early years at Kfar Vitkin. Benny recorded the interview, edited it, and printed it up for the family. Sonia barely touched on her feelings; she said little about the agony she endured during the Shoah and nothing about Arik's death. But her voice comes through clearly: the voice of a woman who has lived courageously, suffered unbearably, and who has made peace with her tragedies. The confidence and conviction of the pioneer never left her. "She did not count her difficulties," says Benny. "She never looked for a comfortable life. Bringing children, grandchildren and great-grandchildren into life in the Land made her happy. She taught us to know, to forgive, not to be angry or carry a grudge." Sonia was truly one of the mothers of a nation.

Among the descendants of Shimon Dov, Sonia had lost more than anyone, yet she lived her final years in tranquility. Family brought her not only warmth but also peace. In the interview with Benny and Rotem, Sonia called her mother, Beyle, "a *tzadeke*—a very charitable God-fearing woman"—and in her own way, Sonia was a *tzadeke* too. She was religious, she honored the ways of her ancestors, she loved her parents and sisters deeply, and yet she was willing to break all her past ties for the cause she believed in.

Sonia and Chaim realized their dream. They brought the line of the scribe to Palestine and played a part in the violent metamorphosis of Palestine into Israel. After the Shoah, Sonia felt it was her obligation to have more children so that her family would have a stake in Israel's future.

Early in 1996, Sonia traveled to Jerusalem to visit the grave of Yitzhak Rabin, the Israeli statesman and Labor prime minister who had signed the Oslo Accords with PLO leader Yasser Arafat and was assassinated in November 1995. It was her last trip. Sonia fell and broke her hip at the family Passover seder in the first week of April 1996. The doctors refused to operate because of Sonia's weak heart. She spent her last weeks immobile but clear in mind and memory and surrounded by her entire family. Her three surviving children were with her the day before she died at the age of eighty-six. Sonia had outlived her son Arik by twenty-three years, her husband, Chaim, by thirty-one years, her sister, Doba, by fifty-three years, and her sister, Etl, by fifty-four years. Her gravestone in Kfar Vitkin's cemetery bears the names and dates of the mother and sisters who perished without graves or prayers to mark their passing.

EPILOGUE

The family that Sonia and Chaim started in Palestine when they married in 1933 continues to flourish in the Land. They currently have thirty-two living descendants, and the number keeps growing.

The American family has also been fruitful. The six children of Abraham and Sarah who lived to maturity—Itel, Ethel, Harry, Sam, Hyman, and Lillie—all married and had children of their own, and most of their children have children and grandchildren. At last count, there are 101 of us scattered around the country, mostly on the coasts. My limb of the family tree is a crowded one: my grandfather Sam had four children with his first wife and one child, a daughter named Leona, with his second wife, Gladys. Leona married Meyer Laskin in 1948 and gave birth to four sons, of which I am the third. So Shimon Dov is my great-great-grandfather, Itel my great-aunt, and Doba, Etl, and Sonia my first cousins twice removed.

I thought a lot about the family tree when I traveled to Israel in the spring of 2010 to meet with Sonia and Chaim's three children. I was fifty-six years old, married, the father of three grown daughters myself, a vigorously secular Jewish American writer embarked on a new book. I had never been to Israel before, but it seemed like the place to begin researching the family story. After all, it was my Israeli cousin Shimon (technically my second cousin once removed) who inspired the idea when he told me that the evil Lazar Kaganovich was not part of the family but that seventeen victims of the Shoah were. Shimon assured me that he and his sister, Leah, and brother Benny would do whatever they could to help. So I bought plane tickets for me and my oldest daughter, Emily.

We landed in Tel Aviv on a warm afternoon in May. Shimon collected us from our hotel in Netanya and drove us to his brother's house in nearby Avi Hayl. The greetings at the door were cordial but awkward. Benny's wife, Orna, suggested we sit outside on the patio in the shade behind the house. She served us mint tea (the mint leaves were from her garden), hummus, and carrot cake. For one jet-lagged instant I wondered what I had gotten myself into. Shimon and I had met once, many years earlier, at my grand-parents' apartment, but I would have walked right by him on the street. All I knew about Benny was that he was the baby of his family, born three years before me, and that he liked basketball ("Benny speaks NBA," a young American relative who had studied in Israel told me when I asked about Benny's English). I had never met Orna or heard her name. These three were perfect strangers. Yet here we were sipping tea and sharing intimate knowledge about the people and history we had in common.

I had worried, beforehand, that the Israelis would find me intrusive, insensitive, presumptuous. Needlessly, as it turned out. There was never any ice to break. As soon as we got to family, everything flowed naturally and rapidly between us. Benny, a tame bear with a child's flashing grin and stormy impatience, reminisced about Gladys and Sam playing cards with Sonia and Chaim. "It was very important to Sam and Gladys to see my parents and their children. Gladys liked to take a little drink of whiskey while she played." (My grandmother—*whiskey*?) We blew by the small talk and jumped right into the thorny genealogical questions and ambiguities and gaps in the record we'd both been puzzling over. Benny gave me a copy of the memoirs he had written about his parents' lives based on the inter-view he and Rotem had done with Sonia in 1992. He had had the memoirs meticulously translated into English before our arrival. Together we thumbed through a sheaf of family photos. By the end of the afternoon, I realized that I had found not only a cousin—I had found a friend and a collaborator.

"We have letters," Benny let drop right before we went back to the hotel, "many letters from the family in Rakov and Volozhin. The last was a postcard that Doba sent my mother right before the Nazis invaded in 1941. But there is a problem. All of the letters were written in Yiddish [Benny pronounced it "Iddish"] so none of us can read them." *This is a problem we will solve*, I was thinking. It took a year and a half, but eventually, between us, the Israelis and I had all 281 letters translated into both Hebrew and English.

In the week that followed, Shimon and Benny took Emily and me on a tour of all the places their parents had lived, the colonies and settlements where they had learned to farm, the house and the fields at Kfar Vitkin, the moshav cemetery where their brother and grandfather and parents are buried under stones bearing the hands of the Kohanim. We stood together over the trickle of salty water that had once sustained the tiny precipitous Kvutza Har Kinneret, where Chaim had come as a boy of eighteen. We drove up the coast as far north as we could and got out of the car at Rosh HaNikra just steps from the Lebanese border, so we could take in the same panorama that had dazzled Sonia when she made aliyah by taxi in 1932. We sat together at kitchen tables amid stacks of photos, bundles of letters none of us could read, notebooks, pages printed off the Web. It was at these kitchen tables in Israel that I felt the presence most intensely of those who came before—not only the impossibly beautiful pioneer couple, but also their anxious families back in Poland and my great-grandfather Avram Akiva sending checks from America, keeping tabs on his niece and nephew in Kfar Vitkin, reading with amazement letters written from a land he knew inch by inch from the Bible but would never see with his own eyes. I felt them bearing down on me, these generations of pious, bearded Kohanim scribes, as I stood by the Western Wall in Jerusalem with the slip of a prayer I folded and stashed in a crack already wadded with prayers. To pray by the Wall would have crowned their lives. *Why me and not them?*

They would have found the answer to such a question in God—I look to history, family history, family story. Stories arise because something happened—but to close the circle, someone needs to discover what happened and be willing and able to say it. Our parents and grandparents could not bear to tell the story of the branch that was destroyed. But Benny and I, independently and then in partnership, committed ourselves to bringing our shared story to light.

The following year I returned to Israel for a week, this time with my three brothers, my oldest brother's wife, and their firstborn son: a trip to honor our father, who had died at the end of 2010. Benny picked me up from the airport and together with Shimon we went to the archive and museum of the Ghetto Fighters' Kibbutz (Beit Lohamei Haghetaot) to research Klooga. I told Benny that I had plans to go to Belarus and Lithuania to see the places where our European relatives had lived and died. Halfway through the week, Benny decided to join me on what he called the "roots trip," and by the end of the week Shimon and his oldest son, Amir, and Benny's son Rotem had signed on too. I enlisted my daughter Emily, who speaks Russian. In the middle of May 2011, the six of us met at a small wooden inn deep in the lush green Belarusian countryside. Together we visited Rakov and Volozhin; we walked through the crumbling hall of the Volozhin yeshiva, which has survived two world wars and the death of its students and teachers; we scouted out the street near Rakov's brick Catholic church where Sonia, Doba, and Etl grew up. We traveled to Vilna—now Vilnius, the capital of Lithuania—and searched out the two apartment buildings where Doba and Shepseleh lived and raised their sons. We drove out to Ponar to say kaddish at the cratered pit where Shepseleh and tens of thousands of Lithuanian Jews lie buried. We walked to a hillside at the edge of Volozhin and said kaddish over the pit where Chaim's brother Yishayahu may have been shot. We said kaddish in the small grassy clearing where the Rakov synagogue burned with Etl and her children inside.

Over dinners, we talked about how this could have happened. How could Germany have changed so radically between the First and Second World Wars? Would the Shoah have happened without Hitler? "One man can change history," Shimon said many times. But why would God have created Hitler and allowed him to triumph so brutally? The more we knew of the horrors, the less we understood its perpetrators.

In Rakov, after much searching in the tangled grass of the cemetery of exile that had depressed Sonia, we found the grave of our common ancestor, Shimon Dov. Shimon and Benny had come prepared. They scrubbed the headstone with steel wool, placed candles and Israeli flags around it, and we said kaddish for the patriarch as well.

Our parents and grandparents never made this trip. It wasn't that they couldn't face what had happened. They were inventors, entrepreneurs, pioneers, explorers, survivors. Tough-minded realists. Courageous fighters. Extravagant givers. But the telling of the story fell to us.

The pulse of history beats in every family. All of our lives are engraved with epics of love and death. What my family gained and lost in the twentieth century, though extreme, was not unique. War has touched all of us. Fate and chance and character make and break every generation. The Shoah was not the only genocide. America is not the first land of opportunity nor will it be the last. Warring peoples have fought over the Holy Land for thousands of years, all of them claiming to have God on their side. In a family history written by Palestinian Arabs, Chaim and Sonia and their fellow Zionists would be oppressors; the Koran, not the Torah, would be the holy book; Jerusalem would be a besieged, stolen city. Open the book of your family and you will be amazed, as I was, at what you find.

My ancestors believed that the book that sustains the Jewish people is the Word of God, but it was they who copied God's words and kept the book alive. Long ago, I walked away from their book, their faith, and their traditions, but in middle age I have come back to their stories. I used to think these stories could never be mine because fundamentally we had little in common: they were strangers with my DNA, these short, dark, striving men and women with their burning eyes and fierce desires. I had left their path and chosen my own. I don't pray. I don't observe the cycle of the Jewish year. I rarely read the Bible. Thoughts of God, when I have them, arise not in synagogue but in wild solitary places. It often occurs to me that my life, my beliefs and irreverent spirituality, would make them snort and shrug. We're so different. I don't belong—*we* don't belong. But in middle age—*late* middle age, as my wife likes to remind me—I've changed my mind. The last of Shimon Dov's European descendants was shot and incinerated at Klooga nine years before I was born. I lived fifty-five years without knowing his name, without wondering about his story, without seeing how his story is bound to mine. "All the days ordained for me were written in your book before one of them came to be," the Bible tells us. My days and the days of my cousin Shimon and the days of my grandfather Sam and his siblings and cousins in Israel are written in that book. *My* book, *this* book, is the only way I know to search the radiant lines inscribed for us, to bring into consciousness some glimmer of our light.

In telling their story I have made it my own. Even my own brothers would have different versions. It would be foolish to believe that I, that we, that our generation alone can see and say the truth. I know there are events we refuse to acknowledge, tragedies we steer clear of, facts we deny at our peril, fictions we entertain to deceive ourselves. Our children will laugh—or weep—at the walls we have built and huddle behind. And yet, just as we cannot unblind ourselves, so we cannot will our curiosity or channel its consequences. We don't choose our stories any more than we fashion the moment in which to tell them.

I have told this story out of reverence for my family but also, to be honest, because I can. It is their story, but in writing it I have claimed it. For now, thanks to Benny, this story is in my hands. But it doesn't belong to me. It belongs to all of us.

ACKNOWLEDGMENTS

Where to begin?

With my mother, of course. My mother, Leona Cohen Laskin, is and always has been a great storyteller (*a great embellisher*, my father, Meyer, liked to add—to which my mother invariably countered that embellishment was what made a story good) and the stories that ground this book originated with her. So thanks, Mom, for telling, embellishing, editorializing, remembering, and yes, repeating those family stories—they all lodged somewhere in my brain, even if I sometimes rolled my eyes or nodded off when you told them. And thanks for connecting me to such a lively, colorful family—who knew your relatives would provide so much material?

Sonia's sons, Shimon and Benny Kaganovitz, were my guardian angels throughout: without their partnership, this would have been a very different, and much poorer, book. I really don't know how to thank them enough. Shimon got the whole thing started when he corrected the notion that Lazar Kaganovich was in our family—and he and Benny have been beyond supportive every step of the way. Shimon, Benny, and their sister Leah were the ideal hosts and guides on my two trips to Israel—they deftly organized a tour of all the places where their parents had lived; they arranged interviews with key people from Kfar Vitkin, Herzliya, and the Kinneret Colony; they helped me navigate the archives at Ghetto Fighters' House; they translated for me on many interviews; and they patiently answered hundreds of questions before, during, and after the trips. Benny, to whom this book is dedicated, kept the nearly three hundred family letters that his mother passed down—though he had never read them because they were all in Yiddish. At my urging Benny had them translated and shared the translations with me. We spent many an hour in Israel and on Skype puzzling over dates, details, and interpretations of these marvelous, heartbreaking letters. Benny and his oldest son, Rotem, interviewed Sonia in 1992, and Benny used this interview as the basis for two beautifully written memoirs of his parents' pioneer days, which he graciously had translated for me. Benny's wife, Orna, wrote me in a recent e-mail that "I try to help Benny when I can in his mission to help you with your book"—and I truly have felt that Benny and his whole extended family in Israel have made this book their mission. All of us were strangers two and a half years ago—and now, as Orna writes, "we are really family in our feelings." This has been a priceless gift. So a huge *toda* to Shimon and Riki, Benny and Orna, Leah and Avi. I would also like to thank Shimon's oldest son, Amir, and Benny's son Rotem for joining us on our roots trip to Lithuania and Belarus. Thanks also to Leah and Avi's daughter, Galit, for her hospitality and insights into her grandmother Sonia—and to all of the other relatives who treated us with such warmth and love during our stays in Israel.

My oldest daughter, Emily, has been a collaborator from the get-go. Since Emily knows Russian and has a deep grounding in Russian history, I roped her into research early on—in fact, before the beginning. Emily ascertained beyond a doubt that the evil Lazar was not part of our family; she helped me navigate through the various Russian revolutions of the twentieth century; she recommended relevant Russian history books as well as fiction (including Isaac Babel's brilliant "The Story of My Dovecote"); and, despite a broken leg, she put up with my warp-speed travel pace on the first trip to Israel. Emily also accompanied me and the Israeli relatives on our roots trip, and her Russian came in extremely handy in Belarus. My paternal heart burst with pride when Bella, our tireless Belarusian guide, pulled me aside to confide, "You know Emily is something very special—and her Russian is perfect." Emily denies it—but she did pick up some new salty expressions from Bella.

Family! How could I have written this book without them? I began my research in Palm Beach, Florida, by interviewing my cousin Susan Schechet and her father Sol Rubenstein—who, sadly, has since passed away. Sol was the oldest surviving first cousin of the generation that included Itel, Sam, Sonia, Doba, and Etl—and he worked for Maidenform for many years, so he was the logical place to start my search. Sol and Susan led me to Rose Rubenstein Einziger, Sol's sister—another of the first cousins of that generation—and I interviewed her and her daughter Laurie Bellet next in Walnut Creek, California. The other two survivors of that generation are Len and Seymour Cohn, the sons of Herman, the youngest son of Shimon Dov, and I had rewarding conversations with the two of them as well. A special extra thank you to Susan Schechet, who is a family historian in her own right and has answered scores of questions and supplied many dates over the years. It has been great to get to know her branch of the family, including her cousin Ruth Grant and her uncle Irving Guyer. Thanks to Ken Schechet for his hospitality in Palm Beach.

I tried to talk to all the descendants of Avram Akiva and Gishe Sore who might know something about the old days, and I'm pretty sure I succeeded. A special thank you to Barbara and Mort Weisenfeld for help, hospitality, kindness, warmth, and their closeness to my mom all these years. Gail Cohen was among the joyous discoveries of this book—a wonderful relative I never knew I had. Many thanks to Gail and her husband, Richard Cohen, for their hospitality and exuberance. And more thanks to Gail for arranging what proved to be a crucial interview with her mother, Inda Epstein Goldfarb, and her late father, Irving Goldfarb. Sallie Cohen was on board all the way and supplied stories, photos, confirmation of family stories/myths, and crucial bits of information including Itel's shoe size. Sallie's husband Michael welcomed us warmly on our visits to Portland, Oregon. Many thanks to Marvin Sleisenger, husband of the late Lenore Cohen Sleisenger, for crucial insights, anecdotes, family photos, and hospitality at his lovely home in Marin County, California. My cousin Gary Cohen has been a terrific help—it was great to reconnect with him and get to know his wife, Lori, and their three kids. Gary presided over my illuminating interview with his father, Marvin Cohen, from whom I gleaned much useful information and many insights. Thanks also to my cousin Jeff Cohen.

Dick Salwitz has been terrific in sending me interviews that his wife, Kathryn, conducted with Maidenform employees and in answering questions about Itel and William. Many thanks also for the family photos.

Other family members who helped include Jay Epstein, the late Adrian Epstein, Rochelle Rogart, Chuck Cohen and his son Laurence, and Bert Cohen.

In the course of researching the book, I connected (through the wonders of the Internet and Twitter) with the "lost" branch of the family—the descendants of Avram Akiva's brother Jasef Bear. Many thanks to Devorah Bayer, Jasef Bear's great-granddaughter, for her enthusiasm for this project and for tons of family lore, genealogy, and affection.

I'd also like to thank the extended Rakov family—Adi Grynholc, Ruth Wilnai, Dan Horowitz, Judy Horowitz Katz, Art Levine, and Linda Kaminsky. A special thank you to Tsipora Alperovich, a heroic and brilliant woman who survived the Shoah and granted me two illuminating and unforgettable interviews in Tel Aviv.

Closer to home, I'd like to thank my brothers, Bob, Dan, and Jon, and Bob's wife, Sue, and oldest son, Isaac, for moral support, listening to long convoluted reconstructions of the family tree, and above all for accompanying me to Israel. In the course of this trip, we honored the memory of our father, Meyer Laskin, who died in November 2010—and we talked and thought a great deal about our family and the meaning of family. Bob and Sue's son Gabe did a crucial interview for me in Israel and answered my questions about the balance sheets and the finances of A. Cohen & Sons during the Depression—so a big thank you to Gabe as well.

I have great friends—and patient friends—who have listened to me blather on about "the family book" for all these many years. Ivan Doig has furnished moral and professional support and invaluable advice and enthusiasm at all stages. I have followed every suggestion Ivan made—and I know I have written a better book for it. Thanks to Ivan and his wife, Carol, for innumerable dinners during the course of composition. My dear friend Jack Levison has cheered, advised, commiserated, bolstered, listened (endlessly), and generally had my back in more ways than I can count; our long rambling talks about writing, religion, Bible, spirituality, fate, character, and the manifold magic of alliteration are a continuing source of joy and knowledge and fresh air. Jack's wife, Priscilla Pope-Levison, has shared insights into how to bring historic figures to life on the page. Thanks to my oldest friends, Jim and Mary Moran, for just being there—always. Many thanks to my writer chums Lyanda Lynn Haupt and David Williams for literary comradeship and for sharing many tricks of the trade. Erik Larson has pointed me toward sources of information on the early Nazi years and shared his wisdom on narrative nonfiction, research, and the publishing process over many an enjoyable lunch. It is a privilege to belong to "the mystic company of the Unspeakables—long may we lunch, dish, and bolster each other.

Thank you Danielle Mattoon of the *New York Times* for giving me the opportunity of turning my "roots trip" to Israel into an article for the Travel Section.

Many thanks to Dr. Bennett Kaplan for insights at every critical juncture.

I'd like to thank the superb guides who organized our roots trip to Belarus and Lithuania: in Belarus, Bella went above and beyond the call of duty in tracking down family sites and locating people to interview, and Yuri Dorn was helpful as well. In Vilnius, the charming and professional Yulik Gurvitch did an excellent job of merging history with our particular family interests. Thanks also to Galina Baranova for research in the Vilnius archives. In Rakov, I'd like to thank Lutsina, the students of the Ninth Form of the Rakov Pubic School, the director of the Art Gallery Museum, and the man who led us to the site of a Nazi massacre and recounted his boyhood memories. I'm sorry I did not record his name.

Thanks to Mulik Moher at the Kinneret Colony in Israel.

This is the second book for which Jonathan Sarna of Brandeis University has been my "go-to" person for all things Jewish; I'd like to thank him for his generosity, promptness, and superb scholarship.

John LaMont at the Seattle Public Library helped me kick-start my genealogical research. Jewish Gen helped in more ways than I can count: this is a fantastic resource for anyone doing family research, Shoah research, or any type of Jewish genealogical research. Stanley Diamond and Jackie Williams also helped me jump into genealogical research. Eilat Gordin Levitan maintains a wonderful Web site devoted to the shtetlach of our region of Belarus, including Rakov and Volozhin, and she is a wizard with genealogical research who has helped me in many ways over the years. The staff of the Bayonne (New Jersey) Public Library helped with research into Maidenform. At the Smithsonian I'd like to thank the staff of the Archives Center at the National Museum of American History for helping me access the Maidenform Collection and Nancy Ellen Davis for letting me handle and photograph historic bras and the pigeon vest in the museum's Textile Division.

Aza Hadas did a masterful job of translating the family letters from Hebrew to English and helped me puzzle through various nuances and thorny questions.

I'd like to thank Ben Anolik, Tola Grynholc Urbach, and Adele Grynholc Jochelson for critically important interviews on the Vilna ghetto and the Klooga concentration camp.

For assistance with the history of the Great War and the First Division's role in it, I want to single out Tom Gudmestad: he is a walking encyclopedia of World War I and more than generous in sharing books, knowledge, and insight. Thanks also to Jim Nelson for sharing his in-depth knowledge of the First Division in the Great War and Phyllis Goodnow for doing research at the National Archives. Mary J. Manning, reference librarian at the Colonel Robert R. McCormick Research Center, First Division Museum at Cantigny (Illinois), did research and provided documents on the military careers of Private Hyman Cohen, Captain Joseph Quesenberry, and Captain Len Cohn.

Thank you Salah Mansour of Palestine Remembered for alerting me to the controversial history of the land sale involving Kfar Vitkin.

My neighbor and friend Ewa Sledziewski helped me with all things Polish, including translation—thanks!

A special thanks to the staff in charge of interlibrary loans at the King County Library System here in Western Washington. We are blessed with fantastic libraries—I could not have written this book without the King County libraries, Seattle Public Library, and the huge collection at the University of Washington libraries, especially the Suzzallo and Allen libraries.

Jerry Pruden shared stories and information about Maidenform. David Mann at the Hebrew Institute of Riverdale answered questions about

Avram Akiva's involvement in the founding and the early days of the synagogue that used to be known as the Hebrew Institute of University Heights.

Mary Whisner, the goddess of research, helped with a key bit of research into the land sale that included Kfar Vitkin. I've lost track of how many books of mine Mary has helped me with now—three? four? I appreciate it all.

Jen Taylor Friedman, a working *soferet* (female Torah scribe), welcomed us into her New York home and answered many questions about the art, craft, and traditions of the Torah scribe.

I relied on a number of museums and archives for research into the Shoah; in particular I'd like to thank Paul Shapiro, Nancy Hartman, William Connelly, and the staff of the library at the U.S. Holocaust Memorial Museum in Washington, DC; David Silberklang, Estee Yaari, Zvi Bernhardt, Leah Teichthal, and Rita Margolin at Yad Vashem in Jerusalem; the people who work at the archives of Beit Rishonim (Founders' House) in Herzliya; and the staff of the archives at the Ghetto Fighters' House in Israel. I'd also like to thank the staff of the YIVO Institute for Jewish Research at the Center for Jewish History in New York, in particular Leo Greenbaum for his expert research assistance, Ella Levine for tips on traveling to Eastern Europe, and YIVO's executive director Jonathan Brent. Also helpful in providing tips and answering questions about heritage travel to Eastern Europe were Howard Margol, Stephanie Bernstein, Ruth Ellen Gruber, and Jonathan Young.

Jill Kneerim is the dream agent and I can't imagine—don't want to imagine—my life without her. Jill totally "got" this project from the first whisper, masterfully stage-managed the proposal and contract process, and connected me with the perfect editor—Penguin's Kathryn Court, who has been a dream to work with as well. Ben George, with his keen eye for both minute details and big-picture structural elements (not to mention extraneous em dashes), did an exemplary job of line-editing the book. Jill, Kathryn, and Ben are my ideal team and I can't begin to express my gratitude for and admiration of their brilliance and professionalism. I'd also like to thank Jill's former assistant Caroline Zimmerman, Kathryn's former assistant Tara Singh, and her current assistant Scott Cohen (a distant relative, perhaps). And thanks to my cover designer, Jason Ramirez, and my copy editor, Nina Hnatov.

Finally, the home team: my wife, Kate O'Neill, and our three daughters, Emily, Sarah, and Alice. By the time I was done writing this book, Kate knew as much about the Kaganovich family as I did—her unflagging interest and curiosity helped keep my nose to the grindstone. Kate always believed in this project—and believed that I could pull it off, even when I had my doubts. She helped me puzzle out all sorts of emotional, moral, and legal quandaries, let me unload and vent and imagine to my heart's content, pushed me (lovingly) to go deeper and try harder, held the fort during my many trips, read the manuscript before anyone else, and made me feel loved and happy during the years I spent researching, writing, and agonizing. As for our three daughters—wonderful brilliant young women in their own right—to quote Doba, "What can I say, my children, may they be healthy, are the greatest joy of my life."

GLOSSARY

Aliyah: "ascent" to the Holy Land; to make aliyah means to move to the Land, or more loosely "to visit"

Bris: the rite of circumcision performed shortly after birth on Jewish male babies; usually the occasion for a family celebration

Bochur (plural bochurim): a yeshiva (q.v.) student

Cheder: Jewish elementary school

Cohen: the English form of Kohain (q.v.)

Dacha: a country vacation cottage

Diaspora: the dispersal of the Jewish people after their exile from the Holy Land

Frum: Yiddish for observant, religious

Gymnasium: a European secondary school that roughly straddles American high school and the early years of college

Halutz (plural halutzim): a male Zionist agricultural pioneer

Halutzah (plural halutzot): a female Zionist pioneer

HeHalutz: an international organization of Zionist agricultural pioneers

Kibbutz: a Jewish agricultural collective in Palestine (and Israel after statehood)

Kinneret: Hebrew form of the place name Galilee, a region in northeastern Israel surrounding the Sea of Galilee

Kohain (plural Kohanim): a member of the Jewish priestly caste, descended from Aaron, the brother of Moses. Used in various forms as a last name: Cohen, HaKohen, Kaganovitch, Kagan, etc.

Ma'apilim: Clandestine Jewish immigrants to Palestine

Mezuzah (plural mezuzot): a tiny Torah scroll in a protective case hung on the door-post of Jewish homes

Moshav: a Jewish cooperative agricultural village in Palestine (Israel after statehood)

Pogrom: an outburst of anti-Semitic violence

Shiva: the period of mourning

Shoah: "catastrophe," another term for the Holocaust

Shtetl (plural shtetlach): Hebrew for little town

Talmud: a compendium of sacred Jewish texts that includes the recorded oral law based on the Torah (q.v.) and extensive commentaries; Talmud is the primary subject of study in yeshivot (q.v.)

Tefillin: small leather boxes containing prayers that observant Jewish men wear during prescribed morning prayers

Torah: the first five books of the Bible

Tzaddik (female, tzadeke): a righteous, upstanding person

Yeshiva (plural yeshivot): a school for Jewish learning, devoted primarily to Torah (q.v.) and Talmud (q.v.)

NOTES

Family stories are the primary source for this book. I started with the stories that I grew up hearing from my mother, Leona Cohen Laskin, and her parents, Sam and Gladys Cohen, and went on from there in wider and wider circles. Once I committed to writing this book, I set about trying to gather as many stories as I could from the entire extended family, including lots of relatives I never knew I had. I can't claim to have interviewed all one hundred–odd living descendants of my great-grandfather or the thirty-two descendants of Shalom Tvi—but I did speak with everyone who knew anything about the "old days."

Among any family's stories there are bound to be a fair number of what Huck Finn called "stretchers"—and my challenge throughout has been to try to separate truth from things that got, well, stretched a bit. Sometimes this has been relatively easy: my great-uncle Hyman Cohen writes on the second page of his self-published memoir, *As I Recall* (1967), that Avram Akiva's grandfather was Chaim the Volozhiner, the founder and head of the Volozhin yeshiva. Two minutes of research online revealed that this was a stretcher. But many other bits of information and conflicting accounts, both large and small, have been more difficult to resolve. For the sake of the narrative, I have written in the body of the text what I believe is the most likely version—and I use the notes that follow to present alternate versions and explain the basis of my choice.

As I indicated in the Epilogue, my Israeli cousins provided two essential sources of material without which I could not have written this book: the memoirs of Chaim and Sonia's early years that Benny wrote based on his 1992 interview with his mother; and the nearly three hundred letters written primarily by Doba, Etl, Beyle, Shepseleh, and Shalom Tvi between 1932 and 1946. In most cases the letters were incompletely dated: the correspondents usually omitted the year and sometimes the month, heading the letter simply "14 June" or "Rosh Hashanah Eve." Benny has performed the invaluable service of dating all the letters based on internal evidence or by correlating events described in the letters to the history of the time. In a very few cases I have contested the dates Benny assigned. I have not footnoted the letters or the family memoirs.

This is a work of history but I have taken some liberties. In order to make the narrative more vivid, I often put myself inside the minds of family members at crucial points in their lives. Examples of this include Gishe Sore's arrival at her Lower East Side tenement; Shimon Dov's experience of the first winter of the Great War; Chaim's adventures in the Kinneret during his first months in Palestine. Though I imagine these and other experiences, I do not invent. I based Gisha Sore's reaction to the cold-water flat on Madison Street on the account that Hyman recorded in his memoir; Chaim's experiences are built on what his son Benny wrote and told me, and so on. I have bolstered and deepened these scenes by researching the accounts left by others—and in the notes that follow I indicate which memoirs, letters, articles, and works of fiction have been most useful. None of the dialogue quoted in the book has been invented: all dialogue in quotation marks comes from accounts either written or recounted by family members. I use italics for dialogue or thoughts for which I have no source: I don't put words in my characters' mouths, but I do give them italicized reactions or expressions that strike me as likely or logical.

In the notes that follow, I indicate the major secondary sources that I have relied on in each chapter. I footnote only long quotations, controversial issues, and incidents or historic events for which I have found conflicting accounts or claims. These are not intended to be strict academic footnotes—but readers who need to know where I came by a crucial fact or assertion or who want to delve deeper into a particular issue will have the citations they need to do so.

INTRODUCTION

2 **"the Wolf of the Kremlin":** In 1987, American journalist Stuart Kahan published a book called *The Wolf of the Kremlin: The First Biography of L. M. Kaganovich, the Soviet Union's Architect of Fear* (New York: Morrow, 1989). Kahan, claiming to be a relative of Lazar Kaganovich, wrote a highly colored account of "the Wolf's" relationship with Stalin and his role in the Ukraine famine as well as pogroms. Kahan's claim that he was a nephew of Lazar, as well as many other assertions in the book, were debunked by Kaganovich's family in the Soviet Union.

2 **"beguiled . . . rifling around in the past":** Alice Munro, *The View from Castle Rock* (New York: Knopf, 2006), p. 347.

6 **"We (I speak of Jews now and not merely of writers)":** Letter from Saul Bellow to Cynthia Ozick, July 19, 1987, in *The New Yorker*, April 26, 2010, pp. 59–60.

CHAPTER ONE: VOLOZHIN

My description of Volozhin and the Volozhin yeshiva is based on the following sources: *Wolozyn: Sefer shel ha-ir-shel yeshivat "Ets Hayim"; Wolozin: The Book of the City and of the Etz Hayyim Yeshiva*, edited by Eliezer Leoni and written by former residents of Volozhin living in Israel and the United States (Tel Aviv: 1970). This is the so-called Yizkor book of Volozhin: after the Shoah, survivors of many shtetlach and towns assembled "memory books" describing the life and institutions of their communities before the war, recounting their destruction under the Nazis, and listing the names of the dead. Many of these books are available online through Jewish Gen, *the* first stop for anyone doing Jewish family research. Some of the Volozhin Yizkor book is available online at http://www.jewishgen.org/yizkor/volozhin/volozhin.html. Henceforth I will cite this source as Volozhin Yizkor book.

I relied on these books for background on shtetl life in the nineteenth century: *There Once Was a World*, by Yaffa Eliach (Boston: Back Bay Books, 1998); *These We Remember: Yizkor Book of Ivenets, Kamin, and Surroundings*, translated by Florette Lynn (Emerson, NJ: Shoah Literature Press, 2008); *The Jews in Poland and Russia*, vol. 1 and 2, by Antony Polonsky (Portland, OR: Littman Library of Jewish Civilization, 2010–2012); *From a Ruined Garden: The Memorial Books of Polish Jewry*, edited by Jack Kugelmass and J. Boyarin (New York: Schocken Books, 1983); *The World of Sholom Aleichem*, by Maurice Samuel (New York: Knopf, 1943); *Twenty-one Stories*, by S. Y. Agnon (New York: Schocken Books, 1970); *Shtetl*, by Eva Hoffman (Boston: Houghton Mifflin, 1997); and *Life Is with People: The Culture of the Shtetl*, by Mark Zborowski and Elizabeth Herzog (New York: International Universities Press, 1952).

For the history of the Volozhin yeshiva and its place in the revival of yeshivot in Lithuania I used the following: *Reb Chaim of Volozhin*, by Rabbi Dov Eliach (Brooklyn, NY: Mesorah Publications, 1993); *Torah Lishmah: Torah for Torah's Sake*, by Norman Lamm (Hoboken, NJ: Ktav, 1989); and *My Uncle the Netziv*, by Rabbi Baruch HaLevi Epstein (Brooklyn, NY: Mesorah Publications, 1988).

For background on the work of the Torah scribe: *Scribes and Schools: The Canonization of the Hebrew Scriptures*, by Philip R. Davies (Louisville, KY: Westminster John Knox Press, 1998); *A Torah Is Written*, by Paul and Rachel Cowan (Philadelphia: Jewish Publication Society, 1986); and *Sofer: The Story of a Torah Scroll*, by Eric Ray (Los Angeles: Torah Aura Productions, 1986). I gleaned additional information from an interview with working Torah scribe Jen Taylor Friedman at her home in New York City, on August 4, 2011.

9 **since science and scripture eerily concur:** Sharon Begley, "The DNA of Abraham's Children," *Newsweek*, June 3, 2010, online version, p. 3, www.thedailybeast.com/newsweek/2010/06/03/the-dna-of-abraham-s-children.html.

10 **"All day he sat . . .":** "The Tale of the Scribe" in Agnon, *Twenty-one Stories*, pp. 9, 18.

10 **"You must never, ever touch anything":** This quote and other details of Shimon Dov in Volozhin come from the unpublished manuscript "History of Louis Rubenstein, Recorded by Rose Einziger," shared by their family. Louis Rubenstein and Rose Einziger are two of the children of Shimon Dov's only daughter, Leah Golda.

10 **Precisely 304,805 letters:** www.torahscience.org/newsletter7.html; other sources put the number of words in the Torah at 79,976.

13 **In 1803, a yeshiva:** Gershon David Hundert, ed., *The YIVO Encyclopedia of Jews in Eastern Europe* (New Haven, CT: Yale University Press, 2008), entry on Volozhin yeshiva, by Shaul Stampfer, pp. 1984–1985. Other sources date the founding of the yeshiva to 1801 or 1802.

13 **the most renowned and revered:** Lamm, *Torah Lishmah*, p. 26.

13 **to live beside the Volozhin yeshiva during its golden age:** To understand Shimon Dov and the religious atmosphere of Volozhin, it helps to have some background on the conflict between Hasidim and *mitnagdim*—opponents of Hasidism—that emerged in the late eighteenth century and shaped the religious atmosphere and pedagogy of the Volozhin yeshiva.

Around the same time that the Gaon of Vilna became prominent, another great spirit arose to beckon the Jews down a different path. Israel ben Eliezer—the charismatic seer known as the Ba'al Shem Tov (Master of the Good Name), who is credited with the founding of Hasidism—is a figure cloaked in reverent mystery. Popular tradition has it that the Besht (an acronym for Ba'al Shem Tov) was a poor, orphaned, barely educated youth who received the call from God to bring ecstatic worship to the Jewish masses— but the rags-to-radiance story may have been fabricated or embellished later to lend a populist aura to the emergence of Hasidism. What is clear is that the Besht opened the way for a more joyous, more immediate, more inclusive, more intimately mystical form of Judaism that inspired the soul of Eastern Europe from the end of the eighteenth century to the beginning of the twentieth. Followers of the Besht believed that the way to approach God was not to shut yourself in a darkened room with your feet in ice water but to sing and dance and shout and pray with such heart-lifting fervor that the very words on the page dissolved into shimmering spirit. God is present everywhere in His creation, the Besht told his followers—pray and study joyously, live a life full of honesty and love, make worship a "joyous service of the heart," and you will find Him. Jews who felt excluded by the pedantry and snobbishness of the Pale's scholarly aristocracy embraced the Besht as a tzaddik—a seer who had the power to deliver man's messages directly to God. When the Besht prayed, "everyone saw that the water was rippling," wrote one of his followers. "The Shekinah [the divine presence of God] hovered over him and as a result the earth trembled." (Dov Ber ben Samuel, *Shivhei Ha-Besht*, trans. and ed. by Dan Ben-Amos and Jerome Mintz, Bloomington, IN: 1970, pp. 50–51; quoted in Moshe Rosman, *Founder of Hasidism: A Quest for the Historical Ba'al Shem Tov*, Berkeley: University of California Press, 1996, p. 37). The Besht traveled through the Pale performing miracle healings and purging the possessed of evil spirits; he foretold the future through his dreams; he dazzled the downtrodden with his radiant sweetness. Hasidism—Hebrew for "piety" or "loving kindness"—burst forth from the teaching and examples of this holy man and quickly gained popularity among poor, humble, yearning Ashkenazi Jews. By the 1750s, the Hasidic fire was spreading into Poland and from Poland throughout the Russian Pale.

But the flames flickered and died when they reached the icy footbath of the Gaon. "When a man studies or prays," the Hasidim rhapsodized, "the word should be uttered with full strength, like the ejaculation of a drop of semen from his whole body" (quoted in Paul Johnson, *A History of the Jews*, New York: Harper & Row, 1987, p. 297). To the Gaon and his followers, such passion was an abomination. Abominators of Hasidism began calling themselves *mitnagdim*—opponents, no need to specify what or whom they opposed—and the Gaon of Vilna stepped, or was dragged, forward as their leader. To the *mitnagdim*, Hasidic ecstasy was an insult to the Almighty, Hasidic visions were delusions, Hasidic reverence for tzaddiks a form of idolatry. In 1781, the Vilna Gaon issued a *cherem* (ban) condemning the Hasidim (Eliach, *Reb Chaim of Volozhin*, p. 158). He ordered their books to be burned in public, he forbade pious Jews from intermarrying or doing business with them, he made formal pronouncements excommunicating them from Jewish communities. "It is the duty of every believing Jew to repudiate and pursue them with all manner of afflictions and subdue them," the Gaon declared, "because they have sin in their hearts and are a sore on the body of Israel" (quoted in Johnson, *A History of the Jews*, p. 298).

According to many accounts, the Volozhin yeshiva, founded by the prime disciple of the Vilna Gaon, was a bastion of *mitnagdim* sentiment, though in recent years scholars have noted that Chaim the Volozhiner tolerated and may even have welcomed Hasidic students in his yeshiva. So, like a lot of scholarly and religious disputes, it's complicated.

14 **"It was the Torah center of the great Russian Jewry":** Volozhin Yizkor book, p. 7.

14 **mixed their essence with gum arabic:** My description of the scribal process is based on the books cited above as well as my interview with Jen Taylor Friedman, a working Torah scribe, in her apartment in New York City on August 4, 2011.

15 **Avram Akiva duly enrolled in the yeshiva:** There is a faint shadow of doubt in my mind as to whether Shimon Dov and Avram Akiva actually attended the yeshiva. My great-uncle Hyman Cohen in his memoir *As I Recall* claims that his father Avram Akiva studied there—but he also said that Chaim the Volozhiner was Shimon Dov's father, which was most definitely not the case. Shimon Dov's and Avram Akiva's names do not appear on the lists of yeshiva students from the nineteenth century that have come down—but these lists are fragmentary and incomplete. There is, however, strong circumstantial evidence and a bit of documentary evidence to support the idea that Avram Akiva and at least some of his brothers were enrolled in the yeshiva. While he was in the United States, Avram Akiva's brother

Shalom Tvi indicated on a U.S. immigration form that he had attended the Volozhin yeshiva: if a younger brother went, it's very likely that the oldest brother went as well. There is also the fact that Avram Akiva became a renowned Talmudic scholar in later life and that the synagogue he helped found, the Hebrew Institute of University Heights, named its religious school after him. It seems likely that so distinguished a scholar would have received his training at the most revered yeshiva in Europe, especially because that yeshiva was located in his hometown.

15 **Under the Netziv:** Lamm, *Torah Lishmah*, p. 28.

16 **Without the work of the scribe . . . the linguistic historian:** Johnson, *A History of the Jews*, pp. 82, 90.

18 **"Hashem, His will, and His word . . .":** Quoted in Eliach, *Reb Chaim of Volozhin*, p. 170.

CHAPTER TWO: THE MOVE TO RAKOV

19 **"I have no desire for any understanding . . .":** Quoted in Eliach, *Reb Chaim of Volozhin*, p. 75.

19 **marched to the house of the Netziv . . .:** Details on celebrations in Volozhin from Eliach, *Reb Chaim of Volozhin*, p. 103.

20 **"Jewish kingdom of strength":** Volozhin Yizkor book, p. 114.

20 **one third will die:** Howard M. Sachar, *A History of Israel: From the Rise of Zionism to Our Time* (New York: Knopf, 2007), p. 12.

21 **the family went by the name Kagan:** According to records in the Minsk National Historical archive in Belarus, Sarah's father's name was Zelick-Movsha Kagan. However, on Sarah's Certificate of Death provided by the Bureau of Records, Department of Health, New York City, her father's name is given as Selig Moses Shapiro.

21 **choice of four synagogues:** I have based my supposition that Rakov had four synagogues on evidence provided in *Rakov Community Memorial Book* by former residents of Rakow in Israel and the United States, edited by Haim Abramson, translated by Ruth Wilnai (Tel Aviv, Israel: 1959)—hereafter the Rakov Yizkor book. I am guessing that the Old Shul was the Great Shul, though I have not been able to confirm this.

22 **A barrel of herring and a barrel of kerosene:** Details on a typical shtetl shop from Lynn, *These We Remember*, p. 6.

23 **The students had organized:** Eliach, *There Once Was a World*, p. 183.

23 **in the holy city of Tzvat:** The Volozhin Yizkor book says the community was in Jerusalem.

23 **Even the Netziv:** Rabbi Dr. Jacob J. Schacter "Haskalah, Secular Studies and the Closing of the Yeshiva in Volozhin in 1892" in *Torah U-Madda Journal*, January 1, 1990, p. 104.

24 **"Don't manage me":** *New York Post*, September 6, 1964, clipping on file with the

Maidenform Collection, 1922–1997, the Archives Center, National Museum of American History, Washington, DC. Hereafter, Maidenform Collection.

24 **Gishe Sore was a famously bad cook:** The story of Gishe Sore's lousy cooking comes from my mother, Leona Cohen Laskin, who lived in the flat below Gishe Sore as a child. The story of Itel taking charge of the younger children and forcing them to eat their mother's bread comes from an unpublished biographical essay on Itel called "Ida Rosenthal: A Remembrance," undated and unattributed, but apparently written in 1977 by Hy Lieberman. Hereafter, Itel's Story.

26 **Kaganovich and Rubilnik:** My cousins in Israel speculate that Rubilnik may have been Beyle's mother's maiden name.

CHAPTER THREE: THE MAKING OF A REVOLUTIONARY

28 **Itel took it for granted:** From Itel's Story.

30 **the number of Jewish students capped:** In *Beyond the Pale: The Jewish Encounter with Late Imperial Russia* (Berkeley: University of California Press, 2002), Benjamin Nathans says that when quotas were first instituted, "Jewish female students were not regarded as warranting such drastic action," though quotas for them started in the 1890s; pp. 266–267.

30 **published in underground Jewish newspapers:** See *The Jewish Bund in Russia from Its Origins to 1905*, by Henry J. Tobias (Stanford, CA: Stanford University Press, 1972), p. 251, for a discussion of the Jewish press at the turn of the last century.

31 **Nails were driven into the heads:** Nora Levin, *While Messiah Tarried: Jewish Socialist Movements, 1871–1917* (New York: Schocken Books, 1977), p. 305.

31 **"The riot was now at its height":** www.shsu.edu/~his_ncp/Kishinev.html. Korolenko describes the Kishinev pogrom of 1903, from "Kishineff: The Medieval Outbreak Against the Jews" in *The Great Events by Famous Historians*, vol. 20 (n.p.: National Alumni, 1914), pp. 35–49.

31 **the citizens of Kishinev killed forty-nine Jews:** Statistics, facts, and background on the pogrom come from http://kehilalinks.jewishgen.org/kishinev/kishinev-pogrom.html.

31 **It was "the last pogrom . . .":** www.forward.com/articles/8544/. "Kishinev 1903: The Birth of a Century," by J. J. Goldberg, *Jewish Daily Forward*, April 4, 2003. This article also provides text for some of Bialik's poem, "In the City of Slaughter."

33 **She was twelve years old:** I have made an educated guess of Itel's age here. The Bund was founded in 1897; so assuming the push for membership happened in 1898, Itel would have been twelve.

33 **One Friday evening:** The account of the young Bundist with the mole is from the Rakov Yizkor book.

35 **"organize armed resistance":** Tobias, *The Jewish Bund in Russia*, p. 226.

38 **Bundists were being arrested:** Ibid., p. 229.

38 **"the halo of heroism":** "Memories of the Zionist movement and the Bund," in the Rakov Yizkor book.

38 **Students took to the streets:** Abraham Ascher, *The Revolution of 1905: A Short History* (Stanford, CA: Stanford University Press, 2004), pp. 19–20.

38 **the Rakov Bundists held secret meetings:** Rakov Yizkor book and Itel's Story (which has details about weapons and target practice in the forest).

39 **Jews taken up arms:** Tobias, *The Jewish Bund in Russia*, p. 343.

39 **Wolf was drafted:** From Itel's Story.

39 **to agitate from within:** Levin, *While Messiah Tarried*, p. 306.

40 **happened to be Itel's nineteenth birthday:** Correlating Itel's birth with Bloody Sunday raises a rather sticky chronological question. Before the Communist Revolution of 1917, Russia did not use the Gregorian (also known as new style—NS) calendar that had long been standard in the West and in the United States but rather the slightly different Julian, or old style (OS), calendar. Itel always gave her birthday as January 9, 1886—but it's unclear whether this was OS or NS. Bloody Sunday fell on January 9, 1905, OS—but the NS date was January 22. So if Itel was born on January 9, NS, then her birthday was not on Bloody Sunday after all. Specialists in Russian-Jewish genealogy consulted on this matter have pointed out that birth dates were notoriously imprecise for our immigrant ancestors. Many Russian Jews used the Hebrew calendar to mark their children's birthdays—and then rough correlations were made to the Julian and/or Gregorian calendar. Some simply invented or changed their birthdays. There was no official agency in the United States that translated OS birth dates to NS birth dates. Given Itel's character and politics, it's possible that she recorded her birthday as January 9 precisely *because* it coincided with Bloody Sunday—but the exact date is impossible to ascertain.

40 **the official government count:** David Floyd, *Russia in Revolt* (London: Macdonald & Co, 1969), p. 64.

41 **"Attack the stores . . .":** Quoted in Tobias, *The Jewish Bund in Russia*, p. 295.

42 **"It could achieve everything":** Quoted in Tobias, *The Jewish Bund in Russia*, p. 309.

43 **In the first years of their marriage:** I have guessed at the year of Shula's birth. In the memoir that Sonia's son Benny wrote, Sonia states: "Shula, the oldest, died of an illness when she was 4 or 5 years old." She had to have been born before 1902, since Doba was born in 1903.

CHAPTER FOUR: THE BOYS

45 **"The root of all evil . . .":** Quoted in Tobias, *The Jewish Bund in Russia*, p. 312.

45 **"A young muzhik was smashing . . .":** Isaac Babel, "The Story of My Dovecote" in *The Complete Works of Isaac Babel* (New York: Norton, 2002), p. 610. Khariton Efrussi is surely a reference to the Ephrussi family that Edmund de Waal belongs to

and wrote about in his recent family history, *The Hare with Amber Eyes*. Though there is no Khariton on de Waal's family tree, the Ephrussi family did make their fortune in Odessa and had a prominent house there.

45 **"torrent of Jewish blood":** Quoted in Levin, *While Messiah Tarried*, p. 328.

46 **"brazen, insolent way":** Quoted in Floyd, *Russia in Revolt*, p. 93.

47 **"Repairing watches or clocks is fascinating . . .":** Hyman Cohen, *As I Recall* (self-published, 1967), p. 5.

CHAPTER FIVE: LOWER EAST SIDE

54 **East River, smelling of fish:** *All-of-a-Kind Family*, by Sydney Taylor, quoted in *Tenement*, by Raymond Bial (Boston: Houghton Mifflin, 2002), n.p.

54 **Half a million Jews:** Johnson, *A History of the Jews*, p. 372.

55 **350 square feet between them:** Lawrence J. Epstein, *At the Edge of a Dream: The Story of Jewish Immigrants on New York's Lower East Side, 1880–1920* (San Francisco: Jossey-Bass, 2007), p. 46.

58 **Even on Kol Nidre night:** Albert Waldinger, ed., *Shining and Shadow: An Anthology of Early Yiddish Stories from the Lower East Side* (Selinsgrove, PA: Susquehanna University Press, 2006), pp. 67–68.

59 **On a special occasion:** Epstein, *At the Edge of a Dream*, p. 177.

59 **barely 12 percent of Jews:** Tony Michels, *A Fire in Their Hearts: Yiddish Socialists in New York* (Cambridge, MA: Harvard University Press, 2005), p. 13.

59 **"Success, American style . . .":** Harry Roskolenko, *The Time That Was Then: The Lower East Side, 1900–1914, An Intimate Chronicle* (New York, Dial Press, 1971), p. 33.

60 **Zionism remained strong:** Rakov Yizkor book, pp. 14–15.

61 **it should have been Samuel:** There is some confusion over my grandfather's name in Yiddish. In a letter to Sonia, Shalom Tvi refers to him as Shalom—and in fact the names Shalom and Solomon are closely related. My mother had always told me that her father's name was Shmuel in the Old Country—which became Samuel or Sam in America—but it's possible that his Yiddish name was Shalom or Solomon, not Shmuel, and he chose to Americanize it as Sam.

CHAPTER SIX: THE BIRTH OF A BUSINESS

Many of the details on the founding or A. Cohen & Sons and its early years come from Hyman Cohen's *As I Recall*.

63 **"Machines, needles, thread, pressing cloths . . .":** Roskolenko, *The Time That Was Then*, p. 69. Other details on sweatshop and pay, from Roskolenko, *The Time That Was Then*, chap. 3.

66 *I have over a thousand dollars:* The exact sum and how much various relatives chipped in is much debated in the family.

66 "**the sentimental heart and the battling mind . . .**": Roskolenko, *The Time That Was Then*, p. 120.

68 "**the capital of capitalism . . .**": Michels, *A Fire in Their Hearts*, p. 10.

CHAPTER SEVEN: SOCIALIST IN A BLACK SATIN DRESS

I relied on Itel's Story for many details in this chapter.

71 "**The Jewish needle . . .**": Quoted in Roskolenko, *The Time That Was Then*, p. 63.

73 "**I am a socialist because . . .**": Quoted in *How We Lived: A Documentary History of Immigrant Jews in America*, by Irving Howe and Kenneth Libo (New York: Richard Marek, 1979), p. 190.

74 "**A man either had God or socialism . . .**": Roskolenko, *The Time That Was Then*, p. 111.

CHAPTER EIGHT: FIRST WORLD WAR

77 **When the news reached Volozhin:** Volozhin Yizkor book, p. 343.

78 **When Russia mobilized:** S. Ansky, *The Enemy at His Pleasure: A Journey Through the Jewish Pale of Settlement During World War I* (New York: Metropolitan Books, 2002), p. ix.

78 "**swaying back and forth . . .**": Quoted in *The Long Way Home*, by David Laskin (New York: Harper, 2010), p. 92.

80 **Some 600,000 Jews were sent packing:** Ansky, *The Enemy at His Pleasure*, p. ix.

80 **Cossacks were desecrating:** Ibid., p. 281.

81 **Again and again, a story was repeated:** Ibid., cited in Laskin, *The Long Way Home*, p. 92.

82 **In a neighboring shtetl:** Krasnoe Yizkor book.

82 **A letter appealing for emergency aid:** *On Foreign Soil: An Autobiographical Novel*, by Falk Zolf at www.eilatgordinlevitan.com/rakov//rkv_pages/rakov_stories_onfor.html.

83 **In March of 1916:** Details from *The Eastern Front, 1914–1917*, by Norman Stone (New York: Scribner, 1975), pp. 228–229, 231.

83 **Shalom Tvi managed to secure:** No papers or photos exist to document Shimon Dov's move to Rakov, but there is one compelling piece of physical evidence. It is the Jewish custom to bury the dead within twenty-four hours of their passing, and even in fine weather it would have been difficult to transport a body from Volozhin to Rakov that quickly in the days of horse-drawn carts. In February 1917, with the roads drifted over in snow, Volozhin sealed off on the front line, and the Pale crippled by war, such a move would have been next to impossible. Since Shimon Dov was buried in Rakov, he must have been living there at the time of his death. Aside from this evidence, family customs and habits also support the idea that Shimon Dov moved to Rakov during the war. His son Avram Akiva lived with his children

in New York, so it seems logical that Shimon Dov, a widower in time of war, would have moved in with his last son remaining in Europe.

85 **It was International Women's Day:** Orlando Figes, *A People's Tragedy: The Russian Revolution 1891–1924* (New York: Penguin, 1996), p. 308.

85 **Police and Cossacks were called in:** Sheila Fitzpatrick, *The Russian Revolution* (Oxford: Oxford University Press, 1994), p. 44.

85 **no one had thought to issue whips:** Figes, *A People's Tragedy*, p. 308.

85 **February 23 in the old-style Julian:** Dates in the old-style Julian calendar are thirteen days earlier than dates in the new-style Gregorian calendar (see footnote above); hence in Russia, which was still using the Julian calendar, it was known as the February Revolution—even though in the West the date fell in March.

85 **The Petrograd chief of police:** Figes, *A People's Tragedy*, p. 310.

86 **As of March 15, 1917:** Geoffrey Jukes, *The First World War: The Eastern Front, 1914–1918* (Oxford: Osprey Publishing, 2002), p. 60.

87 **"There is nothing more to discuss . . .":** Quoted in Laskin, *The Long Way Home*, p. 119.

91 **Russia must withdraw immediately:** Fitzpatrick, *The Russian Revolution*, p. 51.

91 **In the first week of July:** Ibid., p. 57.

94 **"the worst possible material . . .":** Quoted in Laskin, *The Long Way Home*, p. 135.

97 **"it will be a shameful peace":** Quoted in Figes, *A People's Tragedy*, p. 544.

97 **Russia lost not only all of its western territories:** Figes, *A People's Tragedy*, p. 548.

97 **The regime change came as a huge relief:** Some of the details here were supplied by my maternal grandmother, Gisri Sore Galpierjn. Gisri Sore was the daughter of a prominent family in the shtetl of Krasniki—fifty-five miles north-northeast of Minsk. During the Great War a gentlemanly German officer was billeted in their house. The officer told the family that he would help them in any way he could after the war and he made good on his promise. When Gisri Sore decided to immigrate to America in 1921 at the age of eighteen, she contacted the German officer and he helped her arrange passage. In America she Americanized her name to Gladys Helperin. Gladys married Sam Cohen shortly after the death of his first wife Celia, raised his four children, and bore him a daughter, my mother, Leona Pauline Cohen, in 1926.

98 **When Passover came:** *The Jews in Poland and Russia, Volume III: 1914 to 2008*, by Antony Polonsky (Oxford: Littman Library of Jewish Civilization, 2010), p. 19.

98 **"On the earth this is the last part . . .":** Arnold Zweig, quoted in *War Land on the Eastern Front*, by Vejas Gabriel Liulevicius (Cambridge: Cambridge University Press, 2000), p. 191.

98 **There were stories:** Liulevicius, *War Land*, p. 120.

98 **"Jews are living here in considerable numbers . . .":** Ibid., p. 120.

102 **"The shelling did not come in bursts . . .":** Captain Ben H. Chastaine, *History of the 18th U.S. Infantry, First Division 1812–1919* (New York: Hymans Publishing), p. 47.

102 **For a week they lived on:** Jeremiah M. Evarts, *Cantigny: A Corner of the War* (Privately printed, 1938), p. 2.

102 **The shriek was directly overhead:** Details on shell explosion from Evarts, *Cantigny*, p. 73.

102 **A soldier with Company K:** Testimony of Corporal Fidelis H. Elder, on file in National Archives and Record Administration, College Park, Maryland.

102 **But Hyman gave a different account:** Hyman's account in *As I Recall*, pp. 32–41, has a number of errors: he puts the date of Quesenberry's wounding and death a month later than it actually occurred; the part about Quesenberry's refusing aid in the church basement seems unlikely since Corporal Fidelis H. Elder, in sworn testimony, describes him being removed in an ambulance in which he died on the way to the hospital. Hyman states at the start of the book that he was writing "from memory" and the events of the Great War had occurred a half century earlier.

103 **The hard part would be fending off:** *History of the First Division During the World War, 1917–1919*, compiled by the Society of the First Division (Philadelphia: Winston, 1922), p. 83.

105 **"No more glorious task . . .":** Chastaine, *History of the 18th*, p. 59.

105 **"Blinding flashes of lightning . . .":** Ibid., p. 61.

105 **the serene neoclassical façade:** Evarts, *Cantigny*, p. 86.

106 **"No man is fearless in battle . . .":** Charles H. Abels, *The Last of the Fighting Four* (New York: Vantage Press, 1968), p. 77.

106 **Casualties mounted:** Chastaine, *History of the 18th*, p. 63.

107 **"like insects fleeing to the rear":** quoted in Laskin, *The Long Way Home*, p. 220.

107 **Captain Robert S. Gill:** Hyman mistakenly identified him as Captain Gilbert in *As I Recall*.

107 **horrific flanking fire:** Chastaine, *History of the 18th*, p. 64.

107 **"so exhausted . . . that it was often necessary":** Douglas V. Johnson II and Rolfe L. Hillman, Jr., *Soissons 1918* (College Station: Texas A&M University Press, 1999), p. 126.

108 **only seventy-nine returned:** Chastaine, *History of the 18th*, p. 66.

108 **The First Division Infantry as a whole:** *American Armies and Battlefields in Europe* (Washington, DC: Center of Military History, 1992), p. 87.

108 **For the first time since September 1914:** Johnson and Hillman, *Soissons*, p. 125.

109 **The blisters raised by the mustard gas:** In *As I Recall*, p. 39, Hyman mentions the permanent scar on the lower part of his chin; his daughter Barbara Weisenfeld remembers scars on his neck behind his left ear.

CHAPTER NINE: PIONEERS

For background on Maidenform's founding and early years, I relied on Itel's Story, the Maidenform Collection: *They Made America*, by Harold Evans (New York: Little, Brown,

2004), pp. 308–315; *Past and Promise: Lives of New Jersey Women*, edited by Joan N. Burstyn, Women's Project of New Jersey (Metuchen, NJ: Scarecrow Press, 1990); *Uplift: The Bra in America*, by Jane Farrell-Beck and Colleen Gau (Philadelphia: University of Pennsylvania Press, 2002); "At the Curve Exchange," by Vicki Howard in *Beauty and Business: Commerce, Gender and Culture in Modern America*, edited by Philip Scranton (New York: Routledge, 2001); and "Her Half-Billion Dollar Shape," by Pete Martin, *Saturday Evening Post*, October 15, 1949.

For background on Zionism, HeHalutz, and the early collective Jewish colonies in Palestine, I relied on the following: *My Country: The Story of Modern Israel*, by Abba Eban (New York: Random House, 1975); *A History of Palestine: From the Ottoman Conquest to the Founding of the State of Israel*, by Gudrun Kramer (Princeton, NJ: Princeton University Press, 2002); *The Return to the Soil: A History of Jewish Settlement in Israel*, by Alex Bein (Jerusalem: Youth and Hechalutz, Department of the Zionist Organisation, 1952); *Land, Labor and the Origins of the Israeli-Palestinian Conflict, 1882–1914*, by Gershon Shafir (Cambridge: Cambridge University Press, 1989); *Berl: The Biography of a Socialist Zionist, Berl Katznelson, 1887–1944*, by Anita Shapira (Cambridge: Cambridge University Press, 1984); *Arrow in the Blue*, by Arthur Koestler (New York: Macmillan, 1952–1954); *Palestinian Identity*, by Rashid Khalidi (New York: Columbia University Press, 1993); *Overthrowing Geography: Jaffa, Tel Aviv, and the Struggle for Palestine 1880–1948*, by Mark Levine (Berkeley: University of California Press, 2005); *A History of Zionism*, by Walter Laqueur (New York: Schocken Books, 2003); *Imagining Zion: Dreams, Designs, and Realities in a Century of Jewish Settlement*, by S. Ilan Troen (New Haven, CT: Yale University Press, 2003); *A Tale of Love and Darkness*, by Amos Oz (Orlando, FL: Harcourt, 2004); *The Blue Mountain*, by Meir Shalev (New York: Asher Books, 1991); *Pioneers and Homemakers: Jewish Women in Pre-State Israel*, edited by Deborah S. Bernstein (Albany: State University of New York, 1992); *Pioneers in Israel*, by Shmuel Dayan (Cleveland, OH: World Publishing, 1961); *The Promised Land: Memoirs of Shmuel Dayan*, by Yael Dayan (London: Routledge, 1961); *The Plough Woman: Records of the Pioneer Women of Palestine*, by Rachel Katznelson-Shazar (Hanover, NH: University Press of New England, 2002); *Pioneer Youth in Palestine*, by Shlomo Bardin (New York: Bloch Publishing, 1932); *The Israelis: Founders and Sons*, by Amos Elon (New York: Penguin, 1983); *Moshava, Kibbutz and Moshav*, by Dov Weintraub (Ithaca, NY: Cornell University Press, 1969); and *The Moshav in Israel*, by Maxwell I. Klayman (New York: Praeger Publishers, 1970).

112 **Some twenty-eight thousand tons of metal:** Evans, *They Made America*, p. 311.

115 **equal shareholders in a newly incorporated:** According to a document titled "Minutes of First Meeting of Incorporators and Subscribers," in the Maidenform Collection, this happened on August 31, 1922—but other sources including Evans, *They Made America*, and an entry on "Ida Rosenthal" in *Great Lives from History: American Women Series*, Vol. 4, by Catherine Coleman Brawer (Pasadena, CA:

Salem Press, 1995), pp. 1547–1550, say that the partnership began in 1921. Brawer puts the year in which Itel and Enid stopped making dresses as 1925.

116 **Mrs. Bissett had a brainstorm:** Maidenform salesman Jack Zizmor in an interview with Hy Lieberman on June 27, 1973, transcribed and edited by Kathryn Salwitz, in March 1986, said that Mrs. Bissett "got the idea of the first bra from a dance set that she used to wear." In *Uplift*, Farrell-Beck and Gau date brassieres, or at least breast supporters, back to 1863. In the intervening decades there had been various types of support including "breast puffs" and so on.

116 **Mrs. Bissett christened the garment:** Evans, *They Made America*, p. 312.

118 **In 1924 they registered:** Brawer, *Great Lives from History*, p. 1548.

119 **"same old story":** Isaac Babel, *1920 Diary* (New Haven, CT: Yale University Press, 1995), p. 12.

120 **the Tarbut Gymnasium:** *Tarbut*, the Hebrew word for culture, was an interwar network of Hebrew-language schools that prepared students for life in Palestine through a grounding in modern spoken Hebrew and a mainstream Zionist curriculum; Chaim's older brother Yishayahu was one of the founders of a Tarbut school in Volozhin in 1925.

122 **He felt not the slightest twinge:** Some of the details of the train ride and voyage, and the phrase *dust of exile* are from S. Y. Agnon, *Only Yesterday* (Princeton, NJ: Princeton University Press, 2000), p. 21.

124 **"still mostly stony desert":** Koestler, *Arrow in the Blue*, p. 138.

124 **"but thorn and thistle, ruined cities . . ."** Elon, *The Israelis*, p. 85.

125 *Was it I who long ago . . .*: Ra'hel, *Flowers of Perhaps* (New Milford, CT: Toby Press, 2008), p. 47.

128 **"We dreaded comfort":** Quoted in Katznelson-Shazar, *The Plough Woman*, p. 61.

129 **"In those days we were a band . . ."** Dayan, *The Promised Land*, pp. 17–18.

130 **depression and suicide were "rampant":** Elon, *The Israelis*, p. 143.

130 **They had "dreamed of a life rich in heroic deeds . . .":** Katznelson-Shazar, *The Plough Woman*, p. 60.

130 **"Every single person who left . . ."** Dayan, *The Promised Land*, p. 18.

130 **Then he called it quits:** A third group of *halutzim* tried to make a go of Har Kinneret in 1927, but they also gave up after a couple of years. "Most of the last remaining settlers up there were crazy," remembers one old-timer whose father pioneered the first lakeshore colony. "By 1929 only one family remained. When Smoshkavitz, the last settler, died of malaria, that was the end of Har Kinneret." Today groves of mango, eucalyptus, and date palms stand on the slope where the Har Kinneret *halutzim* tried to farm. Nothing of the settlement is left and nothing has replaced it. Beside the dirt track that wanders past where Chaim and Etl and their comrades once lived, there is a sign in Hebrew and English that reads "Switzerland," referring to a bit of nearby forest with a fabulous view funded and maintained by a Swiss group. But for the wind and the drone of insects, the silence is complete.

133 **"Joe Bissett was, in my opinion, a hot and cold sales manager":** Jack Zizmor interview, June 27, 1973.

133 **"I understand you're with Maidenform":** Robert A. Brawer, *Fictions of Business: Insights on Management from Great Literature* (New York: Wiley, 1998), pp. 70–71.

133 **Family lore has it that Itel:** "Uplift" (support of women's breasts by undergarments) had been around for half a century by the 1920s. Maidenform's signal innovation was to provide uplift from above.

134 **"Two stitches more or less...":** Martin, "Her Half-Billion Dollar Shape," pp. 28–78.

135 **Then the chills returned:** Dayan, *The Promised Land*, p. 9.

136 **feasting on the hemoglobin:** Sonia Shah, *The Fever: How Malaria Has Ruled Humankind for 500,000 Years* (New York: Farrar, Straus & Giroux, 2010), pp. 18–19.

136 **"We worked and suffered":** Katznelson-Shazar, *The Plough Woman*, p. 63.

136 **"the enchantress-bride...":** Shapira, *Berl*, pp. 58–59.

138 **It was like the Model T:** Brawer, *Great Lives from History*, pp. 1548–1549. This new "section work" production process is not to be confused with the piecework pay scale that was implemented in 1937.

139 **Abraham and Sarah made the classic hopscotch:** It has been impossible to ascertain Abraham's and Sarah's birth years definitively because of discrepancies in the documentary evidence. In the 1920 census Abraham and Sarah both gave their age as fifty-five, which would indicate a birth year of 1865; in the 1930 census he is sixty-five and she is sixty-two, which would put his birth year at 1865 but hers at 1868; on Abraham's death certificate the birthday is omitted but his age at time of death in 1940 was given as seventy-eight, which would put his birth year at 1862; Sarah's death certificate gives her birthday as February 7, 1862.

140 **Arab village of Ijlil al-Qibliyya:** For more about this village, which Palestinian sources say was abandoned by its Arab inhabitants on April 3, 1948, because they feared for their safety under the new Israeli regime, see the Palestine Remembered Web site, www.palestineremembered.com/Jaffa/Ijlil-al-Qibliyya/index.html. The Web site says that the original village was "completely destroyed and defaced" by the Israelis.

140 **"You want to found a state without bloodshed?":** Quoted in Elon, *The Israelis*, p. 161.

144 **"not a Jewish soul":** Maurice Samuel, *What Happened in Palestine: The Events of August, 1929: Their Background and Significance* (Boston: Stratford, 1929), p. 120.

145 **The casualties on both sides were heavy:** Statistics from Mark Tessler, *A History of the Israeli-Palestinian Conflict* (Bloomington: Indiana University Press, 2009).

145 **the end of a Zionist era:** Shapira, *Berl*, pp. 166–167.

145 **Self-defense now occupied:** Anita Shapira, *Land and Power: The Zionist Resort to Force, 1881–1948* (New York: Oxford University Press, 1992), p. 177.

145 **The idea of peaceful coexistence:** Ibid.

145 **Sam's buy was thirteen shares:** Cohen, *As I Recall*, p. 61.

146 **10 billion dollars in stock value:** T. H. Watkins, *The Hungry Years* (New York: Holt, 1999), p. 32.

146 **America's Jewish community was emerging:** Johnson, *A History of the Jews*, p. 460.

CHAPTER TEN: THE DEPRESSION

147 **Unemployment more than doubled:** Watkins, *The Hungry Years*, pp. 43–44.

148 **right parietal lobe:** Lewis Rosenthal death certificate, August 4, 1930; additional information on Lewis's death came from interviews with Drs. Leona Laskin and Jay Epstein.

148 **respect for Abraham and Sarah:** According to Inda Epstein Goldfarb (Ethel and Sam Epstein's daughter), Abraham and Sarah were on summer vacation in the Catskills in South Fallsberg and unable to get back in time for the funeral; but Leona Laskin recalls that the men went to South Fallsberg only on weekends and returned to work during the week—so since the funeral was on a Tuesday, Abraham would have been around; as a Kohain he was forbidden to enter a cemetery but he could have attended the memorial service beforehand.

150 **The year 1930 was bad:** Watkins, *The Hungry Years*, p. 44.

150 **Stocks continued to sink:** Robert T. Patterson, *The Great Boom and Panic 1921–1929* (Chicago: Regnery, 1965), p. 194.

150 **That summer, drought decimated grain crops:** Ibid., p. 191.

150 **New York City soup kitchens . . . 40 percent of Chicago's workers . . . in Detroit it reached:** Watkins, *The Hungry Years*, pp. 44–45, 59.

152 **Dow Jones industrial average bottomed out:** Patterson, *The Great Boom and Panic*, p. 194.

152 **over a quarter of the nation's population subsisted:** Watkins, *The Hungry Years*, p. 44.

153 **the biggest parade in its history:** *The Jersey Journal*, October 17, 2009.

CHAPTER ELEVEN: "WE WILL BE GLAD TO TAKE YOU BACK"

157 **a considerable sum:** An authority on Polish economic history notes that teachers earned an average of three hundred zloty a month then.

CHAPTER TWELVE: IN LOVE IN THE LAND

163 **the bitter women in the kitchen:** Bernstein, *Pioneers and Homemakers*, p. 64.

165 **even the priest:** In Sonia's Story, the memoir written by her son Benny, Sonia says that Shepseleh played chess with the son of the Catholic priest but this must be an error.

173 **He found his checkbook and wrote out a check:** The dates here are extrapolated from the letters; it's possible he wrote the check somewhat earlier since in a letter sent before Sukkoth—which started the evening of October 4 in 1933—Shalom Tvi

wrote Chaim that Avram Akiva still had not received a receipt from him, Chaim, for the two hundred dollars he had sent. Actually, he could have sent the check in midsummer, given the slowness of mail in those days.

175 **Back in the autumn of 1929:** This date comes from the Kfar Vitkin Web site. According to "The Tenants of Wadi Hawarith: Another View of the Land Question in Palestine," by Raya Adler (Cohen), *International Journal of Middle East Studies*, vol. 20, no. 2 (May 1988), p. 204, the date of first plowing may actually have been September 6, 1930. Adler writes that settlers "were able to continue their work only under the protection of a British security force." The protests continued—when the Jews tried to plow during the winter of 1931–1932 Bedouins "threw themselves in front of the tractors" (Adler [Cohen], "The Tenants of Wadi Hawarith," p. 206). Police came in and twenty-six members of the tribe were arrested. Adler (Cohen) writes on p. 207: "The violent incidents against the Jewish settlers in Wadi Hawarith resulted above all from the tenants' spontaneous resistance to their miserable existence. . . . The tenants reacted with the only weapon at their disposal—their power to sabotage their neighbors' fields."

Adler (Cohen) notes that the British government floated a number of resettlement ideas to the Wadi al-Hawarith Bedouins, including ones guaranteeing appropriate housing and compensation for crops—but all were rejected by the tribe.

176 **a Bedouin woman struck the landlord and drove him off:** This is from the history section of the Kfar Vitkin Web site, www.kfar-vitkin.org.il/.

176 **moved quickly—and perhaps unscrupulously—to snap it up:** "Mandatory Land Policy, Tenancy and the Wadi al-Hawarith Affair, 1929–1933," by Raya Adler (Cohen), "*Studies in Zionism*, vol. 7, no. 2, 1986, pp. 233–257. On pp. 233–234 of this article, Adler (Cohen) writes: "In secret collusion with Yehoshua Hankin acting on behalf of the JNF [Jewish National Fund], and for the consideration of a bribe, the lawyer representing the claimants . . . succeeded in foiling a compromise between the creditors and the landowners. This ploy led to the outright sale, in the guise of a public auction, of the Wadi al-Hawarith land to the JNF." Adler (Cohen) goes on to point out that "a forced sale by order of the court" "annulled the tenant farmers' rights to protection under the Protection of Cultivators Ordinance, as well as their right of first purchase of land put up for sale (the right of preemption under Ottoman law)."

176 **The tenant farmers fought:** Adler (Cohen), "Mandatory Land Policy" says the total number of Bedouins dispossessed was two thousand.

176 **"the basis of justice":** Albert M., Hyamson, *Palestine Under the Mandate, 1920–1948* (London: Methuen, 1959), p. 39. Hyamson also states on p. 87 that "the urgency" of legislation to protect Arab farmworkers' rights "was due to the relatively large purchases of land that were being made by Jewish agencies from large landowners resident in Paris, Beirut and Cairo, without any regard for the moral if not legal rights of their tenants who had been long established on their land. . . . The

vendors, having no local interests, were, of course, anxious to sell at the highest prices. They quickly found at small cost a means of circumventing the legislation" and protecting tenants.

176 **"directly through the courts":** Adler (Cohen), "The Tenants of Wadi Hawarith," p. 202. Adler (Cohen) presents a full and nuanced account of the sale: "In fact, the land had secretly already been sold to Hankin for three times (£136,000) the sum fixed by the courts for the auction. Thus, the entire transaction was extremely profitable for the Tayan family . . . and since it was ostensibly carried out by a court auction order, it was not considered a voluntary sale of land to Jews . . . by making the purchase directly through the courts, the JNF was granted automatic ownership. Accordingly, the tenants' right to preemption (i.e., priority of tenants according to Ottoman law to buy the land they cultivated when it was offered for sale) was null and void."

176 **another parcel fifty miles away:** Adler (Cohen), "Mandatory Land Policy," p. 203.

177 **camped out at the side of the highway:** Adler (Cohen), "Mandatory Land Policy," p. 240.

177 **a large traditional Arab agrarian community:** Adler (Cohen), "The Tenants of Wadi Hawarith," p. 203, reports that the head of the Jewish Agency's Settlement Department stated that the tenants were not deeply rooted in the area, and that in 1929 "the Wadi Hawarith tenants numbered 850 persons who cultivated one-tenth of the land." On pp. 214–216, Adler (Cohen) points out that "the Zionist aim was to attain political control of the country rather than merely formal ownership of the land," hence they offered and accepted no compromise with Bedouin neighbors. "The Wadi Hawarith affair illustrates how problematic the question of Jewish land acquisition became when this entailed eviction and how central it was in exacerbating the conflict between the Zionist and Palestinian Arab national movements. . . . The Wadi Hawarith tenants were fighting with all their might to maintain their traditional tribal framework and to stay in their place of birth. . . . Had the JNF compromised with the tenants and allowed them to cultivate part of the land as they demanded (and as was proposed by a Jewish peasant journal), the affair might have ended differently. But the JNF's goals were national rather than economic: it could not content itself with legal ownership; Jewish settlers had to replace the Arab tenants. The displacement of the Bedouin violated the customs of Arab society and united the community in protest against this blatant injustice."

I would like to add a personal note. I was initially alerted to this battle by Salah Mansour, whom I contacted through the Palestine Remembered Web site. Mansour wrote me, in rather inflammatory language, that the Bedouins of Wadi al-Hawarith were "the first to be dispossessed and thrown out by the Jewish colonizers in the early to mid-30s. . . . Many came to my village Qaqun in the mid-thirties and became day laborers (an insult to a proud farmer). You can find most of them in Tulkarm refugee camps and in Baq'a' refugee camp in Jordan. What a terrible experience; it should have been an early warning to all Palestinians. We have paid dearly for it. . . . Zionism is a terrible disease of mind. I feel sorry for whoever carry [sic] this dangerous ideology."

I find Mansour's rhetoric offensive, but as a result of his message, I was able to track down Adler's (Cohen's) articles and report on the legal battle that accompanied this sizable and highly controversial land deal. The history of land transfers in Palestine has become explosively politicized, which makes it all the more critical to bring the facts to light.

177 **third-largest land deal:** Adler (Cohen), "Mandatory Land Policy," p. 233. In "The Tenants of Wadi Hawarith," p. 200, Adler (Cohen) goes on to state that the main difference in the Wadi al-Hawarith purchase was that "communal lands . . . were being purchased, thus undermining the infrastructure of the countryside . . . its purchase involved the eviction of a large number of tenants, and the fact that it became an issue for the Palestinian national movement makes it relevant to the struggle against the displacement of Arabs in the 1930s." Adler (Cohen) further notes on p. 213 that the tension with Arabs and the isolation were exhausting and debilitating for the Jewish settlers, including, presumably, Chaim and Sonia and their comrades at Kfar Vitkin: "Irritated by constant tensions with the resentful neighbors, exhausted by the work of swamp drainage, and socially isolated—for geographical reasons—from other Jewish settlements, the settlers were not able to increase their numbers significantly" in the first years. In 1934, there were only one thousand Jews in "11 pioneering groups living there."

177 **In the spring of 1930:** These details on the birth of the baby and the first Passover come from the Kfar Vitkin Web site, www.kfar-vitkin.org.il/, translated by Aza Hadas.

180 **"It is necessary that we have a language . . .":** Quoted in Sachar, *A History of Israel*, p. 82.

180 **Hebrew became a badge of honor:** Donna Robinson Divine, *Exiled in the Homeland* (Austin: University of Texas Press, 2009), p. 125.

180 **excruciating internal warfare:** Sachar, *A History of Israel*, p. 83.

182 **Haganah had arranged to meet:** www.jewishvirtuallibrary.org/jsource/History/irgunill.html.

182 **Under cover of night:** Shapira, *Land and Power*, p. 229.

184 **"We are fated to live in a state of constant battle . . .":** Quoted in Yosef Gorny, *Zionism and the Arabs: 1882–1948* (New York: Oxford University Press, 1987), p. 246.

185 **British commissions radically pared back:** Sachar, *A History of Israel*, p. 118.

CHAPTER THIRTEEN: RETURN TO RAKOV

187 **Sales picked up again after the brief stumble:** Maidenform Collection.

187 **Production tripled:** Evans, *They Made America*, p. 314.

188 **This is what he wrote after the visit:** Rakov Yizkor book.

189 **Gentile shop owners now displayed signs:** Ezra Mendelsohn, *The Jews of East*

Central Europe Between the World Wars (Bloomington: Indiana University Press, 1983), p. 73.

189 **Members of the fascist anti-Semitic ONR . . . routinely attacked:** Mendelsohn, *The Jews of East Central Europe*, pp. 70, 73.

191 **A big family wedding was celebrated:** Interview with Tsipora Alperovich, Tel Aviv, June 2010. Tsipora remembered it as Etl's wedding but she was mistaken.

192 **Vilna's Jews accounted for a substantial percentage of the population:** According to http://kehilalinks.jewishgen.org/vilna/vilna.htm#jewstatistics, 40 percent of the 154,532 residents were Jewish in 1897; 43.5 percent in 1916; 45 percent at the time of Sonia's visit. But Dov Levin, "The Jews of Vilna Under Soviet Rule, 19 September–28 October 1939" in *Poles, Jews, Socialists: The Failure of an Ideal*, and Polin, in *Studies in Polish Jewry*, vol. 9, edited by Antony Polonsky, Israel Bartal, Gershon Hundert, Magdalena Opalski, and Jerzy Tomaszewski (London: Littman Library of Jewish Civilization, 1996), p. 108, says 37 percent of 200,000 residents were Jewish prior to the Second World War.

196 **But another, more shadowy motive:** See Giles MacDonogh, *1938: Hitler's Gamble* (New York: Basic Books, 2009), p. 217, for the possible homosexual connection.

CHAPTER FOURTEEN: "THE WORLD OF TOMORROW"

199 **A "special inquiry":** U.S. Citizenship and Immigration Services, File Series A-File, File Number A-2958053, records relating to Sholom Kahanowicz. The documents in this file detail the special inquiry hearing, the issuance of the bail and the tourist visa, and so on.

200 **Now just to visit he needed:** Saul S. Friedman, *No Haven for the Oppressed: United States Policy Toward Jewish Refugees, 1938–1945* (Detroit: Wayne State University Press, 1973), p. 23.

202 **The 1939 World's Fair:** Details on the fair from *1939: The Lost World of the Fair*, by David Gelernter (New York: Free Press, 1995); and *Trylon and Perisphere*, by Barbara Cohen, Steven Heller, and Seymour Chwast (New York: Abrams, 1989).

203 **the seventy neon signs:** Farrell-Beck, *Uplift*, p. 77, and Tom Reichert, *The Erotic History of Advertising* (Amherst, NY: Prometheus Books, 2003), p. 145.

CHAPTER FIFTEEN: SECOND WORLD WAR

210 **Vilna, which had flown God knows how many flags:** Dov Levin, "The Jews of Vilna," p. 111.

213 **"Vilna is congested with refugees . . .":** Quoted in Dov Levin, "The Jews of Vilna," p. 126.

213 **wounding 200 and killing 1:** Yehuda Bauer, *American Jewry and the Holocaust: The American Jewish Joint Distribution Committee, 1939–1945* (Jerusalem: Institute of Contemporary Jewry, 1981), p. 108.

213 **Meanwhile, 14,000 Jewish refugees:** The statistics in this paragraph come from

Bauer, *American Jewry*, p. 112; *Shtetl Jews Under Soviet Rule*, by Ben-Cion Pinchuk (Oxford: Basil Blackwell, 1990), p. 37, which places the number of refugees at ten thousand; and *Vilna*, by Israel Cohen (Philadelphia: Jewish Publication Society of America, 1943), p. 471. The quote on "the spiritual elite of Polish Jewry" is from Pinchuk, *Shtetl Jews*, p. 37.

213 **"The food supply is being rapidly depleted":** Quoted in Dov Levin, "The Jews of Vilna," p. 119.

220 **Vilna's travel agents arbitrarily stopped:** Cohen, *Vilna*, p. 473.

220 **a total of 137 Vilna Jews had immigrated to all countries:** Bauer, *American Jewry*, p. 116. But this figure is far from definitive. Herman Kruk in *The Last Days of the Jerusalem of Lithuania: Chronicles from the Vilna Ghetto and the Camps, 1939–1944* (New York: YIVO Institute for Jewish Research, 2002), p. 49, describes how the Joint arranged for refugees to get out by traveling through Siberia; and Pinchuk, *Shtetl Jews*, p. 38, says "many" refugees found a way out to the West and Palestine—though no number is specified. Doba also indicated that many were getting out. There is no easy way to reconcile these discrepancies. My conclusion is that the American family could have done more but that Doba and Shepseleh were timid and indecisive, burdened with two young boys and unwilling to run big risks or take unorthodox paths like traveling via Siberia or Shanghai.

CHAPTER SIXTEEN: UNDER THE BIG ONES

229 **Young Jews and the Jewish "working intelligentsia":** Pinchuk, *Shtetl Jews*, p. 51.

229 **"had lost their Jewish essence . . .":** Quoted in Volozhin Yizkor book, "Under the Soviet Regime."

233 **"Nonproductive elements" disappeared:** Pinchuk, *Shtetl Jews*, p. 34.

233 **"Within an hour, in one stroke . . .":** Quoted in Pinchuk, *Shtetl Jews*, p. 44.

233 **"We assembled the pieces":** Volozhin Yizkor book, "Under the Soviet Regime."

234 **Khost was ordered to introduce special classes:** Pinchuk, *Shtetl Jews*, p. 85.

CHAPTER SEVENTEEN: "THEY SNATCH WHOLE STREETS"

238 **Reuven Rogovin was such a Jew:** Volozhin Yizkor book, "Under the Soviet Regime."

241 **Next came tanks:** Mendel Balberyszski, *Stronger Than Iron: The Destruction of Vilna Jewry 1941–1945: An Eyewitness Account* (Jerusalem: Gefen Publishing, 2010), p. 13.

241 **Khost and the others were taken prisoner:** There are conflicting bits of testimony concerning the fate of Khost. In the "Testimony by Uri Finkel," http://rakowshtetl .com/UriFinkel_8.htm, Rakov survivor Uri Finkel writes the following: "Thus did our shtetl lose the active ones of our Jewish community still in the first days of the fascist occupation. Further on, in addition to the 255, the shtetl lost the active Soviet educators from the Jewish school and a few other employees, who were evacuated

and then overtaken by the Germans near Minsk and were with the Minsk Jews as the first victims. Among them were the teacher Kehas Goldshteyn [Khost]. . . . Together with them were about a dozen Rakov intellectuals and a dozen young men who arrived to be mobilized into the Red Army and ended up with the rest. Of these I know Sholem Finkel (Fayves), M. Chayet (Ade . . .), I. Kaplan (Israel Moshakhezes), Aizik Katz, and others. The ten who remained alive escaped from the Minsk ghetto. The relatives of 50 Rakov families were in the Minsk ghetto. A much larger number ran away to other shtetls, many to Krosne, not believing the provocations of the commander, that the Jews who were sent to a work-camp would not be killed. Many of these were murdered along the way, not knowing where to turn." But another Rakov survivor named Hillel Eidelman wrote to Sonia from Rakov on July 20, 1945: "I was with your brother-in-law [Khost] in the German camp, where the murderers killed him. I would write more, but my hands are trembling as I tell you such terrible news." Eidelman does not specify which camp it was. Khost's fate after June 27 is unknown, but from Eidelman and Finkel it seems clear that he was captured outside Minsk and killed in a camp in the vicinity of Minsk—most likely Maladzyechna.

242 **the Lithuanian police were on hand to divide shoppers:** Kruk, *The Last Days*, p. 51.

242 **every Jew in Vilna had to wear two badges:** Balberyszski, *Stronger Than Iron*, p. 25. Dates and details about patches versus armbands differ slightly from one account to the next. See Kruk, *The Last Days*, p. 57. What is clear is that the Nazis kept changing the rules in order to confuse the ghetto prisoners and provide themselves with excuses for roundups and murder.

243 **"They Snatch Whole Streets":** Kruk, *The Last Days*, p. 52.

244 **"What is happening in Ponar?":** Kruk, *The Last Days*, p. 66.

245 **a paramilitary police force that reported directly to Hitler:** Richard Rhodes, *Masters of Death: The SS-Einsatzgruppen and the Invention of the Holocaust* (New York: Knopf, 2002), p. 4. My account of the organization of the Einsatzgruppen and the killing pits at Ponar relies heavily on Rhodes. I also consulted *The Einsatzgruppen Reports: Selections from the Dispatches of the Nazi Death Squads' Campaign Against the Jews: July 1941–January 1943*, by Yitzhak Arad and Shmuel Krakowski (New York: Holocaust Library, 1989), pp. vi–vii.

245 **Dr. Alfred Filbert, a lawyer:** It's not entirely clear that Filbert was in charge of Vilna. Filbert was head of Einsatzkommando-9 at the time and this was the unit assigned to Vilna, but his name does not appear in any records attached to this period. The Web site deathcamps.org says that Horst Schweineberger and Martin Weiss were in charge of the Sonderkommando of EK-9 situated at 12 Vilenskaia Street in Vilna—but Weiss and Schweineberger seem to have come later. Balberyszski in *Stronger Than Iron* confirms that Weiss and Schweineberger came later and that Schweineberger directed the establishment of the ghetto in September 1941.

Rhodes in *Masters of Death*, p. 223, notes that Filbert later had a nervous break-down.

245 **an auxiliary force of 150 men cherry-picked from the Lithuanian political police:** Rhodes, *Masters of Death*, p. 54.

245 **"The graves are to be leveled . . .":** Quoted in Rhodes, *Masters of Death*, p. 48.

246 **"between about twenty and fifty. . . . These prisoners were really quite well-dressed . . .":** Quoted in Rhodes, *Masters of Death*, pp. 54–55. I rely heavily on Rhodes's account, p. 55, of Ponar at the time of the killings and for eyewitness accounts. I visited Ponar in 2011, but the pits had been smoothed over and trees had grown up. Old photos from the war also helped me visualize the scene. I used Rhodes's vivid and carefully documented account as the basis for what I imagine were the circumstances of Shepseleh's death, though the exact details will never be known. The idea that he was rounded up early in the occupation and killed at Ponar is speculative—but Tsipora Alperovich, who was in the ghetto, said during our interviews in Tel Aviv that this was his fate (though she did not see him snatched).

247 **"We all said to one another . . .":** Quoted in Rhodes, *Masters of Death*, p. 57.

CHAPTER EIGHTEEN: "AKTION"

249 **"Until further notice, about 200 persons are being liquidated daily":** *The Einsatzgruppen Reports*, p. 52.

250 **The prisoners, according to one account:** "Testimony by Uri Finkel."

250 **rounded up fifty-five Rakov Jews:** The size and composition of the group varies from account to account: In "Testimony by Uri Finkel" Finkel states there were forty-nine victims, most of them young men; The Einsatzgruppen Operational Situation Report No. 36 puts the number at fifty-eight. My account is a composite of Finkel and "Rakov Under Nazi Occupation" in www.eilatgordinlevitan.com/rakov/rkv_pages/rakov_stories_occupation.html.

250 **A Rakov Jew named Moshe Pogolensky:** "Rakov Under Nazi Occupation" in www.eilatgordinlevitan.com/rakov/rkv_pages/rakov_stories_occupation.html.

252 **One day the Germans announced:** "Rakov Under Nazi Occupation," Ibid.

252 **Some of the tortures could have been concocted only by madmen:** Details from Eliach, *There Once Was a World*, pp. 580, 584.

252 **People were "driven out of their minds":** Balberyszski, *Stronger Than Iron*, p. 44.

253 **Some boys put on their father's work clothes:** Ibid., p. 53.

253 **"The children did not complain":** Ibid., p. 47.

254 **"Who has inflicted this upon us?":** Anne Frank, *The Diary of a Young Girl* (New York: Bantam Books, 1993), p. 207.

CHAPTER NINETEEN: VILNA GHETTO

255 **On August 6 he told the Judenrat:** Balberyszski, *Stronger Than Iron*, p. 35.

255 **"Lines of people march on both sides . . .":** Kruk, *The Last Days*, pp. 83, 86.

256 **In the course of two days Hingst evicted:** Balberyszski, *Stronger Than Iron*, p. 58.

256 **The Einsatzgruppen report broke down the numbers:** Rhodes, *Masters of Death*, p. 137.

256 **wild new rumors:** Kruk, *The Last Days*, p. 95.

256 **"Better stop thinking":** Kruk, *The Last Days*, p. 96.

257 **"a picture of the Middle Ages":** Yitskhok Rudashevski, *The Diary of the Vilna Ghetto: June 1941–April 1943* (Tel Aviv: Ghetto Fighters' House, 1973), p. 30.

257 **"A bundle was suddenly stolen . . .":** Rudashevski, *The Diary*, pp. 31–32.

257 **"The Lithuanians drive us on . . .":** Ibid., p. 32.

257 **Anyone who could not be crammed:** Balberyszski, *Stronger Than Iron*, p. 83.

CHAPTER TWENTY: YOM KIPPUR, 1941

259 **Maiden Form, now one of the largest family businesses:** Evans, *They Made America*, pp. 314–315; Maidenform Collection.

260 **Itel and William bought an eighteen-room mansion:** Details from Maidenform Collection and interviews with Sallie Cohen Goldwyn, various dates, and Marvin Sleisenger, Kentfield, California, November 10–11, 2010.

260 **father was "a wonderful man . . .":** *New York Post*, September 6, 1964, on file at Maidenform Collection.

261 **first accounts of the atrocities:** David S. Wyman, *The Abandonment of the Jews: America and the Holocaust, 1941–1945* (New York: Pantheon Books, 1984), p. 20. The subject of how much was known about the Holocaust in the United States and when is highly complex and controversial. Yehuda Bauer in *American Jewry and the Holocaust*, p. 187, says that "There can be no doubt that anyone who read the papers, listened to the radio, or read the daily reports by the Jewish Telegraphic Agency (JTA) had access to all the information about Europe's Jews that was needed to establish the fact that mass murder was occurring." Bauer notes that Yiddish papers in the United States published "accounts of the mass murders in Vilna as early as March, 1942." "Until June, 1942, all this information was admittedly scattered. Nobody imagined a campaign of mass annihilation, and the information was always presented in a form which allowed for doubts as to its veracity." According to Bauer, the Bund sent the first "authoritative and exact report of a general plan to annihilate Polish and, by implication, European Jewry."

See also Henry L. Feingold, *Bearing Witness: How America and Its Jews Responded to the Holocaust* (Syracuse, NY: Syracuse University Press, 1995). Feingold says in part that the American Jewish community failed to speak out against the Holocaust because the community was disunited, bent on assimilating, had no effective leaders, had shed its communal religious traditions, and thus had no general public forum they could use to oppose the slaughter.

262 **At 8:50 in the morning on September 30:** Details on the Maidenform strike come

from newspaper clippings from September and October 1941, in the Maidenform file of the Bayonne, New Jersey, public library; journal name has been omitted from the clippings, but the articles are apparently from the *Jersey Journal* and *Bayonne Times*. Additional articles, many undated or with the journal name omitted, are from the Maidenform Collection.

263 **Clippers and operators working on the piecework scale:** Clipping from Bayonne library, no title or journal name, November 4, 1941.

265 **A survivor named Uri Finkel:** "Testimony by Uri Finkel."

266 **When all 112 men were dead:** I have relied on the account of the killings recounted in "Rakov Under Nazi Occupation" in www.eilatgordinlevitan.com/rakov/rkv _pages/rakov_stories_occupation.html, but there are several different accounts of this massacre. A survivor named Nachum Greenholtz is quoted as follows in "Rakov Under Nazi Occupation": "I was among the people who were taken from the market in Rakov to the road of Buzmanu, where a hundred and twelve Jews were annihilated. A few others as well as I were able to escape. The Germans shot at us but I ran quickly to the forest. I spent the night there and in the morning I returned home." Greenholtz's relative Adi Grynholc, who has done extensive research into Rakov history, insists that Nachum's accounts of Rakov during the war are the most reliable.

266 **At some point during that Yom Kippur:** My account of Beyle's death and Etl's existence in the Rakov ghetto is based on conversations with my Israeli relatives, and their information in turn came from conversations with their mother, Sonia. Unfortunately, Sonia did not tell her children how she came to know about the killing of Beyle or that Etl and her daughters survived the first rounds of shootings. It's likely that one of the Rakov survivors told her—possibly Hillel Eidelman, who wrote letters after the war about the dire situation in Rakov.

268 **The British adopted a strict policy:** Arthur Koestler, *Promise and Fulfilment— Palestine, 1917–1949* (New York: Macmillan, 1949), p. 59.

268 **Finally, the Turks ordered the ship:** Kramer, *A History of Palestine*, p. 300; Koestler, *Promise and Fulfilment*, p. 63.

270 **"The tortures lasted for hours . . .":** Volozhin Yizkor book, p. 534.

271 **"Life in the Ghetto grew harder . . ."** : Eliezer Leoni, ed., *Wolozin: The Book of the City and of the Etz Hayyim Yeshiva* (Tel Aviv: Wolozin Landsleit Association of Israel and the USA, 1970), p. 32.

CHAPTER TWENTY-ONE: WONDER GIRL

272 **Nazi officers convinced the Rakov Judenrat:** "Testimony by Uri Finkel."

272 **"Many such shameful and worn-out lies . . .":** Rakov Yizkor book.

272 **Murder by gas would be perfected:** Timothy Snyder, review of "The Auschwitz Volunteer," by Witold Pilecki, *New York Times Book Review*, June 24, 2012, notes that Zyklon B was used at Auschwitz-Birkenau, Treblinka, Belzec, and Sobibor.

273 **In the six months between June and December 1941:** Timothy Snyder, *Bloodlands: Europe Between Hitler and Stalin* (New York: Basic Books, 2010), p. 189.

273 **By the end of 1941:** Snyder, *Bloodlands*, p. 186.

273 **Heydrich announced that the Reich's goal:** "The Wannsee Conference and 'The Final Solution,'" U.S. Holocaust Memorial Museum Web site, www.ushmm.org/wlc/en/article.php?ModuleId=10005477.

273 **February 4, 1942:** This date is from *The Yad Vashem Encyclopedia of the Ghettos During the Holocaust*, edited by Guy Miron (Jerusalem: Yad Vashem, 2009); other accounts, including "Rakov Under Nazi Occupation," put the date at February 2, 1942.

274 **all assembled in the courtyard:** Accounts of the liquidation of the Rakov ghetto and the torching of the synagogue have serious discrepancies and I agonized over which account to choose in narrating this event. The essential difference concerns whether the ghetto prisoners were shot outside the synagogue and the corpses then thrown into the synagogue and torched, or whether the prisoners were herded into the synagogue and then incinerated alive. Ultimately, I chose the latter because more sources give this account. I also followed the advice of Adi Grynholc, who has researched this episode thoroughly. It's possible, as my friend Ivan Doig speculated, that both accounts have some truth: it could have been that the Nazis began shooting the prisoners in batches and at some point decided that it was taking too long—there were 950 men, women, and children to kill—and so they herded the remainder into the synagogue and set the place on fire.

275 **A group of six witnesses:** "The Destruction of Rakov Jews" report written in August 1945, in "Memory to Volozhin Region," www.jewishgen.org/yizkor/volozhin1/Volozhin1.html#TOC.

275 **Moshe Pogolensky gave a different account:** "Rakov Under Nazi Occupation."

CHAPTER TWENTY-TWO: BREAKDOWNS

278 **"I was torn," he recalls:** Interview with Leonard Cohn, Stamford, Connecticut, August 5, 2011.

280 **Two rabbis imprisoned in the stifling house:** Volozhin Yizkor book, pp. 33–34.

281 **Itel managed to secure a "declaration of essentiality":** Evans, *They Made America*, p. 314.

281 **Itel's campaign to "safeguard the value and goodwill of Maiden Form's name":** www.apparelsearch.com/names/M/Maidenform/Maidenform_Brands.htm.

282 **Gold, though restricted, was still available:** Cohen, *As I Recall*, p. 80.

283 **Twenty-three years old in 1942, Rose was a pretty:** Interview with Rose Rubenstein Einziger and her daughter Laurie Bellet, Walnut Creek, California, February 27, 2010. Also unpublished diary that Rose Rubenstein kept as a young woman.

CHAPTER TWENTY-THREE: DESPAIRING PEOPLE

285 **another nine thousand souls had been slaughtered:** www.deathcamps.org/occupation/vilnius%20ghetto.html.

285 **"the blood-drenched delusion":** Rudashevski, *The Diary*, p. 36.

285 **Doba had no permit:** Most sources, including www.jewishgen.org/yizkor/terrible_choice/ter002.html, note that only those who held permits were allowed to live in Ghetto 1—the Large Ghetto where Doba and the boys were recorded in the 1942 census. But Tsipora Alperovich, in interviews in Tel Aviv, June 8, 2010, and March 29, 2011, described visiting with Doba and her sons in the ghetto and insisted Doba had no permit.

286 **He was a good man, a confirmed bachelor:** H. Kazdan, ed., *Teacher's Memorial Book* (in Yiddish; New York: Committee to Perpetuate Memory of Deceased Teachers, 1954), pp. 284–285. Yitskhok Senicki is mentioned on p. 233 of Kruk, *The Last Days*; the footnote to this page states that "He was killed in a camp in Estonia."

286 **the average "living space" in Vilna ghetto:** www.deathcamps.org/occupation/vilnius%20ghetto.html.

286 **She remembered that he suffered serious hearing loss:** Tsipora Alperovich in the June 8, 2010, interview said that Shimon suffered hearing loss after contracting meningitis—but from the letters it seems that he suffered some hearing loss after contracting scarlet fever as child. It's possible that Tsipora was mistaken or confused. The extent of Shimon's deafness is unknown.

287 **"the insanely wild conditions of life . . .":** Mark Dvorzhetski quoted in Rudashevski, *The Diary*, p. 16.

287 **"The book unites us with the future":** Rudashevski, *The Diary*, p. 106.

287 **"the same sad ghetto song . . .":** Rudashevski, *The Diary*, p. 73.

287 **"Frozen, carrying the little stands on their backs . . .":** Rudashevski, *The Diary*, pp. 91–92.

288 **"Let us not go like sheep . . .":** www.yadvashem.org/yv/en/exhibitions/vilna/during/responses_to_the_murder.asp?WT.mc_id=wiki.

288 **to arm his Jewish ghetto police with guns:** Kruk, *The Last Days*, p. 562.

289 **"An American incursion has landed":** Rudashevski, *The Diary*, pp. 93–94.

289 **Battle of Kasserine Pass:** H. R. Knickerbocker and Jack Thompson, *Danger Forward: The Story of the First Division in World War II* (Washington, DC: Society of the First Division, 1947), pp. 13, ff.

290 **Seventy years later, Len:** Interview with Leonard Cohn, Stamford, Connecticut, August 5, 2011.

290 **"Today the terrible news reached us . . .":** Rudashevski, *The Diary*, pp. 138–140.

291 **Gens, though by some accounts he secretly supported:** www.jewishgen.org/Yizkor/terrible_choice/ter002.html.

291 "The chase after Wittenberg went on for hours": Balberyszski, *Stronger Than Iron*, p. 241; www.holocaustresearchproject.org/ghettos/gens.html.

292 Gens coined a slogan: Kruk, *The Last Days*, p. xlvi.

292 A throng of "underworld characters . . .": Kruk, *The Last Days*, p. xlvi.

292 "Look, Jews are standing in the street," Abba Kovner told Wittenberg: www .jewishgen.org/Yizkor/terrible_choice/ter002.html.

292 signaled the beginning of the end: Kruk, *The Last Days*, p. xlvi.

292 Of the eighty thousand Jews living in Vilna: deathcamps.org.

292 At Ponar alone, some seventy-two thousand Jews: Snyder, *Bloodlands*, p. 192.

292 "No other Jewish community . . .": deathcamps.org.

293 By then Jacob Gens was dead: Gens remains an extremely controversial and enigmatic figure. Some believe that as the ultimate pragmatist he saved many Jews from death, doing the best he could in an impossible situation. Others write him off as a megalomaniacal collaborator—a traitor, a perpetrator of shameful deeds, and a leader who was taken in by German lies and ended up "pushing others to their deaths." For a good discussion of Gens's contradictions, see www.jewishgen.org/ yizkor/terrible_choice.ter002.html.

293 At seven o'clock on the morning of September 23: Balberyszski, *Stronger Than Iron*, p. 265.

293 "Screaming obscenities . . .": Lily M. Margules, *Memories, Memories: From Vilna to New York with a Few Stops Along the Way* (Annapolis, MD: Lighthouse Press, 1999), p. 69.

293 "As soon as we passed the gate . . .": Balberyszski, *Stronger Than Iron*, p. 265.

294 "It is naïve, absurd, and historically false . . .": Primo Levi, *The Drowned and the Saved* (New York: Summit Books, 1988), p. 40.

294 "Germans tore into our columns": Balberyszski, *Stronger Than Iron*, p. 266.

294 "there were two rows of Gestapo . . .": Sonia Pauline Beker, *Symphony on Fire* (New Milford, NJ: Wordsmithy, 2007) pp. 58–59, quoted in www.untilourlastbreath.com.

294 "I don't know how to describe the sound and the smell of death . . .": Margules, *Memories, Memories*, p. 72.

295 "No, they won't do this to you": Beker, *Symphony on Fire*, pp. 58–59, quoted in www.untilourlastbreath.com.

295 "Ukrainian guards walked among the half-sleeping people . . .": Kruk, *The Last Days*, p. 662.

295 the gas chambers at Sobibor: I have found a number of conflicting accounts about the liquidation of the women and children of the Vilna ghetto. Some sources, including Vilnius Ghetto Lists of Prisoners, vol. 1, Vilnius: Jewish Museum, 1996, say that the women who were not sent to Kaiserwald (labor camp) were exterminated at Majdanek concentration camp—not Sobibor. Balberyszski in *Stronger Than Iron* also cites Majdanek. Other sources, including Howard Margol, a past president of Litvak-SIG at Jewish Gen and a well-known expert on the Vilna ghetto, says the women

were all transported to Ponar and shot there. Dr. Rose Lerer Cohen wrote the following in an e-mail of October 25, 2012: "From *The Holocaust in Lithuania a Book of Remembrance* published by Rose Lerer Cohen and Saul Issroff—I found the following references—between June and November 1943 Jews from the Vilna Ghetto were transported to Kaiserwald and on 23–24 September 1943 3,500 prisoners were transported from the Vilna Ghetto—males to Estonia via Siauliai and women were transported to Kaiserwald. The weak were murdered on the spot. The remaining prisoners were transported to Stuttoff, and from there the children were transported to Auschwitz together with their mothers. Others were transported to Buchenwald, Dachau, Mauthausen, Natzweiler and Neuengamme."

However, Zvi Bernhardt, a researcher with the reference and information services of Yad Vashem in Jerusalem, wrote the following in an e-mail message dated October 31, 2012: "According to [Yitzhak] Arad's 2004 book *History of the Holocaust Soviet Union and Annexed Territories* volume 2, pg. 572–573: 1400–1700 younger women were sent to Kaiserwald, 4000–4500 were sent to Sobibor and a few hundred were shot in Ponar. Arad's 1980 book *Ghetto in Flames* is still considered the authoritative book on the Vilna Ghetto." However, in *Ghetto in Flames* (New York: Holocaust Library, 1982), Yitzhak Arad writes the following on p. 432: "About 1,600–2,000 of the males assembled at Rossa Square were dispatched to camps in Estonia, and 1,400–1,700 women to Latvia, totaling 3,000–3,700 persons. Another 4,300–5,000 women and children were sent to the Majdanek gas chambers, and several hundred elderly and sick people were shot at Ponar."

Many questions remain unanswered—and will never be answered—about the final months of Doba's life and about her death. My narrative choices were based on the following: the majority of the prisoners recorded in the May 29, 1942, census were still alive when the final liquidation of the ghetto was made on September 23–24, 1943—therefore it seems logical to conclude that Doba was among them; Yad Vashem's researcher has identified Arad as the authority on the Vilna ghetto and Arad says in his most recent account that "4000–5000 were sent to Sobibor"—so again, it seems logical to conclude that Doba and Velveleh were among those. I have been unable to resolve the question of whether the women and children of Vilna who were selected to die perished at Majdanek or Sobibor, about which Arad himself offers conflicting accounts.

My intention was that Doba would represent the thousands of Jewish women in Vilna whose stories have never been recorded—so I chose to narrate her final days to reflect the most common experiences.

For details about the gas chambers at Sobibor, I relied on *Sobibor: A History of a Nazi Death Camp*, by Jules Schelvis (Oxford: Berg Press, 2007), pp. 99–113. Schelvis cites two contemporary accounts of transports arriving at Sobibor from Vilna (p. 220).

CHAPTER TWENTY-FOUR: KLOOGA

297 **Gestapo Chief Kittel did the counting:** Balberyszski, *Stronger Than Iron*, p. 268.

297 **One hundred of the old and feeble:** Kruk, *The Last Days*, p. 662.

298 **"People started to cry":** Saul Slocki testimony in the archives of Beit Lohamei Haghetaot (The Ghetto Fighters' House), Israel.

298 **the train halted at Klooga . . . on Wednesday, September 29:** Anton Weiss-Wendt, *Murder Without Hatred* (Syracuse, NY: Syracuse University Press, 2009), p. 301; Balberyszski, *Stronger Than Iron*, p. 286.

299 **The next morning they gave him a cup of chestnut coffee:** These details on life in the camp come from Weiss-Wendt, *Murder Without Hatred*, and from interviews with Tola Urbach, Adele Jochelson, and Michael Turner recorded by the USC Shoah Foundation, Institute for Visual History and Education, archived at Stanford University Library, Palo Alto, California (among other libraries). In *Stronger Than Iron*, Balberyszski noted that roll call was usually held at 6 P.M. and initially was not so bad—only gradually did it become a torture.

299 **Gradually the daily quotas were raised to nineteen, thirty:** Weiss-Wendt, *Murder Without Hatred*, p. 303.

299 **"Everywhere [the strong ones] are the first ones . . .":** Kruk, *The Last Days*, p. 680.

299 **"They would use the roll call to punish 'offenders' . . ."; When Kurt Stacher:** Balberyszski, *Stronger Than Iron*, pp. 286, 301; and Weiss-Wendt, *Murder Without Hatred*, p. 304.

300 **Michael Turner watched SS guards:** USC Shoah Foundation testimony.

300 **"The hunger was unbelievable":** Tola Urbach, USC Shoah Foundation testimony.

300 **The food ration was "neither enough to live on nor to die on":** This quote and details about camp life are from Kruk, *The Last Days*, pp. 685–687, 690.

301 **Occasionally the slaves sang Hebrew songs:** Kruk, *The Last Days*, p. 678.

301 **Some of the men smuggled prayer shawls:** Balberyszski, *Stronger Than Iron*, p. 301.

301 **A few written traces:** These traces were located by research wizards Leah Teichthal and Rita Margolin at Yad Vashem and William Connelly at the U.S. Holocaust Memorial Museum. Mr. Connelly helped me translate the German and interpret the various terms on the forms.

301 **One hundred were shot after three prisoners succeeded in escaping:** Balberyszski, *Stronger Than Iron*, p. 306.

301 **In June 1944, Klooga had 2,122:** Statistics for Jewish forced-labor camps in Estonia, September 1943–June 1944, based on monthly reports by camp chief physician Franz von Bodman, archived at Yad Vashem.

302 **"Everything is being liberated . . .":** Kruk, *The Last Days*, p. 698.

302 **Itel was also doing her bit:** Information on the pigeon vest from Maidenform Collection and Evans, *They Made America*, p. 314.

304 **"mighty explosions and bombardments," "Soon you will be liberated," and "You can sense the front . . .":** Kruk, *The Last Days*, pp. 699, 694, 702, respectively.

304 **transferred to Danzig:** Weiss-Wendt, *Murder Without Hatred*, p. 307.

305 **The 301 healthy men:** My description of the last hours of Klooga comes from Weiss-Wendt, *Murder Without Hatred*, pp. 311–313; testimony of Tola Urbach, Adele Jochelson, and Michael Turner, USC Shoah Foundation. Also Kruk, *The Last Days*, p. 685, and Balberyszski, *Stronger Than Iron*, pp. 314–315. For the appearance of the funeral pyres, I relied on the extensive photo archive at the U.S. Holocaust Memorial Museum.

307 **491 could be identified:** Weiss-Wendt, *Murder Without Hatred*, p. 318.

CHAPTER TWENTY-FIVE: POSTWAR

309 **For Future Generations:** Kruk, *The Last Days*, epigraph.

312 **Shalom Tvi booked the first available passage:** U.S. Citizenship and Immigration Services, File Series A-File, File Number A-2958053, records relating to Sholom Kahanowicz.

313 **hundreds of thousands of Arabs:** The exact number is a source of heated controversy—with estimates ranging from 335,000 to nearly a million depending on the source.

313 **In 1998, an estimated 15,672 refugees:** www.palestineremembered.com/Tulkarm/Wadi-al-Hawarith/index.html.

313 **the Jewish population of Israel almost doubled:** Kramer, *A History of Palestine*, p. 320.

314 **print ads crafted by Mary Fillius:** Reichert, *The Erotic History of Advertising*, p. 145, and Evans, *They Made America*, p. 315. Material at Maidenform Collection, Series 1: Company History, 1922–1990, states that Kitty D'Alessio "worked extensively" on the Dream Campaign and may have originated the idea.

314 **The tagline was so catchy:** Evans, *They Made America*, p. 315.

315 **"The edge of Vilna Street stayed intact":** Zelig Kost in Rakov Yizkor book. Additional information from telephone interview with Estelle Trooskin, December 2011, and interview with Inda Epstein Goldfarb, Freehold, New Jersey, July 26, 2010.

317 **Hyman includes one paragraph:** Cohen, *As I Recall*, p. 82.

317 **"Auschwitz," writes Yale historian Timothy Snyder:** Timothy Snyder, "Holocaust: The Ignored Reality," *The New York Review of Books*, July 16, 2009, www.nybooks.com/articles/archives/2009/jul/16/holocaust-the-ignored-reality/.

320 **"First, I can't afford it":** Maidenform Collection.

EPILOGUE

325 **So Shimon Dov is my great-great-grandfather:** Technically I am not a Kohain because membership in the priestly caste passes from father to son.

INDEX